Transcultural Marketing

Transcultural Marketing

Building Customer Relationships
in Multicultural America

Marye Tharp

Routledge
Taylor & Francis Group

LONDON AND NEW YORK

First published 2014 by M.E. Sharpe

Published 2015 by Routledge
2 Park Square, Milton Park, Abingdon, Oxon OX14 4RN
711 Third Avenue, New York, NY 10017, USA

Routledge is an imprint of the Taylor & Francis Group, an informa business

Library of Congress Cataloging-in-Publication Data

Tharp, Marye C.
  Transcultural marketing : building customer relationships in multicultural America /
by Marye Tharp.
    pages cm
Includes bibliographical references and index.
ISBN 978-0-7656-4299-8 (hardcover: alk. paper)—ISBN 978-0-7656-4300-1 (pbk.: alk. paper)
1. Minority consumers—United States. 2. Marketing—United States—Cross-cultural studies.
3. Target marketing—United States. 4. Customer relations—United States. I. Title.

HF5415.332.M56.T48 2014
658.8′12080973—dc23   2013047525

ISBN 13: 9780765643001 (pbk)
ISBN 13: 9780765642998 (hbk)

Contents

List of Tables and Figures

Tables

Figures

Preface and Acknowledgments

The purpose of this book is to introduce transcultural marketing techniques and to profile American consumer subcultures. In choosing the content for each chapter, the author has drawn from a wide variety of sources. Every effort was made at the time of this writing to include the most up-to-date and reliable information and case examples. By the time you read this preface, many of those sources may seem old. In this fast-changing media and marketing world, it has been impossible to keep all sections about different consumer subcultures current. Therefore, when discussing patterns of media use or purchasing preferences the author has tried to emphasize consumer trends rather than absolute numbers.

The value to readers of this approach is the combination of demographic and geographic information, social identity issues, subcultural values, media habits, and marketing preferences about five age subcultures, three ethnic groups, and one subculture organized around sexual identity. When they are put together, the reader will have a basis for comparing consumers in those subcultures and choosing which ones best match a company's own core values and relationships. In most cases, the reader will be able to update data and extend trend lines of interest by accessing the sources used in this book.

Transcultural marketing strategies and tactics outlined in Chapter 3 focus on knowing your target market both economically and culturally. Knowledge is a commodity available to anyone today with a connection to the Internet. Yet keeping up with "what's cool" in this global, multicultural, interconnected network of information highways and trails is a never-ending quest because cultural boundaries are constantly moving. Marketing success depends on being able to anticipate these environmental changes and to relate to customers culturally as well as economically. Transcultural marketing and the cultural values proposition show companies how to become an institution that plays both economic and cultural roles in its customers' lives.

This project has benefited from having many contributors. I assume total responsibility for the final form, and any mistakes or omissions are my responsibility alone. At the same time, I would like to recognize these collaborators. First, three scholars contributed research and writing to early drafts of the book: Dr. Marilyn Roberts, dean of the College of Communication and Media Sciences at Zayed University; Dr. Olaf Werder, lecturer in the Department of Media and Communications at the University of Sydney; and Dr. Eun Soo Rhee. In addition, several colleagues coauthored sections of an earlier version of this book and I wish to recognize their important role in its content: Ernest Bromley, Dr. Carrie LaFerle, Dr. Weina Lee, Dr. Satomi Furuichi, and Dr. Jerome D. Williams.

Over time, I have discussed many of the concepts in this book with students, ex-students, consulting colleagues, and coworkers. I thank the following people for their (sometimes unknowing) suggestions: Hector Bajac, Dr. Lucy Brown, Paul Bryan, Henry Cadena, Dr. Yolanda Cal, Dr. Horacio Casabé, Dr. Vanessa Fonseca, Dr. Linda Gerber, Kimberly Smith Hilsenbeck, Dr. Robert Hoover, Dr. Victoria Jones, Dr. Jaime Alonso Gomez, Dr. Daniel Kempler, Dr. Youngseon Kim, Dr. John Leckenby, Jessica Robb Massay, Ruben McCoy, J. Moncada, Dr. Hirose Morikazu, Adrienne Pulido, Dr. Marilyn Roberts, Patricia Rose, Liesel Riddle, Gustavo Rubenstejn, Joel Saegert, Trina Sego, Kazue Shimamura, L.J. Shrum, Elizabeth "Gigi" Taylor, WanHsiu Sunny Tsai, Vicente Valjalo, Ricardo Villarreal da Silva, Jorge Villegas, Thomas Vogel, Olaf Werder, and Tai Yun.

I have also had several assistants without whose work this book would have taken much longer. They include Brenda Rodriguez, Charlie Tian, Wendy Boaglio, Daniel ShuHao Liu, and Jessica Ikard, My many students at the following universities deserve a mention for their personal stories and age-cohort perspectives, as they have been my teachers as much as I have been theirs: The University of Texas at Austin, Emerson College, Schreiner University, Universidad Adolfo Ibañez, The University of Texas at San Antonio, and Universidad ORT.

Last, I wish to express my appreciation to my editor, Harry Briggs, whose patience in waiting for a complete draft, and whose faith that it was worth the wait, inspired me.

Transcultural Marketing

1

Crossing Cultural Borders at Home

Transmigration

In the contemporary United States, your age, address, language and accent, skin color or shape of eyes as well as the music you listen to, how and where you worship, or where you work are the tools with which American consumers construct, communicate, and change their social identities. Rather than lifetime, fixed definitions of who we are, these self-made, chosen identities are built upon a constantly changing foundation of personal characteristics and behaviors. It is a lifetime project, always in flux, never finalized, but frequently expressed in how we spend our money and time.

National borders have become less important than the distinctions we make between "them" and "us." The groups with which we identify determine our community boundaries. Our Facebook or Twitter friends are spread all over the world; we share language and Internet savvy but no traditional forms of community. Chinese Americans belong to an ethnic Chinese diaspora that spans the world, but they are hyphenated Americans at home. By donning multiple identities, we have become transmigrants, crossing back and forth across cultural borders almost unknowingly.

The purpose of this book is to explain the concept of "chosen" identity and its relationship to the complex roles that products and services play in our lives and to profile significant American consumer subcultures. The techniques of transcultural marketing navigate the sometimes-contradictory expressions of consumer identity in a multicultural society. We highlight specific American subcultures whose members express their identities in their market-space choices ("bricks and clicks").

Relationships with organizations and their brands constitute a key element in the "identity kit" that people use while shaping their public and private selves. Just as people build and manage their social selves, companies choose their core values and develop strategies for expressing them. Since organizations are not as agile as people are, change is more difficult for them, especially when attempting to build relationships with customers whose self-defining behaviors are in constant flux. Transcultural marketing is a way of developing marketing strategies that allow organizations to transmigrate back and forth across the cultural boundaries created by the value shifts and different groups with which their customers identify.

This chapter underscores the forces shaping our multicultural society. A multicultural society exists where multiple, sometime-conflicting value systems are loosely linked to the chosen social identities of its members. In particular, American individualistic ideals encourage each of us to select ways in which we can both belong and stand out. This topic leads in turn to the key "cultural value systems" whose principles "define" cultural boundaries within the United States. This chapter pays particular attention to the core values of American mainstream culture since it is the foundation shared (to a greater or lesser extent) by all Americans, no matter which other groups they identify with. The chapter closes with a summary and overview of the book presentation plan.

Forces of Change: Stirring up the Melting Pot!

Four forces have converged to stir up our so-called melting pot of American culture: globalization, changing demographics, shifting media economics, and cultural ideals. As a result, we behave more like ingredients in a mixed salad than a soup: We trumpet our differences in the belief that they enrich the whole.

Globalization

Globalization refers to the increasing interconnectivity of national economies composed of businesses, buyers, and other organizations that share products, services, events, ideas, or people. Globalization affects all the other significant change agents—demographic, technological, economic, informational, and cultural. Because of its far-reaching effects, globalization is radically transforming the ways in which we do business and how we construct our personal identities.[1]

Let us first explore what it means to live in a "global" world where national boundaries no longer match cultural borders. Geographical closeness and personal contact no longer determine the limits of our knowledge of where we fit in the world. Increasing access to the Internet offers opportunities to find and communicate with any other like-minded persons in whatever way they choose to label themselves. All kinds of media allow us to "know" our counterparts wherever and however they might exist. For example, eHarmony's long-time promise has been to apply the "science of matchmaking" to finding one's soul mate. Angie's List (www.angieslist. com) extends the feedback from one person's social network on service experiences to a crowd-sourced "social media network of service experiences," and Kickstarter.com finds angel investors for art projects. Many other online sites are now where we first learn about "others" who are among our global citizenry.

Business people and teenagers have long been cited as "global market segments," using the criterion that they fit with one another across the world better than within their original cultures.[2] Through travel, work, global media, and virtual identity on the Internet, we no longer must know people personally to be able to communicate with them and identify them as "just like us." Even age-cohort groups such as baby boomers, long thought to have distinctive values across national cultures, are globalizing the wish for "the simpler days of the 1950s."[3] In other studies, younger consumers in multiple countries have shown less prejudice against foreign products and services than do their older counterparts. Such trends suggest growing evidence of global consumer segments.[4] IKEA is a company that sells "a lifestyle that signifies hip design, thrift, and simplicity. For the aspiring global middle class, buying IKEA is a sign of success"[5] as well as of membership in a global community of brand owners.[6]

Our virtual contacts are immune to traditional cultural and physical barriers, but we are also *physically* moving across national borders. Immigration, diasporas (widespread dispersal of people from one culture and region to other places), and the ideals of individualism erase the dividing lines that used to distinguish the beliefs of different cultural groups. The fastest-growing racial group in recent censuses has been "multiple racial origins." The numerous immigrants from Latin America and Asia to the United States are bringing their own cultural experiences to the American mix. As these new groups integrate into American society, "they will further reduce the distance between America and the rest of the world."[7]

The market spaces (physical and virtual marketplaces) in which we live—where we get our news, information, entertainment, ideas, heroes, rituals, myths, cultural norms, and values as well as goods and services—socialize us into global culture.[8] It is not that the other cultural agents—schools, government, religion, family, social groups, and peers—no longer have influence. We simply learn new and sometimes alternative lessons coming from our market spaces of ideas, people, and things. We experience alternative value-influences at younger ages, and they add a set of global and popular culture values to our learning about where we fit into our primary American culture.[9]

What is becoming a personal and business necessity is to have both "roots and wings," as Pascal Zachary, author of *The Global Me,* argues.[10] His research suggests that those who identify strongly with their "roots" but who use their "wings" to achieve interpersonal and business success are best at adapting to change. Such requirements for success in our global economy enhance our proficiency at crossing back and forth across cultural boundaries.

Immigration, longer lives, and more participation in market-based economies result in our becoming as much strangers from those physically close to us as we are "friends" with people from other countries. To make sense of our places in this global society, we choose to live value-driven lives, full of inconsistency, contrasts, and contradictions. This is not unique to the United States, but it is in full bloom here and is reshaping our business and personal lives. Sourcing decisions—for information, goods and services, persons of influence, and ideas—have become the arena in which we play out our hopes for the future and identities of the moment, within this global culture.

Changing Demographics

The increasing diversity of the U.S. population is the most significant force causing organizations to rethink how they reach American consumers. Our recent past and foreseeable future are reflected in some simple demographic statistics.

Table 1.1 shows that by 2050, the minority population will comprise more than 50 percent of Americans. Likewise, the share of Americans over 65 years old will rise from 8.2 percent in 1960 to about one in five by 2050. Americans over 45 will make up 42.6 percent of the population and Latinos 1 of every 3 Americans. These numbers show merely the tip of the "diversity" iceberg.

The statistics in Table 1.1 also suggest that not all groups are growing as rapidly as others. For example, the share of African Americans in the population is increasing but not as quickly as the share of Asian Americans and U.S. Latinos. U.S. Latinos became the largest ethnic group in the United States in the early 2000s. The large influx of immigrants since 1980 will also continue to expand the number of Asian Americans, even if policy changes slow down new immigration.[11] All three of these groups will have a larger presence than they do today.

Even more significant to businesses than the population numbers, is the increased share of national income received by ethnic citizens. The Selig Center for Economic Growth at the University of Georgia estimates that in 2014 the combined buying power of African Americans, U.S. Hispanics, Asian

Table 1.1

America's Future: Changing Age and Ethnic Distribution, 2010–2050

Population group	2010	2020	2030	2040	2050
All Americans	310,233	341,387	373,504	405,655	439,010
Black Americans	42,103	47,748	53,519	59,454	65,703
	(13.57%)	(13.99%)	(14.33%)	(14.66%)	(14.97%)
Asian Americans	16,472	21,586	27,352	33,722	40,586
	(5.31%)	(6.32%)	(7.32%)	(8.31%)	(9.24%)
Hispanic Americans	49,726	66,365	85,931	108,223	132,792
	(16.03%)	(19.44%)	(23.01%)	(26.68%)	(30.25%)
White, not Hispanic, Americans	209,853	205,255	207,217	206,065	203,347
	(67.6%)	(60.12%)	(55.48%)	(50.08%)	(46.32%)
Americans, < 18 years	75,217	81,685	87,815	93,986	101,574
	(24.25%)	(23.93%)	(23.51%)	(23.17%)	(23.14%)
Americans, 18–44 years	113,807	120,541	129,301	138,431	150,400
	(36.68%)	(35.31%)	(34.62%)	(34.13%)	(34.26%)
Americans, 18–65 years	194,787	204,897	213,597	230,431	248,890
	(62.79)	(60.02%)	(57.19%)	(56.80%)	(56.69%)
Americans, over 45 years	121,209	139,160	156,388	173,238	187,037
	(39.07%)	(40.76%)	(41.88%)	(42.71%)	(42.60%)
Americans, over 65 years	40,229	54,804	72,092	81,238	88,547
	(12.97%)	(16.05%)	(19.30%)	(20.02%)	(20.17%)

Source: U.S. Census Bureau, American Community Survey 2009, www.census.gov/acs/www/data_documentation/2009_release/.
Note: Data were sourced from various Census Bureau tables and these do not always use the same numbers for the same population due to different years as their basis, and to differences between actual counts and projected counts.

Table 1.2

Buying Power Among American Minorities: Dollar Amount, Share of Total, and Percentage Change, 1990–2015

	1990	2000	2009	2015
Total buying power (billions of dollars)	4,239.9	7,323.7	11,123.5	14,118.7
White	3,788.7	6,349.6	11,123.5	11,841.3
African American	316.3	600.2	9,439.3	1,247.4
U.S. Latinos	210.0	499.0	1036.0	1,482.0
American Indian	19.6	40.0	67.7	90.3
Asian	115.4	274.4	543.7	775.1
Multiracial	N/A	59.6	115.5	164.6

	1990–2009	1990–2014	2000–2010	2010–2015
Total buying power (percentage change)	162.4	233.0	51.9	26.9
White	149.1	212.5	48.7	25.4
African American	149.1	294.4	59.5	30.3
U.S. Latinos	392.9	605.3	107.5	43.1
American Indian	246.0	361.5	69.4	33.4
Asian	371.3	571.9	98.1	42.6
Multiracial	N/A	N/A	93.9	42.5

	1990	2000	2010	2014
Total market share (in percent)	100.0	100.0	100.0	100.0
White	89.4	86.7	84.9	83.9
African American	7.5	8.2	8.6	8.8
U.S. Latinos	5.0	6.8	9.3	10.5
American Indian	0.5	0.5	0.6	0.6
Asian	2.7	3.7	4.9	5.5
Multiracial	N/A	0.8	1.0	1.2

Source: J.M. Humphries, *The Multicultural Economy Report 2010* (Athens: Selig Center for Economic Growth, Terry College of Business, University of Georgia, 2010), table 1, 15; table 3, 17.

Americans, and Native Americans will be almost $3.4 trillion. This amount makes up about 26 percent of all American buying power estimates for 2014 and is five times the level in 1990. U.S. Latinos alone are projected to have buying power of $1.3 trillion in 2014. Table 1.2 shows these numbers.

Between 1990 and 2011, while overall buying power increased only 175 percent, Asian Americans gained 434 percent in buying power, Hispanics 457 percent, American Indians 270 percent, and African Americans 237 percent. The growth in minority buying power as a percentage of the total is, as noted by the Center, "important because the higher their market share, the lower the average cost of reaching a potential buyer in the group."[12]

The mature market (persons over 65 years of age) held over 50 percent of U.S. disposable income in 1990. As baby boomers join the "over 65" population, they are increasing this group's disproportionate share of American income. Single parents, married couples without children, multigenerational households, and nonfamily households now outnumber the traditional, nuclear-family household. During the 1990s and 2000s, over 40 percent of firstborn children were born to unmarried parents.[13] Organizations ignore the growing representation of ethnic consumers and new types of households, shown in Table 1.3 at their own peril.

Age- and ethnic-specific populations vary significantly from city to city and state to state. Some states are getting whiter (Nevada, Utah, Idaho, Arizona, Colorado, Georgia, North and South Carolina, Tennessee), and some are getting older (North and South Dakota, Nebraska, Kansas), but these are the exceptions. Metropolitan "ports of entry" like Miami, Los Angeles, and New York continue to attract large numbers of immigrants, and domestic migration is toward the Western and Southern states.[14] The larger trend is toward more diversity (by race, ethnicity, age, and education) in more places in the United States, as illustrated by the patterns shown in Table 1.4. Over 15 percent of marriages in 2010 were multiracial.[15] In 2011 Starbucks and Tassimo (a Starbuck's product) conducted a print advertising campaign that included a multiracial couple as "consumers." When Cheerios did the same in 2013, YouTube had to shut down its video comment board because of numerous abusive comments.[16]

Marketers can reach these consumers cost efficiently by concentrating marketing efforts in particular cities or regions.[17] In some ways, the data refute current thinking about when and how to market to particular subculture groups. For instance, Florida may be a great place for targeting mature Americans, but Hispanics in either Texas or California constitute a larger total population, if not market. The buying power of Hispanics in California has been estimated at more than $214 billion, and in Texas this figure is over $140 billion.[18] A concentrated media effort in California could cost less per contact and reach more U.S. Hispanics than one targeted to mature Americans in Florida.

Another surprise might be how patterns of diversity vary in our major cities and states. According to U.S. Census forecasts, Houston is more diverse than Philadelphia.[19] Florida's African-American population is growing very slowly, while the number of Hispanics and mature Americans is growing more rapidly than the overall population in Florida. By looking at geographic dispersion and demographic predictions together, for at least the top five states, as shown in Table 1.5, we can anticipate where different subculture groups will grow.

Table 1.3

Population and Household Income Shares for Various Americans

Population group	1960		1990		2020	
Total population	179,323		249,439		322,742	
	% of population	Median income[1]	% of population	Median income[1]	% of population	Median income[1]
All Americans	100.0	$5,620	100.0	$29,943	100.0	n/a
African Americans	10.5	49.9	12.1	62.4	14.0	n/a
U.S. Latinos	4.0	n/a	9.0	74.6	19.1	n/a
Asian Americans	0.5	n/a	2.9	128.4	7.1	n/a
Whites	88.4	94.2	80.3	104.3	60.1	n/a
Mature market (65+)	8.2	51.5	21.9	56.3	27.4	n/a
Family HHs*	83.6	100.0	75.4	119.2	n/a	n/a
Nonfamily HHs*	19.1	60.0	29.6	59.1	n/a	n/a
Single parent HHs*	12.8	52.8[2]	28.1	57.92	n/a	n/a

Sources: American Fact Finder, www.census.gov/population/documentation/twps0056/TabA-08.pdf. *American Community Survey*, www. census.gov/statab/freq/98s0012.txt; U.S. Census Bureau, *U.S. Census of Population* (Washington, DC: U.S. Government Printing Office, 1961), PC(1)-1A; U.S. Census Bureau, *1990 Census of Population: Social and Economic Characteristics* (Washington, DC: U.S. Government Printing Office, 1993); U.S. Census Bureau, "Population Projections of the United States by Age, Sex, Race, and Hispanic Origin: 1993 to 2050," *Current Population Reports* (Washington, DC: U.S. Government Printing Office, 1993), P25-1104.

[1]Numbers represent percentages of the dollar median for all Americans.

[2]In 1960 and 1990, single parents were included in two categories: female householders (52.8 percent of family median incomes) and male householders (86.5 percent of family median incomes). Female householders account for over 80 percent of all single-parent homes.

*HH = household.

Table 1.4

Population in Selected Geographic Areas, 2000, 2010, and 2030

City/State	Total population (in 000s)	White Americans (%)	African Americans (%)	U.S. Latinos (%)	Asian Americans (%)	Mature market (%)
California						
2000	35,521	78.5	7.5	32.7	13.2	10.6
2010	36,962	62.7	6.1	37.0	12.5	11.2
2030	49,241	33.3	5.0	45.4	13.4	17.8
Texas						
2000	20,119	84.1	12.6	29.2	2.8	9.9
2010	24,782	73.8	11.5	36.9	3.6	10.2
2030	37,285	30.5	10.5	50.9	n/a	15.6
New York						
2000	18,146	75.8	18.2	15.5	5.7	12.9
2010	19,541	67.4	15.7	16.8	7.0	13.4
2030	20,415	n/a	n/a	n/a	n/a	17.9
Illinois						
2000	12,051	80.8	15.5	10.5	3.5	12.1
2010	12,910	72.5	14.5	15.3	4.4	12.4
2030	15,248	63.9	14.2	16.9	7.2	18.0
Florida						
2000	15,233	82.6	15.3	15.7	1.8	17.6
2010	18,538	76.9	15.6	21.5	2.4	17.3
2030	23,821	79.4	17.1	26.5	n/a	27.1
Los Angeles						
2000	14,532	64.7	8.4	32.4	9.2	9.7
2010	12,874	54.6	7.0	44.8	13.9	10.8
New York City						
2000	7,500	35.0	26.0	29.0	10.0	13.1
2010	19,070	61.3	17.9	21.8	9.5	13.0
Chicago						
2000	8,066	71.6	19.1	13.0	2.5	8.0
2010	9,581	66.2	17.6	19.9	5.4	11.2
Miami						
2000	3,193	76.5	18.5	33.1	1.3	16.6
2010	5,547	71.7	20.4	40.3	2.3	15.9
Dallas						
2000	3,885	75.3	14.3	13.0	2.5	8.0
2010	6,447	68.3	14.0	28.0	4.9	8.5
Seattle–Tacoma						
2000	2,559	86.5	4.8	2.8	6.4	0.7
2010	3,408	75.3	5.5	8.0	10.5	10.6
Atlanta						
2000	2,834	71.3	26.0	1.9	1.8	7.9
2010	5,477	57.8	31.5	10.0	4.3	8.5
Washington, DC						
2000	3,924	65.8	26.6	5.6	5.1	8.5
2010	5,476	57.1	26.0	13.0	8.6	10.0

(continued)

Table 1.4 *(continued)*

City/State	Total population (in 000s)	White Americans (%)	African Americans (%)	U.S. Latinos (%)	Asian Americans (%)	Mature market (%)
Boston						
2000	4,172	89.0	6.3	4.5	2.9	2.4
2010	4,589	80.7	7.0	8.3	6.0	12.6
Houston						
2000	3,711	67.6	17.9	20.5	3.5	7.3
2010	5,865	67.6	16.8	34.4	6.1	8.5
Detroit metro						
2000	4,665	76.5	20.9	1.8	1.5	11.6
2010	4,403	70.9	22.8	3.8	3.3	12.8

Sources: U.S. Census Bureau, "Interim State Populations, 2005–2010" (Washington, DC, 2010), www.census.gov/population/projections/state/; www.census.gov/population/projections/PressTab6.xls; State Projections, http://txsdc.utsa.edu/tpepp/2008projections/; State of California, Department of Finance, "Reports and Research Papers," www.dof.ca.gov/research/demographic/reports/view.php; Proximity, "Demographic Composition and Trends: State Demographic Projections to 2030," http://proximityone.com/st0030.htm; Illinois Department of Commerce and Economic Opportunity, "Population Projections," www.commerce.state.il.us/dceo/Bureaus/Facts_Figures/Population_Projections/; Cornell Program on Applied Demographics, "Projection Data: Charts, Table," http://pad.human.cornell.edu/counties/projections.cfm.

Note: The data for states and cities are based on projected population size in 2010.

Shifting Media Economics

In the past five years, new technologies have changed forever the ways in which we learn about our world. A proliferation of channels on television— once labeled the information superhighway—is no match for today's real explosion of information via the Internet. Our cell phones wirelessly take photos, send and check e-mail, record videos, and show movies and television shows. Billboards send exclusive video and music clips to our cell phones, manhole covers point out nearby sites of interest, games simulate product-use experiences, and taxis change their sideboard ads according to location.[20] In this information context, the charge is "how can we make this brand famous" rather than "where do we put advertising?"[21] This context represents the convergence of hardware and the universal accessibility of software thrown together to the benefit of audiences.

Customizing media content has become the direct avenue for bringing in audiences that seek more relevance from all these new choices. For example, newspapers available to their audiences via cell phone or e-mail alerts are able to retain the loyalty of those audiences.[22] The traditional 30-second spot has become two 15-second or three 10-second spots as networks desperately

Table 1.5

Diversity Growing in the Five Largest States
(numbers represent percentage of total population)

State	African American	U.S. Latinos	Asian American	Mature market
California				
1960	5.6	n/a	n/a	8.8
1990	7.4	25.8	9.6	8.2
2010	6.1	37.0	12.5	11.2
2020	8.0	36.5	20.2	16.5
Texas				
1960	12.4	n/a	0.1	7.8
1990	11.9	25.6	1.9	18.4
2010	11.5	36.9	3.6	10.2
2020	12.6	40.3	4.2	15.6
New York				
1960	8.4	n/a	n/a	10.1
1990	15.9	12.3	3.9	22.1
2010	15.7	16.8	7.0	13.4
2020	21.1	15.9	8.1	20.1
Illinois				
1960	10.3	n/a	0.2	10.9
1990	14.8	7.9	2.5	14.5
2010	14.5	15.3	4.4	12.4
2020	18.4	15.7	6.2	18.0
Florida				
1960	17.8	n/a	0.1	11.2
1990	13.6	12.2	1.2	29.1
2010	15.6	21.5	2.4	17.3
2020	17.9	21.5	3.0	27.1

Sources: Census Bureau, www.census.gov/population/projections/PressTab5; Jennifer Cheeseman Day, "Population Projections of the United States by Age, Sex, Race & Hispanic Origin" (Washington, DC: U.S. Census Bureau, 1996), 25–1130; U.S. Census Bureau, *American Community Survey*, 2009 data release (Washington, DC: U.S. Census Bureau, 2011), www.census.gov/acs/www/data_documentation/2009_release/; www.census.gov/population/documentation/twps0056/tabA-01/.

Note: For the purposes of this table, the mature market is defined as the population 65 or more years old.

try to increase their revenues. Increasing commercial clutter has discouraged more audiences from watching programs to watching movies wirelessly on demand or recording programs to watch later and to playing games and using the television set as part of a home entertainment network. To reach consumers, advertisers are moving where their eyes are. Spending on in-game advertising grew more rapidly than spending in any other medium over the past decade and should exceed $1 billion in 2014.[23]

More and more cable channels have customized content for viewers who seek niche informational and entertainment programming.[24] Through digital programming, cable television ads can be adjusted according to the zip code of viewers.[25] Broadband reaches well over 60 percent of American households, and online advertising in all forms is soaring as a result. Viewers see the same ads on their TV, computer, and cell phone as sponsors try to follow audiences around. Niche e-tailers are collaborating with search engines in moving global buyers to these specialized global sellers.[26]

The old line between content and ads has disappeared in new media and is blurring in old ones like magazines, newspapers, and, of course, product placements in television programs and movies.[27] The media, new or old, no longer have a monopoly on content, either. Audiences are creating content and sharing it on the Internet; many are making this process profitable by selling advertising on do-it-yourself websites.

It is not the number of media alternatives alone but the declining costs of delivering, customizing and receiving information that are a radical departure from the past. A typical network television commercial still costs $400,000[28] on average to produce and a minimum of $4 million to show during the Super Bowl,[29] resulting in a cost of less than $.01 per person reached. In contrast, for $1.12 per click, a niche firm like the online jeweler Blue Nile can "get" a prospect for a $5,000 diamond ring.[30] New media in a variety of formats offer cheaper and measurable ways to reach audiences with customized messages.

Media are no longer just a one-way means to reach out to consumers. Gathering information on buyer likes and dislikes is quicker and cheaper when using interactive media. Company blogs capture customer complaints for free. They also turn complaints into free test sites for "beta versions" of new products, in which early users actually design product improvements. Moving TV programs to the Internet allows more precise measurement of audiences and provides yet more entertainment options for consumers.[31]

Companies like P&G (www.pgestore.com) are taking some of their huge media budgets and putting them to work in social networking websites linked loosely to their brands. These new websites are more like continuing focus groups than websites with brand promotion as the goal. P&G can discover what their target audiences "care about at different life stages" by monitoring the discussions on these websites.[32] Other mass marketers, such as McDonald's, are changing their marketing budgets to cover messages in closed-circuit sport programming at Hispanic bars, custom-published magazines at black barber shops, in-store video networks to captivate shoppers, young athletes, and company-sponsored women's magazines for reaching new mothers.[33]

Major advances have also taken place in the ways in which media audiences are measured. No longer are advertisers limited to Arbitron and Nielsen consumer panels and home-based "people meters." New software measures cell phone, videogame, and other new media audiences.[34] In addition, search advertisers only pay "per click," which gives them a precise metric for the cost of online leads. Nielsen now provides advertisers with three reports of a program's audience: those who watched it when first aired, those who recorded it and watched it later, and those who saw it when it aired and played it back later. [35]

The cost of customization in making and delivering products and services has also declined. Custom design, once the gold standard for luxury, is available to the middle class online. For several years, Land's End offered to design a pair of jeans to fit any person's measurements for $70.

As media usage moves into more parts of our daily lives, we "shop for identity."[36] Media are becoming the center of our social and informational lives in today's globalized culture. Marketers are finding more and cheaper ways to insinuate products and services into the ways that we express who we are and who we want to be. Converging media are how we find community, express our distinctiveness, and apply our values.

Cultural Ideals

The contrast between who we want to be and who we are as a nation could not have been clearer in the recent debates over how to stem illegal immigration. If we are no longer opening our arms to welcome the world's refugees, whom do we allow in and whom do we bar? If the United States is no longer a beacon for all freedom-seeking peoples, what are our new ideals and what rules should govern the distribution of resources among members of our society?[37] The philosophical issues that underlie these political debates point to a growing discrepancy between our beliefs and our behaviors, a radical shift in our common ideals, or a splintering of our ideals.

Throughout the twentieth century, American culture placed increasing emphasis on individual needs, wants, and rights at the expense of communitarian responsibilities.[38] Our analogy for what we share in common ("a melting pot") has been replaced by a more individualistic ideal (a "salad bowl," whose ingredients retain their distinctiveness but enrich the whole as a result). The melting pot analogy suggested that in time and over generations all Americans would "lose" their original culture's influences and "become" Americans, meaning that they would lose their visible ethnic traditions and become "typical" Americans.[39] Until the 1960s, fitting into a nearly unitary middle-class existence with a house and a car was the only real option for American identity.

Contrast the strict definition of "middle-class American" of the 1960s with two groups whose values and lifestyles reflect very different ways of participating in the American middle class. First, a group called "cultural creatives" by some market researchers, promote ideas and behaviors that support the notion of a carbon footprint, recycling, and less visible consumption overall. Members of this group are often innovators and opinion leaders for knowledge-intensive products such as ecotravel, the arts, energy-efficient appliances, and authenticity as a generally valued commodity. They are more altruistic and less cynical than other Americans. As global warming has a stronger economic impact and is not just an environmental concern, these beliefs are influencing other Americans to reconsider the role of consumption in their lives.[40] The three most important values for these Americans are close relationships with other people, security, and stability.

Self-navigators reject traditions and conformity yet are still achievement-oriented with a balance that emphasizes close personal relationships, security, and fun. Self-navigators consider security more important than power, and they choose to build their own reliance networks outside traditional institutions and authorities.[41] Their consumer choices are as eclectic as their values. Their values and affiliations point to divisions in contemporary American culture.

The "American Dream," which continues to attract immigrants, is now expressed in terms of owning a house, business success, and educational attainment.[42] Those at the bottom of the economic pyramid still desire to attain the lifestyle that these achievements represent.[43] Those higher up the pyramid translate the "American Dream" into more personal expressions of identity. As the "The American Dream" website (http://americanragstoriches.blogspot.com) puts it: "Doing what you like and making millions."

Another measure of our changing cultural ideals concerns our participation in formal and informal associations. Robert Putnam argues that in the last third of the twentieth century, many Americans "withdrew from civic life."[44] The result is weakened social capital overall—we feel less trust and engage in less cooperation. Other authors worry about how we have changed the American Dream from an aspiration to liberate man and his mind from tyranny to an expectation of material enrichment.[45] Most Americans today define success as achieving a better standard of living than their parents.[46]

Our loss of faith in the institutions of government, business, politics, and education is reflected in our questioning of these institutions. We want to "do it ourselves"—to buy our own stocks and inform ourselves about retirement options. We want society's problems to be solved but not if we have to make sacrifices or receive unequal benefits as a result of the changes needed to implement those solutions.

The increasing gaps between what we say we believe and what some of us actually seek are evident in our popular culture. For example, who are our heroes? We yearn for experiences and stories of selfless heroic behavior. We consider ourselves generous, compassionate, fair, and tolerant. Our media laud everyday heroes in times of natural and manmade disasters. We speak well of them, but their rewards are less tangible than those other "American heroes" we see "rewarded" in and by our popular culture. The television show *American Idol* displays a version of the "American Dream": Anyone with "talent" can have 15 minutes of fame. We have celebrities who are famous for nothing other than being famous. What we see illustrated, as the rewards for various combinations of achievement, talent, looks, and charisma are power, money, beautiful people, and media attention. The following editorial expresses the paradoxes of our values:

> Look who our heroes are. They aren't the people who volunteer in the soup kitchens; they aren't struggling writers and artists; they aren't the librarians or the nurses or the social workers. Mainly they are the rich and the famous and the successful and the beautiful, the film and sports stars, the Wall Street barons, even the articulate convicts who charm us on talk shows once they've done their time. Perhaps the best indicator of what we really are is what we spend our money on or what we watch on television. Look at what we read. Look at what we choose to do with our spare time. That's what we value.[47]

What were once common ideals in our culture are now up for grabs. "Miss America" is no longer on network television. Mounting separate shows for "newer" Americans did not solve their problem of finding an audience. Maybe we no longer believe "a single person can serve as a living snapshot of an entire country."[48] What has forced this shift is the increasing value that Americans place on individuality and trade-offs that we must then make between personal freedom and equality.[49] American individuality has always meant that we can be anyone we want to be, but what happens when my "self" infringes on yours?

If there is one market but multiple cultures even among American consumers, then how can organizations build profitable relationships with these values-driven consumers? That process is the subject of Chapter 3, where we offer specific suggestions for transmigration by organizations. First, let us explore more deeply the power of values to anchor us while we seamlessly switch social identities.

Value Systems Define Cultural Boundaries

Macro Versus Micro Values

Values and value systems are such overused terms that we must clarify the differences between cultural value systems and personal values in a multi-cultural society. Figure 1.1 shows two types of values that shape individuals'

Figure 1.1 **Macro and Micro Values as Sources of Influence on Consumer Choice**

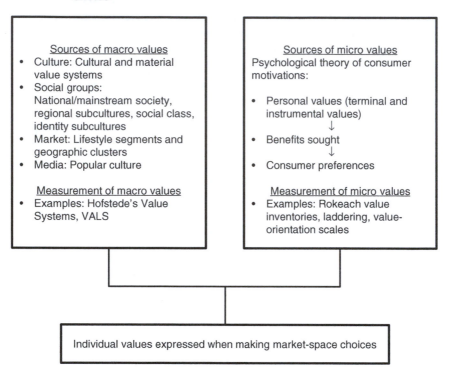

attitudes and behaviors. We each learn our society's macro-level values, to a lesser or greater extent, while micro-level values are value-driven preferences and behaviors chosen by the individual. Both systems of beliefs are at the core of our psychological motivations. Through experience, we translate these beliefs into preferences for specific product or service attributes in the domain of consumption.[50]

The concept of macro-level values as a motivator for consumer behavior is rooted in several fields—prominently anthropology and international marketing practice. Cultural value systems describe the general norms and beliefs of a particular social group, such as a culture, social class, or subculture. For instance, power distance is a cultural value system expressed on a continuum from low (e.g., the United States, Germany, Israel, Sweden, New Zealand) to high (e.g., China, India, Russia, Arab countries, Latin America).[51]

Using global value inventories like those developed by Dr. Geert Hofstede, marketers can compare different cultural groups for similarities and differences (www.geerthofstede.com/culture/). Other macro-level, universal measures such as lifestyle-based VALS marketed by Strategic Business Insights, provide an umbrella under which we can identify unique constellations of values, activities, interests, and opinions shared by peoples across cultures.[52] The next section presents these frames of reference.

Micro values, in contrast, are psychological concepts—personal value systems—to distinguish them from the cultural value systems described above. They anchor our attitudes and, in turn, determine our choices for how to behave. Laddering is a marketing research technique designed to link one consumer's preferences for particular product attributes to benefits that person seeks and, in turn, to values that s/he holds dear.[53]

The insights from laddering help to design communication campaigns that resonate with audiences based on shared values. By connecting values to product preferences one-person-at-a-time, researchers can build a ladder from a person's preferences for particular product features, to benefits desired, both functional and then social, and, ultimately, to the values most important in that person's life. Thus, in this way a personal value inventory can link consumer choices to personal values. For example, the choice of a BMW may be linked to core values of "a comfortable life," "an exciting life," "freedom," or "social recognition." If the individuals seeking these values represent different market segments, and they also identify with different subculture groups, then it may be possible to target different subcultures with unique marketing appeals. Chapter 2 discusses the role of personal values in constructing social identities in detail.

The different origins of cultural and personal value systems yield very different insights into our buying behaviors. For example, the value systems that we learn as members of a particular social group do not necessarily mean that any individual member of that culture is actually motivated by those values at any point in time.[54] These are simply group norms; thus, they do not allow us to predict any single individual's behavior. This gap between community norm and an individual's interpretation or use of it is the source of diversity so evident within most social groups.

However, psychological approaches to values do not suggest how to group people with the same value-structures or how they might be expressed in a market's overall preference for specific product attributes or benefits. Personal values can lead in multiple behavioral directions, reducing their predictive power.[55] Thus some might argue that values are inadequate for purposes of planning a marketing strategy. For this reason, the largest concentration of research in consumer behavior, marketing, and communication theory has been focused on attitudes and attitude change—we can "move the needle" there via marketing tactics.

An important difference between attitudes and values is that values are "semipermanent" while attitudes are changeable. This presents both an opportunity and a barrier for marketers. The opportunity is that if we can understand the motivations that underlie a person's attitude about a particular object by exploring what values it taps into, we can understand how to resonate with consumers on a basis deeper and broader than their current brand preferences, attitudes, or choices. The practical difficulty is that cultural and personal values change only slowly over time, and thus organizations are powerless to change individual preferences using this route. The absence of a direct link between values and actions means there is no direct explanation for why people with particular values do specific things. A large number of attitudes may explain any action, and a behavior may tap into several values simultaneously.

While values are not effective as predictors of an individual's behavior, the concept of a cultural value system highlights the most significant, non-demographic basis on which people determine "us" versus "them." It is this insight that sheds light on how one market becomes a market of consumers from multiple cultures. Some people may choose not to identify with the ethnic group into which they were born, but their personal value system may still reflect that group's cultural norms. Learning about the value inventories associated with different social groups in the United States will help us to learn where some internal cultural boundaries lie and to see how they are shifting over time.

Cultural Value Systems

We begin learning how to be members of a particular culture before we are even born. We recognize music, language, and personal distance as dictated by our primary culture long before we even learn to talk.[56] Beliefs, norms, values, and categories for organizing our world are uniquely arrayed in distinctive cultural environments. Nevertheless, several authors have identified common "etic" (culture-independent) value systems that help us compare multiple cultures.

Geert Hofstede used five value systems to profile the cultural environment in over 70 countries and regions of the world.[57] A continuum from highly individualistic (e.g., Australia, France, the Netherlands, the United Kingdom, the United States) to collectivistic countries (e.g., China, Indonesia, Latin America, South Korea) describes the difference between a "self" constructed by the individual and a "self" defined by the groups to which the individual belongs. This difference has significant implications for how Americans from different subcultures develop their social identities, as discussed in Chapter 2. Nike, the quintessential American brand of sports shoe, emphasizes the "I" in its "Just Do It" campaign, while Adidas, from Germany, preaches the beauty of teamwork, two ways to approach the consumer that resonate with the values of the sports that they emphasize as well as the consumer's culture.[58]

Power distance, from low to high, refers to the distribution of power, prestige, and money across members of a cultural group. Latin America, southern Europe, the Arab countries, and most East Asian societies are high power-distance cultures while northern Europe, Canada, the United States, and Australia are low power-distance zones. Communication in high power-distance cultures emphasizes differences, just as the choice of using *tu* (you, fam.) or *usted* (you, form.) in Spanish or the choice of verb ending in Korean, reflect relative status in the relationship between speaker and listener.

A third value system is anchored on one end by a preference for "risk-taking" and on the other end by "uncertainty avoidance." Uncertainty avoidance is important in countries such as Belgium, Greece, Japan, and Mexico while risk-taking is valued in China, Hong Kong, India, Jamaica, Singapore, the United States, and Vietnam. In cultures emphasizing uncertainty avoidance, rules and experts exist to assist in predicting and ordering behavior. In a risk-taking culture, entrepreneurship and innovation thrive.

Countries that value masculinity (e.g., Ireland, Italy, Japan, Switzerland, the United States) emphasize competition and distinctive gender roles, whereas countries that value femininity (e.g., Chile, the Netherlands, Norway, Russia, Sweden, Thailand) prefer blurred gender roles and cooperation. Romance languages like Spanish and French classify all nouns, animate and inanimate, as masculine or feminine, reflecting the importance in those cultures of distinct gender roles. In countries such as Sweden, public policy supports gender-neutral "new parent" time away from work.

Last, Hofstede recognized the long-term orientation of cultures such as those found in Brazil, China, India, Japan, and Taiwan, in contrast to the short-term horizon that reigns in countries such as Canada, East and West Africa, Germany, the Philippines, the United Kingdom, and the United States. Country scores and comparison profiles for a large number of world cultures are posted on Dr. Hofstede's website (www.geert-hofstede.com/hofstede_dimensions.php).

Another anthropologist, Dr. Edward T. Hall, classified countries into those of high and low "context," his term for the importance of "words" in communicating meaning.[59] People who are brought up in low-context cultures tend to emphasize direct, logical, verbal, and written communication, and most meaning is found in the words themselves (e.g., Germany, Scandinavia, the United States). In contrast, in high-context cultures such as China, Korea, Japan, Native and Latin America, and Southern Europe, how something is said is as significant as what is actually said. Sensitivity to nonverbal messages among these cultures is exemplified in the Japanese tea ritual, in which nothing is said and the meaning is contained in the way in which it is performed.[60] Hall also noted the way people in high-context cultures use personal space to connote power or formality and ritual to structure interaction.[61]

Value Inventories

In a search for ways to segment markets that can be applied across cultures, several marketers and consultants have designed and tested value inventories. VALS, as developed and marketed by Strategic Business Insights, is one of the best-known and most widely applied of these inventories.[62]

VALS classifies buyers into one of eight lifestyle groups based on questions about values, beliefs, activities, interests, opinions, and resources of the individual. The three motivations that distinguish the groups are ideas, achievement, and self-expression. These are then combined with the level of an individual's resources to form the eight groups. More detail about each group is available at www.strategicbusinessinsights.com/vals/ustypes.shtml.

For example, VALS Innovators are described as having high self-esteem, being open to new products and ideas, and being motivated by ideals, self-expression, and achievement to various degrees. Apple products such as the iPhone and iPad are targeted to VALS Innovators.[63] VALS Experiencers tend to be young and seek variety and excitement in their purchases. They are also quick to drop products that no longer express how they see themselves, since their primary motivation is self-expression. A line from an advertisement for a custom-tailored suit claimed it was "a natural aphrodisiac," a perfect appeal to VALS Experiencers. A third VALS group comprises the VALS Believers, who are driven by ideals but are conservative, conventional people whose beliefs underlie their preference for familiar American brands and community organizations. Companies that promise American-made products or who link themselves to Americana such as red, white, and blue or the American flag attract consumers who are VALS Believers. The percentage of any culture's members who fit into a value inventory for Believers, Innovators, or Experiencers naturally varies across cultures, but Strategic Business Insights argues that all cultures include some members of each of the eight groups.

Yet another scholar, Dr. Milton Rokeach, developed a value inventory that can be quantified. He identified 18 terminal (desired end-states of existence worth striving for) and 18 instrumental values (modes of conduct and beliefs socially preferable in all situations). These core values are more reliable than behavior or attitudes since they are stable over time.[64] Yet another value inventory has been developed and tested by the Roper Organization and consists of six "global values segments."[65]

The examples in this section include only a few of the ways in which we use values to distinguish between cultural groups and the individuals who belong to them. According to measures such as VALS, Americans already live in a multicultural society where individuals have different primary motives in the marketplace. The growing diversity of the U.S. population also reflects an increasing number of cultural value systems with origins in other parts of the world, which underlie our motives. In effect, we live in a country with internal cultural boundaries that differentiate cultural and lifestyle-identified individuals. It is not the label used by the person but the beliefs and ideals that s/he is trying to express in market spaces that make up this multicultural society. Understanding and responding to these unseen boundaries is the task of transcultural marketing.

American Mainstream Values

If American consumers see themselves as individuals and identify with other members of American subcultures, then what values do we hold in common? The existence of an "American culture" has been the topic of curiosity since the French historian Alexis de Tocqueville tried to describe Americans to his compatriots in 1831.[66] His conclusion was that we are a "melting pot" with our immigrants' cultural influences all mixed in together. This "melting pot" concept has mistakenly left the impression that there is no such thing as a unique American culture. Nothing could be further from the truth, at least when our unique cultural values are compared to those of citizens of other countries. The next sections present alternative perspectives on exactly what American mainstream cultural values are.

The United States Versus Other Countries

As described earlier, several cultural value systems form the crux of rules and beliefs found around the world. Extensive research programs have documented the country profiles of these interrelated cultural value systems.[67] It is important to understand the substance of mainstream American cultural ideals, since that we judge others and ourselves against them.

An important influence over how the "self" is viewed in any culture comes from the continuum anchored by individualism and collectivism. The United States ranks first in levels of individualism among the countries measured by Hofstede and colleagues.[68] We place importance on standards that apply to all, our rights to privacy, individual initiative, and achievement. These ideals reflect the importance of self-determination in our individualistic culture. Individualism also relates to consumer choices, such as living in detached houses, do-it-yourself activities, and above-average purchases of home and life insurance.[69]

Even a product such as the cell phone, which links us to others, is marketed to Americans as a medium through which to wield influence over others. Verizon used the concept of "conquer with your own signal" in a campaign showing individuals of different genders and ethnicities, emphasizing the power that comes from "being in touch with others."

Countries at the collectivistic end of the continuum are located mostly in Africa, Asia, Latin America, and Southern and Eastern Europe. Americans have led the global trend toward more individualistic societies; at the same time, we are incorporating immigrants from collectivistic regions of the world.

The United States is considered a low power-distance country along with several English-speaking and Northern European countries. We do not tolerate significant inequality in social status, wealth, power, or application of laws. However, we, like other low power-distance cultures, value freedom more than equality, and place less faith in "experts" and more on our own abilities.[70] Americans ignore many variations in social status that members of other cultures do not. Status mobility is a given in American society. These beliefs are in sharp contrast to those of the major sources of America's immigrants: Latin America, Asia, and, to a lesser extent, Eastern Europe and Africa.[71]

The emphasis on individualism in mainstream American culture is replicated in the beliefs that we have about nature and human nature. Americans tend to see human beings as separate from, and more valuable than, the natural world.[72] Thus, the way was paved for us to convert natural resources for our use. It also reflects a strong belief in the value of science, rational thinking, and the use of technology to solve problems. We also believe in the overall goodness of humanity and that with education/training, rehabilitation, self-improvement, and voluntarism, we can make our world better.[73]

The materialism of mainstream American culture is often a topic of critics. It is true that our economic system encourages us to buy and replace things frequently, and we often evaluate people by their material possessions. There are signs that, for younger participants in the American mainstream, "having experiences," especially unique ones, have taken the place of "owning more."[74] Still, we are an action-oriented society. While families complain about the frenetic pace of their lives, they maintain that it keeps them close.[75]

American society is also classified as a masculine one, where there are distinct gender roles and an emphasis on competition over cooperation. Dr. Martin Gannon uses the game of football as an analogy for how success is traditionally achieved in American culture. This model shows the emphasis in our culture on competition, the need for star players, and the ultimate sacrifice of individual rewards for those of the team.[76]

Americans score on the "risk-taking" end of another cultural value continuum, with "uncertainty avoidance" anchoring the other end. We love to break the rules, improvise, and change our minds. These beliefs are behind our large numbers of patents, scientific discoveries, high levels of personal debt, and impulsive purchasing habits. In turn, our love of sports and competition in any form flows from our high level of masculinity on Dr. Hofstede's masculine-feminine continuum.

Last, we live for the future and care little about our history. The short-term but sure horizon is more appealing to us than more-uncertain long-term rewards. Since we believe we can make of ourselves whatever we wish, we undervalue history's lessons.[77] In sum, compared to many other cultures, American culture is individualistic, risk-taking, masculine, and competitive, with a short-term orientation and low tolerance of inequality.

Americans also have distinctive styles of communication, as discussed in more detail in Chapter 2. We are direct, explicit, and both personal and informal. We are quick to come to the point in conversations, whereas Arab, Asian, and Latin American cultures use elaborate greeting rituals to provide social context for discussions.[78] We pay attention to words, less so to the nonverbal signals in communication contexts. Responsibility for clear meaning lies with the speaker rather than the listener, as in high-context societies.

Another unique characteristic of the American style of communication is our "problem-oriented" view of events. We assume problems and solutions are such basic components of reality that we see all events as problems to be "solved." We offer suggestions when someone mentions thinking about going on a diet. In addition, when we are discussing problems, we move quickly to the solution-seeking phase and begin offering options for action. Others see us as impetuous and fear that we rush to judgment before really understanding issues.[79]

Cultural differences have a major impact on how we make decisions. Recent research in cognitive psychology indicates that Asians think more holistically and pay more attention to context, relationships, and experience-based knowledge, while Westerners are more analytic, try to avoid contradictions, and rely on formal logic.[80] A cross-cultural comparison of decision-makers in North America, Asia, and Europe showed that when reasons were requested for decisions, East Asians were likely to choose ones that supported compromise while North Americans used reasons supporting a single interest. The implication is that Americans from different subcultures may draw from differing cultural norms for decision-making. However, the same study warns all consumer behavior researchers that culture can have both active and dormant influences, depending on the situation and the individual consumer's state of mind.[81]

Unique Aspects of American Consumer Culture

A different way of summarizing American culture is to focus on the cultural meanings of consumption. Two different approaches have been developed by different authors.

Josh Hammond and James Morrison defined seven forces that "make up our national character and determine how we respond to everything from new products and ideas to the latest developments in management and leadership."[82] The seven forces paint an American culture whose values easily translate into preferred choices in our market spaces.

First is an insistence on choice as the dominant force in all aspects of life. Second is pursuit of impossible dreams that we "make" come true. Our competitiveness leads to an obsession with "bigger and more," (third) as well as an "impatience with time," (fourth) since we seem to want everything "yesterday." The fifth force is our "acceptance of mistakes," often due to our sixth value, "fixing things up and constantly improvising." Seventh, we are in "perpetual search of the new—identities, ideas, strategies, and products— because they provide new choices."[83] In contrast to a belief that there is no such thing as "an American culture," the authors suggest that these forces not only define us but provide the "glue that keeps us together and the common aspirations that drive us forward."[84]

The energy driven by these cultural forces has been with us since "Plymouth Rock."[85] More than anything, it is our drive for change and the ability to adapt to it that drives Americans. What appears to be cultural change is often only a shift toward the natural restraining forces that limit each of our cultural forces. For example, reality is a limitation on "impossible dreams" just as tradition limits our fixation with "what's new." Ultimately, choice and freedom of choice govern our reactions to cultural change.[86]

Dr. Clotaire Rapaille presents an outsider's view of American culture. He writes that while DNA is unique to every individual and human instincts are universal to all humankind, the middle ground belongs to culture, where we learn the unique meanings of things.[87] He believes that each culture has specific meanings for things within the context of that culture's views of the world. He calls these culture-specific meanings "culture codes."

The codes help uncover the sometimes-hidden importance of choices, such as which car to drive (it defines who we are), why we are fascinated by beautiful people (it saves us from emotionally empty lives), and why we cannot be "too young or too thin" (it is a mask we wear to show that we belong in this culture). In our action-oriented culture, it also makes sense that being healthy means "movement." Our definition of product "quality" is that the product "simply works," but our concept of luxury has more to do with what we feel that we deserve (e.g., a "Starbuck's break") than with product performance or price.

Dr. Rapaille's culture codes do not just help outsiders understand subtle meanings of typical American experiences like being invited to dinner at someone's home; they also suggest where some internal cultural boundaries might lie. For older Americans, the car is "cultural code" for "who I am," as Hyundai recognized with its "your car says a lot about you" campaign. For younger Americans, the culture code for "who I am" may be: "Mac vs. PC?" Social networking websites also play that role for members of Generation Y. "Food as fuel" may not resonate in the same way outside the mainstream or for U.S. Latinos, whose extended family at the dinner table not only "complete their circles" but often symbolize ethnic pride.[88]

Chapter Summary and Book Presentation Plan

Forces such as global economic interactivity, increased population diversity, changing cultural ideals, and new media and marketing options in our market spaces create multiple cultural boundaries in the American consumer market. In this context, we "transmigrate" back and forth across cultural divides to accommodate our complex and departmentalized identities. Consuming is an active part of constructing our self-concept and in allowing us to change them at will. Our new multicultural American society consists of individuals who choose various combinations of mainstream and subculture values to create a constantly changing, socially constructed self.

With this background, Chapter 2 highlights how Americans construct their self-identities and the effect of this on what consumers want from their market spaces. American consumers express who they are and what their values are in their choices from our cornucopia of goods and services. These goods and services must continue to satisfy value and performance expectations in addition to signifying compatibility with customer values and affiliations.

Chapter 3 translates the changes in consumer needs and benefits sought into a manual for building transcultural marketing programs. If marketing's objective is redefined as "building and maintaining partnerships with culturally compatible consumers," strategic options are broadened to include "all programs that communicate brand and corporate values and their symbolic associations."[89] This is the basis of a "cultural values proposition."

The rest of the book is devoted to profiles of American subculture groups that merit investigation as consumer-partners for a large number of organizations. The subculture groups highlighted in this book are quite different from one another. Three chapters profile culturally defined groups: U.S. Latinos (Chapter 4), African Americans (Chapter 6), and Asian Americans (Chapter 8).

The age-cohort chapter (Chapter 5) profiles five subcultures: the mature market, baby boomers, Generation X, Generation Y, and Tweens. Sexual orientation comprises the cultural boundary of the LGBT population (Chapter 7).

Throughout this book are accounts of successful and not-so-successful attempts to market to members of various subculture groups. Whether U.S. Latinos, gay, or mature Americans, or any other groups are good targets for a particular company or brand can be determined only by a careful study of the potential match between the company, its resources, values, products, and services and buyers' values, interests, needs, and behaviors. Our focus in this book is on broad opportunities and requirements represented by the subcultures discussed. While it is not possible in this context to provide enough data for purposes of specific marketing plans, this approach encourages marketers to adopt new ways of thinking about consumer needs and new marketing programs to address our multicultural consumer environment.

Notes

1. P.H. Diamandis and S. Kotler, *Abundance* (New York: Free Press, 2012).

2. T. Levitt, "The Globalization of Markets," *Harvard Business Review* (May/June 1983): 92–102.

3. J. Zogby, *The Way We'll Be: The Zogby Report on the Transformation of the American Dream* (New York: Random House, 2008); C.D. Schewe and G. Meredith, "Segmenting Global Markets by Generational Cohorts: Determining Motivations by Age," *Journal of Consumer Behaviour* 4, no. 1 (2004): 51–63; "Worldwide Cohorts," *American Demographics* (March 2002): 19.

4. D. Kjeldgaard and S. Askegaard, "The Glocalization of Youth Culture: The Global Youth Segment as Structures of Common Difference," *Journal of Consumer Research* 33 (September 2006): 231–247; B.D. Keillor, M. D'Amico, and V. Horton, "Global Consumer Tendencies," *Psychology and Marketing* 18, no. 1 (January 2001): 1–19.

5. K. Capell, "How the Swedish Retailer Became a Global Cult Brand," *BusinessWeek,* November 14, 2005, 96–106.

6. Y. Strizhakova, R. Coulter, and L. Price, "Branded Products as a Passport to Global Citizenship: Perspectives from Developed and Developing Countries," *Journal of International Marketing* 16 (2008): 2–44.

7. A. Davies, and J.A. Fitchett, "'Crossing Culture': A Multi-Method Enquiry into Consumer Behavior and the Experience of Cultural Transition," *Journal of Consumer Behaviour* 3, no. 4 (2006): 316–330; R.D. Kaplan, "Travels into America's Future," *Atlantic Monthly* (August 1998): 37–61.

8. Y. Strizhakova, R. Coulter, and L. Price, "Branded Products as a Passport to Global Citizenship: Perspectives from Developed and Developing Countries," *Journal of International Marketing* 16 (2008): 2–44.

9. R. Walker, *Buying In: The Secret Dialogue Between What We Buy and Who We Are* (New York: Random House, 2008).

10. G.P. Zachary, *The Global Me* (New York: Perseus, 2000).

11. M. Sivy, "What America Will Look Like in 25 Years," *Money,* October 1, 1997, 98–106.

12. J.M. Humphreys, *The Multicultural Economy 2010* (Athens: Selig Center for Economic Growth, Terry College of Business, University of Georgia, 2010), 3.

13. "Unmarried with Children" *Time*, November 29, 1999.

14. W.H. Frey, "Immigrant and Native Migrant Magnets," *American Demographics* 18, no. 1 (1996): 36–41, 53.

15. W. Wang, *The Rise of Intermarriage* (Washington, DC: Pew Research Center, February 16, 2012); Humphreys, *The Multicultural Economy 2010*.

16. J. Faull, "New Cheerios Advert Sparks Race Row After Featuring an Interracial Couple," The Drum, June 1, 2013, www.thedrum.com/news/2013/06/01/new-cheerios-advert-sparks-race-row-after-featuring-interracial-couple/.

17. W.H. Frey, "The Diversity Myth," *American Demographics* (June 1998): 39–43; S. Mitchell, "Birds of a Feather," *American Demographics* (February 1995): 40–48.

18. Humphreys, *The Multicultural Economy 2010*, 5.

19. R. Wartzman, "Houston Turns Out to Be the Capital of the Egg Roll," *Wall Street Journal*, December 7, 1995, A1, A9.

20. M. Esterl, "Going Outside, Beyond the Billboard," *Wall Street Journal*, July 21, 2005, B3.

21. B. Steinberg et al., "How Old Media Can Survive in a New World," *Wall Street Journal*, May 23, 2005, R4.

22. Steinberg et al., "How Old Media Can Survive in a New World."

23. J. Gaskill, "In-Game Advertising to Hit $1 Billion in 2014," G4, May 26, 2009, www.g4tv.com/thefeed/blog/post/695860/in-game-advertising-spending-to-hit-1-billion-in-2014/.

24. Steinberg et al., "How Old Media Can Survive in a New World."

25. B. Steinberg, "Next up on Fox: Ads That Can Change Pitch," *Wall Street Journal*, April 21, 2005, B1.

26. T.J. Mullaney and R.D. Hof, "E-tailing Finally Hits Its Stride," *Bloomberg Businessweek*, December 19, 2004, 26–27.

27. J. Fine, "An Onslaught of Hidden Ads," *Bloomberg BusinessWeek*, June 27, 2005, 24; D. Fonda, "Prime-Time Peddling," *Time*, May 24, 2005, 50–51.

28. Fine, "An Onslaught of Hidden Ads," 22.

29. N. Prakesh, "Super Bowl 2013 Commercials: Watch Them Here!" Mashable, February 3, 2013, http://mashable.com/2013/02/03/super-bowl-2013-commercials/.

30. Mullaney and Hof, "E-Tailing Finally Hits Its Stride," 26–27.

31. J. Caplan, "50,000 TV Channels! The Skype Guys Strike Again," *Time*, March 12, 2007, 52–54.

32. S. Vranica, "P&G Plunges into Social Networking," *Wall Street Journal*, January 8, 2007, B4.

33. A. Bianco, "The Vanishing Mass Market," *Bloomberg BusinessWeek*, July 12, 2004, 52–72.

34. D. Clark, "Ad Measurement Is Going High Tech," *Wall Street Journal*, April 6, 2006, B4.

35. B. Barnes, "New TV Ratings Will Produce Ad-Price Fight," *Wall Street Journal*, December 22, 2005, B1, B3.

36. M. Halter, *Shopping for Identity: The Marketing of Ethnicity* (New York: Schocken Books, 2000).

37. T.L. Friedman and M. Mandelbaum, *That Used to Be Us: How America Fell Behind in the World It Invented and How We Can Come Back* (New York: Farrar,

Straus and Giroux, 2012); C. Murray, *Coming Apart: The State of White America, 1960–2010* (New York: Crown Forum, 2012).

38. J. Meacham, "Keeping the Dream Alive," *Time,* July 2, 2012, 26–39.

39. J.W. Gentry, S. Jun, and P. Tansuhaj, "Consumer Acculturation Processes and Cultural Conflict: How Generalizable Is a North American Model for Marketing Globally?" *Journal of Business Research* 32 (1995): 129–139.

40. P.H. Ray, "The Emerging Culture," *American Demographics* (February 1997): 28–34.

41. C. Walker and E. Moses, "The Age of Self-Navigation," *American Demographics* (September 1996): 36–42.

42. J.N. Boyce, "Nonwhites Wake to 'American Dream,'" *Wall Street Journal,* October 7, 1997, A2, A14.

43. "The Bottom of the Pyramid: Businesses Are Learning to Serve the Needs of Hard-Up Americans," *Economist,* June 23, 2011, www.economist.com/node/18863898/.

44. R.D. Putnam, *Bowling Alone: The Collapse and Revival of American Community* (New York: Simon and Schuster, 2000).

45. Murray, *Coming Apart.*

46. H. Stein, "The American Dream," *Wall Street Journal,* December 24, 1996, 24, A8.

47. N. Fox, "What Are Our Real Values?" *Newsweek,* February 13, 1999.

48. J. Neimark, "Why We Need Miss America," *Psychology Today* (September/October 1998): 40–43, 72, 74.

49. Friedman and Mandelbaum, *That Used to Be Us.*

50. D.E. Vinson, J.E. Scott, and L.M. Lamont, "The Role of Personal Values in Marketing and Consumer Behavior," *Journal of Marketing* (April 1977): 44–50.

51. Hofstede Center, "National Culture: Countries," http://geert-hofstede.com/countries.html.

52. Strategic Business Insights, "US Framework and VALS Types," www.strategicbusinessinsights.com/vals/ustypes.shtml.

53. T.J. Reynolds and J.C. Olson, eds., *Understanding Consumer Decision Making: The Means-End Approach to Marketing and Advertising Strategy* (Mahwah, NJ: Lawrence Erlbaum, 2001).

54. D. Maheswaran and S. Shavitt, "Issues and New Directions in Global Consumer Psychology," *Journal of Consumer Psychology* 9, no. 2 (2000): 59–66.

55. L.J. Shrum, J.A. McCarty, and T.M. Lowrey, "The Usefulness of the Values Construct in Marketing and Advertising: A Re-Examination," in *Proceedings of the 1990 Conference of the American Academy of Advertising,* ed. P.A. Stout (Austin, TX: AAA, 1990), 49–54.

56. Retrieved from www.birthpsychology.com/lifebefore/earlymem.html.

57. G. Hofstede, *Culture's Consequences: Comparing Values, Behaviors, Institutions, and Organizations Across Nations* (Thousand Oaks, CA: Sage, 2001).

58. E. Esterl and S. Kang, "Adidas Extols 'We Over Me' as It Aims at Shoe King Nike's Cult of Personality," *Wall Street Journal,* October 16, 2006, B1.

59. E.T. Hall, *The Silent Language* (New York: Doubleday/Anchor Books, 1959).

60. F. Jandt, *Intercultural Communication* (Thousand Oaks, CA: Sage, 1995), 191–208.

61. Hall, *The Silent Language.*

62. Strategic Business Insights, "About VALS," www.strategicbusinessinsights.com/vals/.

63. M. Pieters, "What Are the Personality Characteristics of iPhone Versus Android Users? (Infographic)," Bandwidth Blog, August 16, 2011, www.band-widthblog.com/2011/08/16/personality-characteristics-of-iphone-vs-android-users-infographic/.

64. K.T. Frith and B. Mueller, *Advertising and Societies* (New York: Peter Lang, 2003), 50–51.

65. Ibid.

66. A. de Toqueville, *Democracy in America* (New York: Penguin Books, 2003).

67. Hofstede, *Culture's Consequences.*

68. Ibid., 215.

69. Ibid., 226, 227, 245.

70. S. Jacoby, *The Age of American Unreason* (New York: Pantheon Books, 2008).

71. E.C. Stewart and M.J. Bennett, *American Cultural Patterns,* rev. ed. (Yarmouth, ME: Intercultural Press, 1991), 89–132.

72. Hofstede, *Culture's Consequences*; G. Hofstede, *Cultures and Organizations: Software of the Mind*, rev. ed. (New York: McGraw-Hill, 1997), 109–138; F. Trompenaars and C. Hampden-Turner, *Riding the Waves of Culture: Understanding Diversity in Global Business,* 2d ed. (New York: McGraw-Hill, 1998), 145–160; M. de Mooij, *Global Marketing and Advertising: Understanding Cultural Paradoxes* (Thousand Oaks, CA: Sage, 1998), 42–125.

73. G. Althuen, *American Ways* (Yarmouth, ME: Intercultural Press, 1988), 12–13.

74. Ray, "The Emerging Culture."

75. S. Shellenbarger, "The American Family: Busy Every Minute and Proud of It, Too," *Wall Street Journal,* August 16, 2000, B1.

76. M.J. Gannon, ed., *Cultural Metaphors* (Thousand Oaks, CA: Sage, 2001), 90–108.

77. W. Strauss and N. Howe, *The Fourth Turning: An American Prophecy* (New York: Broadway Books, 1997).

78. Stewart and Bennett, *American Cultural Patterns,* 155–165.

79. Ibid., 155.

80. E. Goode, "How Culture Molds Habits of Thought," *New York Times*, August 8, 2000, F1.

81. D.A. Briley, M.W. Morris, and I. Simonson, "Reasons as Carriers of Culture: Dynamic Versus Dispositional Models of Cultural Influence on Decision Making," *Journal of Consumer Research* 27, no. 2 (2000): 157–178.

82. J. Hammond and J. Morrison, *The Stuff Americans Are Made of* (New York: Macmillan, 1996).

83. Ibid., 3–21; W. Lazar, *Handbook of Demographics for Marketing and Advertising: New Trends in the American Marketplace,* 2d ed. (Lexington, MA: Lexington Press, 1994).

84. Hammond and Morrison, *The Stuff Americans Are Made of*, 8–10.

85. Ibid., 3.

86. Ibid., 19–21.

87. C. Rapaille, *The Culture Code* (New York: Broadway Books, 2006).

88. Ibid.

89. M.C. Tharp, *Marketing and Consumer Identity in Multicultural America* (Thousand Oaks, CA: Sage, 2001), 2.

2

Who Do You Want to Be Today?

Choosing Products, Creating Identities

This chapter addresses the connection between personal identity and choices from our cornucopia of market spaces. As we learn about, choose, use, and dispose of goods and services, we are simultaneously constructing and communicating who we are. "True identity . . . resides, not in our genes, but in our mind."[1] In this chapter, we first highlight the unique attributes of the American self. Because the construction of our social identities is a constantly changing, lifelong task, we allow economic activities to play significant social and cultural roles in our lives. A luxury watch company (Patek Philippe) asks its target audience, "Who do you want to be in the next 24 hours?"

We then turn to how we "shop for identity."[2] This section of the chapter describes the ways in which we use the dual choices of community affiliations and personal values to express our social selves; we are, in effect, where we belong in society and what we believe. As we express these affiliations in our market-space choices, our economic institutions become sources for creating cultural meaning.

When markets and cultural regions are not in sync, as in a multicultural society, we find that economic institutions play major roles in our socialization into American society and our roles as consumers. Our media and entertainment venues are the locus of American pop culture, another place where we learn about people and things that we do not know through personal experience. These are the subjects of the third section of Chapter 2.

Last we introduce the concept of consumer subcultures to describe the behavioral links between expressions of personal identity and choice of membership in subculture groups. We close this chapter by describing the similarities and differences between these consumer identities as value-driven cohorts.

Americans trumpet individuality and, as a result, are changing mainstream American culture itself. Because we can call ourselves whatever we wish we can similarly belong to whichever subculture we choose. Group labels cannot predict individual behavior. So, *who do you want to be,* and *how do you want to express it?* That is the connection marketers must identify—the relationships among chosen social roles, personal identities, social affiliations, and learned cultural values.

The American "Self" and Social Identity

The American "Self"

The American "self" is grounded in our individualistic culture. Each person is believed to be a biological and psychological being as well as a unique member of the social system.[3] Americans make strong distinctions between ourselves and others, making it hard to understand that individuals in more collectivistic cultures often think in terms of shared characteristics. Since we see ourselves as "unlike anyone else," we construct our identity out of our perceptions of who is like or unlike us as well as the criteria we choose for inclusion and exclusion. In effect, the consumer's self-concept and perception of how others respond to that "self" drive consumption behaviors.[4]

Further, our experience of the self is more intimately attached to what we "do"—our actions and achievements—than to what we know or feel. Americans reinforce each child's sense of self by offering choice at an early age; choosing a preferred cereal teaches independent decision making and expression of identity.[5] Self-actualization is an imperative of the American self, "existing detached from origins and uncommitted to any destiny."[6]

Even compared to the "self" in other individualistic countries, the American self is more autonomous. We believe in setting our own goals and pursuing them independently. Our myths suggest that people who work hard can succeed in accomplishing virtually anything they wish.[7] Products and services are presented as tools for achieving the goals of American consumers.

In spite of the emphasis on the individual, we still find idiocentrics and allocentrics in American society. The idiocentric person emphasizes the motivations of individualism at the personal level whereas allocentrics place more importance on interpersonal effects of behavior and decisions.[8] Idiocentrics in the United States have been found to be happier, to have higher self-esteem, to be more job oriented, to make more impulse purchases, and to be more brand and fashion conscious. Even controlling for gender, allocentrics spend more time cleaning, cooking, and doing laundry than do idiocentrics. In sum, there are both cultural and individual expressions of the self in American society.[9]

Our work is important, too. More than any other peoples, we seek a "feeling of accomplishment" in a job.[10] We strive for higher efficiency and are particularly open to change, with faith that "newer is better." Discipline and control are important in bringing out our goodness; this is why we are so forgiving—we believe that our fundamental nature is open to change and "self-improvement."[11] Our choice of work defines identity to self and others.

Expressing who we are is almost as American as our individuality. In spite of this commitment to a very individual-determined sense of self, groups and organizations play an important role in the process of self-definition. Participating in organizations is a venue for trying out values and making allies in support of our particular interests. We find ourselves through the people and institutions to which we relate. It is thus an irony of American individualism that without the reference point of the groups with which we identify or to which we belong, our self remains incomplete and undefined. We can "feel like a movie star" by wearing Pandora jewelry and wear jeans that are "not our daughter's." We personify brands using descriptions usually reserved for people, such as this description of a Samsung TV: "a colorful character, arrestingly beautiful, razor thin, and highly defined."

American Social Identity

The two major components of social identity in the United States are our values and our affiliations. A self-determined self and American mainstream individualism make Americans unique in our ability to "choose" our own social identity. In the past, personal characteristics such as race, geographic origin, or language spoken predetermined an individual's identity for life. When asked to describe their ethnic identity today, most Americans use labels for themselves that change across social situation and life stage.[12]

Some Americans of different races but of the same age or sexual preference see themselves as more similar to one another than to other members of their own race. Since an individual's perceptions of similarity and identification can change when social conditions do, this complicates the measurement of "ethnic identity."[13] A more accurate predictor of social identity is which population groups a specific consumer chooses to identify with.[14]

Ethnicity is not an important component of social identity for all Americans. White Americans typically do not identify as strongly with their ethnic origins as do most African Americans or U.S. Latinos.[15] African or Asian Americans and U.S. Latinos, who are in the family lifecycle stage of establishing their own families, identify more strongly with their cultural or racial heritage than those same people did during their teenage years.[16] A person who strongly identifies with ethnic heritage is more likely to express this behaviorally.[17] Many individuals also distinguish between public and private behaviors, sometimes reserving expressions of ethnicity for family members and activities at home.[18]

Americans with multiple ethnic origins may choose to identify with some aspects of their heritage over others. This is especially true for groups that are viewed negatively and thus are more distant from the American mainstream. For example, when large numbers of Jewish, Irish, and Italian immigrants came to the United States at the beginning of the twentieth century, mainstream Americans did not consider them "white."[19] It is no surprise that many of these immigrants learned to limit their expressions of ethnicity to home and religious activities.

Some gay and lesbian Americans choose to stay "in the closet" rather than risk the consequences of rejection from mainstream America. At various times, Iranian, German, Japanese, and Iraqi Americans have all found themselves identifying with a country with which the United States was at war. Thus, some Americans choose not to identify with particular aspects of their heritage. Ethnicity in the American context can evolve out of cultural socialization into an ethnic group or from an individual's *choice* to identify with that group.[20]

This last group chooses "symbolic ethnicity" by identifying with an ethnic heritage about which they know very little.[21] The dynamic nature of American social identity is strongly influenced by situational factors.[22] Ethnicity may be foremost in considering where to eat with one's parents on one occasion but not on another; it may affect choices of entertainment or food but not clothing. If a person lives where his or her ethnic group is in the majority, ethnicity or race may be less important to personal identity than for members of the minority subculture. In sum, knowing an individual's ethnic heritage is simply not sufficient information for predicting either marketplace behavior or social identity.

"Shopping for identities" heightens our sensitivity to the cultural meanings of our choices of products, services, memberships, causes, candidates, and related issues.[23] The process of identity formation contributes to perceptions of common cause. Self-labeling as well as labeling by people who are not members of the group have become sensitive issues. Ethnic marketers such as African Pride are identified with the interests of one group. Marketers in multicultural America can target multiple communities simultaneously, always with a risk that the values of these groups lead a firm to support conflicting causes. To be adept at membership in several subcultures, organizations must also learn multiple communication styles and how to segment markets without the usual demographic labels. Our identity choices complete our social selves, yet we still resist being labeled by others, especially outsiders.

Social identity is expressed in the marketplace by the adoption of at least some group norms and patterns of communication and behavior. Table 2.1 presents information about how different Americans spend their time. Personal care is an important activity for all groups, but African Americans, U.S. Latinos, and the millennials spend more time on personal care than do other groups. This leads to consequences for purchases of personal-care products; African Americans, Latinos, and Generation Y spend more on these compared to other groups.[24]

Other differences are also apparent in Table 2.1. For example, Latinos spend more time socializing on weekends than other groups and more time at work and caring for others in the household. African Americans watch more TV and communicate more with others via phone and mail. In their leisure time white Americans read and play games more than others. The youngest Americans have the most leisure time and use it for participating in sports and exercise. By learning about ethnic or other value-defined cohort norms in consumption, many marketers can identify the heavy users of product or service categories.

Products, even media choices, carry both social and individual meanings.[25] African Americans, Generations X and Y, and LGBT consumers are spending more time with media selectively targeted to them, such as BET, Univision, *Essence, HispanicBusiness*, Asianweek.com, Facebook, Out, Gays.com, Blackplanet.com, Brownpride.com, Babycenter.com (new moms), or Egothemag.com (South Asians). Not only do they prefer media that speak their own language, but they also want to shop where they encounter people like themselves.[26] Brick-and-mortar retailers, such as Urban Outfitters, Delias (teen girls), Toys "R" Us, and Tiffany's, and online retailers, such as drjays.com (urban), zebraz.com (lesbian), boomersmusic.com, and Blacklava.net (Asian Americans), help their niche consumers express how they see themselves.

Table 2.2 shows differences across ethnic groups in ownership of electronic products. The table indicates that Asian Americans are much more likely than other consumers to own camcorders, still cameras, MP3 players, projection TVs, and plasma TVs. U.S. Latinos have the highest ownership of home entertainment centers. African Americans purchase less, with the exception of videogames. And although all groups are close to the average consumer in owning television sets, the type of television owned varies by ethnic group (e.g., Asian consumers seem to prefer large plasma and projection TVs while Hispanics are more likely to have LCD TVs).

Table 2.3 shows more differences across ethnic groups, with focus on the types of shopping environments patronized. Everyone seems to have shopped

Table 2.1

Subculture Differences in Time Use, 2012 (average hours per day)

Activity	All	Whites	Blacks	Hispanics	Gen Y	Gen X	Boomers
Personal care	9.49	9.45	9.84	9.90	10.29–9.95	9.30–9.18	9.30–9.17
Eating/drinking	1.24	1.28	0.91	1.19	1.15–1.08	1.18–1.18	1.19–1.30
Household care	1.77	1.85	1.36	1.83	0.72–1.14	1.47–1.92	1.95–2.02
Purchasing goods and services	0.72	0.73	0.71	0.74	0.46–0.61	0.61–0.76	0.73–0.83
Caring for others in household	0.51	0.52	0.39	0.68	0.18–0.44	1.01–1.05	0.44–0.14
Caring for others nonhousehold	0.21	0.21	0.23	0.14	0.16–0.14	0.17–0.20	0.26–0.27
Work and work related activities	3.57	3.63	3.12	3.39	0.88–3.83	4.95–4.60	4.67–3.83
Educational activities	0.47	0.43	0.64	0.71	3.33–0.98	0.37–0.13	0.07–0.03
Orgs, civic, and religious activities	0.35	0.33	0.52	0.27	0.32–0.32	0.24–0.33	0.34–0.36
Phone, mail and e-mail activities	0.16	0.15	0.20	0.10	0.18–0.10	0.12–0.13	0.14–0.20
Miscellaneous other activities	0.29	0.29	0.30	0.27	0.42–0.23	0.34–0.29	0.25–0.27
All leisure and sports[1]	5.21	5.14	5.77	4.79	5.98–5.09	4.24–4.23	4.69–5.55
Leisure and sports: Sports and exercise	0.36	0.39	0.20	0.32	0.75–0.55	0.40–0.41	0.28–0.26
Leisure and sports: Socializing	1.05	1.12	1.10	1.21	1.34–1.13	1.24–1.08	0.87–0.93
Leisure and sports: Watching TV	3.19	3.13	3.74	3.06	2.69–2.40	2.57–2.89	3.24–3.51
Leisure and sports: Reading	0.33	0.42	0.20	0.18	0.12–0.05	0.17–0.20	0.31–0.49
Leisure and sports: Playing computer games	0.44	0.45	0.40	0.32	1.15–0.58	0.40–0.31	0.38–0.34
Relaxing/thinking	0.34	0.30	0.57	0.34	0.20–0.20	0.23–0.24	0.36–0.36
Miscellaneous leisure and sports	0.63	0.65	0.51	0.57	0.81–0.73	0.63–0.57	0.62–0.63

Source: U.S. Bureau of Labor Statistics, "Table 3. Time Spent in Primary Activities 2012," news release, www.bls.gov/news.release/atus.t03. htm; U.S. Bureau of Labor Statistics, "Table 11. Time spent in leisure and sports activities for the civilian population, 2012," news release, http:// data.bls.gov/cgi-bin/print.pl/news.release/atus.t11.htm.
[1]"Average hours per weekend/holiday day."

Table 2.2

Indices for Ownership of Electronic Products for Four Ethnic Groups, 2010

Product ownership	U.S. Hispanics	Whites, non-Hispanic	Blacks, non-Hispanic	Asian, non-Hispanic	Other
Total sample	31,501	154,442	25,275	8,887	3,379
Personal computer	89	103	91	117	98
Cell phone	100	99	102	102	106
Camcorder	110	97	83	153	109
Still camera	83	108	68	115	98
DVD player	94	101	99	98	101
Blu-ray, last 12 months	87	102	97	117	110
DVR (digital video recorder)	85	107	88	74	84
Home theater equipment	120	100	82	101	70
Portable GPS	62	112	60	144	64
MP3/digital media players	103	98	86	154	108
TV set	98	101	99	100	100
TV, type: projection (42 inches or more)	98	98	107	130	86
TV, type: flat panel LCD	70	110	75	99	96
TV, type: flat panel plasma	120	96	95	127	73
TV, type: tube	91	105	89	78	89
Videogames, own or play	97	99	105	110	130
Microwave oven	93	103	95	98	95
Automatic dishwasher	60	114	63	118	80

Source: Experian/Simmons, NCS/NCHS Adult Survey Database, September–October 2010 www.experian.com/simmons-research/consumer-study.html.

Note: The numbers in this table are indexes that compare actual versus expected volume of purchasing, according to that group's share of the population. Any number over 100 means those consumers buy "more than expected" and any number less than 100 indicates they buy "less than would be expected" by their share of the population.

at convenience stores and drugstores in the past four weeks, but Asian Americans show their high-tech preference by heavy visits to electronics stores and shopping malls and by shopping and purchasing online. Hispanics spend more time in shopping malls while white Americans are the largest patrons of home improvement stores.

Data such as those presented in Tables 2.1, 2.2, and 2.3 help quickly spot which consumer groups might be good or bad market opportunities. Those who "over index" (scores over 100) on a product category or type of store should be good candidates for future purchases, and those who "under index" (scores less than 100) may not be as interested in those products or stores. Alternatively, under indexing might indicate a market opportunity, and over indexing can mean the marketer has already missed the boat with these consumers.

Table 2.3

Types of Stores Shopped Across Ethnic Groups, 2010 (last four weeks)

	N/Index	U.S. Hispanics	Whites, non-Hispanic	Blacks, non-Hispanic	Asian, non-Hispanic	Other
Total sample	223,483	31,501	154,442	25,275	8,887	3,379
(Index)	100	100	100	100	100	100
Convenience store	123,032	17,147	85,931	13,906	3,794	2,255
(Index)	100	99	101	100	78	121
Department or /discount store (children's clothing)	119,809	12,706	89,875	10,706	5,225	1,297
(Index)	100	75	109	79	110	72
Drugstore	162,987	22,700	112,154	18,684	7,106	2,344
(Index)	100	99	100	101	110	95
Home electronics store	63,613	8,228	45,097	5,781	3,804	704
(Index)	100	92	103	80	150	73
Home improvement store	116,549	12,107	90,363	8,170	4,545	1,365
(Index)	100	74	112	62	98	77
Supermarket/food stores	207,736	27,975	145,488	22,632	8,529	3,112
(Index)	100	96	101	96	103	99
Shopping malls	113,157	16,876	76,459	12,358	5,737	1,727
(Index)	100	106	98	97	127	101
Gathered shopping information online	44,978	4,365	34,514	2,657	3,006	437
(Index)	100	69	111	52	168	64
Made a purchase online	48,793	4,694	37,236	3,095	2,977	792
(Index)	100	68	110	56	153	107

Source: Experian/Simmons, NCS/NCHS Adult Survey Database, September–October 2010, www.experian.com/simmons-research/consumer-study.html.

Before we build marketing programs on the basis of behavioral data, we need to know more about consumers than their current patterns of behavior. Cultural, demographic, and lifestyle information could provide insight into the numbers. For example, do U.S. Latinos and African Americans not own dishwashers because they lack space, because their families are larger size, because they are unaware of the dishwasher's benefits, or for some other reason? Only a deeper analysis can answer questions like this. Behavioral data have lured many companies into targeting ethnic Americans. Long-term success requires building a relationship with ethnic consumers (or other members of American subcultures) within the context of their values and cultural affiliations.

Personal Communication and Decision-Making Styles

The communication style endorsed by mainstream American culture deserves special attention. We learn through observation and imitation which subjects to talk about, how to have a conversation, and which parts of a message to pay attention to.

The most frequent terms used to describe Americans' styles of interaction are: direct, open, and assertive. Among our preferred topics for discussion with unknown persons are physical surroundings; later, they touch on shared experiences such as favorite entertainments, social lives, hobbies, and jobs. Politics and religion are subjects only for close friends and family. Americans use repartee more than long monologues and employ very few conversational rituals, such as "Nice to meet you."[27] We learn that arguments should be conducted in calm, moderate tones with a minimum of gesturing. Americans can sustain many friendships simultaneously, although often this is at a superficial level of involvement.

We give special weight to messages that are "in writing," while other cultures value oral speaking or verbal ability. People from high-context cultures pay much more attention to the nonverbal aspects of messages and think Americans are "too talkative, too loud and not sensitive enough."[28] A good example of our preference for the personal in conversations is what Americans do first after greeting someone new: We "sift through a number of topics until . . . we . . . find an experience in common."[29] We also self-reveal much more quickly than members of other cultures.

It is not just the way we talk that distinguishes Americans; when making decisions, we are much more likely to rely on facts and logic than on intuition or experience.[30] We place much weight on rational decision making using an empirical approach. We also value personal experience; having seen something "with one's own eyes" is more reliable than evidence from other people. We distrust emotions if they are not supported by facts. Americans are more likely to believe "truth" derived from observed facts, while people in other cultures are more likely to be swayed by theory and ideas, even by insights from meditation.[31]

Shopping for Identities in Our Market Spaces

We learn about our world from the institutions that teach us cultural values. This process, called socialization, takes place mostly while we are children. For immigrants, however, *acculturation*, the term that refers to learning about and adjusting to a new culture, can take a lifetime, even multiple generations. Learning to be a member of a cultural group teaches individuals the options for personal identity and values associated with them.[32]

Learning Culture from Marketers

Cultural socialization is the normal responsibility of institutions such as churches, schools, the family, and government. Their influence as socialization agents is in decline, while peers and the media are playing larger roles. We belong to fewer community organizations, we spend less time socializing with others, and political participation is at an all-time low.[33] Whether we like it or not, communication media and marketing institutions act as primary socialization agents for aspects of our culture that we cannot or do not learn through personal experience.[34] Media images and marketplace experiences are the building blocks of contemporary American culture.

Advertising is a major input into our ideas of what is masculine or feminine and how to act in those roles. Consider the following lines from historical and contemporary advertising: "You mean a woman can open a Heinz cap?" "Deal with it. It's what men do" (Viagra); "I can't cook. Who cares?" (Wonderbra); "Show her it's a man's world" (Van Heusen); "Athletes battle" (Axe); "Subaru is like a spirited woman yearning to be tamed"; "Daddy-like" (Toyota minivan); "Now men adore her milky white skin" (Golden Peacock bleach crème); "Shapely woman and a Gibson guitar"; "Bride and groom dressed in Killer jeans." Can you distinguish past ads from current ones? These differences show how male and female roles have changed over the years.

Radio, television, movies, games, and the other products of media culture provide materials out of which we forge our identities. We use this imagery to develop notions of what it means to be male or female, to belong to a particular social class, ethnicity or race, nationality, or sexual orientation. We use what we learn in media to define who or what is "us" or "them." Media stories reflect what we consider good or bad, positive or negative, moral or evil, using the symbols, myths, and resources of our common culture.[35]

Economic institutions of the marketplace are themselves shaped by their cultural context.[36] Marketing phenomena as diverse as Super Bowl commercials, coupons, price tags, catalogs, web pages, magazines, self-service gas stations, brand names, a YouTube website, and department stores are cultural artifacts. Malls are remaking themselves into entertainment venues to combat the convenience advantages of online competitors.[37] Their economic purpose is to help consumers obtain the goods and services that they want, but while performing this role, marketing institutions transmit and reflect cultural values. Even the relative importance of their economic role is determined by the materialist environment in which they exist.[38]

Sometimes, the cultural reflections seen in our marketing phenomena seem like fun-house mirrors of our real values. We see people go ballistic over a ring-around-the-collar, find true love when they switch to the right brand of toothpaste, or let a passion for one brand of coffee lead to other "passions." Advertising vignettes exaggerate what is true: American culture places importance on cleanliness, physical appearance, and sex appeal. Able to distinguish such distorted images from personal experience, most Americans would be shocked to realize that this is the way we are seen by outsiders. For people who know us only through media images, those images *are* reality.[39]

Recently, a number of writers have pointed to the growing gaps in the way members of different groups think about themselves and their relationships to others in American society.[40] Their refrain is that the lack of a feeling of community across groups in the United States is eroding mainstream American culture and our sense of common purpose. Blacks and whites, Generations X and Y and the baby boomers, the disabled and the mature market all seem to want their unique identities recognized and acknowledged as part of the multicultural America that we have become. While we are "American" in terms of national identity, rarely does patriotism drive our behavior in the marketplace. The "splintering" of our sense of relevant community boundaries reflects the growing importance of subcultures in defining the American mosaic.[41]

The prominent role of the marketplace in American culture reflects a revolution in our cultural institutions and their roles.[42] If culture includes all learned human behavior, then our beliefs, social structure, images of ourselves, choices of government, or economic system all express components of culture and cultural values. But when traditional cultural institutions no longer serve as effective agents of socialization, we look to more accessible subcultures for values, identity, and socialization. We think of ourselves as hyphenated Americans, changing the first part of the hyphen at whim.[43] Depending on what we buy, we can "borrow" cultural artifacts, reaffirm our own heritage, or scramble our mix of identities by symbolically putting "salsa on kosher dishes."[44] Some writers say, "Brands aren't simply in the culture, they are the culture."[45]

We also find substitutes for permanent markers of identity. Cultural change in a multicultural stew is reflected in the more important roles that media and marketers play in people's lives.[46] Programming and advertising in the popular media assume more influential roles as sources of information about what members of different social groups are like. But as we spend more time with selective media, social distance increases in the absence of shared media or personal experiences across ethnic, age, and lifestyle lines. Media portrayals serve as surrogate personal knowledge of other social groups. This is why stereotyping of ethnic, lifestyle, and age groups in the media has such devastating effects on all of us—we see "group members" rather than individuals.[47]

Several studies point to the significance of the marketplace as both cultural "teacher" and manifestation of cultural values.[48] Table 2.4 shows several ways in which the three cultural groups shown value different attributes in purchasing decisions. A company's support of subculture communities is an important influence on where U.S. Latinos and African Americans shop, but not for white Americans. In contrast, all groups want rewards for being frequent shoppers. The lesson in this table is that different subcultures have different expectations of businesses; loyalty may rest on "good value" offered to some consumers, but others want support for "their" community in addition to a "good value."

It is the non–product-linked participation of brands and stores in minority communities where the differences between white and other Americans' criteria for choosing products and stores show up. One of three LGBT consumers reported that they would switch auto insurance providers if another company provided benefits to a partner. Just advertising in gay media strongly influences LGBT consumers to purchase those products. Other sources report that it is important to ethnic shoppers to have employees or models in advertising who are of the same ethnicity as the shopper. About 50 percent of African Americans and U.S. Latinos rate these characteristics as "important," compared to 15 percent of white Americans. This is true as well for bilingual packaging, cultural compatibility in product assortments, participation in ethnic community organizations, and commitment to causes that the shopper cares about.[49]

The marketplace is a major source of learning for immigrants about a new cultural environment.[50] Some evidence also indicates that marketing strategies can teach individuals at a company as well as its customers about cultural phenomena. Volkswagen used the 1970s pop culture phenomenon of hitting someone when a "one-eyed" Volkswagen Beetle drove by, in 2010 ads to introduce new models, to the delight of those who knew what the "cue" meant

Table 2.4

Comparison of Purchasing Influences: African Americans, U.S. Hispanics, and Non-Hispanic Whites, 2010

	African Americans	U.S. Hispanics	Non-Hispanic whites
Importance in deciding where to shop			
Provides discounts or rewards to frequent shoppers	63	68	58
Is a place where my children enjoy shopping	49	61	23
Mails store ads or coupons to my home	51	56	39
Employs people of my race or ethnicity	52	47	15
Has people of my race or ethnicity in their advertising	51	46	13
Carries African-American products and items	62	31	5
Has Spanish-speaking salespeople/customer service reps.	24	59	6
Offers me credit	39	44	20
Carries Hispanic products and items	16	54	3
Sponsors local fairs/festivals/conferences	33	38	17
Has bilingual signage	18	44	4
Has bilingual packaging	20	48	4
Contributes to a charity or my local community	37	45	19

Influences on brand preferences

"Reflects my values, by supporting causes I believe in, in its advertising/marketing communications"	37	37	19
"Sponsors campaigns that raise awareness of human services issues like poverty or domestic violence"	72	72	48
"Is respectful of my cultural background"	37	32	10
"Seems to understand what's important to me and my family, in its advertising and other communications"	45	44	23
"Consistently shows their support and appreciation for the contributions of African Americans and/or Hispanics in the United States, in ads and other communications"	40	40	6
"Gives me emotional satisfaction"	34	33	21

General attitudes

"I wish more companies would stand up for African-American people and communities, even if they are controversial issues"	80	68	39
"I wish more companies would stand up for Hispanic people and communities, even if they are controversial issues"	66	80	32
"Very few brands or companies really care about the state of African-American communities"	63	59	36
"Very few brands or companies really care about the state of Hispanic communities"	59	71	36

Source: Futures Company, Yankelovich Multicultural Marketing Study (New York, 2009), 63–80.
Note: Numbers represent percentages of all respondents within each ethnic group.

and could clue in others who did not "get it." In sum, as the marketplace plays a more important role as cultural "teacher," companies must learn how to recognize the cultural "needs" of buyers alongside their economic reasons for consuming.

Consuming as Cultural Role-Playing

Different age, lifestyle, and ethnic groups inhabit increasingly different informational, technological, marketing, and cultural worlds. These differences are reflected in how their members shop, how they find out about goods and services, the values they seek in the marketplace, and how they respond to organizations' marketing efforts. Buying and owning particular brands are not just expressions of identity; they are part of the process of forming and reinforcing self-identity.[51] Cultural values are the stabilizing force in a fluid social identity, buffeted by situational influences and multiple group memberships. Distinctive beliefs, norms, and worldviews underlie the values of subcultures in multicultural America. While an individual consumer may not consistently engage in group-established norms of behavior, his or her values will likely mirror the ones of groups with which he identifies.

Mature Americans can and do feel alienated in a cultural and media environment that emphasizes youth. AARP (originally called the American Association of Retired Persons), a pioneer in addressing the mature market's needs, has been successful in bundling services and marketing strategies that acknowledge the needs of older Americans. Hispanic marketers have turned Cinco de Mayo (May 5)—the date of an important Mexican victory—into a celebration for all U.S. Latinos. The role of marketing efforts in reinforcing group pride indicates another change in how we form and maintain social identities.

Self-identity is validated through social interaction. Thus it creates a tension between the meanings we create for ourselves and what others interpret.[52] Thus an Asian-American consumer may view luxury possessions as symbolic of achieving the "American dream," while others see them as expressions of achievement by a "model minority." These symbolic meanings of objects and persons may or may not deviate from their cultural meanings.[53]

Consumers are redefining what types of value they seek in the marketplace. Some consumers are loyal to firms that try to reach them in their own language, whether Facebook, Twitter, the blogosphere for Generation Y, Spanish-language advertising for U.S. Latinos, product labels for the information-intense mature market, or designs that are helpful for disabled consumers.[54] Corporate policies regarding all kinds of human rights (e.g., Starbucks's support of child labor laws, "conflict-free" diamonds, or Reebok's human rights awards or "Red" products in 2006), environmental or civic issues, become each organization's "cause marketing mix." These policies provide a new basis for buyers to select or reject a firm's brands. Meeting consumers' needs for this kind of information—values and affiliations—is the central focus of transcultural marketing strategies.

Figure 2.1 outlines how the environment detailed in Chapter 1 affects the "sense of self" of American consumers. Individuals in a multicultural society draw from multiple cultural and personal value systems in defining their own ideals; in turn, what American consumers want from the market-space changes. This new American consumer "values" factors in addition to price and product quality. They might ask, for example, what the company's record is in hiring a diverse workforce. Whoever said that votes in the marketplace must be limited to decisions based on economic criteria alone?

The economy is becoming an arena for implementing domestic social policy. Consumers express their helplessness to effect political change by saying: "I can't seem to get better schools in my neighborhood by paying taxes or voting, but I can buy from the retailer who provides computers for the school. If they all do that, then I can buy from the store that sponsors the school Halloween carnival."

Relationship marketing is focused on the right problem—how to build a perception of shared interests with particular consumers. Still, the emphasis in relationship marketing is on the economic aspects of exchange.[55] Buyers care about how well products perform, but they also value what a product or service does within the context of their social environment.[56] Consumer loyalty is moving from brand to company to the groups with which consumers choose to identify.

The themes that consumers use to define themselves are repeated in their relationships with brands[57] and mirrored in their perceptions of brand personality and symbolism.[58] Brands are used by consumers in symbolic, iconic, and indexical ways. For example, a portrait in her home in which she is wearing a dashiki is both a symbol (the type of garment) and an icon (the photograph itself) of that person's African heritage. The red-green-yellow color combination on the garment is an artificial index of "African-ness."[59] Furthermore, the meanings that brands have in people's lives are multidimensional; cell phones can be valued for their roles as interpersonal media as well as the aesthetic pleasures that they give and the functions that they perform.[60] In a direct link to our culture, products help us perform important rituals at different life stages by providing the artifacts of the ritual and defining its script, players' roles, and the ritual's audience.[61]

Global firms must establish global strategies at the same time that they compete to win loyalty in niche markets. Yet niche consumers can rebel

Figure 2.1　**Consumer Needs in a Multicultural Society**

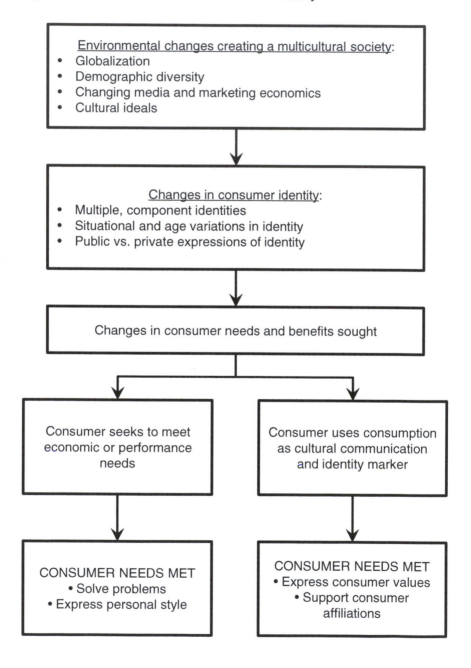

against being a "target market," even though a firm might have taken much care to appeal to their tastes.[62] Over one-third of consumers over age 65 have boycotted firms whose marketing communications portray the elderly in ways that they consider offensive. The economic exchange is only *part* of what determines buying preferences.

The age, lifestyle, ethnicity, regional identity, and other aspects of a consumer's lifestyle provide marketers with a platform for building long-term, broad-based relationships with those consumers. This means supporting the media or events that desired consumers attend, providing the goods and services that recognize the distinctive aspects of their lifestyles, and, in general, speaking their language. In some cases, it means asking consumers to write their own ads in order to get the language and setting into a format that breaks through the media clutter.[63]

Look at the differences in what people from different ethnic subcultures do when they go online. U.S. Latinos remain the least active, and Asian Americans, the most active online. Some relationships between ethnicity and media consumption patterns are shown in Table 2.5. U.S. Latinos and African Americans use the Internet most to look for jobs and access entertainment. Connecting with others on blogs and chat forums, downloading movies, and accessing financial information are the most popular activities for Asian Americans. Non-Hispanic whites have the broadest range of online activities. Members of ethnic groups also spend different amounts of time with different media (television, radio, newspaper, magazines, and the Internet). African Americans spend the most time with TV and radio, while non-Hispanic whites are the largest consumers of newspapers and magazines. Asian Americans spend the least time with traditional media and the most online. Even if some ethnic differences in media usage are converging, these patterns establish "group norms," visible to insiders and outsiders alike.[64]

We must acknowledge communications media and marketing institutions as cultural players in multicultural America. By selecting the organizations that a company supports as partner in buying and selling, this firm expresses values that may or may not resonate with those of its intended customers. Whether this assertive cultural role for business organizations is a good or bad phenomenon in our society, it is characteristic of life in postmodern cultures all over the world.[65]

Media Imagery and Entertainment Venues Create American Pop Culture

While American popular culture is both a reflection and distortion of our cultural values, we do not always recognize the dangers of relying on these

Table 2.5

Online Activities of Four Ethnic Groups, 2010

		Total sample	U.S. Hispanics	White, non-Hispanic	Black, non-Hispanic	Asian, non-Hispanic	Other
Total sample	(000)	223,483	31,501	154,442	25,275	8,887	3,379
	Index	100	100	100	100	100	100
Does your HH own PC? Yes	(000)	185,265	23,132	131,766	18,970	8,646	2,750
	Index	100	89	103	91	117	98
Your HH is online	(000)	185,706	23,389	130,731	19,962	8,548	3,077
	Index	100	89	102	95	116	110
Online activities last 30 days							
Airline/car/hotel info or reservations	(000)	49,762	5,481	36,340	4,000	3,438	503
	Index	100	78	106	71	174	67
Auctions	(000)	21,654	2,383	17,283	836	935	216
	Index	100	78	115	34	109	66
Auto shopping or comparing	(000)	21,737	2,948	15,514	2,011	1,061	204
	Index	100	96	103	82	123	62
Banking	(000)	83,747	8,436	62,857	6,584	5,003	866
	Index	100	71	109	70	150	68
Blogs/blogging(read/write online diaries)	(000)	24,333	2,842	17,207	2,069	1,745	470
	Index	100	83	102	75	180	128
Bulletin/message boards	(000)	20,552	4,184	13,513	1,471	1,025	359
	Index	100	144	95	63	125	115
Chat forums	(000)	17,267	2,773	11,027	1,806	1,359	302
	Index	100	114	92	92	198	116
Digital imaging/photo albums online	(000)	28,108	4,000	20,612	1,759	1,199	538
	Index	100	101	106	55	107	127
Download/listen to podcasts	(000)	15,442	2,610	9,953	1,686	1,000	194
	Index	100	120	93	97	163	83
Download music	(000)	36,334	5,900	23,531	4,204	2,089	610
	Index	100	115	94	102	145	111

Download movies	(000)	13,248	2,169	7,458	2,342	1,022	257
	Index	100	116	81	156	194	128
Employment search	(000)	31,139	5,188	19,444	4,491	1,413	603
	Index	100	125	88	148	77	126
E-mail	(000)	136,628	14,351	101,116	11,693	7,344	2,124
	Index	100	75	107	76	135	103
Financial information/stock trading	(000)	21,329	2,161	16,034	1,240	1,697	197
	Index	100	72	109	51	200	61
Instant messaging (IM)	(000)	28,789	4,521	18,360	3,013	2,257	638
	Index	100	111	92	93	197	147
Lstn/Internet-only radio stations (Inchcst, etc.)	(000)	16,537	3,150	10,382	1,955	836	213
	Index	100	135	91	105	127	85
Listen to satellite radio online (Sirius, XRI, etc.)	(000)	6,371	1,685	3,632	863	133	58
	Index	100	188	83	120	53	60
Listen/traditional radio stations online	(000)	11,647	2,208	7,939	939	323	238
	Index	100	134	99	71	70	135
Medical services and information	(000)	30,350	3,496	22,976	2,289	1,205	384
	Index	100	82	110	67	100	84
Movie information reviews/show times	(000)	39,440	5,738	27,710	3,026	2,343	624
	Index	100	103	102	68	149	105
News/weather	(000)	89,013	9,824	66,984	6,046	5,101	1,057
	Index	100	78	109	60	144	79
Online gambling	(000)	5,316	1,317	2,948	456	283	313
	Index	100	176	80	76	134	389
Personal ads/dating services	(000)	6,292	1,027	4,059	705	331	170
	Index	100	116	93	99	132	179
Play games online	(000)	38,185	4,204	27,522	4,537	1,236	687
	Index	100	78	104	105	81	119
Read magazines/newspapers	(000)	34,716	4,130	25,606	2,362	2,125	494
	Index	100	84	107	60	154	94
Real estate listings	(000)	19,629	1,853	14,870	1,572	1,103	230
	Index	100	67	110	71	141	77

(continued)

Table 2.5 *(continued)*

		Total sample	U.S. Hispanics	White, non-Hispanic	Black, non-Hispanic	Asian, non-Hispanic	Other
Research/education	(000)	37,673	4,790	27,012	2,867	2,476	527
	Index	100	90	104	67	165	93
Send electronic greeting cards	(000)	11,525	1,555	8,071	990	771	137
	Index	100	96	101	76	168	79
Gathered info for shopping	(000)	44,978	4,365	34,514	2,657	3,006	437
	Index	100	69	111	52	168	64
Made a purchase	(000)	48,793	4,694	37,236	3,095	2,977	792
	Index	100	68	110	56	153	107
Sports	(000)	29,796	4,742	20,658	2,879	1,273	244
	Index	100	113	100	85	107	54
Videogame news/reviews/cheat codes	(000)	14,236	2,227	8,908	1,888	891	323
	Index	100	111	91	117	157	150
Yellow pages	(000)	28,034	3,336	20,707	2,651	964	376
	Index	100	84	107	84	86	89
Other activities	(000)	32,001	4,536	22,819	2,767	1,240	639
	Index	100	101	103	76	97	132
Online activities: none	(000)	18,541	3,264	11,248	3,111	565	353
	Index	100	125	88	148	77	126

Source: Experian/Simmons, NCS/NCHS Adult Survey Database, September–October 2010. www. http://www.experian.com/simmons-research/consumer-study.html.

HH = household.

sources for broader cultural lessons.[66] Given the increase in social distance between groups, the vicarious knowledge of "others" that comes via media imagery becomes crucial if we are to relate to each other.

In some ways, American mainstream culture has "become" what the media represent. Critics argue that we construct our own identity according to scripts for popular programming. "Life movies" (fictionalized biographies) and reality TV show us how to organize experience. Entertainment in all its forms has become a "force so overwhelming that it has finally metastasized into life,"[67] making life "no more than a game."[68] Lifestyles displayed in the media may or may not reflect reality but provide the tools that consumers use to realize their own aspirations.[69] The line between media and reality is most blurred by media programming that purports to be "reality."

In the media, high art mixes with folk, modern, and popular arts to become the popular culture of the American mainstream.[70] Advertising as pop culture creates meaning for the objects in our lives. James Twitchell claims that "magical thinking" is the "heart of both religion and advertising" and that consumption of an object often has more to do with meaning than with product function.[71]

The choice of which media to consume is as much a personal statement of identity as a rational search for entertainment and information. A consumer's "media repertoire" describes the variety of media that individual consumes.[72] This mix communicates the person's associations—aspired, actual, and disavowed—as well as ideals and values used to interpret and evaluate the rest of the world.

The broader the choice a consumer has for sources of information, the more relevant to that person's multiple identities media choice becomes. For example, the consumption of Spanish-language programming and advertising may reflect a strong Hispanic identity, not because the individual has no other choice but because a bilingual individual chooses what "speaks to the heart."[73]

In all forms of communication, symbols and myths are used to express the abstract concepts of cultural norms and ideals. Media have always co-opted images and symbols of some people to sell to other audiences.[74] African Americans have been shown as uneducated and hedonistic, the disabled as helpless, U.S. Latinos as lazy, Chinese Americans as hard workers, old people as crotchety, and Native Americans as savage or noble. If these are the only ways that these people are visible in the media, it denies their diversity and reinforces stereotypes.[75] The use of cultural symbols and simplistic media representations are not likely to go unnoticed today, wherever they appear.

Some groups continue to be less visible than others in American media. For example, there is a gap between the percentage of older Americans in our population and their share of images in the media. In contrast, LGBT characters in 2013 were twice their actual percentage of total adult population. Gays and lesbians have been more visible than older Americans, in program stories, and as characters in mainstream programs.[76] By bringing more diversity into media programs and advertising, the stereotyping of these people in popular culture has begun to diminish.[77] The values and associations of mainstream American culture are mutable over time, and media images are important instruments of cultural change.

The act of showing people in the media as members of a particular group acknowledges the significance of that group in American society. Such regard is important to each of the groups discussed in this book. When Walmart uses actors in wheelchairs in its advertising, the benefit is not just more disabled shoppers at Walmart stores but a more active presence for the disabled in American media and popular culture. As media vehicles become more selective, even more American subcultures will want to be recognized by the media as full-fledged participants in our multicultural society.

The dilemma for a multicultural society is how to interact successfully in the face of so many different rules for behavior. When members of particular subcultures within one society represent different value systems, it is personally relevant every day to understand cultural differences as a potential source of misunderstandings. Whose rules will dominate is a constant tension in a multicultural society. This is a good explanation for why mainstream American culture will continue to serve as a common ideal, even while its adherents have varying interpretations of what it means. It is not necessary that we merely accept people with different rituals or foods and music as part of the American mosaic; we must also accept their different ways of "being" American.

The cultural pride of Native Americans, African Americans, or senior citizens is both a reaction to past discrimination and a natural byproduct of a diverse society.[78] Recognizing each group's legal rights further strengthens individual members' retention of culturally distinctive patterns of thought and behavior. While groups activate the legal system to redress discrimination, they also pressure media to diversify the imagery that they reflect.

The Personal Values Link to Social Identity and Market-Space Choices

The link between cultural values, personal values, and chosen affiliations comes full circle when we make market-space decisions to express who we are, who we want to be, or how we want to be seen. This section reviews the relationship between personal values and how we trace their influence on market-space choices.

The Ladder Linking Personal Values to Consumer Choices

One approach to understanding consumer decision making emphasizes the problem orientation of consumers. The belief is that consumers choose various actions (such as choosing a particular brand) to achieve particular goals (e.g., "to have a more efficient home office"), which in turn may lead to broader goals (e.g., "being a successful person"). The theory recognizes that choosing one brand over another may have both functional consequences (e.g., "being able to print faster") and psychological consequences (e.g., the way that person feels after the print job is completed).[79]

The key to mapping these linkages is being able to connect the attributes that were important in the choice of the printer to the functional and psychosocial consequences that person seeks or avoids and ultimately to the personal values that motivate this person. Those personal values derive from the individual's ordering of cultural norms and values according to personal relevance.

Laddering is the research method used to uncover these links between a specific brand choice and the consumer's most relevant personal values. By asking a consumer why particular attributes are important when making a consumer choice, the researcher is able to identify desired and undesired functional and psychosocial consequences that the consumer is trying to achieve or avoid. By continuing to press the consumer for why those consequences are important, the researcher ultimately arrives at the instrumental and terminal values of the consumer. Rokeach identified instrumental values as preferred modes of behavior that lead to terminal values, which are desirable states of existence that the person would like to achieve in his/her lifetime.[80]

Laddering requires skilled and trained researchers who uncover the invisible maps from consumer choices to values, one consumer at a time. Researchers can then compare the ladders of consumers from different segments in a market. Based on data acquired from a small number of consumer laddering interviews, researchers can then observe how closely individual preferences reflect group norms of behavior on a number of demographic and behavioral characteristics.[81]

How Consumers Create and Change Cultural Meanings

One alternative to laddering is finding out what meanings consumers give to consumption activities. By focusing on consumer goals for "having, being or doing," we can identify consumer motivations. For example, "doing" consumption activities can serve as either problem-solving or value-expressive activities. The meanings that consumers attach to such activities and products range from very tangible and functional to more symbolic ones. Laddering approaches only consider how goals are hierarchically related, but discovery of consumer meanings can simultaneously consider the links between various levels of goals with whether products are valued for functional or symbolic meanings.[82]

The cultural world is our source of what "things mean." However, individuals constantly negotiate new meanings for objects, names, events, persons, and institutions, by their experiences with them, and external influences that change from moment to moment. Thus, any efforts to measure consumer meanings capture momentary and multidimensional relationships between the object, the culture, and the individual. A number of qualitative methods such as storytelling, ritual analysis, brand associations, metaphors, and product deprivation can be used to uncover the subtle, individually meaningful meanings of particular activities.

An example can show how the different approaches might yield different findings, but both are avenues toward consumer insight. In a laddering process, a person who recently bought a Volkswagen Jetta revealed the following information. She picked the car because of its "high safety record, quick response, fabulous color choices, and the good deal that was offered through dealer financing." The researcher was able to link these car purchase attributes to functional and psychosocial consequences such as "getting more value, having more choice, less fear entering freeways, and feeling like a smart shopper." Pressed for why those were important, the researcher learned that, for this consumer, it was important to be logical, independent, and fair so that she would feel secure and be respected by others. By deconstructing this purchase for that one person, marketers might learn to seek out consumers with similar personal values of security and respect. Likewise, because respect is so important to this consumer, by extension the marketer should try to identify which partnerships and cultural cues would best resonate with them.

Another researcher might interview the Jetta purchaser, trying to decipher what meanings this purchase has for the consumer. Many seemingly unrelated associations crop up, such as "having her own car lets her be independent," "she feels vulnerable in small cars," "this is the first car that she has bought with her own money," "dealers try to take advantage of female car buyers," "the car came in the same color as her college team's," and "she checked a website showing that the price was close to dealer's costs." The values of respect, independence, and security are echoed in these associations, but there is also information about how this person sees herself in relationship to others. After verifying the centrality of these themes to other buyers who share consumer identities, Jetta will have a broader foundation upon which to build a transcultural marketing program.

Characteristics of American Subcultures

Consumer Identities as Subcultures

The American taste for diversity opens mainstream American culture to new meanings that connect American ideals to those of particular subcultures.[83] The distinctive myths, heroes, symbols, group norms, and ideal values of age, ethnic, lifestyle, and other subcultures are familiar and motivating forces. The marketplace is our public venue for making identity and value statements.[84]

Focus on your own identity for a moment. How do you answer the question "who am I?" to yourself and to others? Most people first think of the social roles that they play: mother, husband, programmer, friend, coach, and so on. These roles, normally associated with prescribed activities, are significant in the way that Americans see themselves; but like other sources of identity, they fluctuate in importance over time and situation. So, they are important but not sufficient for expressing who you are to yourself or to others.[85]

Table 2.6 suggests other possible sources of identity important at various times to every individual's sense of self. Our biological heritage of race and sex provides physical and cultural points of comparison that place all others into "us" or "them" groups. Expressions of ethnicity are a mix of cultural values and norms, along with other influences such as geography, language, and race. The environment where s/he lives or works as well as racial or ethnic heritage may influence an African American's preference for Afro-centric products. Age, physical appearance, disabilities, sexual orientation, and possibly other sources of identity can also express our "us" and "them" accepted behaviors.

In addition to the influence of biology and culture on our social selves, geography, age, sexual preference, occupation, social class, stage in the family life cycle, and education are components of our social identity. Others in our same age group have shared significant experiences that in turn emphasize common values. Members of the World War II cohort save money today even though they may have already saved plenty. Saving for an uncertain future was a value learned from their experiences in the Great Depression and World War II. The millennials and baby boomers experience conflict in the workplace due to their different ways of dealing with hierarchy.

Americans have multiple sources of identity, some related to roles played, some related to ethnic heritage, some related to where people live, grow up, or who they sleep with. Even the U.S. Census Bureau recognizes multiple sources of ethnic and racial identity among Americans today.[86] People reinforce this social identity by the actions they take. The products that people buy, the media programs that capture their attention, the hobbies that they have, or the

Table 2.6

Key Consumer Identities in Multicultural America

Source of identity	Basis of community	Examples of consumer groups
Age cohorts	Shared experiences	Teens, children, baby boomers, mature market, Generation X, Generation Y
Gender	Biology and culturally defined roles	Men, women, boys, girls
Geography	Physical proximity and regional differences	Californians, inner city, small town folks, coastal dwellers, Southerners, Brooklynites, New Yorkers, Chicagoans
Race/physical features	Physical similarities	Blacks, whites, Asians, tall Americans, body builders, blondes, the overweight
Ethnicity/religion	Shared cultural values and/or history	Chinese Americans, U.S. Latinos, German Americans, Cuban Americans, Jewish Americans, African Americans, Muslim Americans, Amish Americans
Lifestyle choices/sexual orientation	Shared AIO[1] or behaviors	Single parents, Christian right, gays and lesbians, condo owners, smokers, DINCs[2]
Disability	Special needs or behaviors	Hearing impaired, mobility impaired, sight impaired, terminally ill, alcoholics, substance abusers, cancer survivors

[1]AIO stands for "attitudes, interests, and opinions."
[2]DINCs stands for "double-income, no children" households.

services that they need. Consumers buy brands they know and like from the companies that they know and like. The increasing importance to consumers of supporting companies that relate to their particular place in the American mosaic creates an unparalleled market opportunity.

Shared Characteristics of U.S. Consumer Subcultures

Table 2.6 shows different aspects of Americans' social identity as the basis of distinctive consumer subcultures. These groups seem to share several qualities that establish their presence as consumers in multicultural America.

First, each group is distinguishable demographically and behaviorally. That is, group membership may not always be important to or declared by an individual, but group distinctions can be made based on media preferences, group norms, responsiveness to particular forms of communication, and participation in community organizations and events. A person over the age of 65 may not consider him or herself as part of the mature market, but if his or her media habits and personal values mirror those of other mature Americans, then group norms are better predictors of behavior than group labels.

Consumers may not agree with the labels used to place them in a group, and they may not consciously identify with that group. But if a group label separates their marketplace preferences from those of others, it is an effective consumer identity for marketing purposes. Still, this presents a number of problems for marketers. For example, where do American-born African and Caribbean blacks belong within the African American subculture? How about Hispanics who do not speak Spanish and have no knowledge of their Hispanic heritage? How do we distinguish the youngest members of Generation X from the oldest members of Generation Y?

These dilemmas about how to define a target market can be answered by marketers armed with knowledge of group cultural norms, values, and community organizations, as well as insight into the cultural meanings connected to product usage. Some examples of advertising that effectively targets members of specific consumer subcultures are as follows: Dodge Ram "voted the Truck of Texas"; mature Americans "can drink now and play later" with V-8; African Americans should "pick this one up" because Coca-Cola is "tall, dark, and cooler than cool"; using "Chinese letters and a kid's drawing of a car" signals Allstate's car insurance message for Chinese Americans.

Second, each subculture group is sensitive to marketers who include too broad a group of people and to ones who draw the lines too narrowly. Should we use the term *U.S. Hispanics* or *U.S. Latinos, Generation X* or *The Free Generation, Gen Y* or *the millennials, disabled* or *physically challenged*

Americans, senior citizens or *the Mature Market, Asian American* or *Chinese American*? Does the U.S. Hispanic market include only Spanish-speaking Americans or all those with origins in Spanish-speaking countries? These label issues are important. The basis or label that a marketer uses to "group" potential consumers may be the very reason that this group does not respond to the marketer's embrace.

Labels often have political meanings as well as cultural ones. Whether a person is called black or African American, Hispanic or Latino, gay or LGBT may affect how he or she responds. One name might be acceptable in some contexts but not in others. The point is that marketers must identify these meanings before choosing to use any label.

Some consumers do not respond to organizations that are not members of the community with which they identify. Consumers can be suspicious of ethnic marketing efforts from firms that do not otherwise "behave" as members of that group would or "should." After Ellen DeGeneres came out as gay in an episode of her TV show *Ellen*, loyal viewers vowed to boycott the companies that withdrew ads from broadcasts of that episode.[87]

A marketer can create antagonism by using the language or symbols of a group when the firm is not an established member of it. Tokenism when marketing to members of a subculture can be devastating for a firm's reputation and destructive to relationships with that subculture community. It has taken Coors over three decades to overcome its earlier reputation as racist, and Denny's is still trying to woo back African-American customers after racist incidents in the early 1990s.[88] It is best to get it right the first time, but there is no "one-size-fits-all marketing solution," as these marketers would likely agree.

A third quality of the subcultures in Table 2.6 is significant diversity within each group. Asian Americans include people of multiple races, religions, and languages; U.S. Latinos encompass people from Spain, Mexico, Cuba, El Salvador, and so on; some came to the United States themselves, while others' families have been here for generations. Generation Y lumps together all 15–26 year olds, in spite of their racial, ethnic, educational, and other differences. Generation gaps between first- and second-generation immigrants or between early and late "baby boomers" can be as wide as their differences from other Americans. Marketers who do not understand such diversity run the risk of stereotyping all members of a particular group.[89]

A fourth quality that these groups share is a certain amount of geographic concentration. One-third of Asian Americans live in California, gay Americans are concentrated in the 25 largest cities and Florida is a haven for the mature market. While U.S. Latinos from Florida, Illinois, New York, Texas, and

California often originate from different parts of Latin America, use different labels for themselves, and speak Spanish and English with very different accents, these five states are home to 67 percent of all U.S. Latinos.[90] As a result of geographic concentration, even subculture groups with small numbers can be viable marketing targets.

A fifth quality shared by subcultures in multicultural America is their distinctive patterns of media usage. The preference of Asian Americans for word-of-mouth sources means that personal selling may be key to penetrating this market. African Americans have positive attitudes about the value of advertising and the enjoyment of shopping, and they spend more time with electronic media than any other group.[91] Younger customers consume multiple media simultaneously and depend on social networking websites to learn about pros and cons of products. As all media usage moves from mass to niche programming, there are fewer opportunities to share media experiences across subcultures. Members of Gen Y who got to know Betty White via social network websites embraced the 91-year-old, well-known television star. They voted online for her to serve as guest host on *Saturday Night Live* in 2010. This is how information flows when mass media no longer reach mass audiences. Media offer symbolic highways for marketers to take as they become members of a subculture and its community.

What makes age so important in this new America is that American culture changes with time and technology.[92] People of similar ages have a community of shared experiences whereas Americans of different ages are products of different American "subcultures."[93] Key events during late adolescence shape the worldview and values of American age groups. Media availability shapes how those people seek information about their world. Thus our media repertoires are formed during adolescence but are buffeted by technological change over our lifetime. Age is a powerful mediator of media habits and preferences.

Last, each of these groups has a unique process for making consumption decisions.[94] Asian Americans and U.S. Latinos give special weight to word of mouth about different products or services; African Americans enjoy shopping and advertising. The mature market likes a lot of information to be available, even when it results in information overload. Gays and lesbians prefer to buy from firms that contribute to gay rights or AIDS projects. As consumers, they are often influenced by information on corporate giving and human resource policies. Not all members of these groups respond in such easily predicted ways, but the stronger the consumer's affiliation with a group, the more likely he or she is to adopt group norms and patterns of behavior.[95]

Differences Among American Consumer Subcultures

Some aspects of consumer identity result in significant differences in how members of subcultures relate to mainstream American culture. One example is that distance from the "mainstream"—both perceived and cultural—varies for each American subculture. Chinese Americans find more distance between their beliefs and those of mainstream America than do immigrants from Germany; other Americans also are likely to see Chinese Americans as more "foreign" than German Americans. This variability affects the self-perceptions of members of a particular subculture as well as the ways in which other Americans perceive them.

Race is a socially constructed concept in American culture. Just as Italian, Irish, and Jewish immigrants "became" white over time, the groups that are perceived as insiders and outsiders in mainstream society can change over time. LGBT Americans are visible participants in American popular culture, but some of their legal rights are still resisted by other Americans. African Americans, women, Asian Americans, and U.S. Latinos have all fought at various times for treatment equal to that of their fellow Americans. These experiences within a subculture's current and historical relationships to mainstream America, as well as current inequities, leave a residue of heightened sensitivity to discrimination and distinctive treatment.

Another issue is the changing importance for any American of particular social identities. Age and stage in the family life cycle are key moderators of the importance of ethnicity to social identity.[96] However, neither our age nor our stages in the family life cycle are the same as they were fifty years ago. The health and wealth of today's senior citizens defy age-appropriate labels. More than half of college students now move back home for a period before moving out permanently. Divorce and remarriage at all ages are becoming, if not the norm, at least normal. In short, transmigrating across cultural boundaries is a byproduct of our constant renegotiation of who we are. Constantly enacting our "identity of the moment" is the new normal, and it is spreading to the rest of the world via our brands, media, and market spaces.

A third point of distinction for consumer subcultures is the role of "symbolic" identity among various subculture groups. For many white Americans of European heritage, ethnic identity may not play a major role in an individual's sense of self. Plenty of "Irish Americans" know nothing more about their Irish heritage than the green shamrock for "good luck" and St. Patrick's Day as an ethnic celebration. Other examples include people who classify themselves as members of a particular ethnic group (e.g., Native American or U.S. Latino) when membership has some immediate benefit (e.g., scholarships), but who neither identify as Hispanic nor have knowledge of that culture's values. These examples reflect symbolic rather than culture-based identity since they are not founded on cultural knowledge and socialization into the culture.[97] Nevertheless, these symbolic identities can influence some of our consumer choices even if this occurs inconsistently. Symbolic identity is the easiest to turn on and off, further compounding the task of understanding nuances of diversity within every group.

Summary: The Multicultural Identity Formula

This chapter has reviewed many influences on social identity. Four elements are vital when consumers use their market-space choices to construct and communicate identity. Our first and most basic influence is our socialization or acculturation into mainstream American culture. Second, we learn group norms and cultural values from our memberships in multiple subculture communities. Third, we are motivated by our personal goals. And, fourth, we choose affiliations in American society to express where we belong. This then is the multicultural identity formula:

What I believe (cultural values + subculture values + personal values) + Where I belong (my chosen communities) = Who I Am

This formula emphasizes knowledge of consumer values and the cultural context of shopping and consuming as basic information that marketers must master. Figure 2.2 puts the multicultural identity formula into a broader model of the relationship between American social identity and market-space choices by individual consumers.

In our increasingly diverse society, individuals find their identities within the multiple groups, based on age, gender, sexual orientation, race, ethnicity, or geography, to which they choose to belong. Consumers look to media images and goods and services to symbolically express who they are or want to be. Self-identity has become a constantly changing mix of values, attitudes, and behaviors, making it virtually impossible to predict behavior as a function of group membership alone.

Consumers enter market spaces to satisfy their needs for products and services to perform expected functions and to express personal style as they always have. However, in addition they use consumption and media choices to express their cultural values and group affiliations. Marketers must adapt to this environment by changing how organizations set goals and choose tactics. Chapter 3 discusses new approaches to marketing in a multicultural setting and presents the rationale for and examples of transcultural marketing.

64

Figure 2.2 **A Model of Social Identity and Consumer Choice**

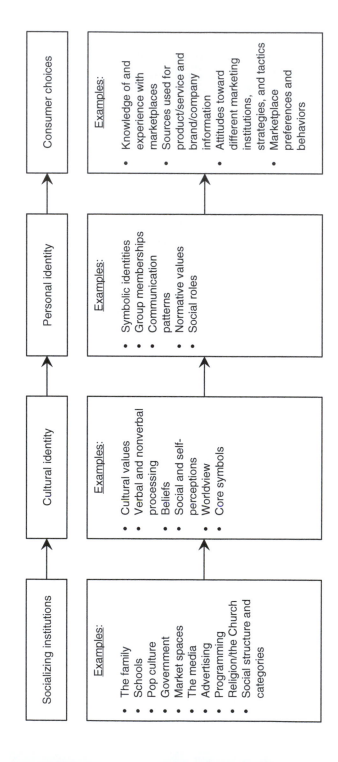

Notes

1. C.A. Miranda, "Diving into the Gene Pool," *Time*, August 28, 2006, 45.

2. M. Halter, *Shopping for Identity: The Marketing of Ethnicity* (New York: Schocken Books, 2006).

3. C. Clausen, *Faded Mosaic: The Emergence of Post-Cultural America* (Chicago: Ivan R. Dee, 2000); M.J. Bennett and E.C. Stewart, *American Cultural Patterns*, rev. ed. (Yarmouth, ME: Intercultural Press, 1991), 129.

4. J.L. Aaker, "The Malleable Self: The Role of Self-Expression in Persuasion," *Journal of Marketing Research* 36, no. 1 (1999): 45–67; M.R. Solomon, "The Role of Products as Social Stimuli: A Symbolic Interactionism Perspective," *Journal of Consumer Research* 10, no. 3 (1983): 319–329.

5. Bennett and Stewart, *American Cultural Patterns*, 132–133.

6. M.J. Sirgy, "Self-Concept in Consumer Behavior: A Critical Review," *Journal of Consumer Research* 9, no. 3 (1982): 287–300; Bennett and Stewart, *American Cultural Patterns*, 143.

7. F.E. Jandt, *Intercultural Communication: An Introduction*, 3d ed. (Thousand Oaks, CA: Sage, 2000), 211–232.

8. H.C. Triandis and M.J. Gelfand, "Converging Measurement of Horizontal and Vertical Individualism and Collectivism," *Journal of Personality and Social Psychology* 74, no. 1 (1998): 118–128; S. Shavitt, A.K. Lalwani, H. Zhang, and C.J. Torelli, "The Horizontal/Vertical Distinction in Cross-Cultural Consumer Research," *Journal of Consumer Psychology* 16, no. 4 (2006): 325–356.

9. M.J. Dutta-Bergman and W.D. Wells, "The Values and Lifestyles of Idiocentrics and Allocentrics in an Individualist Culture: A Descriptive Approach," *Journal of Consumer Psychology* 12, no. 3 (2002): 231–243.

10. H.C. Triandis, *Individualism and Collectivism* (Boulder, CO: Westview Press, 1995).

11. D.M. Stayman and R. Deshpandé, "Situational Ethnicity and Consumer Behavior," *Journal of Consumer Research* 16, no. 3 (1989): 361–371; G. Miller, *Spent: Sex, Evolution, and Consumer Behavior* (New York: Viking, 2009).

12. K.T. Tian, W.O. Bearden, and G.L. Hunter, "Consumers' Need for Uniqueness: Scale Development and Validation," *Journal of Consumer Research* 28, no. 1 (2001): 50–66; M.C. Waters, *Ethnic Options: Choosing Identities in America* (Berkeley: University of California Press, 1990).

13. A. Reed II, M.R. Forehand, S. Puntoni, and L. Warlop, "Identity-Based Consumer Behavior," *International Journal of Research in Marketing* 29, no. 4 (2012): 310–321; V. Chattaraman, S.J. Lennon, and N.A. Rudd, "Social Identity Salience: Effects on Identity-Based Brand Choices of Hispanic Consumers," *Psychology and Marketing* 27, no. 3 (2010): 263–284; R. Deshpandé and D.M. Stayman, "A Tale of Two Cities: Distinctiveness Theory and Advertising Effectiveness," *Journal of Marketing Research* 31, no. 1 (1994): 57–64; W.J. McGuire et al., "Salience of Ethnicity in the Spontaneous Self-Concept as a Function of One's Ethnic Distinctiveness in the Social Environment," *Journal of Personality and Social Psychology* 36, 5 (1978): 511–520.

14. R. Deshpandé, W.D. Hoyer, and N. Donthu, "The Intensity of Ethnic Affiliation: A Study of the Sociology of Hispanic Consumption," *Journal of Consumer Research* 13, no. 2 (1986): 214–220.

15. P. Perry, "White Means Never Having to Say You're Ethnic: White Youth and the Construction of 'Cultureless' Identities," in *Life in America: Identity and*

Everyday Experience, ed. L.D. Baker (Malden, MA: Blackwell, 2004); R.D. Alba, *Ethnic Identity: The Transformation of White America* (New Haven: Yale University Press, 1990).

16. Waters, *Ethnic Options.*

17. Deshpandé, Hoyer, and Donthu, "The Intensity of Ethnic Affiliation."

18. F. Subervi-Velez, "The Mass Media and Ethnic Assimilation and Pluralism: A Review and Research Proposal with Special Focus on Hispanics," *Communication Research* 13, no. 1 (1986): 71–96.

19. Waters, *Ethnic Options.*

20. M. Tharp, "Theories of Ethnicity: Identity Versus Culture" (paper presented at 2003 American Academy of Advertising Conference, Boulder, CO, April 2003).

21. R. Villarreal and R.A. Peterson, "Hispanic Ethnicity and Media Behavior," *Journal of Advertising Research* 48, no. 2 (2008): 179–190; M. Tharp and R. Villarrreal de Silva, "Questioning the Construct of Hispanic Identity" (paper presented at 1998 International Trade and Finance Association Conference, Atlantic City, NJ, May 1998).

22. Waters, *Ethnic Options.*

23. Deshpandé and Stayman, "A Tale of Two Cities."

24. Experian Simmons, National Consumer Survey/National Consumer Household Survey, July 2009–September 2010.

25. R. Elliott and K. Wattanasuwan, "Brands as Symbolic Resources for the Construction of Identity," *International Journal of Advertising* 17, no. 2 (1998): 131–144; M.R. Solomon, "The Role of Products as Social Stimuli: A Symbolic Interactionism Perspective," *Journal of Consumer Research* 10, no. 3 (1983): 319–329.

26. R.O. Crockett, "Invisible and Loving It," *BusinessWeek,* October 5, 1998, 124–128.

27. Bennett and Stewart, *American Cultural Patterns,* 22–34.

28. Ibid., 22–34; H.N. Seelye and A. Seelye-James, *Culture Clash: Managing in a Multicultural World* (Lincolnwood, IL: NTC Business Books, 1995).

29. Bennett and Stewart, *American Cultural Patterns,* 158–159.

30. G. Althen, *American Ways: A Guide for Foreigners in the United States* (Yarmouth, ME: Intercultural Press, 1988), 22–23.

31. Ibid., 22–34; Seelye and Seelye-James, *Culture Clash.*

32. J.M. McLeod and S.R. Chaffee, "The Construction of Social Reality," in *The Social Influence Processes,* ed. J.T. Tedeschi (Chicago: Aldine-Atherton, 1972), 50–99.

33. R.D. Putnam, "Tuning in, Tuning Out: The Strange Disappearance of Social Capital in America," *PS: Political Science and Politics* 28, no. 4 (1995): 664–683.

34. V. Manusov and N.K. Rivenburgh, "'Our Lives Create Our Selves': Conceptualizations of Cultural Identity from an International on-Line Dialogue" (paper presented at Intercultural and International Division, National Communication Association, New Orleans, LA, 2002); T.C. O'Guinn and L.J. Shrum, "The Role of Television in the Construction of Consumer Social Reality," *Journal of Consumer Research* 23, no. 4 (1997): 278–294.

35. G.P. Moschis and G.A. Churchill Jr., "Consumer Socialization: A Theoretical and Empirical Analysis," *Journal of Marketing Research* 15, no. 4 (1978): 599–609; D. Kellner, "Cultural Studies, Multiculturalism and Media Culture," in *Gender, Race, and Class in Media: A Text-Reader,* ed. G. Dines and J.M. Humez (Thousand Oaks, CA: Sage, 1995), 5–6.

36. L. Peñaloza and M.C. Gilly, "Marketer Acculturation: The Changer and the Changed," *Journal of Marketing* 63, no. 3 (1999): 84.

37. J. Ginsburg, "Xtreme Retailing," *BusinessWeek*, December 20, 1999, 120–128.

38. G. McCracken, "Culture and Consumption: A Theoretical Account of the Structure and Movement of the Cultural Meaning of Consumer Goods," *Journal of Consumer Research* 13, no. 1 (1986): 71–83; J.B. Twitchell, *Adcult USA: The Triumph of Advertising in American Culture* (New York: Columbia University Press, 1996).

39. W.M. O'Barr, *Culture and the Ad: Exploring Otherness in the World of Advertising* (Boulder, CO: Westview Press, 1994).

40. R. Hughes, *Culture of Complaint: The Fraying of America* (New York: Oxford University Press, 1993); J. Kotkin, *Tribes: How Race, Religion and Identity Determine Success in the New Global Economy* (New York: Random House, 1993); A.M. Schlesinger Jr., *The Disuniting of America: Reflections on a Multicultural Society* (New York: W.W. Norton, 1992).

41. J. Turow, *Breaking up America: Advertisers and the New Media World* (Chicago: University of Chicago Press, 1997).

42. Peñaloza and Gilly, "Marketer Acculturation."

43. P.C. Judge, "Is the Net Redefining Our Identity?" *BusinessWeek*, May 12, 1997, 100, 102.

44. D. Cyr, "Cutting Across Ethnic Lines," *Catalog Age* 11, no. 7 (1994): 155.

45. A. Zolli, "Rip. Mix. Brand," *American Demographics* (November 2004): 44–45.

46. W. Leiss, S. Kline, and S. Jhally, *Social Communication in Advertising: Persons, Products and Images of Well-Being* (Toronto: Methuen, 1986), 259–297; Turow, *Breaking up America.*

47. Turow, *Breaking up America.*

48. R.W. Belk, K.D. Bahn, and R.N. Mayer, "Developmental Recognition of Consumption Symbolism," *Journal of Consumer Research* 9, no. 1 (1982): 4–15; M. Richins, "Social Comparison and the Idealized Images in Advertising," *Journal of Consumer Research* 18, no. 1 (1991): 71–83; M. Richins, "Valuing Things: The Public and Private Meanings of Possessions," *Journal of Consumer Research* 21, no. 3 (1994): 504–521; M. Tharp and L.M. Scott, "The Role of Marketing Processes in Creating Cultural Meaning," *Journal of Macromarketing* 10, no. 2 (1990): 47–60.

49. Futures Company, *Yankelovich Multicultural Marketing Study 2009* (New York, 2010); J. Ricker and B. Witeck, *Understanding the Gay, Lesbian, Bisexual, and Transsexual Marketing and How It Influences Marketing Communications* (New York: Harris-Heritage Study, 2003).

50. L. Peñaloza, "*Atravesando fronteras*/Border Crossings: A Critical Ethnographic Exploration of the Consumer Acculturation of Mexican immigrants," *Journal of Consumer Research* 21, no. 1 (1994): 32–54.

51. B. Mittal, "I, Me, and Mine—How Products Become Consumers' Extended Selves," *Journal of Consumer Behaviour* 5, no. 6 (2006), 550–562; Sirgy, "Self-Concept in Consumer Behavior"; Judge, "Is the Net Redefining Our Identity?"; and D. Kellner, *Media Culture* (New York: Routledge, 1995).

52. M.S. Rosenbaum, "The Symbolic Servicescape: Your Kind Is Welcomed Here," *Journal of Consumer Behaviour* 4, no. 4 (2005): 257–267.

53. C.L. Wang, T. Bristol, J.C. Mowen, and G. Chakraborty, "Alternative Modes of Self-Construal: Dimensions of Connectedness-Separateness and Advertising Ap-

peals to the Cultural and Gender Specific Self," *Journal of Consumer Psychology* 9, no. 2 (2000): 107–115; T.M. Lowrey, B.G. Englis, S. Shavitt, and M.R. Solomon, "Response Latency Verification of Consumption Constellations: Implications for Advertising Strategy," *Journal of Advertising* 30, no. 1 (2001): 29–39.

54. P. Roslow and J.A.F. Nicholls, "Targeting the Hispanic market: Comparative Persuasion of TV Commercials in Spanish and English," *Journal of Advertising Research* 36, no. 3 (1996): 67–77; T. McCarroll, "It's a Mass Market No More," *Time*, December 2, 1993, 21; M.L. Rossman, *Multicultural Marketing: Selling to a Diverse America* (New York: AMACON, 1994); J.D. Zbar, "Special Report: Marketing to Hispanics," *Advertising Age*, March 18, 1996, 27–29; J. Lipman, "Ads Aimed at Older Americans May Be Too Old for Audience," *Wall Street Journal*, December 31, 1991, B4; G.P. Moschis, *Marketing Strategies for the Mature Market* (Westport, CT: Quorum, 1994); G.B. Woods, *Advertising and Marketing to the New Majority* (Belmont, CA: Wadsworth, 1995).

55. S. Rapp and T.L. Collins, *MaxiMarketing: The New Direction in Advertising, Promotion, and Marketing Strategy* (New York: McGraw-Hill, 1988); D. Peppers and M. Rogers, *The One to One Future* (New York: Doubleday, 1993).

56. G. McCracken, "Culture and Consumption: A Theoretical Account of the Structure and Movement of the Cultural Meaning of Consumer Goods," *Journal of Consumer Research* 13, no. 1 (1986): 71–84.

57. S. Fournier, "Consumers and Their Brands: Developing Relationship Theory in Consumer Research," *Journal of Consumer Research* 24, no. 4 (1998): 343–360.

58. T. Frank, "Brand You: Better Selling Through Anthropology," *Harper's Magazine* (July 1999): 74–79; Elliott and Wattanasuwan, "Brands as Symbolic Resources for the Construction of Identity"; J. Aaker, "Dimensions of Brand Personality," *Journal of Marketing Research* 34, no. 3 (1997): 347–357; Fournier, "Consumers and Their Brands"; R.W. Belk, "Possessions and the Extended Self," *Journal of Consumer Research* 15, no. 2 (1988): 139–168; J.W. Schouten, "Selves in Transition: Symbolic Consumption in Personal Rites of Passage and Identity Reconstruction," *Journal of Consumer Research* 17, no. 4 (1991): 412–425; Sirgy, "Self-Concept in Consumer Behavior."

59. S. Schembri, B. Merrilees, and A. Kristiansen, "Brand Consumption and Narrative of the Self," *Psychology and Marketing* 27, no. 6 (2010): 623–637.

60. M. Tharp and L.M. Scott, "The Role of Marketing Processes in Creating Cultural Meaning," *Journal of Macromarketing* 10, no. 2 (1990): 47–60.

61. S. Youn and H. Kim "Antecedents of Consumer Attitudes Toward Cause-Related Marketing," *Journal of Advertising Research* 48, no. 1 (2008): 123–137; D.W. Rook, "The Ritual Dimension of Consumer Behavior," *Journal of Consumer Research* 12, no. 3 (1985): 251–263.

62. S. Mitchell, *Generation X: The Young Adult Market* (Ithaca, NY: New Strategist, 1997).

63. S. Vranica, "Marketers' New Idea: Get the Consumer to Design the Ads," *Wall Street Journal*, December 14, 2005, B1, B4.

64. F. Korzenny, B.A. Korzenny, H. McGavock, and M.G. Inglessis, *The Muticultural Marketing Equation: Media, Attitudes, Brands, and Spending* (Tallahassee, FL: Center for Hispanic Marketing Communication, Florida State University, 2006), 24.

65. L.J. Shrum, ed., *The Psychology of Entertainment Media: Blurring the Lines Between Entertainment and Persuasion* (Mahwah, NJ: Lawrence Erlbaum, 2004); Turow, *Breaking up America*, 157–200.

66. F.D. Ginsburg, L. Abu-Lughod, and B. Larkin, eds., *Media Worlds: Anthropology on New Terrain* (Berkeley: University of California Press, 2002).

67. N. Gabler, *Life the Movie: How Entertainment Conquered Reality* (New York: Knopf, 1998).

68. A.L. Penenberg, "Everyone's a Player," *Fast Company* (December 2010/January 2011): 135–141.

69. M.A. Stelzner, *2011 Social Media Marketing Industry Report: How Marketers Are Using Social Media to Grow Their Businesses* (Social Media Examiner, April 2011); B.G. Englis and M.R. Solomon, "Where Perception Meets Reality: The Social Construction of Lifestyles" in *Values, Lifestyles and Psychographics*, ed. L. R. Kahle and L. Chiagouris (Mahwah, NJ: Lawrence Erlbaum, 1997), 25–44.

70. M.F. Jacobson and L.A. Mazur, *Marketing Madness* (Boulder, CO: Westview Press, 1995); M.P. McAllister, *The Commercialization of American Culture* (Thousand Oaks, CA: Sage, 1996); T.M. Lowrey, L.J. Shrum, and J.A. McCarty, "The Future of Television Advertising," in *Marketing Communication: New Approaches, Technologies, and Styles*, ed. A.J. Kimmel (New York: Oxford University Press, 2006), 113–132.

71. J. Berger and C. Heath, "Where Consumers Diverge from Others: Identity Signaling and Product Domains," *Journal of Consumer Research* 34, no. 2 (2007): 121–134; Twitchell, *Adcult USA*, 32.

72. E.G. Taylor, "A Cross-Media Study of Audience Choice: The Influence of Traits, Needs, and Attitudes on Individual Selection of Media Repertoires" (Ph.D. dissertation, University of Texas at Austin, 1999); R.X. Weissman, "The Kids Are All Right—They're Just a Little Converged," *American Demographics* (December 1998): 30–32.

73. P. Roslow and J.A.F. Nicholls, "Targeting the Hispanic market: Comparative Persuasion of TV Commercials in Spanish and English," *Journal of Advertising Research* 36, no. 3 (1996): 67–77; H. Cisneros, "Being Hispanic," (keynote speech delivered at First Hispanic Observatory, Bromley Aguilar + Associates, San Antonio, TX, April 30, 1997).

74. W.M. O'Barr, *Culture and the Ad: Exploring Otherness in the World of Advertising* (Boulder, CO: Westview Press, 1994).

75. O'Barr, *Culture and the Ad*.

76. S.G. Beatty, "VW Is Not Steering Clear of 'Ellen' Episode," *Wall Street Journal*, April 25, 1997; N.C. Webster, "Playing to Gay Segment Opens Doors For Marketers," *Advertising Age*, May 30, 1994, 1.

77. Kellner, *Media Culture*; R.J. Donovan and S. Leivers, "Using Paid Advertising to Modify Racial Stereotype Beliefs," *Public Opinion Quarterly* 57, no. 2 (1993): 205–218.

78. J.D. Williams and W.J. Qualls, "Middle-Class Black Consumers and Intensity of Ethnic Identification," *Psychology & Marketing* 6, no. 4 (1989): 263–286; W.J. McGuire et al., "Salience of Ethnicity in the Spontaneous Self-Concept as a Function of One's Ethnic Distinctiveness in the Social Environment," *Journal of Personality and Social Psychology* 36, no. 5 (1978): 511–520; Deshpandé and Stayman, "A Tale of Two Cities."

79. T.J. Reynolds and J.C. Olson, eds., *Understanding Consumer Decision Making: the Means-End Approach to Marketing and Advertising Strategy* (Mahwah, NJ: Lawrence Erlbaum, 2001), 1–23.

80. M. Rokeach, *Beliefs, Attitudes, and Values: A Theory of Organization and*

Change (San Francisco: Jossey-Bass, 1968); Wikipedia, "Rokeach Value Survey," http://en.wikipedia.org/wiki/Rokeach_Value_Survey/.

81. For more detail on laddering, see T.J. Reynolds and J.C. Olson, eds., *Understanding Consumer Decision Making: the Means-End Approach to Marketing and Advertising Strategy* (Mahwah, NJ: Lawrence Erlbaum, 2001).

82. J.E. Escalas and J.R. Bettman, "Self-Construal, Reference Groups, and Brand Meaning," *Journal of Consumer Research* 32, no. 3 (2005): 378–389; M. Ligas, "People, Products, and Pursuits: Exploring the Relationship Between Consumer Goals and Product Meanings," *Psychology & Marketing,* 17, no. 11 (2000): 983–1003.

83. B.G. Englis and M.R. Solomon, "To Be and Not to Be: Lifestyle Imagery, Reference Groups, and the Clustering of America," *Journal of Advertising* 24, no. 1 (1995): 13–28.

84. L.R. Oswald, "Culture Swapping: Consumption and the Ethnogenesis of Middle-Class Haitian Immigrants," *Journal of Consumer Research* 25, no. 4 (1999): 303–318.

85. Sirgy, "Self-Concept in Consumer Behavior."

86. I. Teinowitz, "Special Report: Multicultural Marketing," *Advertising Age,* November 16, 1998, s2.

87. Beatty, "VW Is Not Steering Clear of 'Ellen' Episode."

88. A. Brown, "Coors Cools Hispania," *Marketing and Media Decisions,* June 30, 1990; C. Hawkins, "Denny's: The Stain That Isn't Coming out," *BusinessWeek,* June 28, 1993, 98–99.

89. B. Weinstein, "Ethnic Marketing: The New Numbers Game," *Profiles* (May 1994): 51–54; L.R. Kahle, "Observations: Role-Relaxed Consumers: Empirical Evidence," *Journal of Advertising Research* 35, no. 3 (1995): 59–62.

90. U.S. Census Bureau, "American Community Survey," November 3, 2010, www.census.gov/acs/www/.

91. W.-N. Lee, C. La Ferle, and M. Tharp, "Ethnic Influences on Communication Patterns: Word-of-Mouth, Traditional and Non-Traditional Media Usage," in *Diversity in Advertising,* ed. J.D. Williams, W.-N. Lee, and C.P. Haugtvedt (Mahwah, NJ: Lawrence Erlbaum, 2004), 177–200.

92. Twitchell, *Adcult USA;* J.W. Smith and A. Clurman, *Rocking the Ages: The Yankelovich Report on Generational Marketing* (New York: HarperBusiness, 1997).

93. G. Meredith and C. Schewe, "The Power of Cohorts," *American Demographics* (December 1994): 22–27.

94. M.C. Tharp, *Marketing and Consumer Identity in Multicultural America* (Thousand Oaks, CA: Sage, 2001).

95. J.H. Leigh and T.G. Gabel, "Symbolic Interactionism: Its Effects on Consumer Behaviour and Implications for Marketing Strategy," *Journal of Consumer Marketing* 9, no. 1 (1992): 27–38.

96. Waters, *Ethnic Options;* Stayman and R. Deshpandé, "Situational Ethnicity and Consumer Behavior."

97. Alba, *Ethnic Identity;* M.J. Collier, "Cultural Identity and Intercultural Communication," in *Intercultural Communication: A Reader,* 7th ed., ed. L.A. Samovar and R.E. Porter (Belmont, CA: Wadsworth, 1994), 36–44; M.L. Hecht, M.J. Collier, and S.A. Ribeau, *African American Communication: Ethnic Identity and Cultural Interpretation* (Newbury Park, CA: Sage, 1993), 1–81.

3

Transcultural Marketing

Developing a Cultural Values Proposition

*At USAA we believe honor is not exclusive to the military and
commitment is not limited to one's military oath. The same
values that drive our nation's military are the ones we used
to build USAA Bank. . . . We know what it means to serve.*[1]

The USAA quotation from its website represents a cultural values proposition from USAA to current and past military families. This kind of cultural
compatibility is the foundation upon which marketing plans are made when
the "market" is multicultural. This chapter details how to acquire and exercise
the skills of transmigration across often-invisible cultural boundaries. Shifting identity is natural for people in multicultural societies. Teenagers easily
switch from an ethnic-influenced world at home to cohort-determined values
at school. It is more difficult for marketing organizations to express multiple,
sometimes conflicting, values.

We begin by recommending the adoption of a "border mentality" with
which companies can address the cultural context of their desired customers.[2]
Interpreting what things mean depends on knowing their cultural context.
Transcultural market planning adds cultural analysis to activities designed
to understand and appeal to potential customers. Adjusting company goals
and organization structure are keys to infusing a cultural perspective at
all levels of market planning. The tools for transcultural marketing strategy include the original "4 Ps" (product, prices, promotion, and place) as
well as all decisions that express corporate values and partnerships, to all
publics, including target customers. We propose three choices for building
a cultural value proposition and provide examples of companies whose

marketing programs include both cultural and economic value propositions. The last part of this chapter sheds light on ethical dilemmas in situations where target marketing across consumer subcultures has broader societal impact.[3]

Key Themes in Transcultural Marketing: Values and Affiliations

"I know what it *costs*; what does it *mean*?" "I know what it *does*, but what does it *say*?" "I know *who* sells it; *who else* buys it?" Among consumers, answers to these questions represent two attributes—cultural meaning and group associations—that express the cultural roles played by products and their sellers. To make these an explicit part of brand positioning, organizations must adopt a "border mentality" at every step in the planning process.

The "Border Mentality"

People who "grow up" in more than one subculture (e.g., children of immigrants, members of the LGBT subculture, and people who live as minorities in geographic communities) learn naturally to question the cultural context of phenomena. Individuals in multicultural settings learn that what something means is *situational*—its meaning depends on issues such as whether it is said in English, Spanish, or Spanglish; whether it is a message in mainstream media or comes from a subculture source; and the characteristics, motivations, and status of the person/s who said it. The process of acculturating for immigrants, changing geographic or social communities while young, and racial differences between African or Asian and other Americans represent situations that allow these Americans to develop a high-context approach to interpreting meaning.[4] All of us use our "border mentality" on occasion; most of us would not use the same language or tell the same stories with our grandmothers as with our friends.

   People and organizations in a multicultural society *interpret* cultural meanings and group associations before formulating appropriate responses. This "border mentality" is a valuable tool for navigating between and among U.S. subcultures of gender, age, disabilities, sexual orientation, geography, race, and ethnicity.[5] Individuals, who find their social identities at the intersection of at least two salient subcultures, use their bicultural skills to bridge those worlds.[6] That consumers "reside" simultaneously in multiple cultures presents an opportunity for marketers to participate in the cultural role of the marketplace as a medium for expression.

Applying the "Border Mentality"

For an organization to cater to both the cultural and economic needs of individuals, it, too, must use the border mentality in developing marketing programs. Companies can nurture the border mentality among their decision makers by emphasizing a "different-but-equal" attitude about group differences and appreciation of "meaning" from multiple perspectives. Organizations must act as multicultural entities when choosing resources, capabilities, and goals.[7]

If products and services express their desired consumers' social identities, then marketers must reconstitute marketing plans to communicate that brand's or company's values and affiliations.[8] Large organizations have vast resources with which to build a presence in specific subculture communities, using shared ideals, symbols, heroes, myths, rituals, and other sources of cultural meaning.[9] By mirroring the cultural meanings and group associations that reflect situational identities of a desired market, brands assert their role as cultural media. Whether it is Leonardo di Caprio's endorsement of Tag Heuer watches because the firm supports environmental charities, Budweiser's support of soccer fans during the year of a World Cup competition, or Target's giving 5 percent of sales to local schools, companies are trumpeting their shared interests with members of American subcultures.

In some situations, the market space itself contributes to an experience of crossing cultures. Consider the new experiences that technologies such as the Kindle, Skype, the smartphone, Ikea sun-blocked clothing, or Nike plasma TVs might offer consumers. New product categories or changing configurations of brands in familiar product categories, new types of retailing and even shopping conventions (e.g., norms for special pricing on "Black Friday") are sources of new cultural experiences. Products also define such American cultural rituals as watching the Super Bowl or having Thanksgiving dinner.

Consumers respond to newness in different ways: adopting new patterns of behavior, selectively adopting new behaviors, and resisting change completely.[10] Transcultural marketing recognizes the socialization role of the marketplace by building marketing strategy on both an economic and cultural basis. Advertisements use men and women in roles that either challenge or teach cultural norms for gender. The sellers intend to persuade audiences that their products can solve buyer problems and meet their needs. Nevertheless, these ads are also cultural agents that illustrate appropriate/inappropriate masculine and feminine behaviors.

Managing global brands requires skill in perceiving and adapting to cultural differences in meaning as context shifts from one market segment or country to another. "Think Global, Act Local" suggests that brand strategy can be standardized across country markets while tactics must be designed in response to the differing cultural contexts that surround unique market segments or countries. Transcultural marketing brings this aspect of the planning process—evaluating the impact of different cultural settings—to the segmentation, target market selection, and market positioning processes of market planning in a national market. The objective, then, of transcultural marketing is to use the tools of cultural analysis from global market planning to planning strategy in any multicultural market.

Budweiser's appeal to all "premium" beer drinkers was successful for many years. However, the brand that was the 16th most valuable in 2003 ranked 220th by 2010, as high-price beer buyers switched to craft beers. In other trends, the price-conscious beer drinker traded down, and others switched to light beers.[11] Bud now has different "faces" for these different beer drinkers. Bud tries to win "under 30" drinkers by giving away free samples in trendy bars and a free beer on a consumer's birthday. For craft-beer drinkers, Budweiser promotes itself as the "American Ale." Budweiser addresses ethnic consumers in the United States with separate websites for U.S. Latinos, African Americans, and Asian Americans. These websites link Budweiser to key issues and organizations of different ethnic and age communities. They also show Budweiser's support of education, music, and cultural traditions, economic development, and, of course, responsible use of alcohol—the same values that are important to people in all American subcultures.

McDonald's also has designed separate websites for Asian Americans (www.myinspirasian.com), African Americans (www.365black.com/365black/index.jsp), U.S. Latinos (www.meencanta.com), and tweens (www.mcworld.com/en_US/). On each site, McDonald's shows how it participates in the "cultural" community groups with which these target consumers identify.

Put succinctly, transcultural marketing is about being different things to different people, but with a core set of values and partnerships.

Transmigration for Marketers: Behaving as a Cultural Institution

In order to cross back and forth across cultural boundaries, individuals anticipate the possibility of differences in meaning, accept those differences, and respond to them in culturally compatible ways. Companies must first have a commitment to understanding and responding to cultural differences. It is essential that corporate leaders assert the roles that businesses play in their customers' cultural lives. A recognition of diverse meanings and behaviors must permeate an organization's choices of analytical tools, human resources, and organizational structure.

With a commitment to becoming culturally fluent, companies can then expand their expertise in identifying consumer subcultures and learn what it takes to construct a successful cultural values proposition for them. A broad knowledge of major American subcultures, along with their demographic and psychographic profiles, is a basic requirement, followed by primary research that can capture this particular company's cultural roles. This fluency requires new tools for analyzing consumer trends and attitudes. Hiring more diverse employees and, specifically, hiring people who have experience crossing cultural boundaries can create opportunities for transmigration experiences throughout an organization. Company structure must ensure that the right people are in the right places to identify and analyze opportunities to create cultural compatibility.

The following sections of this chapter provide more detail about how to reorient a firm to take on a role as a cultural institution. Presenting customers with an economic as well as cultural value proposition is the goal of transcultural marketing. Nike's economic value proposition is delivering performance benefits in exchange for the price of running shoes, but its cultural value proposition for runners mirrors runners' values and affiliations. This "cultural values" proposition is expressed by Nike's actions, such as supporting running associations and sponsorship of events, Nike's ads showing runners setting and achieving goals, stories about the Nike CEO who is a runner, and the firm's financial, human resource, philanthropic, and environmental policies.

The Values of Transcultural Marketing

Transmigration is the process in which organizations, brands, and their decision makers become "fluent" in multiple cultures. Since it is difficult to predict situational influences on a specific consumer or purchasing occasion, organizations and brands must construct *their own cultural identities* and make potential buyers aware of them.

An example of a company that acts as a multicultural entity is Burger King. Burger King "acts" as an authentic member of the U.S. Latino community through different methods of communications—handing out coupons at the Calle Ocho festival in Miami, constantly advertising in Spanish-language and U.S. Latino–oriented media, and participating in community programs that contribute to schools in Hispanic neighborhoods. Burger King hires Latino, Chinese, and African Americans as franchise operators, making it an "extended" member of those subculture communities as well.

Such policies communicate Burger King's group associations, position its services within a cultural context, and nurture the "border mentality" of its managers. Ethnic customers do not eat Whoppers® simply because Burger

King advertises in a familiar language. However, if they view hamburger brands as similar, extra incentive to choose one over another could be provided by a company's participation in ethnic festivals, visibility in ethnic media, and support of relevant causes. Transmigration allows managers at Burger King to tune its marketing programs to subculture community interests and values.

Figure 3.1 shows how business organizations can adopt the process of transmigration to meet both economic and cultural needs of consumers. The left side of the figure shows how the changes in social identity discussed in Chapter 2 impact what consumers want from market spaces and products and services. The right side indicates how organizations must adapt to consumers in a multicultural market. The traditional marketing "mix" (product, price, place, and promotions) must be expanded to include other programs and decisions that express corporate values and group associations. The result is an economic and cultural value proposition tailored to buyers who identify with specific groups in a multicultural society.

The fluidity with which organization and brand identity move from one criterion to another is a key characteristic of transmigration.[12] Opinion leaders in multicultural America are people and organizations that can *communicate with* and *interpret for* more than one subculture group.[13] Many of the ideas in this chapter are not new but suggest the advantages of redefining terms like "market," "profits," or "market share." That is the "border mentality"—finding multiple meanings in familiar concepts. It exemplifies a "best" practice for communicating with people who identify with multiple subcultures.

Measuring Results: Shared Interests Added to Long-Term Profitability

Transcultural marketing differs from niche marketing in its emphasis on constructing a cultural values proposition and efforts to share customer values and affiliations. Niche marketers design programs that retain loyal buyers by providing price/quality combinations, performance benefits, and customer services. The competitive benefit of niche marketing is knowing customers' needs and wants better than the competition does. The extra costs of niche marketing are worthwhile when a mass-market approach is not effective in securing a large share of all potential buyers in a market.[14] Cultural compatibility programs are left to public relations, human resources, or other interfaces with community groups, as if the consumer's affiliations were not relevant to purchase decisions. That view of buyer decision making is in direct conflict with surveys that report that three out of four consumers would "switch to a brand associated with a good cause."[15] A brand's "niche" must be redefined

Figure 3.1   **Consumer Needs and Marketing Strategies in a Multicultural Market**

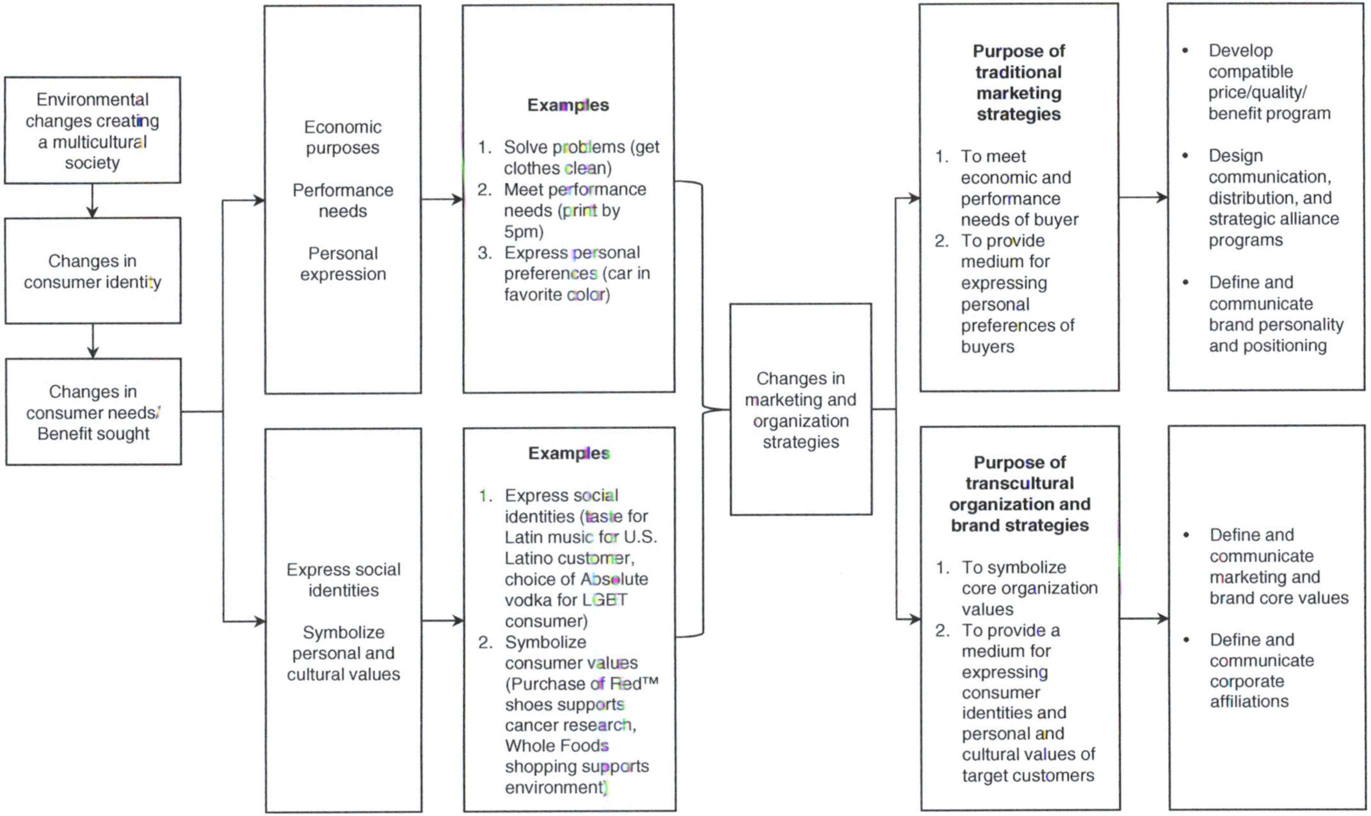

Purpose of traditional marketing strategies

1. To meet economic and performance needs of buyer
2. To provide medium for expressing personal preferences of buyers

- Develop compatible price/quality/benefit program
- Design communication, distribution, and strategic alliance programs
- Define and communicate brand personality and positioning

Purpose of transcultural organization and brand strategies

1. To symbolize core organization values
2. To provide a medium for expressing consumer identities and personal and cultural values of target customers

- Define and communicate marketing and brand core values
- Define and communicate corporate affiliations

Changes in marketing and organization strategies

Examples

1. Solve problems (get clothes clean)
2. Meet performance needs (print by 5pm)
3. Express personal preferences (car in favorite color)

Examples

1. Express social identities (taste for Latin music for U.S. Latino customer, choice of Absolute vodka for LGBT consumer)
2. Symbolize consumer values (Purchase of Red™ shoes supports cancer research, Whole Foods shopping supports environment)

Economic purposes
Performance needs
Personal expression

Express social identities
Symbolize personal and cultural values

Environmental changes creating a multicultural society

Changes in consumer identity

Changes in consumer needs/Benefit sought

as *buyers who seek a proposition or solution that offers economic value and cultural compatibility.*

Some organization policies may seem peripheral, even unrelated to decisions to buy one brand of soft drink over another or to stop at one movie theater and not another. Nevertheless, technology allows us to search for whatever information we want from endless sources.[16] The only perceived difference between one brand of laptop and another, two insurance companies, or two car models may be with which groups' media or social causes the brands are associated. While automobile companies use their recyclability or low environmental impact as attributes that distinguish their models from those of competitors, the impetus for those policies has frequently come from executive offices, not their design or marketing staff.[17]

Table 3.1 shows how shopping priorities can differ across ethnic groups. For example, buying products made with recycled paper is more important to Asian Americans, who also read labels, change brands for novelty, and advise other shoppers. White, non-Hispanic consumers are more likely to advise others, but less likely to ask for advice. Hispanics are brand switchers for fun and tend to believe that advertising gives a "true picture of products." African Americans are the most style conscious and are concerned with what their neighbors think about what they buy. Current data like those in the table can be purchased from Experian/Simmons or from similar companies that provide data to help fine tune marketing strategies for unique market segments

The criteria for setting goals and measures of success must change when practicing transcultural marketing. Setting dollar sales and market share objectives indicate a firm's economic goals, but they do not explain how desired customers evaluate their cultural value proposition. Do current customers believe that a firm whose brands they buy contributes to their overall quality of life? If not, their loyalty may not extend beyond the next transaction. A competitor can more easily match a price/quality relationship than a company's role as cultural insider within a consumer subculture.[18]

Transcultural marketing calls for measuring whether stakeholders, including customers, believe they "share interests," an element that is missing from economic models of profitability. The long-term survival of companies and brands comes from a perceived ability to *share customer values*, not its inherently short-term ability to cater to a profitable niche. The costs of inviting repeat purchases from current customers are less than the marketing costs of attracting new customers, so it makes sense to retain the loyalty of current customers whenever possible.[19] When that loyalty is linked to customers' perceptions that a brand/company is culturally compatible, there is a double bond—economic and cultural. And it is less vulnerable to competitor actions than a relationship based solely on economic criteria.

Table 3.1

Shopping Priorities of Four Ethnic Groups

		Total sample	U.S. Hispanics	White, non-Hispanic	Black, non-Hispanic	Asian, non-Hispanic
Total sample	(000)	223,483	31,501	154,442	25,275	8,887
	Index	100	100	100	100	100
I buy products that use recycled paper.	(000)	89,504	14,055	61,140	8,673	4,424
	Index	100	111	99	86	124
I shop for specials/bargains.	(000)	122,157	16,231	86,681	12,406	5,079
	Index	100	94	103	90	105
I keep up with changes in styles/fashion.	(000)	54,254	8,775	33,894	8,334	2,461
	Index	100	115	90	136	114
I plan ahead for expensive purchases.	(000)	133,133	16,096	98,050	11,760	5,202
	Index	100	86	107	78	98
I don't buy unknown brands to save money.	(000)	75,156	11,140	51,877	7,847	3,339
	Index	100	105	100	92	112
I often buy on the spur of the moment.	(000)	82,942	9,967	60,376	8,836	2,780
	Index	100	85	105	94	84
I change brands often for variety/novelty.	(000)	40,654	8,396	24,182	5,223	2,208
	Index	100	147	86	114	137
I always look for brand names.	(000)	69,974	10,561	47,783	8,350	2,513
	Index	100	107	99	106	90
I usually read information on the label.	(000)	98,714	13,758	68,794	10,049	4,613
	Index	100	99	101	90	118
Advertising gives a true picture of products.	(000)	35,093	6,992	20,249	5,735	1,585
	Index	100	141	83	144	114
I prefer to buy what neighbors approve of.	(000)	26,944	5,104	15,231	3,999	2,168
	Index	100	134	82	131	202
I ask advice before.	(000)	96,729	10,865	71,073	8,785	4,651
	Index	100	82	106	114	108
People come to me for advice before buying.	(000)	48,148	7,212	31,588	6,335	2,172
	Index	100	106	95	113	116

Source: Experian/Simmons, NCS/NCHA Adult Survey Database, September–October 2010, www.experian.com/simmons-research/consumer-study.html.

Table 3.2

Measures of Shared Interests Between Customers and Marketers

Consumer perceptions and behavior	Measures of "shared interests" in cultural domain
Category usage patterns	• Product use as expression of group identity • Usage differences across subculture groups • Subculture meanings associated with product use
Perception of competitive product differences	• Attributes consumers include in their perceived price–value ratios • Perceptions of firm and competitors as members of subculture communities • Awareness of firm policies that affect subculture community • Reputations of competitors in subculture community • Comparative brand ratings on cultural criteria • Brand and user image and perceived compatibility with subcultures
Brand loyalty and perceived brand value	• Importance of price–value ratios in consumer choice • Awareness of targeted marketing efforts • Perception of performance differences across brands on both economic and cultural criteria • Brand preference as expression of group identities • Brand preference as expression of community support
Cultural identity	• Perceptions of organization's presence in community • Perceptions of corporate aesthetics • Perceptions of groups/causes supported by corporate philanthropy • Perceptions of corporate human resource policies • Perceptions of corporate environmental impact and policies

There is no "best" measure of how a marketer's actions reflect shared customer values. The appropriate benchmark must vary for different types of products, firms, and community groups.[20] Table 3.2 shows some possibilities for incorporating "shared interests" into economic estimates of customer value. Some of the measures in the table are in common use, such as product usage differences across age or ethnic groups. Comparative brand ratings on important attributes are another common measure, and such data can be purchased on an ongoing basis. Other measures, such as cultural meanings of brand or product use and perceptions of shared interests between a particular firm and customers identifying with specific subculture communities, can be added to the firm's primary research and dialog with buyers.

One example shows how the concept of shared interests might explain brand preferences and suggest corrective actions. Data on patronage at fast food restaurants are shown in Table 3.3. According to the index numbers in the table, McDonald's appeals to all groups, while Carl's Jr.'s and Jack in the Box attract larger percentages of African-American and U.S. Latino consumers. Burger King is popular with all groups except Asian Americans, while Wendy's and Sonic seem to have trouble attracting U.S. Latinos and Asian Americans.

Assume that Wendy's or Sonic wants to grow its share of the fast food market. It will have to find out why its restaurants are not currently popular with Asian Americans and U.S. Latinos, as these two groups constitute the fastest-growing segments of U.S. population. It could be that stores are not convenient to Asian and Latino neighborhoods, but there are other possible explanations that only primary research could reveal. The lack of a presence of these restaurants in Asian or Latino community and media organizations positions them as "outsiders."

The same database shows how the popularity of pizza, chicken, breakfast, and other fast food restaurants varies across ethnic groups. Domino's and Little Caesars are popular with U.S. Latinos, while Papa John's Pizza and Pizza Inn are most popular with African Americans. African Americans eat more chicken than other ethnic groups across all restaurants. Asian Americans are more likely to have breakfast at Au Bon Pain or Starbuck's, and African Americans are more likely to be at Dunkin' Donuts and Krispy Kreme.

These brands are successful due to effective, traditional marketing strategies. Adding a cultural analysis of ethnic consumers' current behaviors would explain how or if those preferences are linked to cultural compatibility. McDonald's and Burger King have been tapping into black and Hispanic culture in their advertising for many years. They also support scholarship programs in those communities and community traditions such as Black History month and Cinco de Mayo celebrations. McDonald's is even using advertising developed for ethnic markets in mainstream media today.[21] It is able to do this, it says, because ethnic groups are the "trendsetters" in this business. It tries out new menus and ads, first with ethnic groups and then nationally.

An audit of how different consumer groups view the values of these fast food restaurants can uncover negative or unintended associations that are meaningful to a particular ethnic group. However measured, perceived cultural compatibility is more predictive of long-term loyalty than strictly economic measures.[22]

The AARP informs the mature market about social issues of interest through its lobbying efforts reported on its website, via e-mail alerts and in *AARP The Magazine* (formerly *Modern Maturity*). In the same issue of that magazine or on its website, AARP offers low-interest-rate credit cards, pharmacy by mail, travel planning, and health insurance, among other services. Readers do not distinguish these as product- and non–product-related

Table 3.3

Fast Food Restaurant Preferences of Four Ethnic Groups

		Total sample	U.S. Hispanics	Whites, non-Hispanic	Blacks, non-Hispanic	Asian, non-Hispanic
Total sample	(000)	223,483	31,501	154,442	25,275	8,887
	Index	100	100	100	100	100
Fast food and drive-in restaurant use	(000)	188,378	25,368	132,143	21,310	6,864
		84%	81%	86%	84%	77%
	Index	100	96	102	100	92
Burgers						
Burger King	(000)	81,316	11,446	55,286	10,590	2,696
	Index	100	100	98	115	83
Carl's Jr.	(000)	16,320	4,457	8,607	1,505	1,426
	Index	100	194	76	82	220
Jack-in-the-Box	(000)	22,818	6,382	11,803	2,779	1,258
	Index	100	198	75	108	139
McDonald's	(000)	127,749	16,503	90,449	14,513	4,477
	Index	100	92	102	100	88
Sonic	(000)	29,069	3,620	20,393	3,449	698
	Index	100	88	102	105	60
Wendy's	(000)	64,578	6,677	46,964	8,109	1,669
	Index	100	73	105	111	65
Pizza						
Domino's Pizza	(000)	31,789	6,483	18,403	4,757	1,383
	Index	100	145	84	132	109
Little Caesar's	(000)	19,723	4,479	11,574	2,561	668
	Index	100	161	85	115	85
Papa John's	(000)	19,079	2,556	12,520	2,619	807
	Index	100	95	95	121	106
Pizza Hut	(000)	45,210	6,604	30,214	5,914	1,808
	Index	100	104	97	116	101
Pizza Inn	(000)	5,262	800	2,441	1,495	289
	Index	100	108	67	251	138

Chicken					
Boston Market	(000)	12,832	2,111	7,110	2,862	536
	Index	100	117	80	197	105
Chick-fil-A	(000)	29,938	2,441	21,611	4,753	757
	Index	100	58	104	140	64
Church's Fried Chicken	(000)	11,665	2,745	4,011	4,345	224
	Index	100	167	50	329	48
KFC	(000)	58,019	6,966	38,816	8,731	2,327
	Index	100	85	97	133	101
Popeye's	(000)	16,763	3,024	6,841	5,515	1,048
	Index	100	128	59	291	157
Breakfast					
Au Bon Pain	(000)	4,803	848	2,473	962	326
	Index	100	125	75	177	170
Dunkin' Donuts	(000)	27,307	3,363	18,518	3,851	953
	Index	100	87	98	125	88
Krispy Kreme	(000)	12,546	1,550	7,544	2,644	498
	Index	100	88	87	186	100
Starbuck's	(000)	28,034	4,092	19,200	1,964	2,115
	Index	100	104	99	62	190
Other Fast Foods					
Long John Silver's	(000)	16,908	1,951	12,153	1,893	582
	Index	100	82	104	99	87
Arby's	(000)	41,398	2,785	33,013	3,875	1,216
	Index	100	48	115	83	74
Quiznos Sub	(000)	17,809	2,360	12,133	2,164	711
	Index	100	94	99	107	100
Subway	(000)	69,667	8,312	50,934	6,767	2,496
	Index	100	85	106	86	90
Chipotle	(000)	14,266	2,141	9,064	1,810	1,025
	Index	100	106	92	112	181
Taco Bell	(000)	64,672	8,627	46,105	6,551	2,326
	Index	100	95	103	90	90
Other fast food restaurants	(000)	40,460	5,614	27,800	4,842	1,484
	Index	100	98	99	106	92

Source: Experian/Simmons, NCS/NCHA Adult Survey Database, Sept.–Oct. 2010, www.experian.com/simmons-research/consumer-study.html.

bits of information. An AARP credit card in the pocket of a senior citizen supports an organization that keeps its consumers informed about *relevant* topics. It is a "win-win" economic exchange that includes shared interests and member concerns.

Planning Process: Matrix Market Planning

Matrix market planning is a cost-effective and relationship-driven alternative to both mass and niche marketing. The matrix comes from a strategy of cumulating niches as the means to high market share, a concept best described in *The Long Tail*.[23] Matrix market planning explores the appropriateness of marketing strategies and tactics for each group of potential customers whose economic and cultural interests an organization wishes to share. The objective is to develop a multifaceted partnership with consumers from different subcultures, built upon meeting those buyers' economic and cultural needs.[24]

An example of the matrix that McDonald's has built is shown in Table 3.4. For the time being, there is no indication it has a unique corporate strategy to establish a presence in the American LGBT community, though it does tailor promotions to local neighborhoods. Its approach to the mature market is to include more senior citizens in ads and among personnel. McDonald's current marketing and communications target traditional family households, African American, Asian American, and U.S. Latino communities. Each subculture strategy is supported by a variety of culturally appropriate tactics. Unique McDonald's websites for tweens, U.S. Latinos, and Asian and African Americans showcase McDonald's ability to tailor its communication style while emphasizing the match between McDonald's family environment and the importance of family to consumers from these three different subcultures.

Goya's success at marketing to U.S. Latinos illustrates the advantages of being a cultural insider. Goya Food Products has a high share of canned fruit sales among Latinos in New York, not because its prices or product qualities are necessarily superior to those of its competitor Del Monte. It is a *familiar brand* to immigrants from Puerto Rico and other Caribbean countries and has strong *distribution in the bodegas,* which are the preferred shopping outlets of U.S. Latinos. Wells Fargo Bank's penetration of Chinese-American consumers in San Francisco has increased in response to its employment of Mandarin-speaking tellers and support of community events in Chinatown. What matrix market planning does in these cases is suggest a broader mix of marketing tactics as economic and cultural foundation for a relationship with buyers.[25]

Table 3.4

McDonald's Marketing Matrix of Markets, Strategies, and Tactics

Market niche	Marketing strategy	Examples of niche tactics
Mature market	Adjunct to mainstream	• Use of mature Americans in communications • Hiring of mature Americans
African Americans	Identification with African-American community	• Hiring of African-American communication firms • Use of African-American targeted media • Use of African-American communication styles • Use of African-Americans in communications • Support of African-American causes and events • Website for African-American community • Recruitment of African-American franchisees and employees
U.S. Latinos	Identification with Latino groups	• Use of Spanish-language multiple communications • Use of Hispanic cultural settings and media • Use of U.S. Latinos in communications • Support of Hispanic-American causes and events • Recruitment of U.S. Latino franchisees and employees • Hiring of Hispanic communications firms • U.S. Latino website and community • Use of U.S. Latino-targeted media • Use of U.S. Latino communication styles
LGBT consumers	No unique strategy	• Mainstream marketing mix • U.S. news releases of gay male targeting in France • Use of Asian-Americans in ads
Asian Americans	Identification with multiple Asian-American groups	• Support of Asian-American community events • Use of Asian languages in communications • Website for Asian Americans and community
Family households	General market strategy Facility design (playground) Corporate philanthropy Human resource practice Environmental impact policies	• All brand contact points; 4 Ps • Website for young children • Ronald McDonald Houses • Website for tweens
Nonfamily households	No unique strategy	• New product development (e.g., Arch Deluxe) • Media placements and message design

Internal Focus: Market Knowledge and Market Specialists

> *The brand is merely a beacon for a set of values*
> *in the broad spectrum of choices.*[26]

Product and brand images reinforce consumer self-identity. A buyer's choice of product or technology to meet a specific need is framed within this communication and cultural context.[27] There are as many choices as there are meanings that the consumer wishes to communicate to others.[28] From a buyer's perspective, there are infinite "choices" to be made.[29]

Marketing strategy does not have to be built around the cost dimensions of production, communication, and delivery, if we are able to use other areas of distinctive competence.[30] One illustration of marketplace diversity from the consumer's point of view is the need to quench thirst. There are not just many varieties of soft drinks, but also teas, coffees, fruit juices, fruit drinks, beers, wines, liquors, tap water, bottled waters, and carbonated waters. There are infinite numbers of places, quantities, and combinations in which the consumer can acquire any of these drinks in myriad sizes and formats. Which one is picked on a specific occasion depends on the nature of the consumer's thirst, his or her perceptions of the different options available to meet that need, and the significance of the choice of drink in expressing identity at that particular moment.[31]

Not only do the things that people own symbolize their group affiliations, but they also distinguish them from those of members of other groups. Usage or nonusage of a product category, brand or store choices, frequency of product/brand purchases, or usage occasions can all express aspects of social identity. Thus, they are significant decisions in communicating "who I am" to other people in a consumption-oriented society.[32] The Apple campaign for Macintosh computers positioned this brand against all other personal computers. A bloated, middle-aged guy, who can't move fast, resists change, uses only computer-speak, and ignores the cries for help from his users represented the typical personal computer. The Mac "guy" seen in the ads, was young, spry, casual, easy to relate to, open to change, and very friendly.[33] Consumers often choose the same brands that they believe are used by others in the groups with which they identity.[34] Buyers use the cultural meanings of particular brands and products to reduce the number of choices that they must make in a market space and media cornucopia.[35] Information about users of brands, patrons of stores, and employees of producers is increasingly important to consumers. Such information provides a "rationale" for how to deal with information and choice overloads—a consumer will define something as either "me" or "not me" and put one brand in the shopping basket but leave another one on the shelf.[36]

Integrated marketing communications planning has evolved in companies that wish to maximize synergy from their communication activities.[37] This approach offers consumers a consistent message about cultural values and associations. In order to coordinate IPOs with new product announcements, press coverage of new CEOs, advertising campaigns, plant openings, dealer incentives, and advertising with social networking events, marketing managers must design communications for today's broader media mix.[38]

Transcultural marketing plans hinge on the ability to identify all points of contact between customers and brands that affect brand or company perceptions. A joke about the brand on a popular talk show, a story in the tabloid press about someone identified as a brand user, the products next to the brand on store shelves, celebrity endorsers of the brand on Twitter, a new product design or package, layoffs at the brand's maker—these are just a few examples of "contact points." Marketers do not control all these points of contact, but integrated communications planning brings the broadest array of communication media into the marketing plan.[39]

To gather information about how subculture identities influence buyers, organizations must go beyond focus groups, secondary databases, and quantitative studies. Online communities can be a valuable source of quick information. Yahoo uses immersion groups, "a small number of selected consumers who work with the company's staff in studying how people use their products." P&G sends its researchers into the field for two weeks to talk to women, taping the conversations for colleagues back in the office.[40]

Figure 3.2 shows marketing contact points as both economic and cultural bases for exchange with buyers. Our traditional marketing toolkit was developed to meet buyers' needs for brand-related information. It ensures that marketers will have the right bundle of attributes and utility, for a targeted group of buyers, at the right price, at the right time, in the right place, and buyers will be informed about how these attributes match their needs. The figure illustrates the impact of both brand and organization contact on how marketing strategy is designed. Niche and relationship marketing emphasize an "economic" value proposition, while ethnic and transcultural marketing strategies focus on creating a "cultural" value proposition.

Transcultural marketing adds tactics that express the brand and its seller's own cultural affiliations and values. Companies show the public their cultural values, often without realizing what messages they send. A few examples of decisions that buyers use to evaluate an organization or brand's cultural compatibility are hiring/firing decisions and procedures; geographic location and design of production or service facilities; civic or political activities of a firm or its local affiliates; the environmental impact of a firm's activities; and participation in social or community events and causes. A compatible com-

Figure 3.2 **Comparison of Relationship, Niche, Ethnic, and Transcultural Marketing Strategies**

Objective of Marketing Strategy

	Transactions +	Ongoing Relationship
Brand contact points Traditional marketing mix (price, product, distribution, communications), plus strategic alliances	**Niche Marketing**	**Relationship Marketing**
Brand contact points + Organization contact points Traditional marketing mix plus: strategic alliances, philanthropy, human resources, corporate aesthetics, environmental impact of organization	**Ethnic Marketing**	**Transcultural Marketing**

(left axis label: **Domain of marketing strategy**)

munity profile in these areas helps organizations realize cultural partnerships with desired buyers.

Figure 3.2 contrasts four types of niche marketing strategies in terms of meeting economic and cultural needs of buyers. Niche marketing best describes programs designed to appeal to one or more segments of a larger market, using the traditional marketing mix. Using online media, niche marketers can go beyond the limited merchandise mixes of local specialty stores to win the loyalty of the growing number of consumers who buy online. Marketers use the same raw materials (the marketing mix and strategic alliances) to identify and satisfy a broader array of their target consumers' economic needs as part of relationship marketing strategies. Marlboro's specially designed merchandise with Marlboro insignias and experiences such as "smoker-only" travel adventures are examples of how Marlboro has found goods and services that meet their current customers' needs for related products and experiences. These two forms of marketing do not necessarily generate a mutually beneficial *cultural* exchange. Consumers define the extent of their relationships with the brand and marketers respond, rather than the other way around. The competitive advantage of online firms is the data that they can mine from their current customers for opportunities to customize and presell other products to them. It is also a valuable asset in attracting strategic alliances.[41]

Ethnic marketers use a broader mix of marketing, public relations, and management policies to appeal to consumers who identify as members of targeted subculture groups. Levi's, for example, contributes to ethnic community organizations and trumpets its diversity commitments in ethnic-directed media. Their interests remain focused on an economic basis for exchange, even though they use cultural compatibility in their marketing mix to capture the attention of U.S. Latino, Asian-American, and African-American consumers.[42] Support of ethnic media, recognition of ethnic community leaders, and tailored communications maximize a company's access to a subculture group in exchange for goods and services. The organization's other "contact points" (such as Levi's environmental impact or human resource policies) may or may not be compatible with the interests of these subculture communities.

Only transcultural marketing formulates a strategy that covers all points of contact with external groups. It acknowledges the mutual role that consumers and organizations play in each other's economic and cultural lives.[43] Marketing programs reinforce consumer perceptions that the firm is an extended member of their community and lifestyle. People frame current information about a company or brand in the context of past marketer efforts and community beliefs about them.[44] While not all offers of a "cultural values proposition" generate positive customer responses, they position a company as sharing in the cultural and economic lives of target consumers.

The selection of which communities to align a firm's values with from among the age, ethnic, and lifestyle subcultures evolving in American society is fraught with risk. Some subculture groups are still too small or too diverse to make them profitable in the short term. Some groups respond negatively to commercially motivated offers of cultural alliance.[45] Nevertheless, competitors that are willing to court buyers by endorsing the groups with which they identify, and mirror their values, may beat more conservative organizations to the beachhead of shared allegiance.

Pioneers in multicultural America range from large multinational organizations such as AT&T, whose efforts benefit from synergy with its international marketing activities, to smaller organizations such as Overlooked Opinions, a specialist in research on the LGBT market. An investment in whatever it takes to acquire expertise in the values, concerns, and behaviors of consumer subcultures pays off in increased consumer loyalty or brand preference. Separate research studies of the mature market, U.S. Latinos, gay and lesbian buyers, African Americans, teenage consumers, and Asian Americans confirm the preference for culturally compatible marketers.[46] Buyers cite activities such as having a voice in specialized media, tailored product designs or advertising messages, and support of important issues as examples of organizations with a presence in their community.[47]

The multiple and situational identities characteristic of American consumers present special problems for "defining the market opportunity." The first step in the process is estimating the size and value of market segments.[48] Our situational identities mean that subculture group identities and affiliations for most people are not mutually exclusive. They may also defy the rule for "distinctive behavior" as justification for unique marketing programs.[49] There is as much diversity of values and behaviors within the Hispanic or Asian or mature market as there are differences between members of the three groups.

Tastes in soft drinks and coffee offer an example of how difficult it can be to predict marketplace behavior with a superficial understanding of group values. For over 50 years, coffee drinking rose with age and soft drink consumption declined. As the baby boomers age, we would normally expect them to be drinking more coffee. Rooted in their orientation toward youthful imagery, boomers rebel against the rule and continue to drink sodas into old age.[50] When we add ethnicity or geography as subcultural influences, coffee-versus-soft-drink consumption may stray significantly from the norms of an age or ethnic cohort. Customers may respond differently to marketing offers that they receive at different times. People can also share values, but not necessarily behaviors, with other members of an identity group.

Transcultural marketing research should help identify cultural reference points that an organization can reinforce to communicate shared interests. Why do bilingual U.S. Latinos feel more positive about firms that advertise in Spanish? More influential than language skills was the symbolic value of recognizing the contributions of Hispanics to multicultural America.[51] Such symbolism resonates within high-context cultures, where how something is said is as meaningful as what is said.[52] Cuban Americans see Spanish-language usage as having political significance, while it can have class connotations among Mexican Americans. Without fluency in such variations of meaning among different Hispanic groups, Spanish-language ads may reach bilinguals, but they could be communicating different cultural meanings.

Using a broader array of research tools can uncover the relationships between buyers' social identities and their media and marketplace choices. Two middle-class, teenage African Americans may vary greatly in how strongly either one identifies with teen and African-American subcultures. That difference may be critical when each one reaches for snack foods, due to the interactive relationship of brand choice and user imagery, consumer identities, group associations, and cultural meanings.[53]

Cultural research emphasizes qualitative data gathering and interpretation. Qualitative data gathered from focus group discussions, ethnographic observations, ritual studies, semiotic analyses of word and image meanings, in-depth interviews, and cultural partnering can be paired with quantitative product-usage information to find out which product needs and buyer perceptions match an organization's ability to offer those benefits. Social media networks provide direct access to large and small subculture communities.[54]

A market-focused organization offers the best structure for transcultural marketing. Rarely do marketing managers have authority over decisions regarding corporate philanthropy, corporate architecture, human resources, or even public relations. The typical brand- or service-focused company does not allow authority over the types of decisions that express a company's cultural identities and affiliations.[55] A transcultural marketing manager must bring *cohesion* to the multiple ways in which an organization communicates its cultural value proposition. Sears's director of multicultural marketing says, "You need to have the people who have the expertise, the education, the sensitivity, and the understanding of the marketplace involved in the process from start to finish."[56]

Market managers can learn through secondary research and training how different subculture groups respond to different aspects of the "marketing mix." For example, U.S. Latinos have been cited for their strength of brand commitment and Asian Americans for their aversion to trying new products.[57] Some people are as likely to patronize a firm that hires a diverse workforce, contributes to relevant causes, or advertises in their native language as they are a company that offers the lowest prices.[58] Because cultural meanings are constantly in flux and American individualism encourages us to deviate from norms, the "average" is not a strong predictor of individual behavior.

Market specialists focus on the ways in which their brand and company policies express cultural meanings. This provides the insights required to design and implement cultural aspects of marketing programs.[59] Having more diversity in an organization's extended community of employees, buyers, and suppliers is another source of cultural learning. At the same time, ethnicity, or any other characteristic of decision makers, is not a substitute for expertise in bridging cultural differences. A better strategy than hiring people based on ethnic origins is to seek out people with experience or training in navigating between cultures or subcultures.

The account planner's role in integrated marketing communications agencies is similar to that of market specialists. The account planner's job is to represent the target audience and its concerns during the process of deciding the "what-when-where-how-who-to whom-with what effect" of communication programs.[60] Account planners bring consumer insight into play at each step of program design. Market specialists focus on each interface of that company with potential customers or community groups.

External Communication: Consumer and Public Dialogs

The firms that understand, listen to, and speak directly to consumers rise above the cacophony of commercial chatter in our daily lives. To develop economic and cultural relationships with buyers requires communication programs that meet buyers' desires and needs for information. Messages and media choices break through to their targets when they are culturally relevant and share subculture communication styles and values.

Everything a company does that affects the image a person might have of it or its products, services, activities, facilities, or personnel is a chance to influence that person and his/her chosen communities. Any means of communicating with potential buyers should address all these occasions and locations.[61] Many companies apply the concept of "brand contact points" when designing integrated communications programs, but this focus is too narrow.[62] A company's employees and managers, members of its board of directors, the media that it currently uses, past advertising, office locations, and social networking media may affect how a person views this company. The idea of "organization contact points" is more appropriate as a foundation for transcultural communication strategy.

One excellent example of how an organization's "contact points" can affect perceptions of cultural compatibility is the case of British Petroleum. British Petroleum changed its name to BP in order to emphasize alternative sources of energy in which British Petroleum was investing. A significant communication and branding effort was made to reposition BP as "more than an oil company." Then its oil rig the Deepwater Horizon suffered an explosion in the Gulf of Mexico in April 2010, and BP became an "oil company" again in the eyes of the public, and not an honorable oil company at that. While BP dallied in cleaning up the Gulf coast, it was spending millions of dollars on public relations touting its efforts to contain the spill. The public was angry, and the government threatened criminal prosecution. Much of the anger was linked to BP's choice to spend money for advertising while not fully compensating the people most affected by the spill. Although the ads said BP was "taking responsibility" for the spill, its actions said this was just another case of "spin." BP cannot act one way in one community and another way in others without injuring public trust and communicating a confused value system.

A contrast with BP's inconsistency across communities is Coors and the steps that this company has taken to change its values and group affiliations. Before the 1980s, Coors had earned a reputation as discriminatory employer. U.S. Latino and African-American workers sued Coors multiple times, and to no one's surprise its beer was not very popular among Hispanic and black consumers. When Coors announced that the 1980s would be the "Decade of Hispanics," Hispanics were not the only skeptics.[63] Coors changed its personnel policies. The company has now spent over thirty years advertising in Spanish and English, using cues from the cultural context of Hispanic beer drinkers and highlighting and financially supporting leaders in Latino communities. Today, Coors's brands are among the preferred beers of U.S. Latinos.[64] There are no corporate secrets today from Internet surfers in constant search of new and relevant content.[65]

Social media serve important cultural roles in their users' lives. Facebook meets the need for "community" among its one-billion-plus members.[66] The kinds of information Facebook has about its members is the kind of data essential to keeping up with constantly changing tastes.[67] In addition to social media, information collectors are a more recent source of information for and about customers.[68] CompareNet is one such service, which allows users to make direct comparisons on over 20,000 products.[69] Someone looking for companies that are supportive of relevant causes/issues will find many websites that satisfy that need. One example is www.gayfriendlymarketing. com, for targeting LGBT persons; another is the Virtual Asian American Business Community at www.national-caaba.org. Customized content to meet consumer information needs in customized media is the new "gold standard" for being relevant online.[70]

The constant shifting of consumer identities sends mixed messages about values, priorities for cultural compatibility, and media (or gatekeepers) for disseminating information. A dialog with current and past customers is the best way to note changes in target customers' perceptions, behaviors, and values. Customers are not the only stakeholders whose opinions matter; all influences on organization contact points are important to monitor. As marketing authors who emphasize relationship building have pointed out:

> Individual customers teach the company more and more about their preferences and needs, giving the company an immense competitive advantage. The more customers teach the company, the better it becomes at providing exactly what they want—exactly how they want it—and the more difficult it will be for a competitor to entice them away.[71]

Most firms control outsider access to information about costs, safety tests, and other proprietary information. In the new media environment, buyers acquire whatever information they find relevant and use it as leverage with sellers. In automobile purchasing, consumers use web sources about dealers' costs to negotiate how much they are willing to pay. Few Ford dealers would be prepared in the showroom to answer questions about Ford's ethnic hiring policies. They probably will not be asked a direct question about this, because future car buyers will decide whether Ford offers cultural compatibility long before they choose which showrooms to visit. Marketers must anticipate and address buyer interests in various types of cultural and economic information.

Customers can be quite unforgiving of token efforts to win their dollar votes.[72] The best competitive advantage in multicultural settings is acquiring and applying insight to a target group's values, beliefs, attitudes, and behaviors. Hiring employees and partner organizations with that expertise and collecting primary and secondary research are the foundation of transcultural marketing planning. A strategy of cultural compatibility requires constant adjustments to a broader mix of decisions. Just as the experience curve provides economies of scale to early manufacturers, experience in multicultural markets generates information and experience portfolios that are valuable sources of distinctive competence.

Consumer social identity has a strong influence on some purchases but not on others. How simple it would be if there were a list of products "not affected by" and another one of products "with" strong cultural associations. Cultural meaning is not limited to the inherent qualities of products because meaning moves from the product to the consumer's cultural frame of reference.[73] As an example of the range of possibilities, Kwanzaa dolls express African-American identity, while yoyos seem to reflect no group-specific identity. The Kwanzaa doll may have to find some appeal other than self-identity to attract buyers other than African Americans. One possibility is that the values represented by Kwanzaa customs (e.g., self-determination or loyalty) are compatible with those of other subculture groups. The yoyo brand could use tactical moves, such as advertising in ethnic-directed media, to build in cultural associations. In the case of marketing the Kwanzaa doll to non–African Americans, the cultural values of Kwanzaa are the message, while the yoyo can use a standard message delivered via ethnic-oriented media in order to target a specific ethnic group.

Collecting and interpreting information about the tug of social identities on buyer behavior are valuable competitive tools. Behavioral research among consumer subcultures can identify major differences in group norms (e.g., data showing discount store patronage by different ethnic groups). Nevertheless, product usage data contain no information about what products or stores *signify* to their buyers.

Marketers cannot rely on media to supply the kinds of information needed to plan marketing programs in multicultural settings. The media's demographic and lifestyle audience data provide little insight into situation-specific influences over buyers or the roles that a product and media play in expressing identity. Nevertheless, increasing competition in media and selectivity by media users are already forcing smaller and smaller distinctions to be made across audiences. As a result, the media, too, will be forced to learn more about their viewers in order to sell space and time.[74] In the meantime, a better approach than measuring reach in terms of audience and target demographics is to monitor perceptions of organization contact points and determine how people think about and use them. Lifestyle information can pinpoint heroes and ideals of a group, but only insight leads to effective decisions about how to use these symbols in designing a cultural values proposition.[75]

Many methods are available for capturing and analyzing cultural meanings and consumer values. Geert Hofstede categorized the cultural values of most countries of the world into five scales, with individualism/collectivism, risk taking/rule abiding, low-/high-power distance, feminine/masculine, long-/short-term orientations as end points (www.geert-hofstede.com). These values can be compared to those of the U.S. mainstream to highlight likely value differences for members of a subculture.

Cultural sayings such as "A rolling stone gathers no moss" or "The nail that sticks up gets hammered down" also provide insight into a subculture's cultural values. Framing consumer activities with products and shopping as "rituals" is another avenue to deciphering the cultural meanings of those activities. Providing consumers with opportunities for role playing can also highlight the cultural significance of different product or brand constellations. Last, standard qualitative techniques such as consumer observations, product deprivations, in-house audits, and pantry tours, as well as laddering, belong in the toolkit of transcultural marketers.

Diversity within groups presents the greatest reason for following up secondary research with detailed qualitative and quantitative analysis. The symbolic meanings of brands vary with the source of a buyer's cultural reference points. Whether a company's best strategy is to strongly identify its brand with one subculture, multiple groups, or a broader swath of buyers, depends on the extent of within-group variability in meaning.[76] The dilemma of companies like Anthropologie or The Gap is how to decipher cultural influences and desired affiliations for urban teens, who are the opinion leaders for casual fashions. The intersection of urban, ethnic, and age sources of identity for this target market makes it essential to understand what a particular brand signifies about those identities and their ideals.

Consumer preferences regarding timing and format of marketing communications create situations full of cultural significance. What is the relative effectiveness of a storyline about a brand during an episode of *The Office,* a product placement of that brand during the program, or a commercial during a program break? Does the effectiveness vary across baby boomers or Asian Americans? The question is not only which occasions and formats are most effective but also how they vary across and within groups with which your target customers identify.

Collecting intensive market information is hampered by the homogeneity of marketing decision makers. The average copywriter is about 30 years old, and most marketing managers come from middle-class, white-collar, college-educated backgrounds. Ethnographic research relies more heavily on the interpretive skills of the researcher than quantitative analysis. The participation of ethnic minorities in marketing positions remains low, and the costs of gaining experience in cultural analysis are high—presenting yet another reason for more diversity in an organization's human resources.

Given the complexities of gaining insight into people in different ethnic, age, or lifestyle subcultures, marketers must develop substitutes for personal knowledge of those subcultures. The profiles in Chapters 4–8 present information about the distinctive demographic, value, and behavioral characteristics of several important American subcultures. This information does not pretend to predict any group's potential for a company or its products and services, but it can guide businesses to market opportunities that justify more detailed market planning.

Putting Transcultural Marketing into Action

The Transcultural Marketing Mix: The 4 Ps Plus . . .

The traditional marketing mix places the economic needs of buyers at the core of an organization's market strategy. In a multicultural market, an organization's economic "value proposition" must be supplemented with strategies that communicate a "cultural values proposition"—its corporate values and social affiliations. The 4 Ps are the tools with which organizations build a "value proposition." A "cultural values proposition" presents a set of corporate values and affiliations that express the organization's corporate culture.

The ways in which an organization expresses its values and affiliations include such decision areas as philanthropy and financial strategies, personnel and human resource policies, corporate aesthetics, and the economic and environmental "footprints" of the firm. In short, a transcultural marketing program consists of the 4 Ps that build in economically attractive value propositions and the other aspects of the organization that suggest its "cultural values proposition." The next paragraphs illustrate how these traditionally nonmarketing functions can enhance or damage the appeal of a firm's transcultural marketing program.

Economic and Environmental Footprints

Buying local is a way to reduce fuel and transit costs, and it has the side benefit of spreading the wealth to local businesses. Reducing energy costs and the overall "carbon footprint" of companies has become a competitive advantage as well as a values statement.[77] Unilever says, "Now there's a more sophisticated understanding that environmental and social practices can yield strategic advantages in an interconnected world of shifting customer loyalties and regulatory regimes."[78] Company "sustainability" has become defined as a firm's ability to be seen as "doing well by doing good;" these efforts must be visible to and benefit that firm's targeted customers.

Customers and interested stakeholders use boycotts to prompt companies to change. Today's global nonprofit organizations, such as the Rainforest Action Network, Greenpeace, PETA, or Campaign Against the Fur Trade, publicize their boycotts in venues like Facebook and Twitter, thus informing people how to take action with respect to issues that they care about. In the early 2000s, the Rainforest Action Network organized a boycott of Mitsubishi to persuade the firm to change its wood and paper purchasing policies; it also drove the company to withdraw from an environmentally questionable investment in Mexico. Staples, Royal Caribbean Cruises, Zara department stores, and Kimberly-Clark are other companies hit by boycotts that convinced them to change procurement policies.[79]

Size alone, especially a dominating presence in the U.S. economy, can influence how different cultural groups feel about a firm and its products. As a "touch point," size can have both positive and negative consequences. Walmart's everyday-low-price policy hurts small-town businesses even as its citizens switch to Walmart for lower prices. The Walmart policy of placing freestanding stores outside established business districts has redirected the economic growth of small towns across the country. Large companies like Walmart generate attention from media and politicians, who, in turn, influence where people shop and what brands they buy. Even President Barack Obama admonished BP over its oil spill in the Gulf of Mexico. Microsoft receives media attention when it introduces new versions of commonly used software like Microsoft Office or its operating system Windows long before these products are available for purchase. Early published reviews of the operating system Vista were so negative that many people and companies decided to avoid it and stick with Windows XP, its predecessor. In 2011 Bank of America proposed charging its customers a fee for using debit cards, but had to retract the policy after negative publicity generated a higher than usual number of account closures.[80]

The economic footprint of most large companies is multilayered, with potential impacts on local, regional, national, and global competitors and suppliers. As a result, companies are likely to have a different reputation with different publics. For example, Walmart may dominate a small-town economy, but it competes against other giant retailers in the global arena. Consumers change their purchasing choices when a company's economic or environmental activities are meaningful in their values and social identities. After the BP oil spill in 2010, only 28 percent of consumers said they would stop purchasing gasoline from BP. The important question for BP was to find out who comprised those customers and where this issue fits into their values and affiliations. Discovering what different publics think about a company and which policies are "touch points" for them brings these activities into the toolkit for building a cultural values proposition.

Public Relations and Media Presence

Creating word of mouth is the most important way to build a community presence. Sometimes, simply a presence in ethnic media can "create buzz" or position a brand as an "insider" within a subculture community. Ultimately, though, person-to-person communications—verbal, visual, or digital—are where buzz begins and stimulates authentic viral marketing.[81]

Companies courting people who identify as members of U.S. minorities should know that these people are persuaded more when they perceive the source of a message to be an organization with which they identify. Pepsi has leveraged its historical place in African-American communities more recently by supporting Black History Month. One year it offered scholarships to winners of a "Write Your Own History" contest as well as Dell computers, software, and 12-packs of Pepsi. The next year it offered Apple computers as prizes.[82] What Pepsi shows by these activities is that it shares the same ambitions that its customers have for their children and that it understands the importance of education and access to technology in the African-American community.

Marketing communications reach both target and nontarget audiences and the cultural context for the two groups may be quite distinctive.[83] Communication audits of cultural meaning can be designed to capture these variations in meaning across time, cultural groups, and even individuals. A cultural analysis involves the deconstruction of the parts of corporate communications that communicate who the source is (any endorser, celebrity, company, institution, or alliances referred to) to determine what meanings these might have for a new target audience. An audit then addresses the nonsource parts of the message (including all cultural content in the form of words, images, music, and language style). The result is a measure of the values and affiliations communicated by marketing communications as organization contact points.[84]

Corporate Aesthetics

People develop preferences for color, fashion, architectural and artistic styles, music, and humor in the process of socialization or acculturation. Individuals develop unique constellations of preferences. Everything about a company or brand's logo, color and style of employee uniforms, background music that plays while a customer is waiting on hold in a phone call, building design, website graphics, and so on communicates information about that company's cultural preferences. Therefore, these and other organizational contact points should be audited for cultural compatibility with each of a firm's chosen markets.

Different colors, styles, and even numbers can have different meanings in American subcultures.[85] Customers' aesthetic judgments of the same products change depending on the person's cultural context.[86] Starbucks changed its logo in 2010 by removing the words "Starbucks coffee" and rounding the well-known logo. Although many Americans reacted negatively to the change, rounded designs are preferred in Eastern cultures, where Starbucks is growing the most rapidly.[87]

It is not just the logos or colors that a brand uses that communicate cultural significance. Food odors, taste, and scents in general are culturally defined as pleasant or unpleasant. Touch points for consumers include smell, sight, sound, taste, and touch—any one of which can generate a culturally nuanced reaction. Some customers spend more time and buy more in stores that they believe "smell good" and in stores near "good smells." However, strong smells can easily deter other customers.[88] Changes in logo designs seem to upset committed customers more than other people.[89] Strong colors are preferred by teens but may interfere with readability for older consumers.[90]

Retailers have long understood the need to fit into a neighborhood and the role of retail space as customer entertainment. The store can stand out as an outsider (a big store in a small store strip mall) or fit in (same language spoken by employees and neighbors) using many tactics to make such adjustments. Even Walmart adapts to its locality with weekend "farmer's" markets for primarily Hispanic neighborhoods and wider aisles and quieter loudspeakers for their upscale suburban stores.[91] Macy's has centralized buying but has authorized local store managers to request special items for its local inventory. By doing this, it has increased profits and same-store sales while developing customer loyalty and encouraging repeat visits.[92]

Online companies can "fit in" with their online communities too. Pinterest invites users to submit images of companies where its members work in order to generate buzz about the company.[93] Having an appropriate "tone of voice" on a website communicates that firm's personality and differentiates it from competitors.[94]

Financial and Philanthropic Choices

Important clues to a company's cultural identity are the choice of politicians and social causes supported and where and how the firm acquires financing. These issues may be very important to groups like gays and lesbians, who specifically seek out companies that donate to AIDS causes. Corporate philanthropy may be of little importance to some people and groups, but, for others, support of a particular cause may be the rationale for a boycott. Even American religious groups have encouraged followers to boycott companies like P&G, which was mistakenly reputed to use devil symbols in its logo.

Pharmaceutical companies claim that their policy of delaying the licensing of patent drugs as generics allows them to invest in newer, unproven drugs. Their current customers pay higher prices to subsidize their growth. This policy makes the industry appear to jeopardize its role as caretaker of its customers.[95] Such trade-offs between competing corporate objectives send messages to subculture communities about corporate identity.

Strategic alliances in a company's supply chain can change customers into competitors. For example, responding to the popularity of tablets by other companies, such as Apple, Microsoft entered the market with its own tablet, the Surface, in 2012. Its longtime hardware partners, such as Acer, were so threatened by the software giant's move into their markets that they threatened to abandon "the Windows platform" and their partnerships with Microsoft.[96] Wal-mart developed a prepaid card for its customers in conjunction with American Express. Walmart's debit card addressed customer complaints about high bank fees and reinforced the retailer's "everyday low prices" value proposition.[97]

Making alliances with nongovernmental organizations can bring positive media attention, but doing so can also place a company in a position of "taking sides" when there is a controversial issue. "Returning to the core values of who they are and what they stand for" is the only successful option in the long term.[98] While customers are more likely to react when a firm acts irresponsibly, their "sense of well-being" is enhanced even when they are walking through a store that supports a cause they believe in.[99]

Companies are able to support politicians and legislation that is in their interest via lobbying and financing of campaigns. What some politicians have found is that the companies have valuable customer databases. By tracking the websites visited by customers, politicians can anticipate how that person will vote or, at least, reach him/her as a swing voter. "A Wal-Mart Store's shopper is likely to be socially conservative, pro-gun, and exurban or rural, while a Bloomingdale's or Neiman Marcus customer is probably upscale, urban, and socially liberal. A Target regular is an independent-minded, style-conscious, cost-conscious suburbanite."[100] This common interest can, of course, be "held against" the company or politicians when either the company or the politician is in disfavor.

How an organization finances its operations is a subject not normally considered part of "marketing" strategy and tactics. In today's information-rich context, with an overload of consumer choices, even sources of financing can position a company as an insider or outsider in a subculture community. This has always been the case in small towns, where it is important for customers to "buy local" and for businesses to "keep the money in our community." Now that such "communities" exist online, it is incumbent on companies to consider the impact of their financial choices on the effectiveness of their marketing plans.

Personnel and Human Resource Policies

For service firms, employees are tangible symbols of the service provided, and therefore, they are the "face" of the company. The personnel that a company hires shows potential customers who the company "is" as well as what some of its values are. Showing that there is a match between workforce and consumers is a strong message about shared membership in subculture communities. Showing that the employees in marketing communications are diverse resonates with diverse audiences.

An example of this interplay between a company's employees and how customers view that firm is Microsoft and its relationship with members of the LGBT community. Microsoft was one of the earliest U.S. companies to offer domestic benefits to gay employees. However, when a law was proposed to force companies in Washington state to pay benefits for all domestic partnerships, Microsoft refused to support it. Its workers reacted by overwhelmingly signing petitions in support of the legislation, and subsequently Microsoft reversed its opposition to the law.

Many subculture communities rate companies as whether they are good places to work and publicize this information on their websites. The LGBT Human Rights Campaign[101] is an example, as is Diversity, Inc.[102] for African Americans, *HispanicBusiness*[103] for U.S. Latinos, the national Association of Asian American Professionals for Asian Americans,[104] Aging Hipsters for baby boomers,[105] among others. We do not know much about how this information is used by people in general, but 72 percent of LGBT consumers surveyed say it is important for companies that advertise to the LGBT community to "demonstrate effective corporate citizenship by supporting the community's causes."[106]

Another area of controversy is top management. The CEO, his/her salary or opinions, the choices of a firm's board of directors, and their compensation are topics of discussion in the business press and online. In 2012 the media publicized the beliefs against gay marriage by Chick-fil-A's CEO. Boycotts that followed hurt company sales in several cities and helped them in the Midwestern states. The mayors of Chicago and Boston claimed that the firm was not welcome in their cities.[107] Negative publicity like this can influence consumers' views that a company does or does not share their interests.

One of the most successful NGOs, Race for the Cure, has raised millions of dollars for breast cancer research through a race/walk event organized locally all over the country. In 2012 the CEO of that organization decided to stop funding Planned Parenthood because it offers information on abortion to clients. Many people were "troubled by the way this organization handled" the decision, and event participation declined by 30 percent.[108]

Strategic Options for Transcultural Marketing

Recognition of the need to adapt to a changed environment is the first step in implementing a transcultural marketing program. Policies to build in and nurture "the border mentality" as well as transmigration expertise are accommodations to a multicultural setting. Firms can use this expertise to build a strategy of alliances with particular subcultures that match economic opportunities in the market and the cultural heritage of the organization. Aligning a firm with different community groups when cultural meaning is in flux is risky, and it takes both economic and cultural programs to build partnerships with customers.

No single strategic alternative in a multicultural market is inherently superior. The best choice depends on factors such as what competitors are doing, what the firm's unique resource mix is, what the size and diversity of needs in a market are, and the feasible alternatives.

The first, obvious option is to make no adaptation in marketing programs to attract buyers among members of subculture groups. This is the way that mainstream marketing works in most American consumer goods' markets. This strategy assumes that most buyers in a target market, 25 to 34 year olds, for example, are likely to respond as a homogeneous, mass market.

When customers do not see a brand as valuable in expressing how they see themselves, the "one-for-all" strategy is appropriate. For products such as home appliances, which are not visible to other people when bought or used, there may be little opportunity to use the transcultural marketing techniques discussed in the prior sections of this chapter. It is still important to research which cultural meanings might be associated with *the company* that makes those appliances. There may also be *products* for which cultural meanings do not vary much across subculture communities (e.g., cleaning products, canned and frozen foods, or automotive services), even though there are significant differences in the meanings associated with product *usage* ("do it yourself" versus "buy it"). Banking and financial services are other areas where *use* or *nonuse* ("unbanked" people) has meaning while the choice of supplier may not. In 2008, 23 percent of U.S. Latinos were unbanked versus 10 percent of Americans in general. The difference is due to cultural beliefs about the safety of banks as well as to lack of familiarity with the array of services available.[109] In many situations, it simply may not be profitable to adapt products or services and their marketing programs.

The "one-for-all" strategy in a multicultural environment should trumpet inclusiveness at every organization contact point. This invitation to all potential buyers can be delivered via traditional marketing strategy or through the other functional areas that communicate a cultural values proposition or both. Many social issues have broad appeal (e.g., education or environment), as does inclusive hiring. It is also possible for companies to stake their identity on a geographic, rather than demographic, basis, targeting "Texans," for example, rather than ethnic or age-defined markets. Ford, Dodge, Toyota, and General Motors market "Texas" edition trucks, appealing to just about all age and ethnic communities that are proud to be Texan.[110] All-inclusive marketing communications messages often contain a racially mixed group of actors and position their brands for everyone, no matter what color or age.

Many companies are using these techniques to attract buyers from multiple subculture groups. Schick, Pepsi, Fruit of the Loom, Tonka, Hasbro, FedEx, Xerox, and USAIR include actors of multiple ethnic origins in their ads in general market media.[111] Verizon shows its diverse workforce in print media that reach large audiences (e.g., *People*). This "all-inclusive" strategy is particularly effective in media with broad audiences, such as network and cable.

Given the absence of minority representation in both media programming and advertising in the past, the inclusiveness strategy captures the attention of ethnic minority consumers, who react positively to seeing people who share their ethnic origins.[112] They are more likely to see those firms as "good companies to work for," though there is little evidence yet that they are more likely to buy their products.[113]

The second strategy in multicultural markets positions an organization as an "insider" in its targeted subculture community. It involves making tactical changes in the marketing mix: targeted price discounts and promotions; different types of communications messages, media, and languages used; different methods for distribution, retail, and online services; and different models or settings for communications, for example.[114] One of its successful practitioners, Procter and Gamble, calls this "micro-marketing."[115] Miller Brewing Company tried unique ads for black, Hispanic, and Asian consumers in the 1990s, but later decided to return to a single approach to target 21 to 28 year olds. It helps that it is reaching an age cohort that already shares many values and attitudes about beer drinking.[116] In contrast, supported by a sophisticated computer tracking system, Target redesigns its store merchandise mixes to satisfy consumer preferences in different ethnic, racial, and lifestyle neighborhoods.[117] The "insider" strategy uses cultural cues and models that match the target market to capture the attention of a subculture target.

Cosmetics usage varies to a great extent across ethnic and age groups as a function of differing needs and cultural attitudes about makeup. Companies in the broader personal care product and services industry can gain a competitive advantage by adjusting product and communication programs. This is evident in the efforts of Mary Kay and Avon to appeal to African-American, U.S. Latino, and Asian-American consumers. Both companies' reliance on personal selling has led them to diversify their sales staffs also.

It is essential that the insider strategy is supported by an organization's alliances and values. The quickest way to being branded by members of a subculture community as "inauthentic" is to ignore the issues that are important to them. Even competitors with inferior value propositions can lure consumers when their favorite causes or community organizations will benefit.

Even when companies do not develop unique marketing strategies for consumers who identify with specific subculture communities, it may be necessary to adjust communication and distribution aspects of a mainstream strategy. A minority of Asian Americans and U.S. Latinos can be reached only through ethnic media. Some retailers find their natural trade area composed of people from only one subculture, while other members of the same retail franchise may have a totally different neighborhood. In all these cases, the tactics used for the "insider" strategy have to differ. As noted earlier in this chapter, Budweiser and McDonald's try to match unique websites, unique slogans, even support for different causes, with their various ethnic and age target markets.

Market specialists can recommend compatible policies to managers outside the traditional marketing domain. For this purpose, companies can perform a cultural compatibility audit for each contact point relevant to its target customers.

The third option for multicultural markets is a redesign of overall marketing strategy, incorporating the traditional marketing mix and tools of transcultural marketing. The earliest practitioners of ethnic marketing were ethnic advertising and communications agencies. They opened the door to transcultural marketing, by counseling mainstream clients to build a presence in target communities.[118] They suggested that clients support important community issues, use specialized media and languages to reach ethnic audiences, and implement diversity in hiring.[119] In those early years, ethnic agencies were hired for their cultural expertise but excluded from the design of mainstream strategies for U.S. consumers. Thus, there was no mechanism for a planning strategy using a matrix to decide strategies and tactics for different market segments in the mainstream. The legacy of "ethnic marketing" is the "insider" strategy—the traditional marketing mix and points of cultural compatibility.

Transcultural marketing takes a more holistic approach by emphasizing organization contact points. This is a two-step process—identifying contact points and cultural meanings associated with them, then designing targeted programs to communicate corporate values and affiliations. There is no consensus about how best to organize this matrix planning process. Some companies acquire cultural expertise in-house while others depend on their market-specialist partners. Some companies put their subculture market budgets within ongoing marketing plans, while others set up special divisions. Anheuser-Busch organizes its ethnic marketing efforts under a vice president for emerging markets, which includes foreign markets, while Procter & Gamble and Levi's put their targeted programs under a vice president for ethnic markets.

Transcultural marketing is about choosing where a company's future lies in terms of its customer base. Since customer relationships are based on both economic and cultural shared interests, the costs of building those relationships pay off in more sustainable marketing overall. Since the focus of transcultural marketing activities is building relationships, over time the return on marketing efforts should increase and average marketing costs per transaction should decline. In the case of a mass retailer like Walmart, transcultural marketing may also consist of many inconsistencies in the merchandise mix, attention to subculture differences among customers, and differing roles as a cultural agent for its broad base of consumers.[120]

Ethical Challenges in Transcultural Marketing

Today, the marketplace is anywhere, anytime, at the touch of a finger. Purchasing decisions are not so different from voting, contributing to causes, or any choices about how to spend limited time, money, or emotion. Naturally we prefer choices that "mean something" and that support the groups and values in which we believe. The boundaries between the cultural, economic, political, and social parts of our lives are as porous as our identities. Transcultural marketing asserts a role for businesses (and other organizations) in the cultural lives of consumers. Is this a healthy allocation of responsibilities in our society? What role should these organizations play in changing overall societal values? Should consumers' marketing partners sell information about those consumers to their strategic partners?[121] Is it acceptable for buzz marketing to use unknown people who are being paid to pull in ethnic or age markets without revealing that they are being paid?[122] These are some of the "gray" areas of transcultural marketing.

At the broadest level of American life, transcultural marketing intends to distinguish members of different subcultures, thus bringing attention to our differences rather than our similarities.[123] The potential for mistaking group membership for individual preferences is great. The impact on our sense of shared community, of signaling social division by images, media, and content chosen to attract ever-smaller groups of consumers, is open to speculation. In *Breaking up America*, Joseph Turow feared that Americans will lose sight of our diversity and citizens will "join their own image tribes apart from other image tribes."[124] One irony of the multicultural marketers' recognition of increased American diversity could be the loss of our national sense of community.

One major difficulty in implementing transcultural marketing programs is our dependence on and preference for quantitative measures of consumer behavior or characteristics. From a client's point of view, for example, the U.S. census is a more objective count of U.S. Latinos in Los Angeles than estimates of English- or Spanish-dominant Hispanics in Los Angeles by a Hispanic market specialist. Even though a client may recognize the importance of ethnic identity or language use in predicting behavior, third-party product-usage data and size of an age or ethnic group have more sway over resource commitments. It is easier and cheaper to measure how people behave than what they think. Not understanding the complex relationship of consumer identity to what people want and do in the marketplace ignores the intervening importance of cultural values and symbolic affiliations. This omission ignores opportunities to participate at a deeper and more significant level in consumers' lives and to be less vulnerable to competitors.

Many proponents of multicultural marketing are among the ethnic market specialists in advertising agencies, research firms, and niche brands. One of their frequent complaints is how little the decision makers who make budget recommendations in large firms know about ongoing changes in our society or the growth of diverse communities in the United States. Many people who work in marketing jobs are young, with limited business and life experiences.[125] Our lingering stereotypes continue to substitute for deeper understanding of ethnic consumers. African-American market specialists have to convince decision makers to buy their expertise by overcoming a perception that African Americans are reached effectively by more generic advertising on network TV.[126] Training and awareness programs that educate corporate managers can reduce these misperceptions.

One concern has to do with the qualifications of people in multicultural marketing. Do experts in marketing to consumers in a subculture group have to be members of the subculture? Some people and companies expect all members of a racial or ethnic subculture to be "experts" about what works and does not work in marketing to members of their subculture.[127] In contrast, some marketers with experience in ethnic marketing say it counts against them with clients, who discount their rational arguments for more spending: "You're just saying it of course because you're Asian . . . and so you're going to push that."[128] At the other end of the spectrum are people who believe that the only credible expertise is educational background and business experience. Without training in cultural analysis and appreciation of the cultural roles that brands play, subculture members are often as poorly equipped as anyone else to decipher and translate cultural meaning. While they may understand the unique worldviews and subtleties of their subculture, they must be able to translate it for marketing planners.

Participation in subculture communities must be visible to its members. However, extracting an economic quid pro quo can discredit the authenticity of community membership. Uptown cigarettes designed for African-American smokers, Dakota smokes for blue-collar women, and the *Reality Bites* movie about Generation X are examples of products that suffered a public backlash from their "target market."[129] The firms marketing these products were seen as exploiting the targeted group. This is the danger of a narrow focus in ethnic marketing. Marketers who seek only dollar votes ignore the real benefits gained from cultural compatibility.[130]

One good example of the challenge posed by transcultural marketing is Pepsi's attempt to market healthier snack foods in inner-city areas, where the majority of its customers are members of minorities. In view of the high rates of obesity among African Americans and U.S. Latinos, Pepsi's efforts to encourage them to adopt healthier eating and lifestyles would seem to be at odds with the majority of its merchandise mix: soda and snack foods. Pepsi must first convince its sales force, whose income depends on sales, to switch store buyers from salty snacks and colas to these healthier products. Pepsi was the first fast food company to take out trans fats from its snacks, and in 2004 it began labeling its lower calorie, fat, salt, or sugar items with a green circle. So ultimately Pepsi's core values are consistent with its search for how to market healthier snack foods.[131]

Summary

Being able to understand cultural differences and adjust to them are essential skills for both consumers and marketers in a multicultural society. Having a "border mentality" alerts us to cultural differences in meaning without necessarily judging one interpretation as the better one. Transmigration describes the process that an organization can use to build in cultural compatibility with buyers in different subculture groups. It requires a broader palette of marketing tools and conscious planning of communicative points of contact between any organization and its brands and stakeholders.

To measure success in a multicultural marketplace, organizations must add a measure of "shared interests" to their estimates of long-term profitability. Market planners can start by determining the best strategy and tactics for one subculture niche and then expand by accumulating market niches among consumers from different subcultures. Meeting the information needs of buyers in a multicultural setting means reformulating how a firm "speaks" from a cultural point of view.

These shifts in emphasis highlight the need for a broader responsibility for marketing decision makers. Market expertise must be acquired so that there is knowledge of different subcultures and their value systems as well as variability within the subcultures. Authority for marketing must be broad enough to cover areas not traditionally part of the market mix. Planning must originate with market specialists. Communication and information systems must be designed to provide constant adjustments to changing cultural meanings and consumer perceptions of the firm and its brands.

There is no inherently superior strategy for building relationships with people who identify with American subcultures. Some companies will decide that their general market strategies are the most cost-efficient way to reach these consumers, while other firms may decide to concentrate their resources for a strategy of cultural compatibility with one subculture. Inclusive and insider market strategies are often a company's first steps toward the more holistic matrix planning, market specialists, and incorporation of nonmarketing functional areas that constitute transcultural marketing. In sum, in the process of developing programs of cultural compatibility, companies become multicultural entities themselves. Implementing a program of transcultural marketing opens the door to questions about skills and experiences to seek in employees and potential negative effects on our social and cultural environments.

Notes

1. USAA, "Military Values," video, September 1, 2011, www.youtube.com/watch?v=eb3ql0sCORU/. USAA is headquartered in San Antonio, with global insurance and financial services operations; its original market was military officers and families. Today it serves current and former military families of all ranks. The quotation is from a USAA ad targeting veterans and was part of its 2012 television advertising campaign.

2. L. Peñaloza and M.C. Gilly, "Marketer Acculturation: The Changer and the Changed," *Journal of Marketing* 63, no. 3 (1999): 84–104.

3. J. Turow, *Breaking Up America: Advertisers and the New Media World* (Chicago: University of Chicago Press, 1997); J. Turow, "The Dark Side of Target Marketing," *American Demographics* (November 1997): 51–54.

4. For acculturation's effect on cultural meaning, see L. Peñaloza, "*Atravesando fronteras*/Border Crossings: A Critical Ethnographic Exploration of the Consumer Acculturation of Mexican Immigrants," *Journal of Consumer Research* 21, no. 1 (1994): 32–54; for the unique styles of communication of African Americans, see M.L. Hecht, M.J. Collier, and S.A. Ribeau, *African American Communication: Ethnic Identity and Cultural Interpretation* (Newbury Park, CA: Sage, 1993); for discussions of low- versus high-context cultures: E.T. Hall, *Beyond Culture* (Garden City, NY: Anchor, 1976); F.E. Jandt, *Intercultural Communication: An Introduction*, 3d ed. (Thousand Oaks, CA: Sage, 2000), 201–203; L.A. Samovar and R.E. Porter, *Communication Between Cultures* (Belmont, CA: Wadsworth, 1991), 232–236; W.B. Gudykunst, *Bridging Differences: Effective Intergroup Communication*, 2d ed. (Thousand Oaks, CA: Sage, 1994), 124–129; W.B. Gudykunst and S. Ting-Toomey, *Culture and Interpersonal Communication* (Thousand Oaks, CA: Sage, 1988), 43–45.

5. D. Tannen, *You Just Don't Understand: Women and Men in Conversation* (New York: Ballantine Books, 1990); S.A. Ribeau, J.R. Baldwin, and M.L. Hecht, "An African-American Communication Perspective," in *Intercultural Communication: A Reader*, 7th ed., ed. L.A. Samovar and R.E. Porter (Belmont, CA: Wadsworth, 1994), 140–147; R.E. Majors, "Discovering Gay Culture in America," in ibid., 165–172.

6. J.D. Williams and W.J. Qualls, "Middle-Class Black Consumers and Intensity of Ethnic Identification," *Psychology & Marketing* 6, no. 4 (1989): 263–286.

7. G.P. Zachary, "Mighty Is the Mongrel," *Fast Company*, July 2, 2000, 270–284.

8. C.B. Bhattacharya and S. Sen, "Consumer–Company Identification: A Framework for Understanding Consumers' Relationships with Companies," *Journal of Marketing* 67, no. 2 (2003): 76–88; Peñaloza and Gilly, "Marketer Acculturation."

9. S. Randazzo, *The Myth Makers: How Advertisers Apply the Power of Classic Myths and Symbols to Create Modern Day Legends* (Chicago: Probus, 1995).

10. A. Daview and J.A. Fitchett, "Crossing Culture: A Multi-Method Enquiry into Consumer Behavior and the Experience of Cultural Transition," *Journal of Consumer Behavior* 3, no. 4 (2004): 315–330.

11. B. Horovitz, "Latest Ad Strategy to Freshen Budweiser's Image: Free Beer," *USA Today*, September 23, 2010, www.usatoday.com/money/advertising/2010-09-22-freebud22_ST_N.htm.

12. Peñaloza and Gilly, "Marketer Acculturation."

13. Y.R. Cal, "The Market Maven: Implications for a Multicultural Environment" (Ph.D. dissertation, University of Texas at Austin, 2003), http://hdl.handle.net/2152/11919/.

14. G. Lantz and S. Loeb, "An Examination of the Community Identity and Purchase Preferences Using the Social Identity Approach," in *Advances in Consumer Research*, vol. 25, ed. J.W. Alba and J. W. Hutchinson (Provo, UT: Association for Consumer Research, 1998), 486–491; G. Albaum et al., *International Marketing and Export Management*, 2d ed. (Reading, MA: Addison-Wesley, 1994), 281–291; G. Harris, "International Advertising Standardization: What Do the Multinationals Actually Standardize?" *Journal of International Marketing* 2, no. 4 (1994): 13–30; V. Terpstra and R. Sarathy, *International Marketing*, 7th ed. (Fort Worth: Dryden Press, 1997), 195–248.

15. S. Youn and H. Kim "Antecedents of Consumer Attitudes Toward Cause-Related Marketing," *Journal of Advertising Research* 48, no. 1 (2008): 123–137; K. Heubusch, "Switching for a Cause," *American Demographics* (April 1997): 26–27.

16. C. Lawton, "TV + Social Network = ?" *Wall Street Journal*, October 27, 2008; G. Imperato, "Shopping for a Cause," *Fast Company* (December 1999): 446; J. Kaufman, "The Omnipresent Persuaders," *Wall Street Journal*, January 1, 2000, R26; A. David, "Shopping Smart," *People*, July 14, 1997, 37.

17. D. McGinn, "The New Ford," *Newsweek*, November 23, 1998, 56.

18. J.C. Collins and J.I. Porras, *Built to Last: Successful Habits of Visionary Companies* (New York: HarperBusiness, 1994).

19. A traditional definition of marketing is "the process of planning and executing the conception, pricing, promotion, and distribution of ideas, goods, and services to create exchanges that satisfy individual and organizational goals," from P.D. Bennett, *Marketing* (New York: McGraw-Hill, 1988), 10. Also, see R.J. Best, *Market-Based Management: Strategies for Growing Customer Value and Profitability* (Englewood Cliffs, NJ: Prentice Hall, 1997), 405–406.

20. J. Cayla and E.J. Arnould, "A Cultural Approach to Branding in the Global Marketplace," *Journal of International Marketing* 16, no. 4 (2008): 86–112.

21. B. Helm, "Ethnic Marketing: McDonald's Is Lovin' It," *Bloomberg BusinessWeek*, July 8, 2010.

22. B. Saporito, "Wrestling with Your Conscience," *Time*, November 15, 1999, 71–74.

23. C. Anderson, *The Long Tail* (New York: Hyperion, 2006),

24. S. Hample, "Fear of Commitment," *Marketing Tools* 2, no. 1 (1995): 6, 8–10.

25. Z. Schiller, "Stalking the New Consumer," *BusinessWeek*, August 28, 1989, 54–58, 62; N. Carr-Ruffino, *Managing Diversity: People Skills for a Multicultural Workplace* (Cincinnati: South-Western, 1996).

26. J. McManus, "Tapped In, Tapped Out," *American Demographics*, December 6, 1998.

27. Turow, *Breaking Up America*.

28. E. Schonfeld, "The Customized, Digitized, Have-It-Your-Way Economy," *Fortune*, September 28, 1998, 115–124; M. Tharp and L.M. Scott, "The Role of Marketing Processes in Creating Cultural Meaning," *Journal of Macromarketing* 10, no. 2 (1990): 47–60.

29. R. Narisetti, "Too Many Choices: P&G, Seeing Shoppers Were Being Confused, Overhauls Marketing," *Wall Street Journal*, January 15, 1997, A1, A8; C. Power, "How to Get Closer to Your Customers," *BusinessWeek/Enterprise* (1993): 42–45; M.R. Solomon, "Building Up and Breaking Down: The Impact of Cultural Sorting on Symbolic Consumption," in *Research in Consumer Behavior*, vol. 3, ed. J. Sheth and E.C. Hirschman (Greenwich, CT: JAI Press, 1988), 325–351; J. Solomon, *The Signs of Our Time* (Los Angeles: J.P. Tarcher, 1988); Randazzo, *The Myth Makers*.

30. Schonfeld, "The Customized, Digitized, Have-It-Your-Way Economy"; E.W. Brody, *Communication Tomorrow: New Audiences, New Technologies, New Media* (New York: Praeger, 1990).

31. D.E. Schultz and B.E. Barnes, *Strategic Advertising Campaigns*, 4th ed. (Lincolnwood, IL: NTC Business Books, 1995), 3–26, 61–80; R. Batra, J.G. Myers, and D.A. Aaker, *Advertising Management*, 5th ed. (Englewood Cliffs, NJ: Prentice-Hall, 1996), 219–263.

32. A.M. Brumbaugh, "Source and Nonsource Cues in Advertising and Their Effects on the Activation of Cultural and Subcultural Knowledge on the Route to

Persuasion," *Journal of Consumer Research* 29, no. 2 (2002): 258–269; L. McAllister, "Ethnic Customs Influence How Ethnic-Americans Gift," *Gifts & Decorative Accessories* (July 1993): 52–53, 77–79; T. Mccarroll, "It's a Mass Market No More," *Time,* December 2, 1993, 80–81.

33. To see the four-year campaign, see T. Nudd, "Apple's 'Get a Mac,' the Complete Campaign," *AdWeek,* April 13, 2011, www.adweek.com/adfreak/apples-get-mac-complete-campaign-130552/.

34. D.J. Moore and P.M. Homer, "Self-Brand Connections: The Role of Attitude Strength and Autobiographical Memory Primes," *Journal of Business Research* 61, no. 7 (2008): 707–714.

35. Solomon, *The Signs of Our Time*; Randazzo, *The Myth Makers,* 173; C. Moog, *"Are They Selling Her Lips?": Advertising and Identity* (New York: Morrow, 1990).

36. B.G. Englis and M.R. Solomon, "To Be *and* Not to Be: Lifestyle Imagery, Reference Groups, and *the Clustering of America,*" *Journal of Advertising* 24, no. 1 (1995): 13–28.

37. D.E. Schultz, S.I. Tannenbaum, and R.F. Lauterborn, *Integrated Marketing Communications: Pulling It Together and Making It Work* (Lincolnwood, IL: NTC Business Books, 1993).

38. Batra, Myers, and Aaker, *Advertising Management,* 71–107; R. Fizdale, "Integrated Communications: The Whole Picture," *Advertiser* (Summer 1992): 58–62; F.K. Beard, "Conflict in the Integrated Marketing Communications Task Group," in *Proceedings from the 1994 American Academy of Advertising Conference,* ed. Karen Whitehall King, (Tucson, AZ: American Academy of Advertising): 21–31.

39. A. Zolli, "Rip. Mix. Brand," *American Demographics* (November 2004): 44–45.

40. R. Berner, "Detergent Can Be So Much More," *BusinessWeek,* May 1, 2006, 66–68; D. Kiley, "Shoot the Focus Group," *BusinessWeek,* November 13, 2005, 120–121.

41. McManus, "Tapped In, Tapped Out."

42. J. Holland and J.W. Gentry, "Ethnic Consumer Reaction to Targeted Marketing: A Theory of Intercultural Accommodation," *Journal of Advertising* 28, no. 1 (1999): 65–84.

43. I.F. Wilkinson and C. Cheng, "Multicultural Marketing in Australia: Synergy in Diversity," *Journal of International Marketing* 7, no. 3 (1999): 106–118.

44. Holland and Gentry, "Ethnic Consumer Reaction to Targeted Marketing."

45. C. Miller, "Xers Know They're a Target Market, and They Hate That," *Marketing News* 27, no. 25 (1993): 2; K. Ritchie, *Marketing to Generation X* (New York: Lexington, 1995), 158–161.

46. S. Biagi and M. Kern-Foxworth, *Facing Difference: Race, Gender, and Mass Media* (Thousand Oaks, CA: Pine Forge Press, 1997), 205–220; Heubusch, "Switching for a Cause"; C. Webster, "The Effects of Hispanic Subcultural Identification on Information Search Behavior," *Journal of Advertising Research* 32, no. 5 (1992): 54–62; N. Delener and J.P. Neelankavil, "Informational Sources and Media Usage: A Comparison Between Asian and Hispanic Subcultures," *Journal of Advertising Research,* 30, no. 3 (1990): 45–52; H. Kahan and D. Malayan, "Out of the Closet," *American Demographics* (May 1995): 40–43, 46–47; B. Johnson, "Special Report: Marketing to Gays and Lesbians," *Advertising Age,* January 18, 1993, 29–37; S. El-Badry, "The Arab-American Market," *American Demographics* (January 1994): 22–28.

47. Heubusch, "Switching for a Cause"; Webster, "The Effects of Hispanic Sub-cultural Identification"; Delener and Neelankavil, "Informational Sources and Media Usage"; Kahan and Malayan, "Out of the Closet"; Johnson, "Special Report: Marketing to Gays and Lesbians"; El-Badry, "The Arab-American Market."

48. E.J. McCarthy, *Basic Marketing: A Managerial Approach* (Homewood, IL: R.D. Irwin, 1960), 37; P. Kotler, *Principles of Marketing*, 3rd ed. (Englewood Cliffs, NJ: Prentice-Hall, 1986), 263–276.

49. Kotler, *Principles of Marketing*, 65–66; E.W. Cundiff and R.R. Still, *Basic Marketing: Concepts, Environment, and Decisions* (Englewood Cliffs, NJ: Prentice-Hall, 1964), 22.

50. G. Meredith and C. Schewe, "The Power of Cohorts," *American Demographics* (December 1994): 22–31.

51. S. Koslow, P.N. Shamdasani, and E.E. Touchstone, "Exploring Language Effects in Ethnic Advertising: A Sociolinguistic Perspective," *Journal of Consumer Research* 20, no. 4 (1994): 575–585.

52. Hall, *Beyond Culture*; Jandt, *Intercultural Communication*, 201–203; Samovar and Porter, *Communication Between Cultures*, 232–236; Gudykunst, *Bridging Differences*, 124–129; Gudykunst and Ting-Toomey, *Culture and Interpersonal Communication*, 43–45.

53. J.F. Durgee, "Richer Findings from Qualitative Research," *Journal of Advertising Research* 26, no. 4 (1986): 36–44; Solomon, "Building up and Breaking Down," 337.

54. C. Jones, *Clout: the Art and Science of Influential Web Content* (Berkeley: New Riders, 2011); D. Evans, *Social Media Marketing: The Next Generation of Business Engagement* (Indianapolis: Wiley, 2010); E. Rosen, *The Anatomy of Buzz: How to Create Word of Mouth Advertising* (New York: Doubleday, 2000); R. Flinn, "The Big Business of Sifting Through Social Media Data," *BusinessWeek,* October 25, 2010, 20–22.

55. R. Gulati, "Silo Busting: How to Execute on the Promise of Customer Focus," *Harvard Business Review* (May 2007): 98–108.

56. I. Teinowitz, "Multicultural Marketing," *Advertising Age*, November 16, 1998, s6.

57. Webster, "The Effects of Hispanic Subcultural Identification"; Delener and Neelankavil, "Informational Sources and Media Usage"; B. Wiesendanger, "Asian-Americans: The Three Biggest Myths," *Sales & Marketing Management* 145, no. 11 (1993): 86; J. Saegert, R.J. Hoover, and M.T. Hilger, "Characteristics of Mexican American Consumers," *Journal of Consumer Research* 12, no. 1 (1985): 104–109.

58. L.E. Wynter, "Advocates Try to Tie Diversity to Profit," *Wall Street Journal*, February 7, 1996, B1.

59. Peñaloza and Gilly, "Marketer Acculturation."

60. L. Fortini-Campbell, *Hitting the Sweet Spot* (Chicago: Copy Workshop, 1997), 159–189.

61. J. Kaufman, "The Omnipresent Persuaders," *Wall Street Journal*, January 1, 2000, R26.

62. Schultz and Barnes, *Strategic Advertising Campaigns*, 6–8; Fizdale, "Integrated Communications."

63. W.E. Green, "Reaching Out: Firms Seek to Tighten Links with Hispanics as Buyers and Workers," *Wall Street Journal*, November 10, 1980, A1, A14; A. Brown, "Coors Cools Hispania," *Marketing & Media Decisions* (June 1990): 30.

64. Brown, "Coors Cools Hispania."

65. Randazzo, *The Myth Makers.*

66. R.D. Hof, D.S. Browder, and P. Elstrom, "Special Report: Internet Communities," *BusinessWeek*, May 4, 1997, 64–67, 70, 74, 76, 80.

67. J. Ellis, "That Sound—The Sound of Advertising Being Allowed In—Is the Sound of the Future Being Born," *Fast Company* (December 1999): 368–372; R.H. Cross, "The Five Degrees of Customer Bonding," *Direct Marketing* (October 1992): 33–35, 58f.

68. J.H. Snider, "Shopping in the Information Age," *The Futurist* 26, no. 6 (November/December 1992): 14–18.

69. David, "Shopping Smart," 37.

70. R. Narisetti, "New and Improved: Ad Experts Talk About How Their Business Will Be Transformed by Technology," *Wall Street Journal*, November 11, 1998, S1.

71. B.J. Pine, D. Peppers, and M. Rogers, "Do You Want to Keep Your Customers Forever?" *Harvard Business Review* (March/April 1995): 103.

72. D.K. Davidson, "Targeting Is Innocent Until It Exploits the Vulnerable," *Marketing News* 29, no. 19 (1995): 10.

73. G. McCracken, "Culture and Consumption: A Theoretical Account of the Structure and Movement of the Cultural Meaning of Consumer Goods," *Journal of Consumer Research* 13, no. 1 (1986): 71–83; J.B. Twitchell, *Adcult USA: The Triumph of Advertising in American Culture* (New York: Columbia University Press, 1996); Tharp and Scott, "The Role of Marketing Processes in Creating Cultural Meaning."

74. Ellis, "That Sound—The Sound of Advertising."

75. Randazzo, *The Myth Makers*, 121–158.

76. J.H. Leigh and T.G. Gabel, "Symbolic Interactionism: Its Effects on Consumer Behavior and Implications for Marketing Strategy," *Journal of Consumer Marketing* 9, no. 1 (1992): 27–38.

77. B. Walsh, "How Business Saw the Light," *Time*, January 15, 2007, 56–57.

78. P. Engardio, "Beyond the Green Corporation," *BusinessWeek*, January 28, 2007, 52.

79. Ethical Consumer, "What We Do." www.ethicalconsumer.org/home/whatwedo.aspx.

80. T.S. Bernard, "In Retreat, Bank of America Cancels Debit Card Fee," *New York Times,* November 1, 2011, www.nytimes.com/2011/11/02/business/bank-of-america-drops-plan-for-debit-card-fee.html.

81. R. Dye, "The Buzz on Buzz," *Harvard Business Review* (November/December 2000): 139–146.

82. W.F. Gloede, "The Art of Cultural," *American Demographics* (November 2004): 27–33.

83. S. Grier and A.M. Brumbaugh, "Noticing Cultural Differences: Ad Meanings Created by Target and Non-Target Markets," *Journal of Advertising* 28, no. 1 (1999): 79–93; G.K. Oakenfull, M.S. McCarthy, and T.B. Greenlee, "Targeting a Minority Without Alienating the Majority: Advertising to Gays and Lesbians in Mainstream Media," *Journal of Advertising Research* 48, no. 2 (2008): 191–198.

84. J.L. Aaker, A.M. Brumbaugh, and S.A. Grier, "Nontarget Markets and Viewer Distinctiveness: The Impact of Target Marketing on Advertising," *Journal of Consumer Psychology* 9, no. 3 (2000): 127–142.

85. C. Cousins, "Color and Cultural Design Considerations," WDD.com, June 11, 2012, www.webdesignerdepot.com/2012/06/color-and-cultural-design-considerations/.

86. V. Chattaraman, N.A. Rudd, and S.J. Lennon, "The Malleable Bicultural Consumer: Effects of Cultural Contexts on Aesthetic Judgments," *Journal of Consumer Behaviour* 9, no. 1 (2010): 18–31; T.J. Madden, K. Hewett, and M.S. Roth, "Managing Images in Different Cultures: A Cross-National Study of Color Meanings and Preferences," *Journal of International Marketing* 8, no. 4 (2000): 90–114.

87. K. Winterich, "New Starbucks logo May Reposition Brand," news release, January 29, 2011, http://news.smeal.psu.edu/news-release-archives/2011/january/new-starbucks-logo-may-reposition-brand/.

88. J.-J. Williams IV, "The Smell of Success," *Baltimore Sun*, January 19, 2012, http://articles.baltimoresun.com/2012-01-19/features/bs-ae-store-scents-20120113_1_scent-branding-smell-scented-candles/.

89. Penn State, "The Starbucks Effect: Committed Customers Don't Like Logo Redesigns, Research Finds," *Science Daily,* January 11, 2011, www.sciencedaily.com/releases/2011/01/110111133015.htm.

90. Fulcrum Marketing Group, "Choosing Colors for Your Website," http://iflair.biz/fulcrummarketinggroupnew/choosing-colors-for-your-website/.

91. A. Zimmerman, "To Boost Sales, Wal-Mart Decides to Drop One-Size-Fits-All Approach," *Wall Street Journal*, September 7, 2006, A1, A17.

92. C. Timberlake, "With Stores Nationwide, Macy's Goes Local," *Bloomberg BusinessWeek,* September 30, 2010, 21–22.

93. A. Morris, "How to Fit into the Pinterest Community," WideDiary.com, August 15, 2012, www.widediary.com/how-to-fit-into-the-pinterest-community/.

94. R. Mills, "Finding Your Tone of Voice," *Smashing Magazine*, August 21, 2012, http://uxdesign.smashingmagazine.com/2012/08/21/finding-tone-voice/.

95. M. Fabio, "Are Drug Companies 'Pay-for-Delay' Tactics Hurting Customers?" LegalZoom.com (April 2012), www.legalzoom.com/legal-headlines/debate-controversy/are-drug-companies-pay-delay-tactics/.

96. K. Mackie, "Acer Wants Communication from Microsoft on Surface Pricing," *Redmond Developer News*, August 13, 2012, http://reddevnews.com/articles/2012/08/13/acer-wants-communication-from-microsoft-on-surface-pricing.aspx.

97. H. Touryalai, "Wal-Mart Targets Unhappy Bank Customers with New Prepaid Card-Should Big Banks Be Nervous?" *Forbes*, October 8, 2012, www.forbes.com/sites/halahtouryalai/2012/10/08/walmart-targets-unhappy-bank-customers-should-big-banks-be-nervous/.

98. J. Greene and M. France, "Culture Wars Hit Corporate America," *BusinessWeek,* May 23, 2005, 90, 93.

99. C.B. Bhattacharya and S. Sen, "Doing Better at Doing Good: When, Why, and How Consumers Respond to Corporate Social Initiatives," *California Management Review* 47, no. 31 (2004): 9–24.

100. R.S. Dunham, "Shop at Target? You're a Swing Voter," *BusinessWeek,* September 25, 2006, 64.

101. Human Rights Campaign, "Best Places to Work 2013," www.hrc.org/resources/entry/best-places-to-work-2013/.

102. DiversityInc, "The DiversityInc Top 50 Companies for Diversity," 2013, www.diversityinc.com/the-diversityinc-top-50-companies-for-diversity-2013/.

103. HispanicBusiness.com, "Top 40 Companies," January 5, 2014, www.hispanicbusiness.com/top40companies/.

104. National Association of Asian American Professionals (NAAAP), "Best Places for Asians to Work," 2011, www.naaap.org/Programs/BestPlacesForAsiansToWork. aspx.

105. Aging Hipsters.com, "50 Best Places to Work If You're an Aging Boomer," December 8, 2005, www.aginghipsters.com/blog/archives/000440.php.

106. Human Rights Campaign, "Business Case: Corporate Reputation and Marketing Opportunities," April 2010.www.hrc.org/resources/entry/business-case-corporate-reputation-and-marketing-opportunities/.

107. M. Morrison, "Chick-fil-A Fast Losing Ground in Marriage Debate," *Advertising Age*, July 26, 2012, http://adage.com/article/news/chick-fil-a-fast-losing-ground-marriage-debate/236335/; M. Bullock, "Chick-fil-A Sites in Tulsa, Elsewhere See Surge in Customers After CEO's Comments Opposing Gay Marriage," *Tulsa World*, August 2, 2012, www.tulsaworld.com/archives/chick-fil-a-sites-in-tulsa-elsewhere-see-surge-in/article_cc0500e2-2ce5-5d19-9821-1197a6253611.html.

108. M. Lepore, "Komen CEO Just Did What She Should Have Done Months Ago . . . Resigned," The Grindstone, August 9, 2012, http://thegrindstone.com/career-management/komen-ceo-just-did-something-she-should-have-done-months-ago-resigned-882/.

109. Latino Marketing Pro, "Banks Pursue Unbanked Latinos," January 2009, www.latinomarketingpro.com/articles/banks-pursue-unbanked-latinos.html.

110. M. Williams, "Ram's Lone Star Edition Hits 10th Year," PickupTruck.com, March 21, 2012, http://news.pickuptrucks.com/2012/03/rams-lone-star-edition-hits-10th-year.html; E.A. Sanchez, "Texas-Edition Trucks: All the Lone Star Half-Tons North of the Rio Grande," *Motor Trend*, June 14, 2013, www.trucktrend.com/features/consumer/163_1305_texas_edition_trucks/; K. Seaman, "Chevrolet Tries to Make Other 49 States Jealous, Introduces 2014 Texas Edition Silverado," *Car and Driver*, May 9, 2013, http://blog.caranddriver.com/chevrolet-introduces-silverado-texas-edition-tries-to-make-other-49-states-jealous/.

111. L.E. Wynter, "Minorities Play the Hero in More TV Ads as Clients Discover Multicultural Sells," *Wall Street Journal*, November 24, 1993, B1, B7; "Hispanic Marketing Wins New Converts," *AdWeek*, February 8, 1988, 30, 32.

112. City of New York, *Invisible People: The Depiction of Minorities in Magazine Ads and Catalogs* (New York: Department of Consumer Affairs, 1991); R.E. Wilkes and H. Valencia, "Hispanics and Blacks in Television Commercials," *Journal of Advertising* 18, no. 1 (1989): 19–25.

113. Wynter, "Minorities Play the Hero in More TV Ads as Clients Discover Multicultural Sells"; T. Whittler, "The Effects of Actors' Race in Commercial Advertising: Review and Extension," *Journal of Advertising* 10, no. 1 (1991): 54–60.

114. Whittler, "The Effects of Actors' Race in Commercial Advertising"; Wilkes and Valencia, "Hispanics and Blacks in Television Commercials."

115. Schiller, "Stalking the New Consumer."

116. R. Melcher, "United Colors of Miller," *BusinessWeek*, May 19, 1997, 96.

117. G.A. Patterson, "Target 'Micromarkets' Its Way to Success; No 2 Stores Are Alike," *Wall Street Journal*, May 31, 1995, A1, A9.

118. Turow, *Breaking Up America*, 55–89.

119. S. Mehta, "Big Companies Heighten Their Pitch to Minority Firms," *Wall Street Journal*, August 23, 1994, B2.

120. C. Oster, "Disabled Group Charges Bias in Insurance Offer," *Wall Street Jour-

nal, July 25, 2001, B1; J.B. Cahill, "Charged Up: Credit Cards Invade a New Market Niche: The Mentally Disabled—Some Just Can't Say No; Leaders Can't Either by Law in Some States," *Wall Street Journal*, November 10, 1998; B. Saporito, "Wrestling with Your Conscience," *Time*, November 15, 1999, 71–74.

121. G.D. Pires and J. Stanton, "Ethnic Marketing Ethics," *Journal of Business Ethics* 36, nos. 1–2 (2002): 111–118; S.H. Wildstrom, "On the Web, it's 1984," *BusinessWeek*, January 10, 2000, 28; L. Peñaloza, "Vulnerable Populations," *Journal of Public Policy & Marketing* 14 (Spring 1995): 83–95.

122. S. Vranica, "Buzz Marketers Score Venture Dollars," *Wall Street Journal*, January 13, 2006, A11; S. Vranica, "Getting Buzz Marketers to Fess Up," *Wall Street Journal*, February 9, 2005, B9.

123. D.J. Ringold, "Social Criticisms of Target Marketing: Process or Product?" *American Behavioral Scientist* 38, no. 4 (1995): 578–593; N.C. Smith and E. Cooper-Martin, "Ethics and Target Marketing: The Role of Product Harm and Consumer Vulnerability," *Journal of Marketing* 61, no. 3 (1997): 1–20; T.J. Rittenburg and M. Parthasarathy, "Ethical Implications of Target Market Selection," *Journal of Macromarketing* 17, no. 2 (1997): 49–64; Davidson, "Targeting Is Innocent Until It Exploits the Vulnerable."

124. Turow, *Breaking Up America*, 199.

125. J.S. Nevid and N.L. Sta. Maria, "Multicultural Issues in Qualitative Research, *Psychology & Marketing* 16, no. 4 (1999): 305–325; Teinowitz, "Multicultural Marketing."

126. T.H. Davenport and J.G. Harris, "The Dark Side of Customer Analytics," *Harvard Business Review* (May 2007): 37–48; Teinowitz, "Multicultural Marketing."

127. N. Byrnes, "Leader of the Packs," *BusinessWeek*, October 31, 2005, 56–58; Vranica, "Getting Buzz Marketers to Fess Up."

128. K.J. Delaney, "In 'Click Fraud,' Web Outfits Have a Costly Problem," *Wall Street Journal*, April 6, 2005, A1, A6; Teinowitz, "Multicultural Marketing."

129. R.G. Matthews, "KFC 'Soul' Ad Poses Global Issue," *Wall Street Journal*, January 27, 2005, B6; R.M. McMath, "Don't Bite Off More Than You Can Chew," *American Demographics* (March 1998): 68; C.C. Wilson II and F. Gutiérrez, *Race, Multiculturalism, and the Media*, 2d ed. (Thousand Oaks, CA: Sage, 1995), 137.

130. S.L. Hwang, "Light Brigades: Tobacco Companies Enlist the Bar Owner to Push Their Goods," *Wall Street Journal*, April 21, 1999, A1, A6.

131. C. Terhune, "Lighten Up: Pepsi Sales Force Tries to Push 'Healthier' Snacks in Inner City," *Wall Street Journal*, October 5, 2006, A1, A17.

4

U.S. Hispanics

Cultural Roots Unite a Diverse Group

In 2003, U.S. Hispanics (or Latinos) officially became the largest ethnic group in the country.[1] In 2007 Garcia and Rodriguez were among the top 10 surnames in the United States.[2] Members of this fast-growing subculture share cultural roots that transcend different countries of origin, races, socioeconomic status, time or generations in the United States, and even languages spoken. The special role of family, pride in ethnic heritage, and retention of the Spanish language symbolize shared Latino values and behaviors. Despite these shared values, Latinos come from multiple races, ethnic identities, countries of origin, social and educational backgrounds, and different stages of acculturation into U.S. mainstream culture. This chapter provides a profile that highlights the similarities that underlie Hispanic cultural roots and the differences that make U.S. Latinos such a challenging target market in multicultural America.

The first part of this chapter describes the potential meanings of labels that express Latino identities. The following section presents geographic and demographic characteristics of U.S. Hispanics and the parameters that frame their social and economic lives. The next section describes Hispanic patterns of acculturation, ethnic identities, and language usage and how those form the basis of key Latino consumer segments. Next, the chapter reviews key Latino cultural values that influence market-space choices and compares their similarities and differences with values of mainstream America. This is followed by an introduction to media issues, such as current preferences of U.S. Latinos for acquiring market-space information and the availability of English- and Spanish-language media vehicles. Last, there is a section addressing Latino search strategies and marketplace preferences.

What Do the Labels "Hispanic" and "Latino" Mean?

The choice of which label to use in grouping together these more than 50 million Americans is full of significance. If we asked individuals of Hispanic heritage whether Hispanic or Latino best expresses how they see their own ethnic identity, a majority would answer, "Neither!" The terms "Hispanic" and "Latino" originated in organizations such as U.S. government agencies in their efforts to classify people of Spanish-speaking origin.[3] A person of Hispanic origin is more likely to see his or her cultural heritage as *dominicano/a*, "Cuban American," "Mexican-American," *nuyorican, chicano/a*, and so on than "Hispanic" or "Latino." Most Hispanics experience no conflict in using one term with family or friends and another term when filling in a standardized form. Nevertheless, these labels also contain political meanings that an individual might or might not share.

A discussion of what to call this group of diverse peoples who share key cultural values provides a short introduction to the multiple facets of Latino ethnicity. Consider the following quotation from Earl Shorris's introduction to *Latinos*:

> There must be one name, a single word that is not objectionable. . . . Geographically, *Hispanic* is preferred in the Southeast and much of Texas. New Yorkers use both *Hispanic* and *Latino*. Chicago, where no nationality has attained a majority, prefers *Latino*. In California, the word *Hispanic* has been barred from the *Los Angeles Times*, in keeping with the strong feelings of people in that community. Some people in New Mexico prefer *Hispano*. Politically, *Hispanic* belongs to the right and some of the center, while Latino belongs to the left and the center. Politically active Mexican-American women in Los Angeles are fond of asking, "Why *HISpanic*? Why not *HERSpanic*?" Historically, the choice went from *Spanish* or *Spanish-speaking* to *Latin American, Latino,* and *Hispanic*. Economically, Rodolfo Acuna, the historian, is correct when he says that *Hispanic* belongs to the middle class, which seems most pleased by the term. Anglos and people who oppose bilingual education and bilingualism prefer *Hispanic*, which makes sense, since *Hispanic* is an English word meaning "pertaining to ancient Spain."[4]

A history of terms used by the U.S. Census also illustrates the confusion, not only as to which label to use for U.S. Hispanics but also with regard to how to count Latinos. At various times, the following criteria have been used to classify U.S. Hispanics: shared language (Spanish), Spanish surnames, race and type of ancestors, national origin, and religious traditions. Until the 1940s, "Mexican" was listed as a race on census forms, and from then until the 1970 census, Hispanics were simply counted as "whites." The 1970 census tried using several criteria simultaneously (Spanish-surname, Spanish-speaking, parentage) to count U.S. Hispanics. To confuse matters further, during the 1970s the label "Hispanic" was treated by other government agencies as if it referred to a distinctive racial group. As a Uruguayan immigrant said, "I thought I was white until I went to college in the U.S. and had to choose between white, black or Hispanic." People whose origins trace to Spain but not to Brazil, Portugal, or the Philippines are now included in counts of U.S. Latinos.

In terms of actual use, the label preferred by about half of U.S. Hispanics is their family's country of origin (e.g., Mexican American). About 26 percent use either "Hispanic" or "Latino," and about 24 percent use only "American" as label for themselves.[5]

The Census Bureau currently uses the term "Hispanic" (as an ethnic, not racial, category) but recognizes that many people self-identify as "Latino" and not as "Hispanic" and vice versa. These changing definitions of who should be counted among U.S. Latinos contribute to the uncertainty of marketers about the size and cultural unity of the Hispanic market. If companies want to measure their success in this market, they must not confuse race with ethnicity; there is no such thing as a "Latino look."

So, where does that leave a firm wishing to develop a partnership with Hispanic consumers? Recognizing the possibility that individuals do not think of their ethnicity in "Hispanic" or "Latino" terms is an important step toward understanding Latino ethnicity. It may be best not to use a label in communications when there is a possibility of stepping into this minefield. When a choice is made to use "Hispanic" or "Latino," there will be trade-offs of inclusion and exclusion.

U.S. Latinos: Population Growth and Increased Buying Power

The U.S. Census Bureau has valuable information about the size and geographic concentrations of the U.S. Latino population and how it differs from other groups of Americans. This section uses U.S. Census data, Pew Hispanic Center publications, and other resources to provide an overview of the size of the U.S. Latino population, its geographic dispersal across states and cities, and major social and economic characteristics. Their websites offer the most up-to-date information.

Influence of Country of Origin on U.S. Hispanic Geography

Different Latin American countries of origin have distinctive political, cultural, and historic traditions. This heritage is an important source of diversity among American Latinos.[6] About 65 percent of U.S. Latinos are of Mexican heritage, 9 percent Puerto Rican, 4 percent Cuban, and over 13 percent come from Central and South America.[7] The original motivation to immigrate as well as timing and patterns of immigration vary across these groups.

For example, economic conditions tend to propel immigration from Mexico and Puerto Rico, but Puerto Ricans are more likely to return to the island after living in the continental United States for a while. In contrast, Mexican immigrants have stayed in the United States for generations. Some Hispanics' ancestors were already living in the American Southwest before the states in that region became part of the United States. Most Cuban immigrants came to the United States as political refugees in the early 1960s or 1980s. The relative portion of U.S. Latinos from different countries changes over time, as do overall levels of immigration. The "push and pull" of Latino immigration responds to external events, such as political unrest in Central America in the 1980s, economic opportunities in the United States in the 1990s, and the Great Recession of 2008–11.

Table 4.1 shows the countries of origin for U.S. Latinos and the states in which they live. The Latino population has grown from 22 million in the 1990 U.S. census to 35 million in the 2000 U.S. census to more than 53 million as of 2013, and it is expected to exceed 132 million in 2050. At present, Hispanics make up over 16 percent of the total U.S. population, but they are expected to reach 20 percent by 2020 and about 25 percent in 2050.

An important characteristic of the Latino population is concentration according to country of origin. Cuban Americans dominate the Latinos of southern Florida (54 percent of Latinos in Miami), Puerto Ricans are the majority Latino group in New York (about 27 percent), and Mexican Americans are the largest number of Latinos in the Southwestern states (78 percent of Hispanics in Los Angeles, 91 percent in San Antonio, and 78 percent in Houston). Chicago also has a large percentage (nearly 80 percent) of Hispanics who originated in Mexico.[8]

Growth in the U.S. Hispanic population remains concentrated in a few states even while new locations are increasing their appeal. Most U.S. Latinos live in urban areas (over 90 percent), and the largest share of Hispanics live in Western (about 41 percent) and Southern (about 36 percent) states. Table 4.2 shows the top states and cities for the Hispanic population.[9] Five states have over 78 percent of U.S. Latinos: New York, California, Texas, Illinois, and Florida. California, Texas, and Florida are home to 55 percent of U.S. Latinos. The geographic concentration of U.S. Latinos makes them easier to reach even as the need to accommodate their diversity is taken into consideration.

Hispanics prefer to migrate to established Spanish-speaking communities in the United States, where newcomers are able to conduct their lives largely

Table 4.1

Hispanic Countries-of-Origin in Selected States (in thousands)

Country of origin for Hispanic population	Total U.S. population	State with highest population	State with second-highest population	State with third-highest population	State with fourth-highest population	State with fifth-highest population
Mexico	31,798.3	CA 11,423.1	TX 7,951.2	AZ 1,658.7	IL 1,602.4	CO 757.2
Puerto Rico	4,623.7	NY 1,070.6	FL 847.6	NJ 434.1	PA 366.1	MA 266.1
Cuba	1,785.5	FL 1,213.4	CA 88.6	NJ 83.4	NY 70.8	TX 46.5
Dominican Republic	1,414.7	NY 674.8	NJ 197.9	FL 172.5	MA 103.3	PA 62.3
Guatemala	1,044.2	CA 332.7	FL 83.9	NY 72.8	TX 66.2	NJ 48.9
El Salvador	1,649.0	CA 573.9	TX 222.6	NY 152.1	VA 123.8	MD 123.8
Other Hispanic	8,162.2	CA 1,393.9	FL 1,221.6	TX 1,030.4	NY 917.6	NJ 516.6

Source: S.R. Ennis, M. Rios-Vega, and N.G. Albert, *Census Briefs: The Hispanic Population 2010* (Washington, DC: U.S. Census Bureau, 2011), tables 4, 8.

Table 4.2

Top Hispanic Cities and Countries of Origin

Metro area	Hispanic population	% share of Hispanics in population	% among Hispanic, share of foreign born	% among those under 18 years, share Hispanic	Top three Hispanic origin groups	% of all Hispanics in metro area
Los Angeles–Long Beach, CA	5,724,000	44.50	42.50	58.50	Mexican Salvadoran Guatemalan	78.40 7.40 4.70
New York–Northeastern NJ	4,243,000	23.90	44.50	29.20	Puerto Rican Dominican Mexican	27.40 20.60 12.90
Houston–Brazoria, TX	2,044,000	36.30	40.80	45.90	Mexican Salvadoran Honduran	78.60 7.20 2.50
Riverside–San Bernardino, CA	2,012,000	47.40	33.00	60.60	Mexican Salvadoran Guatemalan	87.60 3.00 1.50
Chicago, IL	1,934,000	21.10	40.00	29.80	Mexican Puerto Rican Guatemalan	79.70 10.20 1.50
Dallas–Fort Worth, TX	1,746,000	27.90	40.20	37.70	Mexican Salvadoran Puerto Rican	85.50 3.90 2.00
Miami–Hialeah, FL	1,610,000	65.70	66.50	60.90	Cuban Colombian Nicaraguan	53.90 7.50 6.20
Phoenix, AZ	1,136,000	29.70	31.70	43.30	Mexican Puerto Rican Spaniard	89.70 1.90 1.30
San Antonio, TX	1,090,000	55.50	17.80	65.70	Mexican Puerto Rican Spaniard	91.00 1.90 0.70

Metro area	Population				Origin	%
San Francisco–Oakland–Vallejo, CA	1,088,000	22.20	41.80	32.20	Mexican	71.00
					Salvadoran	7.80
					Guatemalan	3.30
San Diego, CA	1,000,000	32.20	37.40	45.70	Mexican	90.40
					Puerto Rican	1.80
					Spaniard	1.50
Washington, DC/MD/VA	774,000	14.00	56.20	17.90	Salvadoran	34.40
					Mexican	15.80
					Guatemalan	6.40
McAllen–Edinburg–Pharr–Mission, TX	707,000	90.70	30.80	95.30	Mexican	97.70
					Spaniard	0.20
					Cuban	0.20
El Paso, TX	662,000	82.30	30.00	87.90	Mexican	96.00
					Puerto Rican	1.00
					Spaniard	0.60
Denver–Boulder, CO	596,000	23.10	29.20	34.10	Mexican	81.80
					Spaniard	4.80
					Puerto Rican	1.60
Las Vegas, NV	571,000	29.20	41.30	42.20	Mexican	76.60
					Cuban	4.20
					Salvadoran	3.70
Fresno, CA	552,000	50.90	31.60	63.30	Mexican	95.10
					Salvadoran	0.90
					Puerto Rican	0.80
Orlando, FL	543,000	25.40	26.00	32.00	Puerto Rican	51.30
					Mexican	11.40
					Cuban	8.30
Atlanta, GA	530,000	10.80	53.80	14.70	Mexican	58.50
					Puerto Rican	
Austin, TX	502,000	31.00	28.90	42.30	Mexican	82.00
					Puerto Rican	

Source: S. Motel and E. Patten, *Characteristics of the 60 Largest Metropolitan Areas by Hispanic Population* (Washington, DC: Pew Research Center, September 19, 2012), www.pewhispanic.org/2012/09/19/characteristics-of-the-60-largest-metropolitan-areas-by-hispanic-population/.

in Spanish. Today's Latino immigrants continue to concentrate according to country of origin.[10] During the 2000s, several states experienced unexpectedly strong population growth attributable to new Latino residents; the new locations were in states such as Alabama, Georgia, Nevada, and North Carolina.[11]

More than 28 cities of over 100,000 now have Hispanic majorities.[12] Patterns of Latino settlement sometimes vary among different cities in one state. For example, Hispanics of Mexican origin comprise over 80 percent of the Latino population in Los Angeles and San Diego, but only about 70 percent in San Francisco. Salvadorans are in second place in San Francisco and Los Angeles, but they are the largest share of Latinos in Washington, DC, and Maryland. In nearby Virginia, Hispanics are mostly of Mexican origin. In the 2010 census, Miami's Latinos were 54 percent Cuban, while the largest number of Hispanics in Orlando and Tampa were from Puerto Rico. Although San Antonio and Austin are only 80 miles from each other, San Antonio is a Hispanic majority city (56 percent) while in Austin Latinos make up only 31 percent of the population.

Members of each country-of-origin group can identify strongest with other Latinos from the same country of origin. They can identify other Latinos by their socioeconomic status, language patterns and accents, knowledge or lack thereof of cultural traditions as well as physical appearance. Countries of origin continue to be strong forces of diversity within U.S. Latino subculture, since their traditions and language preferences vary.

According to the 2010 American Community Survey, more than half the 16 million foreign-born U.S. residents were from Latin America, and most of them are not U.S. citizens.[13] These foreign-born residents from Latin America concentrate in the traditional entry points of California, Texas, Florida, and New York (about 63 percent of Latin American foreign-born). Central America was the source of 69 percent of U.S. Latin American noncitizen residents, and Mexico alone accounted for 55 percent of all noncitizen residents. California had the highest percentage of total population that are foreign-born, about 25 percent of Californians. Foreign-born residents from Latin America on average are older, more likely to be male, and more likely to be married and to have larger families than U.S. Latinos who are born in the United States. Only 32 percent of Latin American residents in the United States are naturalized citizens.[14]

The illegal Latino immigrant population is the most difficult group of U.S. Hispanics to count. Current estimates by the Pew Hispanic Center suggest that there are 40 million immigrants in the United States, and 11.1 million of those are unauthorized.[15] Other sources estimate the illegal population as high as 20 million.[16] The illegal immigrant population peaked in 2007 at 12 million people. Mexico is the source of about 30 percent of all current U.S. immigrants—legal and illegal, about 12 million residents. By 2012 immigration from Mexico was reduced to almost zero.[17] The decline is due to more stringent border controls and the lack of jobs in the United States during the 2008–11 recession. By acquiring identity cards at their consulates, and tax identification numbers from the Internal Revenue Service, illegal residents can open bank accounts, get credit cards, even obtain home mortgages.[18] As consumers, illegal immigrants represent a market opportunity.

Age and Family Size Create Foundation for Future Growth Among U.S. Latinos

Hispanic influx in the United States is reshaping the American demographic profile. The low average age and growing income and education of U.S. Hispanics are making them an important market for the future. Their dedication to family reaffirms the importance of home ownership. These are important difference between U.S. Latinos and other American subcultures.

Compared to other American populations, Hispanics are younger and have a larger average family size and larger household. Seventy-eight percent of Hispanics live in family households, compared to 67 percent of other Americans. The average Hispanic household has 3.3 persons compared to 2.4 persons in non-Hispanic households.[19] Only 20 percent of all American family households have children, while over 33 percent of Hispanic family households have children.[20] In 2011 those under age 20 made up 18.5 percent of the overall American population but over 38 percent of the U.S. Hispanic population.[21] The median age of U.S. Latinos is 27, compared to 36 for other Americans.

Nevertheless, fertility rates among Hispanics are actually declining.[22] In 1990, it was 2.96 births per woman, but in the 2010 Census it was 2.23, compared with the American average of 1.78.[23]

U.S. Hispanics are more likely to rent their homes (52 percent vs. 32 percent for all Americans).[24] Cuban Americans have the highest rates of home ownership, and Dominican, Honduran, and Guatemalan Americans have the lowest rates. This represents a tremendous opportunity in the future as most Latinos aspire to home ownership, as a key component of the Latino version of the "American Dream."[25]

Table 4.3 shows different levels of educational attainment and income levels for U.S. Hispanics compared to foreign-born Hispanics and all Americans. The table indicates that foreign-born Hispanics are the least well educated; almost half of them have less than a high school education. The relationship of education to income is also shown in the table. The lower levels of education

Table 4.3

Education and Income Levels of U.S. Hispanics

Education/income characteristics	U.S. average	Native-born Americans	All U.S. Hispanics	Foreign-born Hispanics
Education level				
Less than H.S.	12.9%	11.0%	37.1%	46.8%
H.S. or equivalent	31.2%	29.7%	29.6%	25.3%
Some college	25.9%	30.9%	19.4%	16.7%
Bachelor's degree or advanced degree	29.9%	28.4%	13.8%	11.2%
Total	95.9%	100.0%	99.9%	100.0%
Median household income	$50,000		$39,000	$35,000
HH < $20,000*	13.2%		25.1%	31.4%
HH > $50,000*	40.5%		21.9%	15.3%
HH below poverty line	15.9%		25.9%	25.8%
Homeowners	64.7%		46.5%	44.0%

Sources: E.M. Grieco, Y.D. Acosta, G.P. de la Cruz, C. Gambino, T. Gryn, L.J. Larsen, E.N. Trevelyan, and N.P. Walters, *The Foreign-Born Population in the United States: 2010,* American Community Survey Report (Washington, DC: U.S. Census Bureau, May 2012); "Table 231. Educational Attainment by Selected Characteristics 2010," in U.S. Census Bureau, *The 2012 Statistical Abstract* (Washington, DC, September 30, 2011), www.census. gov/compendia/statab/cats/education/educational_attainment.html; National Center for Education Statistics, "Fast Facts" (Washington, DC: Department of Education), table 8, http://nces.ed.gov/fastfacts/display.asp?id=27/.
    *HH = household.

among U.S. Latinos compared to American averages lead to lower household incomes and higher percentages of Hispanics living in poverty.

In Los Angeles, Latinos represent three-fourths of children attending public school, and 43 percent of them do not speak English.[26] Latino youth in places like Los Angeles live in two worlds, one Spanish-dominant and traditional and another English-dominant and open to change. This dichotomy creates significant diversity within the youth community. Young Latinos value family above all else and look to personal relationships for acceptance and support. At the same time, they want to change their world to improve themselves and to be heard.[27] They have favorite television shows in Spanish (e.g., *Noticias, Cristina, Sabado Gigante, La Fea Mas Bella*), English (*The Simpsons, Grey's Anatomy, Family Guy,* and *CSI*), and Latino-focused shows in English and Spanish (*George Lopez,* MTV en español, Sí TV).[28]

Economic Profile of U.S. Latinos

U.S. Latinos had $1.1 trillion in purchasing power in 2012, equivalent to that of the twelfth-largest economy in the world. Within three years, they are expected to have $1.5 trillion in purchasing power, equivalent to that of the ninth-largest economy.[29] That purchasing power was about 16 percent of total American purchasing power in 2013, compared with 6 percent in 1990.[30]

Nevertheless, Hispanic family income and education levels are lower than those for blacks, non-Hispanic whites, or Asian Americans, and high school dropout rates remain high (over 50 percent).[31] Latinos are now the largest minority group in colleges and universities, accounting for over 16.5 percent of college enrollments and one-fourth of two-year college enrollments.[32] Median annual income for Hispanic families in 2011 was $38,624, compared with $55,412 for non-Hispanic whites, $32,366 for blacks, and $66,895 for Asian-Americans.[33]

Incomes also vary across national origin, as shown in Table 4.4. For example, while the median household income for Hispanics as a whole is around $40,000, it is $38,700 for Mexican Americans, $36,000 for Puerto Ricans, $40,000 for Cuban Americans, $43,000 for Salvadoran Americans, and $34,000 for Dominican Americans.[34] The second generation of U.S. Latinos has higher education levels, which points toward growth overall in Hispanic incomes over time.[35]

Many Latinos live in family households with income below the poverty line. Between 23 percent and 27 percent of Hispanic children were living in poverty in 2012, compared with 18 percent for all Americans. The percentage of families living in poverty varies across Hispanic countries of origin: 27 percent for Mexican Americans, 27 percent for Puerto Ricans, 25 percent for other Central Americans (not shown in the table), 26 percent for Dominican Americans, and 21 percent for other Hispanics (not shown in the table).[36]

Despite the lower income levels, Hispanic households spend more than other Americans in some product categories. For example, Latinos spend more on telephone services, men's and boys' clothing, children's clothing, and footwear. Also, Hispanics spend a higher proportion of their money than other Americans on food (groceries and restaurants), housing, utilities, and transportation. They spend proportionately less than other Americans on alcohol, health care, entertainment, reading materials, education, tobacco products, personal insurance, and pensions.[37]

Over the past 20 years, many Latino families have become affluent. A major income source for the affluent Hispanic is business ownership. Pollo Campero, a Guatemalan-American fast-food restaurant specializing in chicken, fried plantains, and other Guatemalan delicacies, opened in 2002 and now operates in more than 13 countries, with 27 locations in the United States and over 200 elsewere.[38] A different model of success is Robert Dominguez Jr.'s Ambreco, a construction management firm. This business competes for federal projects using a proprietary technology that allows clients to watch work sites in real time.[39]

Table 4.4

Household Income for U.S. Hispanic Country-of-Origin Groups

Socioeconomic characteristics	All U.S. Hispanics	Mexican Americans	Puerto Ricans	Cuban Americans	Salvadoran Americans	Dominican Americans
Population size (in 000s)	50,730	32,916	4,683	1,884	1,827	1,509
Foreign-born	37%	36%	1%	59%	62%	57%
Median age	27 years	25 years	27 years	40 years	29 years	29 years
H.S. diploma only	26%	26%	30%	29%	24%	26%
Bachelor's degree or higher	13%	9%	16%	24%	7%	15%
English proficiency	65%	64%	82%	58%	46%	55%
Have citizenship	74%	73%	99%	74%	55%	70%
Median HH income*	$40,000	$38,700	$36,000	$40,000	$43,000	$34,000
Living in poverty	25%	27%	27%	18%	20%	26%
No health insurance	31%	34%	15%	25%	41%	22%
Own home	46%	50%	38%	57%	42%	24%

Source: S. Motel and E. Patten, Hispanic Origin Profiles 2010 (Washington, DC: Pew Research Center, June 27, 2012), www.pewhispanic.org/2012/06/27/country-of-origin-profiles/.

*HH = household.

As business ownership has risen over the past few years, so have the numbers of wealthy Latinos. Over 1.5 million Latino households have income over $100,000. Nevertheless, about 40 percent of all Americans have household incomes above $75,000 while only 22 percent of Hispanics do.[40] While non-Hispanic whites comprise 68 percent of the population, they make up 77 percent of households with income above $100,000 and 83 percent of households with income over $250,000. Hispanics constitute 9 percent of American households with income over $100,000 and 5 percent of households with income over $250,000.[41]

Nearly half (45 percent) of affluent U.S. Hispanics are concentrated in five markets: Los Angeles, New York, Miami, Houston, and Chicago.[42] Four subsegments among affluent Hispanics have distinctive demographics and lifestyles. The "Heavy Hitters" range from 50 to 70 years old, and most have incomes over $250,000 per year. They have Ivy League degrees, are executives or entrepreneurs, and are bilingual/bicultural members of the second generation in the United States. The "Young Professionals" have income around $175,000 and are 35–70 years old. They are well educated and bilingual members of the first generation and, like others of their age, are highly mobile. The "Immigrant Entrepreneurs" tend to be between 45 and 70 years old with $150,000 in annual income. They were likely educated in their country of origin and tend to be bicultural and conservative. The "Small Business Owners" are younger (35–65) and have the least formal education. This group prefers Spanish and does most of its business in cash.

Latino Identity, Language Use, and Acculturation Among U.S. Latinos

Latino identity is multifaceted, situational, and symbolic, all of which present challenges to targeting Hispanics as "one" market. Choice of language has practical and symbolic meanings among Latinos. Individual Latinos also vary with respect to their acculturation to the American environment: their motivation, which cultural agents are most influential, and how long it takes. Acculturation describes the process in which immigrants to a new country (or culture) acquire the skills necessary to survive and succeed in the new environment.

Latino Identities

Ethnic identity involves not only self-labeling but ethnic behaviors or practices, feelings about one's ethnic group, commitment to the ethnic community, and contacts with those of other ethnicities.[43] A person's ethnic identity depends on how well that person knows his/her ethnic background, what that person's cultural values are, and how ethnicity is expressed. Expressing ethnic identity is less prevalent when a group is the target of discrimination or for whatever reasons has been stigmatized by members of mainstream culture.[44] Moreover, people may express their ethnicity privately but not in public.[45] In addition, situations can reinforce, denigrate, or have no impact at all on an individual's sense of ethnicity. This inevitably means that there is no uniform way in which Latino ethnicity is expressed.

The act of choosing and using a label for ethnicity communicates ethnic identity to others.[46] The choice of which term a U.S. Latino uses will "prime" how others see that person. A person "avows" who he is when he uses a label, but others "ascribe" that same person's identity according to the label chosen as well as by that person's physical appearance and verbal and nonverbal behaviors. So, Latino identities are created by individuals and co-created through communication with others, who may be Hispanic or non-Hispanic.

The influence of the situation on the strength of ethnic identity modifies how Hispanics respond to marketing efforts.[47] Advertising in Spanish is more influential when a Hispanic audience has been primed to identify as Hispanic. Hispanics will feel their ethnicity more strongly when they are in a minority environment than when they are in places where they are the majority ethnic group.[48] Using Hispanic models in advertising may persuade those who identify strongly as Hispanic to try a low-involvement product (e.g., soft drinks, computer supplies, snacks) but have little effect on persuasion for high-involvement goods (e.g., appliances, electronics, vehicles).[49] Many more studies have identified the influence of cultural context as determinant of a Hispanic person's reaction to information.[50] In other words, while appealing to a Hispanic person's identity as Latino can generate many positive outcomes, the size of the effect depends on other factors.

Figure 4.1 introduces a model of the diversity found among American Latinos with regard to how they identify themselves. As discussed in Chapter 2, Americans can choose parts of their heritage to identify with and others to ignore. Likewise, a person can claim a particular identity without any real knowledge of or socialization into that culture's value system.[51] Thus the figure shows two axes, one ranging from weak to strong Latino identity and the other, from weak to strong Latino cultural values. The groups named in the figure appear to be distinctive but more likely blend into each other at various points along the axes.

As indicated in the figure, "Weak Hispanics" represent the most "mainstream" Latinos who neither emphasize their Hispanic heritage as part of their identity nor were brought up learning typical Hispanic cultural values.

Figure 4.1 **Strength of Latino Identity and Latino Cultural Values**

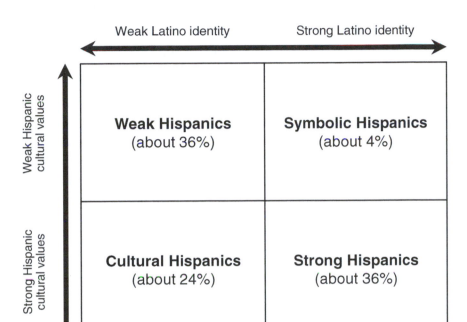

Source: R. Villarreal and R.A. Peterson, "Hispanic Ethnicity and Media Behavior," *Journal of Advertising Research* 48, no. 2 (2008): 179–190; M. Tharp and R. Villarreal, "Questioning the Construct of U.S. Hispanic Ethnic Identity," paper presented at International Trade and Finance Association Meetings, May 1998.

This group is often considered "fully assimilated" into the American mainstream. "Symbolic Hispanics" define themselves as Hispanic but have not really learned Hispanic values. They may have a multiracial or multiethnic background. In contrast, the "Cultural Hispanics" for whatever reasons do not identify as Hispanic yet behave according to Latino values. Some believe that this is due to a "dual" identity as Hispanic and American or a desire to "fit in" mainstream America. The last group ("Strong Hispanics") celebrates Latino identity and is motivated by traditional Hispanic cultural values such as familism, fatalism, *simpatía* (go along to get along), and *personalismo* (importance of personal networks).

Both Latino identity and what might be unique Latino cultural values are topics for more detailed research.[52] Nevertheless, this model provides insight into the diversity marketers might encounter when targeting U.S. Hispanics.

The concept of symbolic identity reveals a paradox in which someone identifies as Hispanic but does not know what beliefs and behaviors are "Hispanic." The "Cultural Hispanics" may have dual identities as members of Latino culture and as Americans by citizenship, but their core values are Latino. Because they choose not to identify as Latino and are unlikely to consume media in Spanish, they may be excluded from efforts to reach Hispanic consumers.[53] This "dual identity" makes it more difficult to isolate Hispanic consumer behaviors from those of non-Hispanics. The different combinations of cultural values and ethnic identities are undoubtedly a contributing cause of conflicting findings in past research about Hispanic consumer behaviors.[54]

One important point is that the four groups identified in Figure 4.1 have different responses to Hispanic-targeted marketing efforts. For example, buying familiar brand names, sticking with well-known brands, and a preference for brands that reach out to the consumer in Spanish are preferences of the "Strong Hispanics." "Weak" and "Symbolic" Hispanics are less responsive to these appeals, as their dual identities motivate them to minimize their differences with other Americans.[55]

Some observers of U.S. Latino styles of consumption have argued that Hispanics have a distinctive expression of their subcultural heritage that represents neither mainstream America nor their culture of origin.[56] It is a "culture of adaptation," reflecting conflicted feelings about belonging to the U.S. mainstream and being of Latin American origins. Several studies, using different methodologies, suggest that Latino cultural values have combined over time with mainstream U.S. values to create a unique U.S. Latino culture that is unlikely to disappear even when the use of Spanish does.[57]

Spanish Usage Symbolizes Ethnic Pride

The United States has the second-largest Spanish-speaking population in the world.[58] While Spanish is an important link between U.S. Hispanics and their shared values, not all U.S. Hispanics speak Spanish. The Pew Research Center reports that 36 percent of younger Latinos are English dominant, 41 percent are bilingual, and 23 percent are Spanish dominant. However, English fluency does not mean that later generations are abandoning the use of Spanish. Almost 80 percent of the second generation of U.S. Hispanics and 38 percent of the third generation report speaking proficient Spanish.[59] In the 2010 Census about 10.4 percent of Latin Americans born in other countries reported being monolingual in English, and 26.6 percent said they speak English "very well."[60] The wide variation in language skills among U.S. Latinos presents a major challenge to companies that want to build relationships with consumers in the Hispanic community.

The idea that U.S. Latinos are either monolingual in Spanish or English or are bilingual in the two languages oversimplifies actual language usage of U.S. Latinos. Among bilinguals, language ability can range from comfort in both languages to strong preferences for speaking, understanding, or writing a first or second language. They may or may not have English accents in Spanish or Spanish accents when speaking English, and this will affect how others perceive their fluency.[61] In addition, there can be "code-switching" among bilinguals, mixing English and Spanish in one sentence. This "Spanglish," as it is known colloquially, is frequently heard in use. A good example would be the language in any of the following situations: Bud Light: "Tan buena como encontrar un parking en frente al building." Or Nescafé's question to Latinas: "Con el chisme con las comadres, ¿Tomes coffee o café?" A Burger King in the Rio Grande Valley announced on a huge sign its discount on a "double cheeseburger con todo." About 70 percent of Latinos report using "Spanglish" when speaking with family and friends.[62]

English fluency varies among different age groups and among native and foreign-born Hispanics. For example, 38 percent of young Hispanics born in the United States (younger than 18) are fluent in English and speak only English at home, compared with only 4 percent of those born outside the United States. And 49 percent of adult, native U.S. Hispanics say they speak English "very well," but only 25 percent of adult foreign-born Latinos report speaking English "very well." Another major language difference is for foreign-born children (younger than 18) versus foreign-born adults: over 63 percent of foreign-born children claim to speak English "very well" while only 25.9 percent of foreign-born adults with Latin American origins speak English "very well."

Language usage also varies among persons from different countries of origin. About 76 percent of Hispanics speak a language other than English at home, but the percentage varies from 92 percent of Salvadorans to 66 percent of Puerto Ricans. And 35 percent of U.S. Latinos are not fluent in English. Hispanics from Central America are the least fluent in English (54 percent); Mexican Americans are the most fluent in English (37 percent), and about 42 percent of Cuban Americans are not fluent in English.[63] Spanish fluency can decline among second-generation Latinos but regain importance to the third generation.[64]

The majority of U.S. Hispanics claim to be bilingual. Latinos who speak only Spanish face barriers to participation in mainstream American institutions. One important distinction is between persons who are bilingual *and* bicultural, compared to those who are bilingual but not fluent in American mainstream culture.[65] Bicultural/bilingual persons are comfortable in the languages of both cultures and can switch between those languages when prompted by the cultural context of a message. This "frame-switching" by a bicultural viewer facilitates processing of information, making information easier to access and thus more likely to have a persuasive impact.[66]

Bilingual persons can express different aspects of their personalities in different languages. For example, participants in one study reported themselves as more assertive and achievement-oriented in English than when questioned in Spanish.[67] Some research indicates that a message in Spanish that switches to English has greater persuasive effect than slogans translated into Spanish.[68] Other research has shown that advertising received in the person's native language has stronger "emotional intensity" than the same message in the person's second language. This effect was not present, however, if the person was not familiar with the terminology in both languages.[69] It is important to remember that some Latinos cannot read or write Spanish, while others read and write it but are not conversationally fluent. Because cultural context can be cued by the choice of language used to reach a consumer, this choice of language should be determined by the situation in which a product or service is consumed.[70]

In spite of many positive benefits for marketers who reach U.S. Hispanics in Spanish, Spanish-language messages to U.S. Latinos do not always lead the audience to believe that the company is Hispanic friendly.[71] In some studies, advertising exclusively in Spanish was found to "arouse Hispanic insecurities about language usage." The implication is that a better formula for relating to Latinos is to use both English and Spanish and to be knowledgeable about the language skills of a specific target audience.[72]

Fluency in Spanish does not mean that young Latinos are not immersed in American popular culture. Younger Latinos prefer English-language television, network or cable, to Spanish-language television programming. In one study, Fox was the most popular network in English and popular shows were *The Simpsons, Grey's Anatomy, CSI,* and *Family Guy.* They even preferred the George Lopez show in English to *Sabado Gigante* or *La Fea Mas Bella,* popular programs from Latin America. Younger Latinos are also fans of mainstream musicians and actors, and eight out of ten Latino gamers prefer videogames in English.[73]

Language use per se (referring to whether an individual is monolingual in English or Spanish or bilingual), should be one consideration for marketers, but another is the language that best persuades members of a specific target market.[74] Consider the findings of Nielsen about the 77 percent of U.S. Hispanics who claim to speak English well.[75] About 60 percent of those supposedly fluent English-speakers speak Spanish at home versus only 17 percent who speak only English. Furthermore, in other research Spanish-dominant consumers tend to be even more influenced by interpersonal sources of information while English-dominant Hispanics are more influenced by marketer-sponsored advertising.[76] Still, because Spanish is the best medium to express pride in being Hispanic, this language may also be best for expressing respect for the Latino community.

Acculturation Influences and Patterns Among U.S. Latinos

In earlier times, marketers considered language use a simple measure of a person's progress in acculturating to the U.S. environment. Today, U.S. Hispanics, among other contemporary ethnic immigrants, are not abandoning their native languages as they adapt to American lifestyles.[77] The way in which Latinos adapt to the American environment is a major source of diversity within the Hispanic community.

In past generations, immigrants to the United States either assimilated or acculturated to life in a new setting. Assimilation meant that over time and generations, an immigrant group abandoned native ways and languages. This concept accurately described the process in which Italian, Irish, and Jewish immigrants moved into mainstream American life. In contrast, U.S. Hispanics tend to acculturate, not assimilate; they adopt new behaviors and adapt old ones to the environment. Over time or generations, there remain ways in which the Latino subculture differs from mainstream American culture. Retention of Spanish-language fluency is an important signal of Latino heritage and ethnic pride, as noted in the last section. Therefore, many firms find that Spanish-language use is an effective way to reach both monolingual speakers of Spanish and bilingual segments within the Latino market.

For a better understanding of U.S. Hispanic diversity, it is important to recognize the many influences over how immigrants adjust to life in today's multicultural America. Several researchers believe that being foreign born is more important than country of origin in determining cultural values among U.S. Latinos.[78] In addition to place of birth, age at the time of immigration is another important influence on acculturation. For example, people who come to the United States as adults are socialized in their countries of origin. In contrast, U.S. Latinos who immigrate to the United States as children are socialized into both cultures (Spanish at home and English outside the home) and often act as the family's translator and bridge to U.S. mainstream culture.[79] It also makes a difference whether immigrants arrive in a port of entry where there is an established community where immigrants can survive without adapting to American ways. Also, well-educated immigrants become bilingual more quickly than blue-collar immigrants.

Because there are so many different influences on an individual's or a family's path toward acculturation in the United States, there is no linear relationship between time in the United States and level of acculturation. Nevertheless, most researchers base their measures of acculturation on a combination of language and cultural orientation. On this basis, about 38 percent of U.S. Latinos are considered "Spanish dominant," 24 percent are English-dominant or "acculturated," and 38 percent are described as "bilinguals." Only 40 percent of U.S. Hispanics live in neighborhoods where they are a minority, suggesting that more families today are comfortable outside Spanish-dominant neighborhoods. About 90 percent of Hispanics believe immigrants need to learn English to be successful in the United States, and 95 percent believe that it is important for future generations of Latinos to speak Spanish.[80]

Hispanic immigrants may begin the acculturation process, but it is their children and grandchildren who express acculturation in their "Spanish lives at home" and "English lives outside the home." Now that immigration has slowed, more attention is being focused on what acculturation means for second-, third-, and fourth-generation Hispanics. Persons of second-, third-, and fourth-generation Hispanic heritage vary widely in their adaptation to the U.S. mainstream. In some cases, the public persona is "typically" American, while the individual still expresses cultural values, at a subconscious level or in private at home.

Many behaviors and preferences other than language reflect acculturation levels when it is defined as a "Spanish dominant," "English dominant," or "bicultural" lifestyle. One example is the choice to live in a Hispanic-majority neighborhood. This is linked to the history of Latinos immigrating to Spanish-dominant neighborhoods in a small number of cities and along the southern border of the United States. Over time, they move for economic opportunities, and perhaps over generations, the need to be in a Spanish-dominant neighborhood dissipates. Easy access to Spanish-language media for news and entertainment sustains connections with countries of origin, and the close proximity of those countries reinforces bicultural and bilingual lifestyles in the United States.[81]

There is a paradox for Hispanics with regard to acculturation into mainstream American lifestyles. There may be benefits in terms of achievement and success, but American lifestyles take a toll on the overall health of Latinos.[82] U.S. Hispanics live longer than their families left in their countries of origin, but they suffer higher rates of obesity, diabetes, and heart disease because of dietary changes. In addition, they have higher levels of addiction to alcohol, drugs, and smoking.[83] Furthermore, when Latinos become as mobile as other Americans the Hispanic extended family is pulled from participation in the daily lives of family members.

Language and Acculturation: Implications for Segmenting the U.S. Hispanic Market

The diversity within the U.S. Hispanic community has always been of interest to firms catering to Latino consumers. Until the 1980s, most companies saw only "country-of-origin" markets (e.g., Cubans in Florida, Mexicans in California and Texas, Puerto Ricans in New York), not a "U.S." market of Hispanics. This section describes why acculturation levels are the basis for most models of how companies segment the U.S. Latino consumer market. In general, researchers have found differences among Hispanics in the amount of acculturation, however measured, to be more meaningful for marketing purposes than cultural variations across Latino countries of origin.[84] Furthermore, the process of "retro-acculturation" means more second- and third-generation U.S. Hispanics speak Spanish but are also perfectly at home in mainstream U.S. culture.[85]

In the early 1980s, many organizations discovered the opportunity that the growing economic power of U.S. Hispanics represents. Hispanic market researchers[86] began to report the similarity of many attitudes, values, and behaviors across country-of-origin Latinos—what have come to be known as their "shared Hispanic values." This focus on similarities rather than differences across Latino countries of origin became the foundation for "acculturation levels" as the conceptual model for how to segment the Hispanic consumer market.

Table 4.5 reports indexes for a variety of media activities and product ownership, for Hispanics of different acculturation levels and for Latinos from different countries of origin. According to the table, Cuban Americans appear to be the Hispanic group that is the most active in social media such as MySpace and LinkedIn and to own smartphones and an iPad. Puerto Ricans play games online more than other Hispanics do. MySpace and radio are popular with Mexican Americans. While these differences may be important for some marketers to know about, there is no consistent pattern of media preferences linked to countries of origin. In contrast, there are clear patterns of differences for Hispanics at different acculturation levels. For example, "unacculturated Hispanics" are the least active in consuming different types of media. With two exceptions (Twitter and MySpace), "acculturated Hispanics" are the most active, and "bicultural Hispanics" fall somewhere in between, regarding use of these particular media.

These data alone are not sufficient to conclude that acculturation level is the best basis for segmenting the Latino market. It is the link of acculturation level to language usage that provides the strongest incentive for marketers to use it as starting point for analyzing diversity within the market. The cost

Table 4.5

Comparison of Media Activities by Acculturation Level and Country-of-Origin for U.S. Hispanics

Media activity	All Hispanics	Cuban Americans	Mexican Americans	Puerto Ricans	Other Hispanics	Acculturated	Unacculturated	Bicultural
Total N	4,062	402	2,399	382	879	1,031	1,083	1,499
Watch TV	92	87	93	93	90	93	95	93
Listen to radio	96	91	105	77	80	106	85	105
Play games online	110	102	104	156	111	162	53	120
Online	92	98	91	85	98	103	84	92
Social media user	96	104	91	94	109	110	84	102
Facebook	87	80	82	87	104	107	69	92
Twitter	104	83	104	86	112	87	99	132
MySpace	112	231	123	117	56	96	81	166
LinkedIn	45	29	38	31	53	74	27	51
YouTube	107	125	105	81	118	135	83	114
Own laptop	95	85	90	107	106	96	74	99
Own iPad	79	107	78	103	70	90	51	78
Smartphone user	104	118	95	104	125	119	92	111
Own iPhone	80	128	69	*56	107	110	49	86
Own Android phone	124	147	113	134	144	147	107	128

Source: Experian Information Solutions, Database: Summer 2012 NHCS Adult Survey, www.experian.com/simmons-research/consumer-study.html.

advantages of a pan-Hispanic approach have attracted more companies to the U.S. Latino consumer market. Marketers are able to match acculturation levels to zip codes, media habits, and shopping preferences. The idea that companies should reach consumers in whatever the appropriate language is, rather than treating all Hispanics as Spanish speakers, is considered common sense today.

Marketing practitioners have applied different versions of acculturation models. One group identified what it believes to be five stages along the "assimilation" route. They named the stages "newcomers," "transitionals," "transplants," "first borns," and "deep roots."[87] Another company coined names for three groups of Latinos: "strong," "moderate," and "weak" Hispanic cultural identification. "Cultural identification" uses language preferences but adds lifestyle influences, such as the density of Hispanics in the consumer's neighborhood, ties to country of origin, and socioeconomic status.[88] Other marketers have applied "familiarity with or preference for" American and Latino cultures.[89] Depending on which Latinos are the best target markets for a client's products, these firms recommend using English, Spanish, or both languages to reach the market.[90]

Most marketers today use some version of measuring and identifying three groups of Latinos: "unacculturated," "bicultural," and "acculturated." These groups are still defined mostly by their use of language: "Unacculturated" Hispanics are considered monolingual in Spanish, "acculturated" Hispanics are thought to be monolingual in English, and "bicultural" Hispanics are divided into Spanish-dominant and English-dominant groups.[91] Newer acculturation models incorporate measures for language usage in different situations and locations. This is necessary information for reaching Latinos in mobile and online media.

Another approach to segmenting the Hispanic market uses a combination of age, birth country, percentage of life lived in the United States, and language preference, rather than acculturation level.[92] The result is five Hispanic consumer segments: "newcomers," "transitionals," "transplants," "maintainers" and "adapters." The first three are foreign-born but vary in the amount of their life spent in the United States and their use of Spanish. The last two groups are American-born, but "maintainers" are bilingual while "adapters" are monolingual in English. The advantage of this approach is that the groups have distinctive media habits, entertainment preferences, and geographic dispersion. For example, 50 percent of Southwestern Hispanics are "maintainers" and "full adapters," while 40 percent of Southeastern, Northeastern and Midwestern Hispanics are "newcomers."

Academic researchers have tackled the issue of acculturation while trying to tease out which preferences, attitudes, and behaviors are uniquely Hispanic and which are not. One common problem has been how to distinguish a "totally acculturated" from a "totally bicultural" Latino.[93] These newer methodologies measure cultural orientation toward both Latino and non-Latino cultures, recognizing a U.S. Hispanic person's *choice* to remain bicultural rather than to fully assimilate into mainstream culture.[94] These cultural orientation scales come in several versions, of which the most common one in academic use is the ARMSA-II scale.[95] Examples of the Hispanic segments that such scales have identified are the following five groups within the Latino market: "totally unacculturated," "somewhat unacculturated," "totally bicultural," "somewhat acculturated," and "totally acculturated." These segments respond uniquely to different marketing tactics in financial services and airlines, but in categories such as beer, acculturation level appears to be unrelated to purchase motivations.[96]

The lack of consensus about the process of acculturation or how best to measure an individual's acculturation status does not mean that it is not valuable for marketing purposes. A good example of this is the relationship of acculturation status and pre-purchase information searches by Hispanic consumers.[97] Persons who live in ethnic enclaves (e.g., "Little Havana" in Miami) are more likely to rely on family for purchasing information and advice. In contrast, those who do not strongly identify as Hispanic are more influenced by imagery in mass media and a broader array of information sources.[98] This is consistent with the Hispanic cultural value of reliance on personal networks.

Young Hispanics represent the future of Hispanic marketing. Hispanic "millennials" comprise 29 percent of all Hispanics, and a majority of them are bicultural/bilingual. For these younger Latinos, language and acculturation levels are less predictive of market behaviors.[99] Product search strategies, product category usage, and media habits of most "millennial" Hispanics differ substantially from those of older Latinos. However, among Generation Y Latinos, there remain differences in market motivations and preferences between consumers who are connected to Hispanic culture ("bicultural") and those who are not ("acculturated").[100] "Millennial" Hispanics in general are technologically active, but personal communications are still preferred by those who remain closest to their Hispanic heritage. For the latter group, technology provides the means for staying in contact with friends and family and, for those who are foreign born, to know what is going on in their country of origin. In addition, the culturally connected "millennials" consider shopping entertainment, prefer shopping with and receiving advice from friends and family, and enjoy purchasing familiar brands.[101]

In contrast to language, age, or time in the United States as bases for segmenting the U.S. Latino consumer market is the option of a multiethnic segmentation scheme. GlobalHue segments the four major American cultural groups (African American, Hispanic, Asian American, and non-Hispanic whites) into seven segments that cross cultural boundaries. Its basis for segmentation is the pessimism or optimism of individuals about their future and their involvement with their respective cultural communities. Hispanics were found to be equally optimistic and pessimistic, but most of the optimistic Latinos were disengaged from the Latino community (named "forward-focused youth" and "techies" in its research). It also found that the most acculturated Hispanics were often the least successful and most isolated from other members of the Hispanic community.[102]

For marketers who hope that cultural differences between Hispanics and other Americans will be erased by the third or fourth generation, there is bad news. The values embedded in the Hispanic culture survive intact from one generation to the next, even when members of it are no longer able to speak, read, or write Spanish. A good example of this is the fatalism identified earlier as characteristic of Latino values. English-dominant Hispanics are significantly more fatalistic than non-Hispanic whites, though much less fatalistic than Spanish-dominant and bilingual Latinos.[103]

The importance of Latino roots and cultural practices to U.S. Hispanics has had an unexpected impact on non-Hispanic Americans and American mainstream culture. This "Hispanization" of American culture means that Latino celebrities, sports stars, actors, music, and musicians have "crossover" appeal to non-Hispanic Americans.[104] These people and trends symbolize the "American dream" and give Latinos their own niche in American popular culture. This fusion of cultures is energizing the expression of *latinidad* by U.S. Latinos. A perfect example of this trend, salsa, has become the favorite condiment of American diners!

Family, Church, and Language Preferences Express Hispanic Cultural Values

U.S. Latinos may be becoming English-dominant among the second and third generations, but certain Latino cultural values remain central to Latino lifestyles. The family and the Church (primarily the Roman Catholic Church) continue to be the center of U.S. Latino social life and calendars. Spanish retention symbolizes strong Hispanic ethnic identity for individuals. These three important cultural institutions anchor many of the values so important to U.S. Latinos.

The Hispanic Family

The Hispanic family differs from an Anglo-American one. Men and women play more traditional roles within the family, and many households include extended family members. Children in Latino families are "expected to be dependent for as long as possible, and therefore they are not asked to act independently until they reach maturity."[105] To a Hispanic mother, a "healthy" baby is chubby, has rosy cheeks, wears shoes or socks, and looks at his mother's eyes, not at the camera. In the same study, non-Hispanic mothers thought that barefoot babies, dressed in diapers or light shirts, who looked all around were "healthy."[106]

Research on Mexican-American families emphasizes the continuing importance of lifecycle rituals (e.g., ceremonies relating to birth, marriage, and death) as markers for stages in Latino life in the United States, regardless of social class.[107] The rituals of baptism, confirmation, *quinceañera* (a ceremony that takes place when a girl turns fifteen years old), marriage, and funerals unite family and religion in the expression of ethnicity. Religion is important in these lifecycle rituals, but traditions are so rooted in communal and ethnic origins that they operate as expressions of ethnicity as much as religious commitments.[108] The celebration of *Las Posadas* (a nine-day celebration) at Christmas or altars in the home for patron saints represent cultural traditions as much as religious fervor.

"New" traditions in Mexican-American culture are distinct from those in Mexico.[109] A good example is the *quinceañera,* an event that celebrates the passage of a young girl into womanhood, her commitment to Catholicism, and her debut in society. The Catholic ritual has a Mexican heritage, but it has been adapted to the American Latino environment. A *quinceañera* in Mexican America is a more social event and may or may not have a religious component.

Another example of the "culture of adaptation" is how Latin American cuisines have been reinvented for the American environment.[110] *Nuevo Latino* is a cross-cultural version of traditional Latin dishes offered by upscale restaurants to cosmopolitan diners. Salsas are now offered in varying levels of spiciness to give diners a choice as to whether they do or do not want the flavor without the heat. Packaged goods companies are substituting convenience for older ways of preparing traditional dishes (e.g., instant Spanish rice, canned refried beans, and ready-to-eat flan), and this has added to their popularity with all Americans.[111]

Other traditional celebrations like the Day of the Dead and Cinco de Mayo have also found their way onto the U.S. Latino calendar.[112] While the extended family may be disappearing from the routines of daily life in Hispanic households, extended family members are still important participants in lifecycle rituals of Hispanic families. In advertising for a car dealer in south Texas, even a beloved nanny is considered "family"; she serves as the ultimate trustworthy source for Mexican-American car buyers.[113] The fiestas that celebrate cultural rituals communicate and reinforce Latino identity. The examples here illustrate Mexican-American customs, but all U.S. Latino country-of-origin groups have home country rituals that have been extended or adapted to their American environment.

In many ways, U.S. Latinos are traditional and conservative Americans.[114] While many Latinas work outside the home, they are still the center of home life. Because adults remain close to their families, they consult with their parents about many decisions. The U.S. Army learned that the best way to attract Hispanic recruits was to talk to their mothers, to de-emphasize distances from home or dangerous jobs, and to emphasize the career benefits of Army life.[115] Parents see the rigors of immigration as worthwhile if their children are able to access the education they could not in their home country. By 2004, 23 percent of third-generation Mexican Americans had completed college; this is the realization of that Latino "American dream" for a better life.[116]

Today many younger Hispanic women seek success outside their homes at the same time that they continue to take pride in their homemaking skills.[117] This deviation from the traditional role of women generates tension with older generations who fear that their daughters and granddaughters will lose their *latinidad*. These young women can find that they are too *latina* in the workplace and too *gringa* at home, leaving them searching for how to define themselves and what path they should take. Successful Latinas such as Sofía Vergara, Selena Gomez, Supreme Court Justice Sonia Sotomayor, and Jennifer Lopez provide important role models.

Table 4.6 contrasts cultural values of U.S. Latinos and those of mainstream America. For the most traditional Hispanics, husbands continue to dominate family decision making for some products and services, but roles are becoming blurred as Hispanic women's income approaches that of their spouse. Care of the home is still considered a female responsibility in most Latino households.[118]

The three institutions of family, religion, and language are cultural points of comparison with those found in mainstream American culture. For example, family is important in both cultures, but non-Hispanic parents encourage their children to become independent and to go out "on their own" as soon as they can. Latino parents encourage close family ties and obligations.[119] The importance of good relationships in Latino culture is linked to the concept of *personalismo*. This value often translates as a Hispanic preference for familiar people and institutions and a distinctive set of behaviors and obligations to insiders versus outsiders. It also highlights the indirect versus direct styles of Spanish and English communication. In English one might say, "Don't do business with your friends," while in Spanish the rule is "Only do business with your friends." Many companies describe their workforce in Spanish as

Table 4.6

A Comparison of American Mainstream and Hispanic Cultural Values

Cultural values	U.S. Latino subculture	American mainstream culture
The Family		
Children	Dependence	Independence
Parents	Authoritarian, mother is nurturer	Egalitarian, mother is nurturer
Family roles	Gender-specific, defined	Diffused
Success		
Shared as a family	Belongs to the individual	
Religion		
Structure	Hierarchical	Egalitarian
Domain	Physical/spiritual/philosophical/daily	Spiritual
Role prescriptions	Defined	Diffused
Role differentiation	Male-dominant	Egalitarian
Language		
Structure	Indirect communication: "It is believed . . ."	Direct communication: " I think . . . "
Nouns	Feminine or masculine	Assigned genders only for living beings
Verbs/pronouns	Dependent on relationships, directs attention to hierarchies	Independent of relationships, egalitarian
Equivalent meaning	More wordy	Less wordy
Nonverbal information	High context, important to interpretation of words	Low context
Worldviews		
Man and nature	Humans dominant over nature	Humans dominant over nature
Science and technology	Random events can disrupt objectivity, adapt to the environment	Events have discoverable causes
Human nature	Man can be good or evil, less subject to change; faith and idealism important	Man is born evil but with potential to be good via self-discipline
Materialism	Possessions express individual style and God's will	Possessions are measure of worth and identity

Time and Activity

Work	"Work to live," to keep what you have, makes the fiesta possible	"Live to work," money is the reward
Efficiency	Longer time horizons	Short-term over long-term goals
Progress and change	Traditions are important, adapt rather than change, more fatalistic	Change is good, new is better than old, future orientation
Time orientation	More to the present and past	Time is resource and must be managed, future orientation
Expectations	More pessimistic, "suffer with dignity"	More optimistic, "create and change the world"
Uncertainty	Avoid risk-taking	Take risks
Motivations	Opportunistic, interdependence	Set and pursue own goals, competitive

Relationships with others

Physical distance	Physical closeness important	More space important
Social hierarchy	Status predetermined, accept your place	Status based on behaviors
Treatment of superiors	Respect	Minimize differences
Conformity	Simpatía, "go along to get along"	Tolerance of deviance
Dealing with conflict	Preservation of relationships more important than solving conflict, passive resistance	Attempt to solve conflict directly
Self-revelation	Reluctant to disclose, makes individual vulnerable, males more reluctant than females	More open, males more reluctant than females
Loyalties	Family, extended family, then in-group, strangers last	Arm's length
Dealing with criticism	Highly sensitive	
Nonverbal communication	Significant part of communication with others	Not as important to effective communication
Leadership style	Responsible for sharing resources and protection	Responsibilities negotiated with followers

Sources: G. Althen, *American Ways: A Guide for Foreigners in the United States* (Yarmouth, ME: Intercultural Press, 1988); N. Carr-Ruffino, *Managing Diversity: People Skills for a Multicultural Workplace* (Cincinnati: South-Western, 1996); J. Hammond and J. Morrison, *The Stuff Americans Are Made Of* (New York: Macmillan, 1996); F.E. Jandt, *Intercultural Communication: An Introduction* (Thousand Oaks, CA: Sage, 1995); E.C. Steward and M.J. Bennett, *American Cultural Patterns*, rev. ed. (Yarmouth, ME: Intercultural Press, 1991); M.I. Valdes and M.H. Seoane, *Hispanic Market Handbook* (New York: Gale Research, 1995); H. Valencia, "Hispanic Values and Subcultural Research," *Journal of the Academy of Marketing Science* 17, no. 1 (1989): 23–29.

a "family" and customers as part of their extended "family." "Being well known," within the context of Spanish values, means "trustworthy."

Adherence to religion, as it is practiced among U.S. Hispanic Catholics, shows acceptance of hierarchy and the status quo. Recently, more U.S. Hispanics have been drawn to new, evangelical denominations, such as the Pentecostals and Jehovah's Witnesses. Wherever formal religious practices take place, the Latino tradition blends spiritual, physical, philosophical, and daily life.

Values in the Spanish Language

Spanish is a high-context language, in which pronoun use depends on relationships and all nouns have an ascribed masculine or feminine gender. These "norms" for interaction are in place, even when Latinos do not speak Spanish. Language is the ultimate "mirror" of cultural values, yet those values can persist in the absence of the original language. Budweiser, in keeping with its positioning as the "King of Beers" in the United States, uses the respectful *usted* to address Budweiser consumers, while Miller appeals to U.S. Hispanics with a more intimate *tu*. Such distinctions in Spanish pronouns for "you" reflect the importance of relative status between speaker and audience. A greater appreciation for and sensitivity to interpersonal status are important values in the U.S. Hispanic subculture, even for Latinos who are not fluent in the Spanish language.

Spanish is the language of the Latino's "heart and soul." The language structure itself expresses emotion and masculinity-femininity in ways that English does not. And whether in English, Spanish, or Spanglish, U.S. Latinos speak more indirectly and are more likely to say what they think someone else wants to hear.[120] Their sensitivity to criticism and frequent use of nonverbal signals to express respect or disgust mean that the language is only one of the ways in which their communication patterns are distinct from those of non-Hispanic Americans.[121]

The values of U.S. Latinos regardless of income level are more "middle class" and conservative than those of comparable non-Latino Americans.[122] This conservatism is evident in the reluctance of many U.S. Latinos to use credit cards and financial services.[123] These patterns of product usage may have evolved from experiences in Latin American countries of origin, where distrust of those institutions was based on personal experience. Many consumer decisions are undoubtedly affected by these risk-averse behaviors: a preference for familiar or well-known brands, word of mouth as an important source of product information and endorsement, and reluctance to complain.[124] Brand "bloc" buying, the informal endorsement of brands by Latino community persons and institutions, is an example of how immigrant consumers reduce purchasing risk in the U.S. marketplace.[125]

The more traditional gender roles of Latino families mean that females are more immersed in the ethnic culture than males are.[126] They are responsible for passing along religious traditions and the Spanish language. Male dominance in decision making is most apparent for expensive decisions, but is tempered by the economic contributions of the partners, especially among middle- and upper-class households.[127]

One important aspect of Hispanic culture is viewing interpersonal relationships within the context of an authoritarian social structure.[128] People who are at the top have more power than those at the bottom, but it is important to preserve good relations with all members. In case of conflict, passive resistance is preferred over direct confrontation. *Simpatía* means keeping everyone happy, even when the news may not be so good. In some cases, this will mean just letting some things be because it is impossible to predict the future. A Spanish phrase that expresses this is "Si Dios quiere" (If God so wills). This fatalistic approach to life has been used to explain the reluctance of some Latinos to set goals and engage in planning.[129] In the consumer realm, this means fewer Hispanics than non-Hispanics take a shopping list to the supermarket.

A print ad for Benson and Hedges cigarettes from many years ago illustrates how meanings can change when words are translated from English to Spanish. The ad shows two "cigarette people" relaxing in a swing on the front porch. In Latin American countries, houses are not open to the street, so there is no tradition of couples sharing the day's events in front of the house. The "cigarette people" in Spanish could even be members of the same sex, because there are no obvious clothing or size or other points of differentiation in the picture. Even the slogan is softer in English ("A moment of pleasure with a 100 mm cigarette") than in Spanish ("The most pleasurable moments are with a 100 mm cigarette").

Cultural values rather than race are at the heart of the U.S. Latino as a consumer. This does not mean there are no prejudices for and against lighter or darker skin, hair color, hair texture, hairiness, and physical size. These physical characteristics vary across Latino country-of-origin groups and thus call for specific research when an advertiser is choosing actors or actresses to represent "typical" members of a target market within the U.S. Latino community.

Latino Sources of Marketplace Information and Media Habits and Availability

The Frito Bandito was "a mustachioed Mexican bandit with six-gun, broad sombrero, and a sinister smile who took Fritos corn chips from unsuspecting mothers."[130] The Frito Bandito was the first Hispanic to be *visible* in main-stream American advertising. The negative associations that he symbolized sparked the first resistance of U.S. Latinos to the ways in which they have been represented, or misrepresented, in American media. Other images in film, literature, comic books, radio, and TV programs have stereotyped Hispanics as lazy (in a sombrero, sleeping midday beside a cactus), as immigrants unable to speak English properly, as professionals festooned in traditional costumes,[131] and as quick-tempered male lovers and oversexed and manipulative female spitfires (Chiquita banana).[132]

These images have damaged all Americans' understanding of Latino culture. However, it is the invisibility of Latinos in the mainstream media that undermines their contributions to American life.[133] In a 2010 study, only 5 percent of all actors on television were Latino, and half of all Hispanic roles depicted someone involved in criminal activities.[134] The act of inserting minorities or minority celebrities in digital advertising offends many Latinos as lacking authenticity.[135] One critic says: "Television tells children where they are in society. If you're not on TV, you're not important."[136]

Advertising in Spanish- and English-Language Media

The growth of Spanish-language media since the 1970s has been nothing short of phenomenal. In 2012 all television advertising was up 8 percent from the prior year, but Spanish-language television spending was up 15 percent.[137] The top ten advertisers in Spanish-language media spent over $1.4 trillion in 2011, only about 25 percent of total spending in Hispanic media by all advertisers.[138] The number of Spanish-language radio stations increased in 2010, and more Spanish-language radio companies are now measured for Arbitron, the standard radio station rating method.[139] The number of Hispanic newspapers is about the same as a decade ago, and Hispanic-targeted magazines are one of the few areas of growth in consumer magazines.[140] Bottom line: traditional media are doing great in the Spanish language!

At the same time that Spanish-language media are prospering, Latinos are tuning into more English-language media. In 2011, the number of "Spanish-dependent" Hispanics was about 20 percent and the number of "English-dependent" Latinos was around 22 percent. The real change was in the bilingual group; 27 percent of them prefer using English-language media, 18 percent prefer Spanish, and 13 percent are truly bilingual.

The differences in language preference in media across Hispanic populations in different American cities are significant. For example, of all the majority Latino cities, Miami has the smallest English-dependent and largest Spanish-dependent and Spanish-preferred percentages of its Latino population.

In contrast, Los Angeles and Chicago also have large Spanish-dependent and Spanish-preferred populations, but they also have large English-dependent and English-preferred Hispanics. New York and Houston have more balance across language preferences.[141] This trend toward more consumption of English-language media will only speed up as immigration slows down and that growth is replaced by growth among second-, third-, and fourth-generation U.S. Hispanics.

Independent researchers claim that advertising in Spanish is 40 percent more effective in increasing awareness levels than commercials in English, among both Spanish-dominant and bilingual viewers of television.[142] Not only is it more persuasive, but Spanish-language advertising increases consumers' perceptions that advertisers are sensitive to Hispanic culture and peoples.[143]

Hispanics are early adopters of new and mobile media, but they still spend more time with television and radio than general market audiences do. Almost a quarter of Hispanics who speak English mostly at home watch between one and three hours of Spanish-language TV a day, and among those who mostly speak Spanish at home, 40 percent watch one to three hours of Spanish-language TV a day. Arbitron's *Hispanic Radio Today 2010* reports that radio's overall reach among Hispanic consumers has remained constant at 94–96 percent since Arbitron began including Hispanic radio stations in 2001. Regardless of whether language preference is Spanish-dominant or English-dominant, radio reaches at least 91 percent of Hispanic men and women in all age categories under the age of 65.[144]

Since spoken Spanish continues to have higher rates of fluency among U.S. Latinos than written Spanish, it is not surprising that radio is such a dynamic medium among Spanish-language media. There is a long tradition in Latin America of radio as a medium for learning how to adapt to a new environment while keeping in touch with immigrant roots.[145] Spanish-language radio today offers a broader music mix and bilingual content.[146] Latino men spend more time with radio than women, with the exception of teens, and the audience peaks at 45 to 54 years old and almost 18 hours listening to radio per week.[147] The most popular formats are regional Mexican, adult contemporary, top 40, and tropical music. Pandora and iHeart Radio, both Internet stations, offer additional options for Spanish-language listeners, as do country-of-origin online stations. Table 4.7 shows the top radio and television markets in Spanish.

The major Spanish-language television networks are Univision, TeleFutura, Galavision (all owned by Univision), Telemundo/Mun2, and Azteca América. Telemundo can be received in over 200 U.S. markets and has transformed its programming from Latin American imports to content created specifically for American Latinos. Univision and its sister station, TeleFutura, attract the most viewers and advertising revenue although its programming draws heavily from

Table 4.7

Top Radio and Television Markets in Spanish

Market area for Spanish TV	Rank for Hispanics	Hispanic TV households	Total TV households	Hispanic % of all households
Los Angeles	1	1,893,810	5,666,900	33.4
New York	2	1,276,130	7,515,330	17.0
Miami–Ft. Lauderdale	3	690,640	1,580,580	43.7
Houston	4	586,120	2,177,220	26.9
Dallas–Ft. Worth	5	526,760	2,594,630	20.3

Radio markets	Hispanic market rank	Overall market rank	Top Spanish stations	Avg. listeners per ¼ hour
Los Angeles	1	2	KLVE-FM	43,500
			KSCA-FM	36,200
			KXOL-FM	
New York	2	1	WSKQ-FM	55,900
			KPAT-FM	40,200
			WXNY-FM	38,200
Miami–Ft. Lauderdale–Hollywood	3	12	WAQI-AM	
			WMGE-FM	
			WCMQ-FM	
Houston–Galveston	4	6	KLTN-FM	
			KGOL-AM	
			KLOL-FM	
Chicago	5	8	WOJO-FM	
		9	WLEY-FM	

Sources: Ad Age Data Center, *Hispanic Fact Pack* (New York: Advertising Age, 2011). Reproduced by permission of Advertising Age. Copyright Crain Communication Co.; G. Otteson, "The State of Spanish Language Media Industries: A Summary of Spanish Language Radio 2011," in *The State of Spanish Language Media: 2011 Annual Report*, comp. Center for Spanish Language Media staff (Denton: University of North Texas, February 2012), 1–8; J. Perrillat, "Spanish Language Television," In Ibid., 9–22. Reproduced by permission of the University of North Texas.

its Mexican affiliate, Televisa. Other affiliated stations in Spanish belong to Azteca America, AméricaTeVe, Estrella TV, and MegaTV and LATV. Cable adds other options in Spanish, such as FoxDeportes, ESPN Deportes, CNN en español, and Nicklelodeon.[148] Since most of these media have multiple platforms available, they invite advertisers to create interactive marketing programs.

In several cities, the radio and television stations with the largest audiences are in Spanish, confirming their effectiveness in covering Latino populations in those cities.[149] Univision has beat the "big four" networks since 2005 with young audiences 18 to 34 years old, yet Univision still does not match their advertising revenues.[150] Ultimately, large audiences for programs such as the premiere of Univision's *Eva Luna* will attract advertisers. In 2010, the series attracted 3.3 million total viewers and 1.8 million adults 18 to 49 years old.

Since the 1990s, Nielsen and Univision have developed systems for counting Hispanic audiences in both Spanish- and English-language media. It is now easier for agencies and clients to estimate reach for Hispanic audiences in both languages. Other problems in U.S. Latino audience measurement and in researching U.S. Latinos have not been resolved. For example, the low home telephone ownership, large quantity of unlisted numbers, low response rates, and Latino cultural tendency to please the researcher reduce the reliability of media audience and market research measurements. With mail surveys, researchers must confront illiteracy, especially in English. It can be difficult to determine a correct dialect of Spanish for interviews. Personal interviews in Hispanic neighborhoods face a higher number of not-at-homes. Most research firms with experience in Latino communities have developed methods for improving reliability and overcoming these barriers to useful data.[151]

American cities with significant Latino populations have multiple Spanish or bilingual television channels, radio stations, and community newspapers. At the same time, mainstream media have learned to court members of the Hispanic market with more culturally sensitive programs in English. The key issues in designing a media program to communicate with Hispanics nationally have become focused on the balance between English- and Spanish-language media and the significant differences in media habits found across geographic locations and age groups.

Table 4.8 reports consumption of English- and Spanish-language media among U.S. Latinos by generation. The first generation of U.S. Latinos uses Spanish at home and mostly Spanish outside the home. They also prefer to read, watch TV, and, to a lesser extent, seek Spanish content online. The second generation speaks mostly English at home and outside the home and looks for English reading material, TV programming, and online sites. The strongest preference for English is with the third generation, only 8 percent of which speak "predominantly Spanish" when at home. While these data suggest that the future will be tilted toward English-speaking U.S. Latinos, Spanish may continue to signify Hispanic pride.

Another trend in media that target U.S. Hispanics are the bilingual and crossover media that afford non-Spanish speakers and non-Hispanics more access to Hispanic-related news and information. CNN's Spanish-language news reports are one example of this programming. Spanish-language television programming mirrors Latin American programming more than North American TV. For example, the largest audiences are for shows like *Sabado Gigante, Siempre en Domingo, Noticiero Univision,* and *Primavera.* Telenovelas and game and talk shows dominate the programming that originates from Mexico and most DVD rentals.[152] The major Spanish-language networks now have programs such as *Ugly Betty,* set in the United States.[153]

The strongest argument for Spanish-language TV advertising is the more than 75 percent of Hispanics who prefer to speak Spanish at home. Florida, New York, and New Jersey have the highest percentage of Latinos who speak Spanish at home—over 85 percent—while Arizona, New Mexico, and Colorado have the lowest percentages. San Antonio and New York are cities where the majority of Latinos consider themselves bilingual.[154] The introduction of Nielsen's Hispanic Family Panel and better measurement of Spanish-language audiences serve as stimuli for even more advertisers to enter the growing U.S. Latino market.

Spanish-language newspapers have a long history in communities such as Miami, San Antonio, New York, and Los Angeles. The number of Spanish-language newspapers—over 25 dailies, 428 weeklies, and 378 less-than-weekly papers—has remained stable, but their circulation and advertising revenue have declined substantially since 2008.[155] More recently, mainstream papers have introduced their own Spanish-language versions. *Nuestro Tiempo* is the *Los Angeles Times*'s Spanish-language medium, and *El Heraldo* is the *Miami Herald*'s entry.[156] In the long term, the newspapers that can follow their readers online will be best positioned for a future in either English or Spanish.[157]

Large majorities of U.S. Latinos say that they prefer to read in English. However, during the Great Recession of 2008–11, many of these Latino-targeted magazines in English folded. The largest magazine readerships are now for vehicles in Spanish: *People en Español, Latina* (English), *Ser Padres, TV y Novelas, Vanidades*, and *Siempre Mujer*. The top products advertised in these magazines are cosmetics, autos, hair care, food, household supplies, skincare, and department stores.[158] Cubans in Miami, who have higher education levels overall, are greater readers of both magazines and newspapers than Hispanics from other countries of origin.

The English-language media for U.S. Hispanics are not just mainstream

Table 4.8

U.S. Latino Media Consumption by Language, Medium, and Generation
(in percent)

Responses (% of total)	All Hispanics	Generation 1	Generation 2	Generation 3
Language spoken in the home by adults				
Only English	14	3	15	47
Mostly English but some Spanish	21	11	34	34
Mostly Spanish but some English	30	42	22	6
Only Spanish	17	28	4	1
Both English and Spanish equally	16	15	24	11
Predominantly English	35	14	49	81
Predominantly Spanish	48	70	26	8
Language spoken outside the home by adults				
Only English	20	8	22	53
Mostly English but some Spanish	37	32	53	35
Mostly Spanish but some English	21	32	8	5
Only Spanish	12	19	1	1
Both English and Spanish equally	9	8	15	6
Language preferred for speaking				
Only English	20	5	56	82
Mostly English but some Spanish	30	20	35	14
Mostly Spanish but some English	27	38	16	8
Only Spanish	22	36	4	3
Language preferred when reading				
Only English	37	13	56	82
Mostly English but some Spanish	22	20	35	14
Mostly Spanish but some English	18	29	6	3
Only Spanish	22	37	3	1
Language preferred when watching TV				
Only English	31	12	43	69
Mostly English but some Spanish	32	29	44	24
Mostly Spanish but some English	23	35	11	5
Only Spanish	14	23	2	2
Language preferred when online				
Only English	50	26	73	87
Mostly English but some Spanish	20	23	22	10
Mostly Spanish but some English	14	22	5	2
Only Spanish	15	28	<1	<1

Source: Ad Age Data Center, *Hispanic Fact Pack* (New York: Ad Age, July 22, 2012), 42. Reproduced by permission of *Advertising Age*. Copyright: Crain Communication Co.

vehicles with the same advertisements and content. Publishers and advertising agencies that place ads in these media advise their clients to "picture their products with Latino foods, celebrities, cultural events, community events, and family traditions, . . . and to adapt the product to make it appear to be a part of the Latino lifestyle in the United States."[159] Both English- and Spanish-language media are important members of the Latino community in the United States. While Spanish continues to play an important role in Latino lifestyles, English is becoming the primary language of artistic and intellectual expression.[160] New advertisers in the Hispanic market responded to the 2010 Census data, boosting revenues for all Hispanic-targeted media.

For companies whose products sell well with direct response advertising, call centers in Spanish, such as provided by CallZilla, reach Spanish-speaking Hispanics. Direct response is now fourth (after television, radio, and print) in Hispanic media spending overall. One direct response brand, "Sin Barreras," has some of the highest recall numbers of any brand marketed to Hispanics.[161] Since U.S. Latinos receive less mail in general, direct mail pieces in Spanish encounter less clutter.[162] In cities such as Miami, New York, San Antonio, and Los Angeles, yellow page publishers have also found a niche among Spanish-language media. The *Paquinas Amarillas en Espanol de Texas* and Houston's *Spanish Telephone Directory*'s 3,700 advertisers list Hispanic and Anglo-owned firms catering to Hispanic buyers.

Billboards in heavily Latino neighborhoods represent a medium that reaches Spanish-dominant Hispanics. Billboards are excellent vehicles for reaching young Hispanics who have low involvement levels while consuming Spanish-language broadcast media.[163] In addition to using billboards, some advertisers are placing televisions in retail stores in heavily Hispanic neighborhoods to reach buyers while they are shopping.

Overall, in 2011 more than $7 billion was spent in Hispanic media, with almost $5 billion going to television. About $400 million was spent in online media to reach Hispanic consumers.[164] The ten largest advertisers in the Hispanic market in 2011 were Procter and Gamble ($220 million), Dish Network ($155 million), Verizon ($115 million), McDonald's ($114 million), AT&T ($110 million), General Mills ($97 million), Broadcast Media Partners ($87 million), Toyota ($86 million), Kraft ($83 million), and General Motors ($79 million).[165]

Latinos Online

U.S. Latinos and African Americans are the early adopters in wireless phone services, use of smartphones, and use of interactive mobile media. Latinos spend more on cell-phone service per capita than any other major U.S. ethnic group.[166] And they are very talkative: "It takes 30 percent more time to say the same thing in Spanish as in English."[167]

Hispanics online are younger and even Spanish-dominant audiences tend to prefer English content. Entertainment, user-generated content, and social networking are the most popular sites for U.S. Latinos.[168] These preferred activities online are shown in Table 4.9 in comparison with activities by non-Hispanic whites, blacks, and Asian Americans. All three minority groups overindex on cell-phone usage. Asian Americans are more likely to have iPhones, while Hispanics and African Americans are more likely to have Android phones. Talking, texting, and visiting websites are the most popular activities for all groups, but the importance of the cell phone for accessing the Internet is most apparent for Hispanics and blacks. Non-Hispanic whites are the most active online, but social media attract the three minority groups. Facebook and Twitter appear to be most popular with Hispanics and blacks, and YouTube appeals most strongly to African Americans. It has been suggested that U.S. Latinos find the interactive aspects of these sites most appealing.[169]

Online research is the "first stop" when Latinos are buying electronics, cell phones, digital cameras, and related merchandise. Some research suggests that U.S. Hispanics are more receptive to online advertising than non-Hispanic audiences. In 2011 Hispanic consumers online grew 7.2 percent and were projected to remain the fastest-growing segment online for the next five years. Hispanics also spend more per online transaction than non-Hispanics.[170] Companies such as Movida are able to attract immigrants who have special needs for international calling and prepaid services that do not require credit checks.[171] Some analysts call the Internet the "ultimate border-less Hispanic market" and the largest in this hemisphere.[172]

Much online advertising targets second- and third-generation Latinos, even though their bilingual and bicultural habits make them harder to understand than the Spanish-dominant Latinos. For them, it is more important to have a culturally nuanced appeal, in the form of "family, food, and music, or gestures such as greeting each other with hugs and kisses," than what language the ad is using.[173] Hispanics in general spend more time online than general market consumers, listening to music, watching video clips, and visiting other web-based entertainment sites.[174] The only factors that seem to be holding Hispanics back from more frequent use of online devices and content is their lower education and income levels.[175] A major barrier that all e-commerce participants must overcome is the lower ownership of credit cards, stock portfolios, or financial advice sought online.[176]

The English-versus-Spanish argument continues unabated. Perhaps the best answer to this dilemma depends on which of the country of origin, age,

Table 4.9

Cell Phone and Online Activities of Different Ethnic Groups

		Total sample	Hispanic	Non-Hispanic white	Non-Hispanic black	Non-Hispanic Asian	
N =		12,333	4,062	6,757	922	362	
Activities with cell phone							
Smartphone user	Yes	51.0%	8.0%	33.4%	6.0%	2.9%	
		(100)	(104)	(98)	(102)	(120)	
iPhone	Yes	11.8%	1.4%	8.5%	0.7%	0.9%	
		(100)	(80)	(108)	(54)	(161)	
Android phone	Yes	18.0%	3.4%	11.1%	2.5%	*	
		(100)	(124)	(92)	(122)		
"To talk"	Very often	10.6%	2.4%	5.3%	2.4%	*	
		(100)	(151)	75	(200)		
	Not at all	42.9%	5.6%	30.8%	4.0%	1.9%	
		(100)	(86)	(107)	(81)	(95)	
"To text"	Very often	12.5%	2.6%	7.2%	2.1%	*	
		(100)	(137)	(85)	(149)		
	Not at all	24.9%	3.0%	18.2%	2.3%	1.2%	
		(100)	(78)	(109)	(80)	(99)	
"To visit websites"	Very often	5.8%	1.3%	3.2%	1.0%	*	
		(100)	(146)	(82)	(149)		
	Not at all	36.0%	4.5%	26.3%	3.3%	1.4%	
		(100)	(82)	(109)	(80)	(85)	
Active Online	Yes	86.1%	12.0%	59.1%	9.2%	4.4%	1.4%
		(100)	(92)	(102)	(93)	(110)	(102)
Social media user		67.1%	9.7%	45.6%	6.9%	3.7%	1.2%
		(100)	(96)	(101)	(89)	(119)	(109)
Facebook		48.8%	6.4%	34.4%	4.8%	2.4%	0.7%
		(100)	(87)	(105)	(86)	(107)	(95)
MySpace		3.0%	0.5%	1.8%	*	*	*
		(100)	(112)	(90)			
Twitter		7.2%	1.1%	4.6%	1.1%	*	*
		(100)	(104)	(97)	(138)		
LinkedIn		6.3%	0.4%	4.6%	0.7%	*	*
		(100)	(45)	(108)	(99)		
YouTube		37.4%	6.0%	24.2%	3.8%	2.8%	0.5%
		(100)	(107)	(97)	(89)	(157)	(88)

Source: Experian Information Solutions, Summer 2012 NHCS Adult Study database, www.experian.com/simmons-research/consumer-study.html.
* Indicates too few observations in that cell to be reliable.

or generational groups are the best target market for a firm's products. A recent survey of Spanish-speakers-at-home found that 46 percent said they were influenced by a Spanish-language television advertisement to make a purchase within the previous month, and 23 percent reported influence from an English-language TV ad.[177] Whether in English or Spanish, programming and market communications should recognize Hispanic lifestyles, leaders, and celebrities in American culture.

Sponsorship of events is another avenue for reaching Hispanics. As African-American attendance at baseball games has declined, Spanish-language web-sites and merchandise for American teams have begun to attract new Latino fans to watch games at stadiums.[178] Cinco de Mayo was originally a Mexican celebration of victory over an invading French army, but it has now become a "pan-Hispanic" symbol of pride in the United States. Major marketers such as McDonald's, Domino's, Hallmark, and Chrysler as well as Mexican brands such as Corona beer and Jose Cuervo Tequila feature campaigns centered on this holiday: "It's an American, not a Mexican, holiday now."[179] The link to Mexican history is less well known than the party atmosphere.

Product placement in sports and other programming is also a valuable investment. For example, Budweiser created *Republica Deportiva*, a sports-news program set in a bar where Bud signs and beers were everywhere.[180] In 2006, Walmart made a smart move by sponsoring World Cup soccer broadcasts and showing the games in stores all over Latin America and in Hispanic-dominant areas of the United States. The World Cup is the world's most-watched sporting event. Walmart stocked up on team-related merchandise, hosted soccer contests where winners were sent to the final games, and even had special foods linked to the countries whose teams made it to the finals. U.S. stores hosted soccer instruction, imprinted soccer balls with the Mexican team's logo, and placed ads on Spanish-language networks that broadcast the games. Clearly the target audience was the 65 percent-plus of Hispanics with Mexican origins.[181]

Early ads to Hispanic audiences tended to be serious and earnest. More recent ads use the same techniques that capture attention from general-market audiences: pranks, edgy humor, and slapstick.[182] Even after the entertainment value of online advertising was enhanced, Hispanics claim that they do not see themselves. Their biggest criticism of online advertising is that it lacks authenticity, especially when ethnic minorities are shown.[183] Even programs developed in English for the U.S. Latino audiences too often base their characters on stereotypes.[184]

Relationships with Hispanic community institutions help Hispanic consumers to see a firm as a member of the extended Hispanic community. It is also a way to keep in touch with what is important to members of that community: "It's not about a transaction with the Hispanic community; it's about a relationship."[185]

Ethnic-oriented media depend on advertising support and thus promote themselves as the best way to reach a group such as U.S. Latinos. Their doing so has been criticized by Latino activists, who believe the media interest in the community is purely exploitative. Their position and ambivalence about advertiser attention to ethnic-minority markets can be summarized as: "Black and Spanish-language media will benefit from the advertising dollars of national corporations only as long as dollars are the most cost-effective way for advertisers to persuade Blacks and Latinos to use their products.[186]

Because U.S. Latinos comprise a growing proportion of the population and have a higher birthrate than other ethnicities, in addition to the continuing high immigration rate, media investment in the U.S. Hispanic market is an investment in the future. U.S. Latinos have become technological-, fashion-, and pop culture leaders. As a result, some marketers are beginning to hire Hispanic ad agencies to do all their advertising. Heinz hired LatinWorks to adapt its Hispanic campaign for the general market, Mars is using it to target all teens for Skittles, and the Texas Lottery hires it for its entire advertising account.[187]

Search Strategies and Buying Preferences of Latino Consumers

The symbolic value to U.S. Latinos of buying and owning products can be summarized as: "The American Dream begins with an education and ends with a good-paying job. Educating oneself and working means money, a home, a car, vacations, entertainment, health care and a secure retirement. The Hispanic Dream should be the same."[188] Owning the same kinds of goods and services as other Americans means being "American." Because their purchasing power is growing and is projected to exceed $1.5 trillion in 2015, U.S. Latinos are essential to success in the American consumer market.

Most U.S. Hispanics are proud of their Latino heritage yet at the same time express that they want to be recognized as Americans. These symbolic roles may seem to be in conflict, but both are the essence of what makes U.S. Hispanic buyer behavior unique. Latino mothers look for and purchase the "best" products for their families. P&G's sampling programs for Pampers include lists of undocumented immigrants, and Pampers has gained 25 percent market share at the expense of Huggies, Mexico's number one brand. Fifty-seven percent of Hispanic consumers are "avid scent seekers," compared with 31 percent of the general market. After learning about these preferences, P&G developed several scents for the Latino market for its Gain detergent. P&G

recognizes that some of its products, such as Bounty paper towels, are new to U.S. Hispanics, so, it makes a special effort to introduce them. In addition to offering free samples and coupons, P&G's magazine *Avanzando con tu familia* is full of recipes and other advice about American lifestyles.[189]

Two product categories with heavier consumption than would be predicted by a position on a continuum between Latin American product use patterns and those of non-Hispanic-Americans, are meat and laundry and cleaning products.[190] Heavy consumption by U.S. Latinos in these categories cannot be explained by assimilation into mainstream America or socioeconomic status. They are examples of the often unexplained differences in Hispanic and non-Hispanic consumption preferences. Other examples follow. U.S. Hispanics are heavy consumers of movies (Hispanics comprise 24 percent of movie audiences),[191] light beer, cosmetics, children's clothing, footwear, fresh fruits and vegetables, food at home, public transportation, and durable goods. The fastest-growing categories among U.S. Latino consumers are software, computers, office equipment, appliances, photo and audio equipment, and home mortgages.[192]

There is a long history of research that suggests the marketplace is an arena in which Latinos seek cultural reinforcement and familiarity.[193] At one point, P&G distributed its brands to 7,000 bodegas in New York, which account for half the groceries bought by Latinos in the city. When they shop in *bodegas* or small neighborhood stores, they can get "not just chorizo, but also gossip." Family and friends are major sources of information about stores, products, and brands. Hispanic consumers may choose to pay a premium for a company's products when the firm recognizes Hispanics' place among American subcultures. Hispanic cultural values emphasize relationships, and it follows that Hispanic consumers prefer familiar products and bands. U.S. Latinos also talk more than other consumers about advertisements that they have seen and are more positive about advertising in general.[194]

Language is not the only key to a positive attitude about a brand. The cultural nuances of communications must be "Hispanicized." The pitfalls of not doing so are well illustrated by an ad for a car phone company. The company merely translated its ad from English into Spanish and showed a man relaxing by his pool while he did business on the phone. Non-Hispanics got the message that having this phone gave them more leisure time, but Cuban Americans thought that the man in the ad was lazy and missed the point about higher work productivity.[195] In contrast, retailers like Sears and Target have found success by "Hispanicizing" their merchandise mix to become more culturally compatible with the neighborhoods in which they have stores.[196] Even a Tequila brand sold in the United States used a theme more in tune with its U.S. target market than with its true Mexican origins: "born in Mexico, raised in

Texas." Food companies such as Frito-Lay, Subway, and Gatorade have been "Hispanicizing" their product lines to appeal to U.S. Latino tastes.[197]

More and more U.S. Latinos have become opinion leaders in their consumption and media behaviors. They enjoy the authentic ethnic foods offered at many restaurants that cater to U.S. Latinos, but they also patronize the nontraditional ethnic cuisines as found in *Nuevo Latino* restaurants.[198] More Latin American companies are distributing brands well known in Latin America to U.S. buyers. One firm makes its rice-based *horchata*, tamarind juice, and hibiscus beverages in Mexico City but distributes them in the eastern United States. As one competitor puts it, "Hispanics living in the U.S. crave the brand names, flavors, and entertainers who remind them of home."[199]

Culture-bound attitudes can travel north even when the retailing environment is totally different in the United States. Many financial services would not have been available to low-income consumers in their countries of origin. Even illegal immigrants to the United States are able to acquire credit cards and home mortgages and have those loans secured by government agencies.[200] An even larger market opportunity is the over 27,000 Hispanic-owned businesses with revenue exceeding $1 million, and who will need financial advice as they take those companies public.[201]

Walmart is cited by U.S. Latinos as their favorite store: 61 percent of Hispanics shop at Walmart or Target more often than other stores.[202] In spite of Walmart's popularity for its everyday low prices, service is very important to Hispanics because it represents the relationship between consumers and providers. For Spanish-dependent consumers, Spanish-speaking employees and signage are essential. Hispanics tend to prefer personal attention, a lot of time for interacting with retail providers, respected and known sources of authority, prestige brands, and, in general, service over efficiency.[203] Even shopping malls are adapting their store and merchandise mixes to appeal more strongly to their Hispanic neighborhoods.[204]

There is also opportunity in bringing shopping environments to the United States that Hispanic consumers preferred in their home countries. H-E-B, a Texas grocery chain, has used its experience in Mexico to adapt its stores in Hispanic areas of the United States. It features store design with Mexican decorations, Spanish-speaking employees wearing Latino-style shirts, in-store restaurants that serve Mexican specialties, and merchandise layouts that look more like a Mexican village than a U.S. grocery store.[205] One underground supply chain brings bottles of Coca-Cola stamped "Hecho en Mexico" to stores in various areas of the United States, and they sell faster than bottles from U.S. bottling plants.[206]

A frequently repeated description of U.S. Latinos is that they tend to be brand loyal. Their preference for well-known brands, familiar within the

Hispanic community is well documented. One study found Hispanics to be more brand loyal to automotive brands than any other American subculture.[207] However, private-label products are challenging the major brands' dominant market share among Hispanics. Brands are an important expression of status and conspicuous consumption when U.S. Hispanics are socializing.[208]

What may seem confusing illustrates the importance of understanding cultural values rather than product behavior. What seemed to be loyalty to well-known brands may in fact have been lack of information about products in the marketplace and a preference for familiar brands. Goya, a well-known Puerto Rican food processor, had a 65 percent market share in categories where it competed in New York until U.S. firms like Del Monte began targeting New York Hispanics, too. Brand name is important to U.S. Latino shoppers as an indicator of quality, especially in unfamiliar situations or product categories.[209]

"Being the first" describes the underlying desire and need for status and respect of Hispanic consumers. That motivation is driving their use of new and mobile media. Both African Americans and Hispanics consider themselves "opinion leaders" in this regard. Marketers need to take advantage of this mindset and think beyond traditional ethnic consumer engagement platforms such as music and fashion. One example of this kind of tactic is how Kraft, Home Depot, and Wendy's came together to sponsor a contest on the Spanish-langue network Telemundo, allowing entrants to pick the ending of one of its telenovelas.[210]

How to best reach Hispanic teens is an important question for marketers whose eyes are on the future. While Latino teens live in Spanish at home and English outside the home, that does not mean they want mainstream companies to translate all their slogans and advertising into Spanish. English-language versions of "Got Milk?" were preferred over Spanish translations by Los Angeles' teens, who are proud of their Hispanic heritage and their fluency in American popular culture.[211] Inner-city Hispanics often share important trendsetting behaviors with African-American teens. Thus, some marketers use "urban" marketing tactics to reach them rather than "ethnic" ones. It is the biculturalism of Hispanic youth as well as their bilingualism that permit such flexibility in marketing.[212] Three key tactics have been used to build familiarity with Latino consumers: hiring practices, support of community events and goodwill, and aggressive sales promotions and celebrity advertising. Coca-Cola has used all of these. It has recruited U.S. Latino employees via Hispanic-targeted media and schools since the early 1980s. It is visible at Hispanic festivals such as Cinco de Mayo in Los Angeles, National Puerto Rican Day Parade in New York, Calle Ocho celebration of Latino foods and music in Miami, and the Tex-Mex Fiesta in San Antonio. Coca-Cola uses various Latino celebrities and music styles to suit the tastes of different country-of-origin groups in different cities.

Advertising that builds awareness of brand names or features is not enough to communicate that the seller is a member of the Latino community family.[213] A fuller complement of communication tools is needed to build a presence in the Hispanic consumer's mind. Sponsoring school programs and events and public service campaigns are other ways to fit into the Latino subculture community.

Like immigrants of all nationalities, Hispanics can have trouble finding products that they recognize unless marketers include pictures of the product and the product category where it can be found in stores, in their commercials. New U.S. Latino immigrants use advertising as well as programming in the media to learn how to consume products American style.[214]

A major tactic for capturing the attention of U.S. Latino consumers is the inclusion of Hispanic celebrities at ethnic events and in marketing communications. Sports figures, such as baseball player Roberto Clemente, boxer Roberto Duran, and golfer Nancy Lopez, as well as actors, such as Eva Longoria, Selena Gomez, Jimmy Smits, Antonio Banderas, George Lopez, Sofía Vergara, Andy Garcia, and Edward James Olmos, and musicians including Jennifer Lopez, Enrique Iglesias, Jose Feliciano, Gloria and Emilio Estefan, Ricky Martin, Shakira, Celia Cruz, Los Tigres del Norte, Tito Puente, and Mark Anthony are well-known role models of American success among U.S. Hispanics. Hispanic celebrities represent "mainstream success and acceptance."[215]

Leisure time in the Hispanic household is frequently spent participating in festivities with family and friends. They may patronize fast food restaurants and eat ready-made American-style foods, but they are likely to cook from scratch for events with an ethnic theme. In this context, event sponsorships have high visibility. The patronage of both fast-food restaurants and ethnic festivals shows the variable influence of ethnic identity in product choices in different consumption situations.

Two aspects of Hispanic consumer identity affect the strength of subculture influence when purchase decisions are made. First, the level of "felt ethnicity" is situational, depending on the social dynamics of purchasing and consumption occasions.[216] Second, there is significant variation in Hispanic self-designated ethnicity, suggesting that cultural influence is minimal when people do not strongly identify as Hispanic.[217] Thus, purchasing decisions for products such as packaged goods in general (analgesics, bar soaps, detergents, toys) may show very little cultural influence and have been successfully marketed to U.S. Latinos using mainstream market strategies. But for other categories (or for particular brands within the aforementioned categories), such as soft drinks, beer, or anything that has a strongly regional or local flavor to it, ethnicity can be a stronger influence on brand choice.

In sum, ethnicity as an influence in Hispanic purchasing decisions varies by product or service category, purchase and use situation, socioeconomic background, language preference, language of advertising, communication medium, individual consumer's strength of ethnic identity, and geographic location. Another way to put this seeming paradox is that cultural values have a pervasive influence on a person's view of the world, which in turn determines that individual's needs and aspirations. In contrast, a person's varying ethnic (or other) identities may or may not explain preferences for one brand over another or different rates of consumption within product categories.

Summary

The U.S. Hispanic market includes people of various different races, countries of origin, economic status, language fluency, and levels of acculturation. These differences provide a foundation for exploring effective ways to segment the U.S. Latino market. At the same time, ethnic expression and behavior tend to vary by individual and by situation. In this context, Spanish has a unifying and symbolic value. Other important cultural values focus on the importance of the family, personalized relationships, and hierarchy as well as conservative and traditional family roles.

Among this ethnic group, which is the most rapidly growing one in the United States, over 60 percent have origins in Mexico, followed by those with roots in other Central and South American countries, Puerto Rico, the Dominican Republic, and Cuba. U.S. Latinos are concentrated in the South and Southwest and around major urban areas such as New York, Miami, Los Angeles, and Chicago. This geographic concentration makes for effective reach via Spanish-language and low-cost regional and online media.

Successful marketers understand that such diversity precludes simple rules of thumb when marketing programs are designed. Language translation may or may not be appropriate to reach a particular Hispanic target market. Equally problematic are communications that are not compatible with Hispanic subculture values. Having a presence in Hispanic-oriented media, aggressive use of sales promotions, participating in Latino community events, and contributing to social causes of interest to Hispanics such as education are cited as effective marketing tools for constructing partnerships with Latino consumers.

Notes

1. H. El Nasser, "39 Million Make Hispanics Largest U.S. Minority Group," *USA Today,* June 19, 2003, http://usatoday30.usatoday.com/news/nation/census/2003-06-18-Census_x.htm; Invisible America, "Shocking Revelation: Latinos Become Largest Minority," March 16, 2001, www.invisibleamerica.com/largestminority.html;

H. El Nasser and P. Overberg, "Twenty Years of Sweeping Change," *USA Today,* August 10, 2011, http://usatoday30.usatoday.com/news/nation/census/2011-08-10-census-20-years-change_n.htm.

2. S. Roberts, "In U.S. Name Count, Garcias Are Catching Up with Joneses," *New York Times,* November 17, 2007, www.nytimes.com/2007/11/17/us/17surnames.html?_r=0/.

3. A. Portes and D. MacLeod, "What Shall I Call Myself? Hispanic Identity Formation in the Second Generation," *Ethnic and Racial Studies* 19, no. 3 (1996): 523–548.

4. E. Shorris, *Latinos: A Biography of the People* (New York: W.W. Norton, 1992), xvi–xvii.

5. P.B. Corbett, *Between Two Worlds: How Young Latinos Come of Age in America* (Washington, DC: Pew Hispanic Center, 2009); T. Gandossy, "The Complicated Measure of Being Hispanic in America," CNN, September 28, 2007, www.cnn.com/2007/US/09/26/hispanic.identity/index.html; P.B. Corbertt, "Hispanic? Latino? Or What?" After Deadline blog, *New York Times,* June 9, 2009, http://afterdeadline.blogs.nytimes.com/2009/06/09/hispanic-latino-or-what/; U.S. Census Bureau, *The Hispanic Population in the United States: 2011* (Washington, DC: U.S. Census Bureau, November 2012), www.census.gov/population/hispanic/data/2011.html.

6. H.O. Rizzo, "Mariachi to Mambo," *Hispanic* (July/August 2000): 55–60.

7. "Table 2. Population by Sex, Age, And Hispanic Origin Type: 2011," in U.S. Census Bureau, *The Hispanic Population in the United States: 2011* (Washington, DC: U.S. Census Bureau, November 2012), www.census.gov/population/hispanic/data/2011.html.

8. Pew Research Hispanic Trends Project, "Hispanic Population in Select U.S. Metropolitan Areas, 2010," www.pewhispanic.org/hispanic-population-in-select-u-s-metropolitan-areas/#map/, based on data from U.S. Census Bureau, *2010 American Community Survey.*

9. U.S. Census Bureau, *The Hispanic Population in the United States: 2011.*

10. D. Foust, "The Changing Heartland," *BusinessWeek,* September 9, 2002, 80.

11. S.R. Ennis, M. Rios-Vargas, and N.G. Albert, *The Hispanic Population: 2010,* 2010 Census Brief (Washington, DC: U.S. Census Bureau, May 2011).

12. E.M. Grieco, Y.D. Acosta, G.P. de la Cruz, C. Gambino, T. Gryn, L.J. Larsen, E.N. Trevelyan, and N.P. Walters, *The Foreign-Born Population in the United States: 2010,* American Community Survey Report (Washington, DC: U.S. Census Bureau, May 2012).

13. Ibid.

14. J. Passel, D. Cohn, and A. Gonzalez-Barrera, "Net Migration from Mexico Falls to Zero—and Perhaps Less," Pew Hispanic Center, April 23, 2012, www.pewhispanic.org/2012/04/23/net-migration-from-mexico-falls-to-zero-and-perhaps-less/.

15. B. Grow, "Embracing Illegals," *BusinessWeek,* July 18, 2005, 56–64.

16. Passel, Cohn, and Gonzalez-Barrera, "Net Migration from Mexico Falls to Zero."

17. Grow, "Embracing Illegals."

18. Association of Hispanic Advertising Agencies (AHAA), "Think Hispanic: Why U.S. Hispanics Represent a Unique Opportunity for Brands," http://ahaa.org/default.asp?contentID=161/.

19. U.S. Census Bureau, "Table 3. Annual Estimates of the Resident Population by Sex, Race, and Hispanic Origin for the United States: April 1, 2000 to July 1, 2009

(NC-EST2009-03)," *National Characteristics: Vintage 2009* (Washington, DC: U.S. Census Bureau, 2009).

20. Ibid.

21. C. Dougherty and M. Jordan, "U.S. Hispanic Population Growth Is Driven by Domestic Birthrate," *Wall Street Journal,* May 1, 2008, A3.

22. "Demographics of the United States," in Wikipedia, http://en.wikipedia.org/wiki/Demographics_of_the_United_States/.

23. U.S. Census Bureau, "Table 3. Annual Estimates of the Resident Population."

24. T.A. Repack, "New Roles in a New Landscape," in *Structuring Latina and Latino Lives in the U.S.,* ed. M. Romero, P. Hondagneu-Sotelo, and V. Ortiz (New York: Routledge, 1997), 247–257; H. Tobar, *Translation Nation: Defining a New American Identity in the Spanish-Speaking United States* (New York: Riverhead Books, 2005).

25. M. Jordan, "California Dreamers: Once Here Illegally, the Laras Savor Children's Success," *Wall Street Journal,* July 20, 2005, A1, A8.

26. R. Quayat, "The Undeniable Importance of Hispanics in the Marketing Mix," *Marketing News* 44, no. 11 (2010): 10; DMB&B, *New World Teen Study: Wave II, a Hispanic Perspective* (1996).

27. New American Dimensions and the New Generation Latino Consortium, "New Generation Latino Media Habits," study, May 10, 2007.

28. D. Nhan, "Buying Power of U.S. Hispanics Worth $1 Trillion Report Says," *National Journal,* May 10, 2012, www.nationaljournal.com/thenextamerica/demographics/buying-power-of-hispanics-worth-1-trillion-report-says-20120508/; Agence France-Presse, "Hispanic Purchasing Power Surges in U.S.: Study," Hispanic Business.com, May 17, 2012, www.hispanicbusiness.com/2012/5/17/hispanic_purchasing_power_surges_in_us.htm; M. Waldman, "Hispanic Consumer Market in the U.S. Is Larger Than the Entire Economies of All But 13 Countries in the World, According to Annual UGA Selig Center Multicultural Economy Study," news release, Terry College of Business, University of Georgia, May 1, 2012, www.terry.uga.edu/news/releases/hispanic-consumer-market-in-the-u.s.-is-larger-than-the-entire-economies-of/.

29. Greater Austin Hispanic Chamber of Commerce, "The Hispanic Market and Its 'Buying Power'?" presentation, www.gahcc.org/fileadmin/files/Hispanic_Market___Its_Buying_Power.pdf.

30. A.D. Kohler and M. Lazarín, "Hispanic Education in the United States," National Council of La Raza; Statistical Brief No. 8 (2007), www.nclr.org/images/uploads/publications/file_SB8_HispEd_fnl.pdf.

31. R. Fry and M.H. Lopez, "Hispanic Student Enrollments Reach New Highs in 2011," Pew Research Hispanic Trends Project, August 20, 2012, www.pewhispanic.org/2012/08/20/ii-hispanic-public-school-enrollments/.

32. U.S. Census Bureau, "Table H-4. Gini Ratios for Households, by Race and Hispanic Origin of Householder," Historical income tables: Households, www.census.gov/hhes/www/income/data/historical/household/.

33. S. Motel and E. Patten, *Hispanic Origin Profiles 2010* (Washington, DC: Pew Research Center, June 27, 2012), www.pewhispanic.org/2012/06/27/country-of-origin-profiles/.

34. Goldman Sachs, "Hispanization of the US: The Growing Influence of Hispanic and Latino Communities in the U.S. Economy," press release, November 26, 2007, http://goldman-sachs-news.newslib.com/2007113123/.

35. S. Aud, M.A. Fox, and A. Kewal-Ramami, *Status and Trends in the Education of Racial and Ethnic Groups,* Report NCES 2010-015 (Washington, DC: U.S. Department of Education, July 2010), 18.

36. U.S. Census Bureau, "Hispanic-Owned Businesses," in *2007 Survey of Business Owners,* www.census.gov/econ/sbo/07menu.html; J.M. Humphreys, "The Multicultural Economy 2009," *Georgia Business and Economic Conditions* 69, no. 3 (third quarter 2009): 10–11.

37. M. Arndt, "Invasion of the Guatemalan Chicken," *Bloomberg BusinessWeek,* March 22, 2010, 72–73.

38. J. Russell, "Bricks & Clicks," *Hispanic Business* (December 2004): 24–28.

39. U.S. Census Bureau, "Table 3. Annual Estimates of the Resident Population."

40. S. Kraus, "Affluency Survey: Diversity Among Affluent Americans," *Ad Age,* April 4, 2012, http://adage.com/article/adagestat/affluency-survey-diversity-affluent-americans/233901/.

41. J. Haar, "The Hispanic Wealthy: The Next Big Wave in Financial Services," HispanicBusiness.com, October 5, 2007, www.hispanicbusiness.com/2007/10/5/the_hispanic_wealthy_the_next_big.htm.

42. J.S. Phinney, "Ethnic Identity and Self-Esteem," in *Hispanic Psychology: Critical Issues in Theory and Research,* ed. A.M. Padilla (Thousand Oaks, CA: Sage, 1995), 57–70.

43. M. Tharp and R. Villarreal, "Psychographic, Universal and Culture-Specific Values: Applications for Marketing to Hispanics," paper presented at the International Trade and Finance Association Meetings, Casablanca, Morocco, May 1999.

44. D. Vallejo, "Beyond Skin Color: Unveiling the Screen of Prejudice and Misconceptions," in *Hispanic Marketing and Public Relations,* ed. E. del Valle (Boca Raton, FL: Poyeen, 2005), 47–83; M.C. Waters, *Ethnic Options: Choosing Identities in America* (Berkeley: University of California Press, 1990).

45. F. Subervi, "U.S. Hispanic Identity," La Chispa Workshop for Tichenor Media, University of Texas, Austin, College of Communication, July 1994.

46. J. Abrams, J. O'Connor, and H. Giles, "Identity and Intergroup Communication," in *Cross-Cultural and Intercultural Communication,* ed. W.B. Gudykunst (Thousand Oaks, CA: Sage, 2003), 209–224.

47. I.M. Torres and E. Briggs, "Identification Effects on Advertising Response," *Journal of Advertising* 36, no. 3 (2007): 97–108; V. Chattaraman, S.J. Lennon, and N.A. Rudd, "Social Identity Salience: Effects on Identity-Based Brand Choices of Hispanic Consumers," *Psychology & Marketing* 27, no. 3 (2010): 263–284.

48. R. Deshpandé and D.M. Stayman, "A Tale of Two Cities: Distinctiveness Theory and Advertising Effectiveness," *Journal of Marketing Research* 31, no. 1 (1994): 57–64; D.M. Stayman and R. Deshpandé, "Situational Ethnicity and Consumer Behavior," *Journal of Consumer Research* 16, no. 3 (1989): 361–371.

49. Torres and Briggs, "Identification Effects on Advertising Response."

50. A.M. Brumbaugh, "Source and Nonsource Cues in Advertising and Their Effects on the Activation of Cultural and Subcultural Knowledge on the Route to Persuasion," *Journal of Consumer Research* 29, no. 2 (2002): 258–269; M. Chattalas and H. Harper, "Navigating a Hybrid Cultural Identity: Hispanic Teenagers' Fashion Consumption Influences," *Journal of Consumer Marketing* 24, no. 6 (2007): 351–357; D. Luna, T. Ringberg, and L.A. Peracchio, "One Individual Two Identities: Frame Switching Among Biculturals," *Journal of Consumer Research* 35, no. 2 (2008):

279–293; N. Donthu and J. Cherian, "Impact of Strength of Ethnic Identification on Hispanic Shopping Behavior," *Journal of Retailing* 70, no. 4 (1994): 383–393; M.R. Forehand and R. Deshpandé, "What We See Makes Us Who We Are: Priming Ethnic Self-Awareness and Advertising Response," *Journal of Marketing Research* 38, no. 3 (2001): 336–348; S.G. Grier and R. Deshpandé, "Social Dimensions of Consumer Distinctiveness: The Influence of Social Status on Group Identity and Advertising Persuasion," *Journal of Marketing Research* 38, no. 2 (2001): 216–224; Chattaraman, Lennon, and Rudd, "Social Identity Salience."

51. Waters, *Ethnic Options*; R. Deshpandé, W.D. Hoyer, and N. Donthu, "The Intensity of Ethnic Affiliation: A Study of the Sociology of Hispanic Consumption," *Journal of Consumer Research* 13, no. 2 (1986): 214–220; P.L. Sunderland, E.G. Taylor, and R.M. Denny, "Being Mexican and American: Negotiating Ethnicity in the Practice of Market Research," *Human Organization* 63, no. 3 (2004): 373–380.

52. H. Valencia, "Hispanic Values and Subcultural Research," *Journal of the Academy of Marketing Science* 17, no. 1 (1989): 23–29; R. Villarreal and R.A. Peterson, "Hispanic Ethnicity and Media Behavior," *Journal of Advertising Research* 48, no. 2 (2008): 179–190; R. Marin and G. Marin, "Influence of Acculturation on Familism and Self-Identification Among Hispanics," in *Ethnic Identity: Formation and Transmission among Hispanics and Other Minorities,* ed. M.E. Bernal and G.P. Knight (Albany: State University of New York Press, 1993), 181–196; G. Marin and B.V. Marin, *Research with Hispanic Populations* (Newbury Park, CA: Sage, 1991); H.C. Triandis, G. Marin, J. Lisansky, and H. Betancourt, "Simpatía as a Cultural Script of Hispanics," *Journal of Personality and Social Psychology* 47, no. 6 (1984): 1363–1375.

53. Stayman and Deshpandé, "Situational Ethnicity and Consumer Behavior"; M. Tharp and R. Villarreal, "Questioning the Construct of US Hispanic Ethnic Identity," paper presented at International Trade and Finance Association Meetings, Atlantic City, NJ, May 1998.

54. Villarreal and Peterson, "Hispanic Ethnicity and Media Behavior"; J.G. Saegert, R.J. Hoover, and M. Tharp-Hilger, "Characteristics of Mexican American Consumers," *Journal of Consumer Research* 12, no. 1 (1985): 104–109.

55. Chattaraman, Lennon, and Rudd, "Social Identity Salience"; R. Villarreal and R.A. Peterson, "The Concept and Marketing Implications of Hispanicness," *Journal of Marketing Theory and Practice* 17, no. 4 (2009): 303–316; Forehand and Deshpandé, "What We See Makes Us Who We Are."

56. A. Dávila, *Latinos Inc.: The Marketing and Making of a People* (Berkeley: University of California Press, 2001); M. Wallendorf and M.D. Reilly, "Ethnic Migration, Assimilation, and Consumption," *Journal of Consumer Research* 10, no. 3 (1983): 292–302.

57. E.J. Rueschenberg and R. Buriel, "Mexican American Family Functioning and Acculturation," in *Hispanic Psychology: Critical Issues in Theory and Research,* ed. A.M. Padilla (Thousand Oaks, CA: Sage, 1995), 15–25; Wallendorf and Reilly, "Ethnic Migration, Assimilation, and Consumption"; R. Piirto, *Beyond Mind Games: The Marketing Power of Psychographics* (Ithaca, NY: American Demographics Books, 1991), 198–201.

58. U.S. Census Bureau News (August 6, 2012). Profile America facts for features: Hispanic heritage month 2012: September 15–October 15. U.S. Department of Commerce. CB12-FF.19, http://www.census.gov/newsroom/releases/archives/facts_for_features_special_editions/cb12-ff19.html.

59. Corbett, *Between Two Worlds.*

60. Grieco et al., *The Foreign-Born Population in the United States: 2010,* figures 12, 15.

61. O. Arrieta, "Language and Culture Among Hispanics in the United States," in *Handbook of Hispanic Cultures in the United States,* Vol. 4: *Anthropology,* ed. T. Weaver (Houston: Arte Publico Press, 1994), 168–190.

62. Corbett, *Between Two Worlds*; D. Durbin, "Toyota Tees Up Bilingual Ad for Big Game," *San Antonio Express News,* January 19, 2006, 3E.

63. U.S. Department of Health and Human Services, "Hispanic/Latino Profile," September 7, 2012, http://minorityhealth.hhs.gov/templates/browse.aspx?lvl=2&lvlID=54/.

64. "Defining Hispanicity: E Pluribus Unum or E Pluribus Plures?" in *Multiple Origins, Uncertain Destinies: Hispanics and the American Future,* ed. M. Tienda and F. Mitchell (Washington, DC: National Academies Press, 2006), www.ncbi.nlm.nih.gov/books/NBK19811/.

65. Luna, Ringberg, and Peracchio, "One Individual Two Identities"; D.A. Briley, M.W. Morris, and I. Simonson, "Cultural Chameleons: Biculturals, Conformity Motives, and Decision Making," *Journal of Consumer Psychology* 15, no. 4 (2005): 351–362; L.G. Lau-Gesk, "Activating Culture Through Persuasion Appeals: An Examination of the Bicultural Consumer," *Journal of Consumer Psychology* 13, no. 3 (2003): 301–316; Brumbaugh, "Source and Nonsource Cues in Advertising and Their Effects."

66. V. Chattaraman, N.A. Rudd, and S.J. Lennon, "The Malleable Bicultural Consumer: Effects of Cultural Contexts on Aesthetic Judgments," *Journal of Consumer Behaviour* 9, no. 1 (2010): 18–31.

67. L. Aaronson, "My Spanish Side," *Psychology Today* 38, no. 4 (2005): 26.

68. D. Luna and L.A. Peracchio, "Sociolinguistic Effects on Code-Switched Ads Targeting Bilingual Consumers," *Journal of Advertising* 34, no. 2 (2005): 43–57; D. Luna and L.A. Peracchio, "Advertising to Bilingual Consumers: The Impact of Code-Switching on Persuasion," *Journal of Consumer Research* 31, no. 4 (2005): 760–765.

69. S. Puntoni, B. deLanghe, and S.M.J. van Osselaer, "Bilingualism and the Emotional Intensity of Advertising Language," *Journal of Consumer Research* 35, no. 6 (2009): 1012–1025.

70. J. Noriega and E. Blair, "Advertising to Bilinguals: Does the Language of Advertising Influence the Nature of Thoughts?" *Journal of Marketing* 72, no. 5 (2008): 69–83.

71. J. Holland and J.W. Gentry, "Ethnic Consumer Reaction to Targeted Marketing: A Theory of Intercultural Accommodation," *Journal of Advertising* 28, no. 1 (1999): 65–79.

72. S. Koslow, P.N. Shamdasani, and E.E. Touchstone, "Exploring Language Effects in Ethnic Advertising: A Sociolinguistics Perspective," *Journal of Consumer Research* 20, no. 4 (1994): 575–585.

73. M. Chattalas and H. Harper, "Navigating a Hybrid Cultural Identity: Hispanic Teenagers' Fashion Consumption Influences," *Journal of Consumer Marketing* 24, no. 6 (2007): 351–357; New American Dimensions and the New Generation Latino Consortium, "New Generation Latino Media Habits," unpublished study, May 10, 2007, http://www.hispanicbusiness.com/2007/5/10/they_dont_want_to_learn_english.htm.

74. F. Korzenny and B.A. Korzenny, *Hispanic Marketing: A Cultural Perspective* (Boston: Elsevier, 2005), chs. 6 and 7.

75. C. Pardo and C. Dreas, "Three Things You Thought You Knew About U.S. Hispanic's Engagement with Media . . . and Why You May Have Been Wrong," Nielsen Company, 2011, http://blog.nielsen.com/nielsenwire/wp-content/uploads/2011/04/Nielsen-Hispanic-Media-US.pdf.

76. C. Webster, "Effects of Hispanic Ethnic Identification on Marital Roles in the Purchase Decision Process," *Journal of Consumer Research* 21, no. 2 (1994): 319–331.

77. F. Subervi and D. Rios, "Latino Identity and Situational Latinidad," in *Hispanic Marketing and Public Relations,* ed. E. del Valle (Boca Raton, FL: Poyeen, 2005), 29–46.

78. Valencia, "Hispanic Values and Subcultural Research"; D.R. Moyerman and B.D. Forman, "Acculturation and Adjustment: A Meta-Analytic Study," *Hispanic Journal of Behavioral Sciences* 14, no. 2 (1992): 163–200.

79. Access Worldwide, *The Culture Markets Report* (Falls Church, VA: Access Worldwide, Communications, Spring 1999), 1.

80. P. Taylor, M.H. Lopez, J.H. Martinez, and G. Velasco, *When Labels Don't Fit: Hispanics and Their Views of Identity* (Washington, DC: Pew Research Hispanic Center, April 4, 2012), www.pewhispanic.org/2012/04/04/when-labels-dont-fit-hispanics-and-their-views-of-identity/.

81. E. del Valle, ed., *Hispanic Marketing and Public Relations* (Boca Raton, FL: Poyeen, 2005), 7–10.

82. E. Horevitz and K.C. Organista, "The Mexican Health Paradox: Expanding the Explanatory Power of the Acculturation Construct," *Hispanic Journal of Behavioral Sciences* 35, no. 1 (2013): 3–34.

83. M. Jordan, "The Beer Industry's Embrace of Hispanic Market Prompts a Backlash from Activists," *Wall Street Journal,* March 29, 2006, B1, B3.

84. W.M. Gomez, "Segmentation by Level of Acculturation," in *Hispanic Marketing and Public Relations,* ed. E. del Valle (Boca Raton, FL: Poyeen, 2005), 153–167; Valencia, "Hispanic Values and Subcultural Research."

85. Gomez, "Segmentation by Level of Acculturation."

86. Some of the "Godfathers of Hispanic Marketing Research" Ernest Bromley and Lionel Sosa in San Antonio, Carlos Arce in Austin, Isabel Valdes, Andrew Erlich, and Felipe Korzenny in California, and SRI in Florida.

87. C. Arce, "infoSource's Hispanic Assimilation Segmentation," paper presented at the New Americas Advertising Forum, University of Texas at Austin, April 1994.

88. Market Segment Research, *The 1992 MSR Minority Market Report* (Coral Gables, FL: Market Segment Research, 1993).

89. J.W. Berry et al., "Acculturation Attitudes in Plural Societies," *Applied Psychology* 38, no. 2 (1989): 185–206; M.F-O. de la Garza, M.D. Newcomb, and H.F. Myers, "A Multidimensional Measure of Cultural Identity for Latino and Latina Adolescents," in *Hispanic Psychology: Critical Issues in Theory and Research,* ed. A.M. Padilla (Thousand Oaks, CA: Sage, 1995), 26–42.

90. E. Bromley, "How to Teach the Language of the Largest Target Market Without Speaking Spanish," in *Proceedings of the 1992 Conference of the American Academy of Advertising*, ed. L.L. Reid (Athens, GA: American Academy of Advertising, 1992), 68–71.

91. Bromley Communications, "True to Its Heritage of Innovation, Bromley Communications Switches into Higher Gear; Celebrates 30-year Milestone," PR Newswire. com, October 12, 2011, www.prnewswire.com/news-releases/true-to-its-heritage-of-innovation-bromley-communications-switches-into-higher-gear-celebrates-30-year-milestone-131592503.html.

92. D. Allen and M. Friedman, "A Deeper Look into the U.S. Hispanic Market," in *Hispanic Marketing and Public Relations,* 85–114.

93. Gomez, "Segmentation by Level of Acculturation."

94. M.C. Waters and T.R. Jiménez, "Assessing Immigrant Assimilation: New Empirical and Theoretical Challenges," *Annual Review of Sociology* 31 (2005): 105–125.

95. I. Cuellar, B. Arnold, and R. Maldonado, "Acculturation Rating Scale for Mexican-Americans II: A Revision of the Original ARMSA Scale," *Hispanic Journal of Behavioral Sciences* 17, no. 3 (1995): 275–304; Chattaraman, Lennon, and Rudd, "Social Identity Salience."

96. Gomez, "Segmentation by Level of Acculturation."

97. K.A. Moore, B.D. Weinberg, and P.D. Berger, "The Mitigating Effects of Acculturation on Consumer Behavior," *International Journal of Business and Social Science* 3, no. 9 (2012): 9–13; L. Cabass, "Measuring Acculturation: Where We Are and Where We Need to Go," *Hispanic Journal of Behavioral Sciences* 25, no. 2 (2003): 127–146; D. D'Rozario and S.P. Douglas, "Effect of Assimilation on Prepurchase External Information-Search Tendencies," *Journal of Consumer Psychology* 8, no. 2 (1999): 187–209.

98. D'Rozario and Douglas, "Effect of Assimilation."

99. D.T. Ogden, "Hispanic Versus Anglo Male Dominance in Purchase Decisions," *Journal of Product and Brand Management* 14, no. 2 (2005): 98–106.

100. B.S. Bulik, "The Cultural Connection: How Hispanic Identity Influences Millennials," Ad Age Insights/Univision, PowerPoint slides, May 13, 2012.

101. Ibid.

102. GlobalHue, "GlobalHue Report Reveals Cultural Map of the New America," PR Newswire, June 6, 2010, www.prnewswire.com/news-releases/globalhue-report-reveals-cultural-map-of-the-new-america-95397619.html.

103. Pew Hispanic Center, *Hispanics: A People in Motion* (Washington, DC: Pew Hispanic Center, January 2005), www.pewhispanic.org/files/reports/40.pdf.

104. Goldman Sachs, "Hispanization of the US: The Growing Influence of Hispanic and Latino Communities in the US Economy"; C. Haubegger et al., "Latino America," *Newsweek,* July 12, 1999, 48–63; H. Stapinski, "Generacion Latino," *American Demographics* (July 1999): 63–68.

105. "Explaining Cultural Differences: Some Common Themes Among Hispanics," *Hispanic Market Report* 3, no. 2 (1996): 2.

106. B. Padilla, "Projective Techniques: Do They Work in the Hispanic Market?" *Quirk's Marketing Research Review* (April 1999): 30–34.

107. N. Williams, *The Mexican American Family: Tradition and Change* (Dixon Hills, NY: General Hall, 1990).

108. M. Wallendorf and D. Nelson, "An Archaeological Examination of Ethnic Differences in Body Care Rituals," *Psychology & Marketing* 3, no. 4 (1986): 273–289.

109. Williams, *The Mexican American Family,* 136–150.

110. V. Fonseca, "Nuevo Latino: Re-Branding Latin American Cuisines," *Consumption, Markets, and Culture* 8, no. 2 (2005): 95–130.

111. Cultural Access Group and About Marketing Solutions, *Grow with America:*

Best Practices in Ethnic Marketing and Merchandising (Coca-Cola Retailing Research Council of North America, 2002), www.ccrrc.org/wp-content/uploads/2012/10/Grow_With_America_Ethnic_Marketing_Study_2002.pdf.

112. R. Vargas, "Families Celebrate the Day of the Dead," *Hispanic* 9, no. 11 (1996): 72–73.

113. M. Jordan, "Gringo, Nanny Court Hispanics with Car Pitch," *Wall Street Journal,* May 24, 2005, B1, B7.

114. N.S. Lansdale and R.S. Oropesa, "Hispanic Families: Stability and Change," *Annual Review of Sociology* 33 (2007): 381–430; Williams, *The Mexican American Family,* 136–150; N. Carr-Ruffino, *Managing Diversity: People Skills for a Multicultural Workplace* (Cincinnati, OH: South-Western, 1996), 322–366; Valencia, "Hispanic Values and Subcultural Research."

115. E. Peter, "Army's Hispanic-Recruitment Ads Cater to Mom," *Wall Street Journal,* May 24, 2002, B3.

116. Jordan, "California Dreamers."

117. R. Maso-Fleischman, "Archetypal Research for Advertising: A Spanish-Language Example," *Journal of Advertising Research* 37, no. 5 (1997): 81–85.

118. Webster, "Effects of Hispanic Ethnic Identification."

119. M. Rodriguez and K. Koslosky, "The Impact of Acculturation on Attitudinal Familism in a Community of Puerto Rican Americans," *Hispanic Journal of Behavioral Sciences* (August 1998): 249–255

120. G.H. Hofstede, *Culture's Consequences: International Differences in Work-Related Values* (Beverly Hills, CA: Sage, 1984); M. de Mooij, *Global Marketing and Advertising: Understanding Cultural Paradoxes* (Thousand Oaks, CA: Sage, 1998); L.A. Samovar and R.E. Porter, *Communication Between Cultures* (Belmont, CA: Wadsworth, 1991).

121. Carr-Ruffino, *Managing Diversity,* 322–366.

122. Valencia, "Hispanic Values and Subcultural Research."

123. "Hispanic 1010," slide presentation by Agencia de Orci, 2007; C. Cartagena, *Latino Boom! Everything You Need to Know to Grow Your Business in the U.S. Hispanic Market* (New York: Ballantine Books, 2005), 206–207.

124. H.O. Pruden and D.S. Longman, "Race, Alienation, and Consumerism," *Journal of Marketing* 36, no. 3 (1972): 58–63; T.C. O'Guinn, R.J. Faber, and F. Imperia, "Subcultural Influences on Family Decision Making," *Psychology & Marketing* 3, no. 4 (1986): 305–317; M.T. Hilger and W.D. English, "Consumer Alienation from the Marketplace," in *Proceedings of 1978 Southern Marketing Association,* ed. R.S. Franz, R.M. Hopkins, and A.G. Toma (Lafayette: University of Southwestern Louisiana Press, 1978), 78–83.

125. C. Webster, "The Effects of Hispanic Subcultural Identification on Information Search Behavior," *Journal of Advertising Research* 32, no. 5 (1992): 54–62; L. Peñaloza, "Immigrant Consumer Acculturation," *Advances in Consumer Research* 16 (1989): 110–118; A.H. Kizilbash and E.T. Garman, "Grocery Retailing in Spanish Neighborhoods," *Journal of Retailing* 51, no. 4 (1975/76): 15–21; L. Lee, "New Immigrants Get Crash Course in Consumerism," *Wall Street Journal,* December 24, 1996, B1; T. Agins, "To Hispanics in U.S., a Bodega, or Grocery, Is a Vital Part of Life," *Wall Street Journal,* March 15, 1985, A1, A17.

126. L.N. Peñaloza and M.C. Gilly, "The Hispanic Family—Consumer Research Issues," *Psychology & Marketing* 3, no. 4 (1986): 291–303; B.R. Flores, *Chiquita's Cocoon* (Granite Bay, CA: Pepper Vine Press, 1990), 21.

127. Flores, *Chiquita's Cocoon*, 58; O'Guinn, Faber, and Imperia, "Subcultural Influences on Family Decision Making."

128. Carr-Ruffino, *Managing Diversity*, 322–366.

129. Flores, *Chiquita's Cocoon*, 38.

130. C.C. Wilson II and F. Gutiérrez, *Race, Multiculturalism, and the Media*, 2d ed. (Thousand Oaks, CA: Sage, 1995), 109.

131. S. Reyes, "Ethnic Stereotypes Have Formidable Staying Power," *Corpus Christi Caller-Times,* August 4, 1994, A11.

132. O.E. Nuiry, "Ban the Bandito!" *Hispanic* (July 1996): 26–32; M. Westerman, "Death of the Frito Bandito," *American Demographics* (March 1989): 28–32; R.J. Astroff, "Spanish Gold: Stereotypes, Ideology, and the Construction of a U.S. Latino Market," *Howard Journal of Communications* 1, no. 4 (1988–89): 155–173; Wilson and Gutiérrez, *Race, Multiculturalism, and the Media,* 161–167.

133. A. Villavicencio, "Latino Stereotypes on TV: The Good, the Bad, the Ugly," Being Latino, January 23, 2012, www.beinglatino.us/entertainment/television/latino-stereotypes-on-tv-the-good-the-bad-and-the-ugly/; "Worst Latino Stereotypes on Television: Will Rob Schneider and Cheech Marin Break the Cycle?" Huffington Post Latino Voices, January 13, 2012, www.huffingtonpost.com/2012/01/06/worst-latino-stereotypes-on-television_n_1190276.html; J. Torres, "Invisible Ink?" *Hispanic* (October 1999): 23–31; City of New York, *Invisible People: The Depiction of Minorities in Magazine Ads and Catalogs* (New York: Department of Consumer Affairs, 1991).

134. E. Monk-Turner, M. Heiserman, C. Johnson, V. Cotton, and M. Jackson, "The Portrayal of Racial Minorities on Prime Time Television: A Replication of the Mastro and Greenberg Study a Decade Later," *Studies in Popular Culture* 32, no. 2 (2010): 101.

135. eMarketer, "Ethnic Groups Don't See Themselves in Advertising, Digital Content," December 22, 2011, http://www.emarketer.com/Article/Ethnic-Groups-Dont-See-Themselves-Advertising-Digital-Content/1008746.

136. R.E. Wilkes and H. Valencia, "Hispanics and Blacks in Television Commercials," *Journal of Advertising* 18, no. 1 (1989): 19–25; H.F. Waters, "Listening to Their Latin Beat," *Newsweek*, March 28, 1994, 42–43.

137. Marketing Charts Staff, "U.S. Ad Spending Grew by 3% in 2012," March 12, 2013, www.marketingcharts.com/wp/television/us-ad-spend-up-3-in-2012-27707/.

138. Kantar Media, "Kantar Media Reports U.S. Advertising Expenditures Increased 0.8 Percent in 2011," March 12, 2012, http://kantarmediana.com/intelligence/press/us-advertising-expenditures-increased-08-percent-2011/.

139. E. Guskin and A. Mitchell, "Hispanic Media Faring Better Than the Mainstream Media," in *The State of the News Media 2011* (Washington, DC: Pew Research Center, 2011), http://stateofthemedia.org/2011/hispanic-media-fairing-better-than-the-mainstream-media/.

140. D. Vasquez, "Behind the Gains by Hispanic Magazines," *MediaLife Magazine*, May 7, 2012, www.medialifemagazine.com/behind-the-gains-by-hispanic-magazines/.

141. A.R. Jacobson, *Hispanic Market Overview—2011* (Miami: Adam R. Jacobson Editorial Services and Research Consultancy, 2011), 9.

142. Ad Age Data Center, *Hispanic Fact Pack* (New York: Ad Age, July 22, 2012), 44; P. Roslow and J.A.F. Nicholls, "Targeting the Hispanic Market: Comparative

Persuasion of TV Commercials in Spanish and English," *Journal of Advertising Research* 36, no. 3 (1996): 67–77.

143. See, for example, Briley, Morris, and Simonson, "Cultural Chameleons"; Lau-Gesk, "Activating Culture Through Persuasion Appeals"; Forehand and Deshpandé, "What We See Makes Us Who We Are"; Grier and Deshpandé, "Social Dimensions of Consumer Distinctiveness"; Brumbaugh, "Source and Nonsource Cues in Advertising and Their Effects on the Activation of Cultural and Subcultural Knowledge on the Route to Persuasion"; Torres and Briggs, "Identification Effects on Advertising Response"; Chattaraman, Lennon, and Rudd, "Social Identity Salience"; Koslow, Shamdasani, and Touchstone, "Exploring Language Effects in Ethnic Advertising."

144. Arbitron, *Hispanic Radio Today: How America Listens to Radio* (Columbia, MD: Arbitron, 2010), www.americanradiohistory.com/radioresearch/Archive-Arbitron/Arbitron-Hispanic-Radio-Today-2010.pdf.

145. J.-M. Barbero, "Latin America: Cultures in the Communication Media," *Journal of Communication* 43, no. 2 (1993): 18–30.

146. J. Trimble, "Internet Radio Must Tune in to the Emerging Hispanic Mainstream," *Advertising Age,* February 6, 2013.

147. G. Otteson, "The State of Spanish Language Media Industries: A Summary of Spanish Language Radio 2011," in *The State of Spanish Language Media: 2011 Annual Report,* comp. Center for Spanish Language Media staff (Denton: University of North Texas, February 2012), http://doczine.com/bigdata/2/1366963229_13ab168f22/sofslm2011.pdf.

148. Jacobson, *Hispanic Market Overview—2011,* 21–31.

149. D. Petrozzello, "Hispanic Radio Formats Going Strong," *Broadcasting and Cable* 126, no. 48 (1996): 60–62.

150. B. Barnes and M. Jordan, "'Big Four' TV Networks Get a Wake-Up Call in Spanish," *Wall Street Journal,* May 2, 2005, B1, B6.

151. For discussion of research methods: Korzenny and Korzenny, *Hispanic Marketing,* ch. 7; Moyerman and Forman, "Acculturation and Adjustment"; H. Morrow, "Among Hispanics, Phone Surveys May Be Preferable to Doing Door-to-Door Interviews," *Marketing News,* August 29, 1988, 23, 26; V. Rodriguez, "Charting Latino Listeners," *Dallas Morning News,* January 16, 1990, 5–6C; J. Saegert and D.P. Deiter, "Response Rates to Mail Questionnaires in an Ethnic Minority Population," working paper, Center for Studies in Business, Economics, and Human Resources, University of Texas at San Antonio, 1980; G.R. Soruco, "Hispanic Consumer Behavior and the Development of Advertising Copy: The Advantages of Qualitative Research Techniques," paper presented at 1990 American Academy of Advertising Conference, Orlando, FL; G.R. Soruco, "Sampling and Non-Sampling Errors in Hispanic Population Telephone Surveys," presented at1990 American Academy of Advertising, Orlando, FL; S.A. Hernandez and C.J. Kaufman, "Marketing Research in Hispanic Barrios: A Guide to Survey Research," *Marketing Research* (March 1990): 11–27.

152. P. Singer, "'Telenovelas' Become a Vibrant New Niche in the DVD Market," *Wall Street Journal,* August 22, 2005, B1, B3.

153. J. Ordoñez, "A turn for Telenovelas," *Newsweek,* September 25, 2006, 42; J. Thottam, "A Telenovela Revolution," *Time Inside Business* (July 2006): A27–A28.

154. Hispanic Market Connections, "Language Segmentation: A Tested Research Tool for the Hispanic Market," *Hispanic Market Report* 2, no. 1 (1995): 2.

155. Guskin and Mitchell, "Hispanic Media Faring Better Than the Mainstream Media."

156. Torres, "Invisible Ink?"

157. Jacobson, *Hispanic Market Overview—2011*, 47–50.

158. Vasquez, "Behind the Gains by Hispanic Magazines."

159. Wilson and Gutiérrez, *Race, Multiculturalism, and the Media,* 129.

160. G. Rodriguez, "The Rising Language of Latino Media: English," *Los Angeles Times,* May 4, 1997, M1.

161. Jacobson, *Hispanic Market Overview—2011*, 55–58.

162. J.D. Zbar, "Hispanic Direct Mail Greeted by Open Door," *Advertising Age,* January 23, 1995, 39.

163. J. Feuer, "Signs of the Times: Hispanic Outdoor Advertising," *AdWeek*, August 15, 1988, 20.

164. Ad Age Data Center, *Hispanic Fact Pack* (New York: Ad Age, July 25, 2011), 6.

165. Ibid., 8.

166. S. Young, "Mobile Mavens: African-Americans and Hispanics are the Early Adopters When It Comes to Wireless Phone Service," *Wall Street Journal,* October 24, 2005, R11.

167. Ibid.

168. "Study Provides Insight to Young Hispanics and the Digital World," January 25, 2008, Diversityspectrum.com, http://diversityspectrum.com/index.php?option=com_content&task=view&id=2152&Itemi/.

169. Bulik, "The Cultural Connection."

170. Batanga Media, "Meet the Digital Hispanic," http://batangamedia.com/meet-the-digital-hispanic/.

171. L. Yuan, "Wireless Providers Tap Niche Markets," *Wall Street Journal,* January 31, 2006, B3.

172. L. Romney, "A Latino Internet Revolution," *Los Angeles Times*, June 22, 1999, A1, A25.

173. S. Kang, "Hispanic Ads Try More Nuanced Strategy," *Wall Street Journal,* January 8, 2008, B7

174. M. Jordan, "Latinos Embrace Web Entertainment," *Wall Street Journal,* April 14, 2004, B3.

175. Economics and Statistics Administration and National Telecommunications and Information Administration, *Exploring the Digital Nation: Computer and Internet Use at Home* (Washington, DC: U.S. Department of Commerce, 2011).

176. V. Hagerty, "Clicking Online," *Hispanic Business* (December 1999): 60, 62, 64.

177. F. Korzenny, "Study Finds Spanish Ads More Effective," *Quirk's Marketing Research Review* (February 1997); F. Korzenny et al. "Hispanic Advertising Effectiveness and Loyalty," *Quirk's Marketing Research Review* (February 1997).

178. M. Hyman, "The Racial Gap in the Grandstands," *Business Week*, October 2, 2006, 78–79.

179. J. Millman, "U.S. Marketers Adopt Cinco de Mayo as National Fiesta," *Wall Street Journal,* May 1, 2001, B1, B4; A. Chozick, "Marketers Join Cinco de Mayo Party," *Wall Street Journal,* May 4, 2005, B8.

180. S. Vranica, "Anheuser-Busch Hopes to Make Bigger Splash with Hispanics," *Wall Street Journal,* October 24, 2005, B4.

181. C. Rohwedder, "Wal-Mart's Big Goal," *Wall Street Journal,* June 7, 2006, B1, B3; A. Zimmerman, "Wal-Mart's Hispanic Outreach," *Wall Street Journal,* May 31, 2005, B9.

182. D. Kiley, "Laughing Out Loud in Spanish," *BusinessWeek*, March 13, 2006, 80–82.

183. eMarketer, "Ethnic Groups Don't See Themselves in Advertising, Digital Content."

184. T. Vega and B. Carter, "Networks Struggle to Appeal to Hispanics," *New York Times*, August 5, 2012, www.nytimes.com/2012/08/06/business/media/networks-struggle-to-appeal-to-hispanics-without-using-stereotypes.html?pagewanted=all&_r=0/.

185. P. Levy, "Mi casa es su casa," *MarketingNews*, September 15, 2010, 19–21.

186. Wilson and Gutiérrez, *Race, Multiculturalism, and the Media,* 135.

187. L. Wentz, "LatinWorks Is Ad Agencies' Multicultural Agency of the Year," AdAge.com, January 28, 2013.

188. Flores, *Chiquita's Cocoon*, 36.

189. S. Gregory, "Viva la familia!" *Time Inside Business* (February 2005): B1–B12.

190. DRI/McGraw-Hill, *Hispanic Consumer Market Growth to 2010* (New York: Univision, 1995); Wallendorf and Nelson, "An Archaeological Examination of Ethnic Differences in Body Care Rituals"; Wallendorf and Reilly, "Ethnic Migration, Assimilation, and Consumption."

191. Bulik, "The Cultural Connection," 21.

192. Cartagena, *Latino Boom!* 49–59.

193. D. Longman and H.O. Pruden, "Alienation from the Marketplace: A Study in Black, Brown, and White," *Journal of Marketing* 36 (July 1972): 616–619; Kizilbash and Garman, "Grocery Retailing in Spanish Neighborhoods"; F.D. Sturdivant, "Business and the Mexican-American Community," *California Management Review* 11 (1969): 73–80; L. Peñaloza and M.C. Gilly, "Marketer Acculturation: The Changer and the Changed," *Journal of Marketing* 63, no. 3 (1999): 84–104.

194. T. Agins, "To Hispanics in U.S., a Bodega, or Grocery, Is A Vital Part of Life," *Wall Street Journal,* March 15, 1986, A1, A17.

195. T.P. Meyer, "Advertising to Hispanics: A Research Agenda for the Next Decade," in *Proceedings of 1990 Conference of the American Academy of Advertising*, ed. P. Stout (Austin, TX: American Academy of Advertising), RC-8.

196. J. Steinhauer, "A Minority Market with Major Sales," *New York Times*, July 2, 1997, C1, C3.

197. E. Porter and B. McKay, "Frito-Lay Adds Spanish Accent to Snacks," *Wall Street Journal,* May 22, 2002, B4.

198. V. Fonseca, "Nuevo Latino: Rebranding Latin American Cuisine," *Consumption, Markets, and Culture* 8, no. 2 (2005): 95–130.

199. T. Carl, "Hispanic Brand Names Burn Deep: Consumers Seek Back-Home Familiarity with Products, Services—Not Quality," *Chicago Sun-Times*, January 22, 2002, 48.

200. M. Jordan, "Legal and Illegal, Welcome," *Wall Street Journal,* October 10, 2007, B1; M. Jordan, "Banks Open Doors to New Customers: Illegal Immigrants," *Wall Street Journal,* July 8, 2005, B1, B2; M. Jordan, "Credito Hispano: Trust in Poor Built Consumer Empire for Israeli Brothers," *Wall Street Journal,* August 20, 2004, A1, A4.

201. B. Grow, "How to Seize a Gran Oportunidad," *BusinessWeek*, December 27, 2004, 110–111.

202. T.J. Soto, *Marketing to Hispanics: A Strategic Approach to Assessing and Planning Your Initiative* (Chicago: Kaplan, 2006), 14.

203. Cartagena, *Latino Boom!* 47.

204. R. Chittum, "Buenos Días, Shopper," *Wall Street Journal,* July 19, 2006, B1, B10.

205. J. Moreno, "H-E-B Turning a Store into a 'Mexican Village,'" *Houston Chronicle,* HoustonChronicle.com, October 5, 2006.

206. C. Terhune, "U.S. Thirst for Mexican Cola Poses Sticky Problem for Coke," *Wall Street Journal,* January 11, 2006, A1, A10.

207. Cartagena, *Latino Boom!* 51; Saegert, Hoover, and Hilger, "Characteristics of Mexican American Consumers."

208. S. Vaezi, "Marketing to Mexican Consumers," *Brand Strategy,* no. 190 (March 2005): 43–46.

209. R.J. Faber, T.C. O'Guinn, and J.A. McCarty, "Ethnicity, Acculturation, and the Importance of product attributes," *Psychology & Marketing* 4, no. 2 (1987): 121–134; J.G. Albonetti and L.V. Dominguez, "Major Influences on Consumer-Goods' Marketers' Decision to Target U.S. Hispanics," *Journal of Advertising Research* 29, no. 1 (1989): 9–21; C. Fisher, "Poll: Hispanics Stick To Brands," *Advertising Age,* February 15, 1993, 6.

210. R. Grover, "The Payoff from Targeting Hispanics," *BusinessWeek,* April 20, 2009, 76.

211. R. Wartzman, "Read Their Lips: When You Translate Got Milk? What Do You Have?" *Wall Street Journal,* June 30, 1999, A1, A8.

212. G.S. Elizondo, "Mosaic Marriages," *Latina* (November 1999): 74–76.

213. Peñaloza and Gilly, "Marketer Acculturation."

214. L. Peñaloza, "*Atravesando fronteras*/Border Crossings: A Critical Ethnographic Exploration of the Consumer Acculturation of Mexican Immigrants," *Journal of Consumer Research* 21, no. 1 (1994): 32–54; Wilson and Gutiérrez, *Race, Multiculturalism, and the Media,* 130–131.

215. Cartagena, *Latino Boom!* 198–199.

216. Stayman and Deshpandé, "Situational Ethnicity and Consumer Behavior."

217. Deshpandé, Hoyer, and Donthu, "The Intensity of Ethnic Affiliation."

5

Age Differences Create Unique Consumer Subcultures

This chapter profiles five consumer subcultures whose community boundaries are created by age differences. There is a special role for popular culture and values reflected in the unique experience that each generation has while coming of age (15 to 25 years old). While people born around the same time plus or minus 20 years constitute a *generation*, it is their unique coming-of-age *experiences* that turn these groups into distinctive *subcultures*. The events and environments that shape a person's lifelong values and priorities differ across time. The result is a shared generational experience that creates generational differences in how people meet their needs for information.[1] How members of an age subculture translate their aspirations and experiences into market-space choices is what completes the picture of age cohorts as consumer subcultures.

The first section of this chapter details the processes that create consumer subcultures out of age-related experiences. Next is a demographic profile of each generation and the cultural influences behind generational value shifts. We highlight the role that collective memory has in spawning generational nostalgia because this emotion connects people within an age cohort. The next sections describe the consumer preferences of tweens, Generation Y, Generation X, baby boomers, and the mature market. Each profile touches on the group's unique media and marketing preferences as well as the marketing tactics and strategies that companies have used to build successful relationships with them.

Shared Experiences and Values Create Consumer Subcultures

The concept of "generational differences" is not new.[2] For over 60 years, marketers have used age-related differences in customer behavior to target consumers in the American market. During this period, the number of generations expanded from two in the 1960s (the Greatest Generation and baby boomers) to at least five in 2014 (the mature market, baby boomers, Generation X, Generation Y, and teens/tweens). The differences in attitudes, values, and behaviors of each generation have continued to diverge as each generation lives out its defining influences. This is a major reason behind the fragmentation of the so-called mass market.[3]

In 1968, the wife of Playtex's president's throwing away her girdle started research into generational differences. Nothing was wrong with the product; it was simply a reflection of shifting values among younger consumers.[4] Thus the idea was born that marketers could improve the effectiveness of their marketing efforts if they understood the differences across generations of consumers in the American market.

Coming-of-Age Experiences Create Generational Sensibilities

"Generational marketing" focuses on the unique market-space behaviors and aspirations of age groups. It is the shared experiences of life during the coming-of-age years (ages 15 to 25) that give a generation its "shared sensibility," which "teaches its members what's funny, what's stylish, what's status, what's taboo, what works and what doesn't, what to aspire to and what to avoid."[5]

Research into generational differences first highlighted unique behaviors linked to the demographic characteristics of age cohorts—income, ethnicity, education, occupation, and gender. Through the use of annual, large-scale surveys, such as Yankelovich's MONITOR, marketers began to flesh out how consumer values and motivations were reshaping those behaviors.[6] Ultimately this type of research has built a "big picture" of each successive generation's "norms" and how shifting social values affect their media choices and the best ways to market to them.

Formative influences can come from pop culture, economic conditions, world events, natural disasters, heroes, villains, politics, wars, or technology.[7] What is significant is that these early experiences are strong enough to influence the rest of our lives. For people age 18 to 30 today, technological innovations, economic instability, and the terrorist attacks on 9/11 have combined to form Generation Y, known as open to new technologies yet engaged (so far) in a lifelong search for safety in an unsafe world. For members of the mature market, it was the Great Depression and two world wars that made that generation sacrifice for our country and save money to make life better for their children, the baby boomers.

The profiles of each generation highlight those key influences. Keep in mind that cohort experiences are just one of three major forces that affect a consumer's values and market-space preferences. As consumers go through different life stages, their commitments and responsibilities change. Likewise, the consumer's current economic situation and macroenvironment will shape that buyer's needs and limit possibilities. Thus it is the combination of these conditions that create similar responses among members of an age cohort and are the basis of generational marketing.

Cycles of Shifting Values Create Social Change

Historians recognize the repetition of four cycles in American history in how people feel about themselves, their culture, the country, and the future.[8] These so-called social moments can be set in motion by secular crises, "when society focuses on reordering the outer world of institutions and public behavior" or "spiritual awakenings, when society focuses on changing the inner world of values and private behavior."[9]

The first cycle is an era of strengthening social and political institutions and weakening individualism, followed by the second phase, when this civic order is challenged by new values and spiritual upheavals. During the third phase, society feels as if it is unraveling, while individualism grows and society's institutions weaken as new values are absorbed. This phase is then followed by a crisis, when new values begin to replace the old ones, and new institutions implement policies aligned with the new values. Then it starts over again.

The Silent Generation was the product of the first phase of this cycle as its members defended and created American power and institutions in the 1940s and 1950s. The baby boomers challenged the Silent Generation's norms in the 1960s and 1970s as they pursued personal growth. Gen X reasserted individualistic values as American social, economic, and political institutions were unraveling in the 1980s. Gen Y now faces the need to rebuild these institutions to align them with new "norms" and values. As these cycles repeat, new generations will take their place in the "turning of generations." This historical perspective shows the mood of the country as an important influence on the shared values of a generation. It also suggests that each generation "reacts" to the values and civic environment of its predecessors.

American Cultural Values Change over Time

Cultural value systems, originally developed to compare cultural differences across countries, provide a means for measuring and comparing shifts in our values over time. They also reflect the different roles played by market spaces in the lives of American age cohorts.[10] For example, younger cohorts (e.g., tweens, Gen Y) actively use products and services to explore and shape their identities, while older consumers focus on issues that affect the well-being of society as a whole.[11] Brands serve as markers of tween identities but may not be as important value markers for Generation X or baby boomers.

Cultural value differences are the source of conflicts at work, as baby boomers bemoan younger workers' lack of respect for experience and authority.[12] Generations X and Y apply this "go-it-alone" approach to shopping. They prefer to use other people's online reviews, rather than trust so-called experts; older consumers are more influenced by expert opinions. Older consumers seek out warranties, well-known brands, and recommendations by experts as their preferred strategies for reducing purchasing risks, while younger generations like to "shop around" on the Internet to find deals, new products to try, and what appear to be "real" customer reviews before buying.[13]

Another area of life where the values and behaviors of different age cohorts differ is with regard to men and women's roles, especially in family decision making. Traditional decision making in an American family was organized around the father as its head, while today's younger families are more like democracies in which even children have a vote on topics such as the family car or where to vacation.[14] The Silent Generation has always thought "long term," while for Gen Y the short-term payoff is of highest priority, and the long term was never too important to baby boomers, who "forgot to save for retirement." Thus as American culture shifts with the passage of time, each generation is socialized into a unique version of our cultural values.

Pop Culture Feeds Consumer Nostalgia

Pop culture is an important source of shared experiences. The films, TV shows, types of games, celebrities, music, fashion, and politics that each age group experienced growing up have a strong appeal throughout their lives. The sentimental attachment that people have for products and entertainments of their youth is a source of opportunity for marketers. Using popular music as background in 15-second ads immediately draws the attention of audiences of a particular age. The most effective brand endorsers are celebrities cherished by members of specific age cohorts because they build trust and familiarity for unknown brands and complex, risky purchases. Even old brands (e.g.,

Vespa) and out-of-fashion products can find a market among buyers whose nostalgia for "the good old days" puts these products in their shopping carts and a nostalgic smile on their faces.

Moon Pies, Necco Wafers, Groovy Candies, Fizzies, and Sugar Daddys are old candy brands experiencing a renaissance in demand from baby boomers longing for their childhood in the 1950s and 1960s.[15] On Halloween one year, adults pretending to be children were shown in a print ad "trick or treating" for Snickers. A print ad for Nestlé Crunch showed a child jumping on the sofa and asked the reader, "Remember finding money in the sofa?" Background music style, use of celebrity performers and popular tunes, and the rewriting of lyrics to familiar tunes serve as "pop culture" cues to members of one age cohort and may also be recognized by persons of all ages.

The advantage for marketers of incorporating age-appropriate pop culture into their marketing strategy is to reach potential customers as an "insider" member of that group and in a voice that rings "true." It says to them: "We understand you and your experiences."

P&G is an example of a company that uses a website (www.peopleschoice.com) to keep up with the popular culture likes and dislikes of different age groups and people at different life stages.[16] Facebook data offer company partners the same data, which helps their partners design marketing programs as "insiders" for their target markets.

Another market opportunity evolves out of key product categories of importance when each group came of age. The baby boomers' identities are still linked to their choice of cars—styles and brands—since they were born into the car culture of the 1950s and 1960s. Cars were the "ultimate expression of freedom and of self."[17] Through every life stage, boomers have used their vehicles to rebel (VWs, muscle cars), to meet their taste for speed (Mustang, Cadillac CTS), to fight global warming (Toyota Prius, Nissan Leaf), to show their success (Lexus, Hummer), or to feel cool (new Camaros, Mustangs, and Challengers), in addition to the importance of their vehicles in their role as family chauffeur (for which minivans and SUVs were developed).[18] Since electronics and technology are important aspects of the identity of Generations X and Y, these products and their brands may remain important to them throughout their lives.

Table 5.1 shows major influences on American consumers as age-based subcultures. This table highlights cultural and pop culture influences on each of the age subcultures. For example, the marketplace is essential for tweens in creating their identities, but it can be a way to connect with other generations for older Americans. Other things to note in the table are the differences in music, heroes, celebrities, causes, and world events across age cohorts. Furthermore, the economic environment at the time of a generation's coming of

Table 5.1

Comparison of Cultural Influences on Age-Based Consumer Subcultures

Defining experiences	Age cohort				
	Tweens to Teens	Generation Y	Generation X	Baby boomers	Mature market
Key role for marketplace	Creating personal identities via brand choices	Creating personal identities and expressing personal style	Getting the best value and personal style expression	Self-expression and connections to others	Meeting personal needs and connections to other generations
Coming-of-age economic environment	Instability	Early 2000s boom, 2008–2011 recession	First oil crisis, corporate layoffs, economic instability	Boom economy, low unemployment	Great Depression, creation of Social Security, postwar boom
Significant world events	Natural disasters, global warming, civil unrest	Natural disasters, terrorist attacks, school shootings	Collapse of communism, latchkey kids	Vietnam war, civil rights movement, youth culture, Woodstock	World War II, American global dominance, move to suburbs
Music	Pop, indie musicians	Hip hop, indie, world	Grunge, rock n roll	Rock 'n' roll	Swing, classics
Celebrities	Justin Bieber, sports and entertainment stars, volunteers	Entrepreneurs, Indie musicians	Entrepreneurs, Silicon Valley, Steve Jobs, Internet entrepreneurs	Donald Trump, Bill Clinton, Stephen King, Oprah Winfrey	Movie and sports stars, political and religious leaders
Heroes	Social networking contacts and Twitter micro-bloggers, civil rights leaders	Creators, innovative online services	Innovators, entrepreneurs	The "Made-it-to-the-top" in careers, world leaders	War, romance, world, and religious leaders

Important causes	Global warming, women's diseases, cancer, favorite entertainers' causes, human rights	Personal and economic security, personal ambitions, "giving back" and volunteering, teamwork and collaboration, global warming, sustainable lifestyles	Family life, recycling, global warming, organics, local sourcing	Retirement financing and lifestyles, environmental issues, aging, giving back, and changing careers	Patriotism, financial security, respect for authority, experiences over things, remaining "active"
Favorite hobbies	Gaming, online browsing, shopping, sports, listening to music, hanging out	Music, gaming, watching movies, hanging out with friends, shopping, watching and joining sports activities	Family activities (e.g., watching and joining sports teams, travel by car, visiting theme parks), extreme sports	Exercise, reading, concerts, eating healthy, watching TV, gardening	Volunteerism, church, charities, grandchildren, watching TV
Most media used	Internet search and interactive websites, social networks, television, games, mobile	Internet search and media sharing sites, social networks, streaming video and videogames, mobile	Internet search, media sharing, consumer advice and news sites, social networks, television, gaming, mobile	Television, Internet search, consumer education and health advice, media sharing and news sites, magazines, newspapers	Television, Internet search, news, health advice, and limited social network sites, newspapers, magazines
Other sources of information	Parents, peers, online reviews, Internet searches, brand websites, videogames	Peers, Internet searches, brand websites, online reviews, parents, grassroots and viral marketing	Online reviews, Internet searches, friends, shopping bots, online product comparisons	Expert websites (e.g., Consumer Reports), children, online reviews, Internet searches	Expert websites (e.g., AARP, sponsored by community organizations), grandchildren, children, friends

age shapes its members' ambitions and fears in unique ways. Perhaps most important of all, media habits are formed while a person is growing up and include only media that exist at that time. Over a lifetime, changes in media habits occur when newer media appear, but older audiences are rarely early adopters of these new sources of information.

Demographic Overview of American Generations

While members of American age subcultures share experiences and values, they also have distinctive demographic profiles. Just as there is tremendous diversity within an ethnic group, there are vast differences in the income, gender distribution, education level, occupation, and family structure of consumers within age cohorts. Table 5.2 highlights the demographic differences both within and across American age subcultures. In addition, the table includes information about purchasing power, cohort size, and birth years.

Tweens do not officially comprise a generation, just a life stage that all adults go through. It is their tastes, technological savvy, and the significant role that brands play in their construction of personal identity that turn them into a consumer subculture. Today's tweens number over 20 million in elementary and middle schools.[19] Their purchasing power consists of $43 billion of their own money, and they influence more than $150 billion of their parents' spending.[20]

Generation Y, also known as the "millennials," represents over 80 million people. About one-third of them are minorities, making this the most diverse American generation. Most of them have not yet fully entered the workforce, and some are still completing their education. Over 60 percent are still unmarried, reflecting their tendency to postpone marriage until after they have established a career. Their direct purchasing power will overtake that of the baby boomers by 2017.[21]

Generation X appears large according to the numbers in Table 5.2, but is actually a much smaller cohort than either Generation Y or the baby boomers.[22] The table is based on census data reported for people in their twenties, thirties, and forties, while Generation X members are currently between 32 and 46 years old. Originally called "Slackers," this group includes the most educated women of all American generations, and they are now known for having a strong work ethic.[23] An unusually high percentage of them have never married, though family is a high priority. They spend more than $700 billion per year, overindexing on personal luxuries.[24]

According to U.S. Census data, Generation X is slightly more male (50.1 percent male vs. 49.9 percent female) than the U.S. average (49.2 percent male vs. 50.8 percent female). It also has a somewhat higher percentage of college and post–college graduates compared to the U.S. average (27 percent vs. 24.4 percent). However, Generation X has fewer homeowners compared to the national average.[25]

Table 5.2 divides baby boomers into early and late boomers. Together the group represents over 79 million persons. They have the highest rate of divorce among all generations—30 percent. Their huge purchasing power (over $2 trillion) and size constitute their great appeal to marketers.

The last age cohort shown in Table 5.2 is the mature market, also known as the "Greatest Generation" or "Silent Generation." These 50 million aging consumers stay active longer and act younger, than any prior group at the same age. Senior citizens find themselves a bit isolated in youth-oriented American culture. They continue to be savers and to be dedicated to family and community. Most important, they still control over 70 percent of the personal wealth and assets in this country and will soon leave over $8.5 trillion in inheritance to the baby boomers.[26]

Tweens Are in Search of "What's Cool"

The term "tween" comes from "between" and "teen." Technically it refers to a life stage—the preteen years. Marketers consider tweens those age 9 to 14 or 8 to 12, depending on the source.[27] In transition from childhood to the teenage years, tweens are eager to grow up, but still act like kids.[28] These characteristics make their marketplace behavior highly symbolic of self-expression and personal identity construction. To successfully target tween consumers, it is important to reach them in their "world."

The current tween cohort is made up of individuals born after Generation Y (roughly 1998–2004). This group—typically the offspring of Generation X or late baby boomers—is currently in middle or elementary school. They share many habits and traits with Generation Y and have also been called "Generation Z," "Generation V" (for virtual), the "Internet Generation," "Gen @," or the "MySpace Generation."[29] While the last three are popular names for this digital youth culture, some of the same terms are used to describe Generation Y.[30]

Some authors have suggested that today's tweens are the "New Silent Generation." This "future" generation shares experiences of the original "Silent Generation" (today's Mature Market), such as coming of age during a time of economic and political instability with an uncertain future.[31] They worry a lot—about money, being accepted, and problems with family, peers, and school. "Generation Now" is another moniker that reflects the group's "culture of immediacy."[32] The term "Generation C" has also been used, with the "C" having multiple, often simultaneous meanings, such as "content,"[33]

Table 5.2

Demographic Comparison of Age Cohorts

Age group (names used for this group)	Birth years[1]	Purchasing power	Population size (000s)	Education levels	% currently married
Tweens aka, Connecteds, Gen @, Generation Z, Generation V "Virtual," The New Silent Generation, MySpace Generation, Generation Now, **Generation C**	1999–2005 (7–14 years)	Direct: $51 billion[2] Indirect: $200+ billion	20,000+ 40% of schoolchildren = minority	grades 3–8	N/A
Generation Y aka, Millennials, Wired Generation, Echo Boomers, Gen @, Net (or Internet) Generation, Nexters, and Nintendo Generation	1984–1995 (18–29 years)	Direct: $200 billion Indirect: $300+ billion	84,000+ 33%+ = minority	HS/M = 34.4% HS/F = 29.4% BA/M = 7.2% BA/F =10.9%	Married (M/F)[3] 32.8%/39.7% Divorced (M/F) 5.3%/8.2% Unmarried (M/F) 62.0%/52.1%
Generation X aka, Slackers, 13th Generation, Latchkey Generation	1965–1983 (30–48 years)	Direct: $125 billion	83,000[4] Most well-educated women	HS/M = 84.5–85.5% HS/F = 88.7–88.9% BA/M = 27–28.9% BA/F = 31.6–34.2%	Married (M/F)[5] 64.0%/64.3% Divorced (M/F) 14.6%/19.4% Unmarried (M/F) 21.4%/16.4%
Baby Boomers II aka, Woodstock Generation	1956–1964 (49–57 years)	Direct: $2 trillion (I & II)	44,000+	HS/M = 86.4% HS/F = 87.9% BA/M = 29.9% BA/F = 27.2%	Married (M/F) 66.8%/64.1% Divorced (M/F) 30.7%/25.2% Unmarried (M/F) 14.0%/10.8%

	Birth years (age)	Assets	Population / Demographics	Education	Marital status
Baby Boomers I	1945–1955 (58–68 years)		34,000+		Married (M/F) 72.4%/62.3% Divorced (M/F) 19.7%/30.7% Unmarried (M/F) 7.9%/7.0%
Mature Market aka, Silent Generation, Senior Citizens States with High concentrations: FL, WV, ME, PA, IO, ND, MN, HI, SD, VT	Before 1945 (over 68 years)	77% of all American assets	39,000+ M = 16,823.6 (42.3%) F = 22,747.0 (57.7%) 80.8% white, not Hispanic, 8.4% black, 6.5% U.S. Latino, 3.2% Asian	HS/M = 75.3% HS/F = 73.4% BA/M = 25.3% BA/F = 14.9%	Married (M/F) 71.4%/41.3% Divorced (M/F) 25%/55% Unmarried (M/F) 4.6%/4.6%

Sources: L.M. Howden and J.A. Meyer, "Age and Sex Composition: 2010," 2010 Census Brief (Washington, DC: U.S. Census Bureau, May 2011); C.A. Werner, "The Older Population: 2010," 2010 Census Brief (Washington, DC: U.S. Census Bureau, November 2011); U.S. Census Bureau, 2009 Data Set, America FactFinder.com, http://factfinder2.census.gov/faces/nav/jsf/pages/index.xhtml.

[1]There is significant disagreement about which years to use to classify each of the American age cohorts. The years used in this table have been chosen in order to fit U.S. Census data and categories.

[2]A. de Mesa, "Marketing and Tweens," *Bloomberg Businessweek,* October 11, 2005, www.businessweek.com/stories/2005-10-11/marketing-and-tweens/.

[3]Marital status for Generation Y includes only persons 20–34.

[4]Most researchers estimate Generation X's size as about 40+ million.

[5]Marital status for Generation X includes only persons 35–44.

"community,"[34] and "creativity."[35] The American Press Association's Media Center describes Gen C as "creating, producing and participating in news in a connected, informed society."[36] Whatever terms stick over time, today's tweens are very young but active consumers, connected to the Internet, and completely at ease in the world of digital technology.[37]

Consumer Tweens Are Shaped by Technology and Global Uncertainties

Numbering nearly 20 million, tweens are an influential buying force in today's marketplace. Although their parents pay for the majority of tween purchases, tweens themselves often research and act as purchasing agents. They are savvy in ways that people of that same age in prior generations never would have been. That Walmart even has its own brand of makeup for this age group may be shocking to persons unfamiliar with tweens' "grownup" buying habits.

Today's tweens make a conscious effort to secure some financial independence from their parents. In addition to earning an allowance at home, 61 percent of tweens perform jobs (e.g., babysitting, pet care, and lawn care) in the neighborhood. Their main sources of income are an allowance, a job, gifts, and their parents. The average tween spends more than $220 per month, making direct tween purchasing power over $11 billion annually.[38]

In addition to having their own disposable income, they also influence their parents' spending. The majority (72 percent) of all tween purchase decisions are made jointly by parent and child. An additional 19 percent of tween purchase decisions are made by parents on their behalf. Parents are this group's heroes. Since parents do not want to buy something that their kids do not want, tweens have direct and indirect ways to influence family decisions. It is estimated that girls 11 to 14 are subjected to 500 advertisements a day.[39] This tween "purchase influence" translates to over $200 billion a year. Even automakers target this age group with toy cars that showcase their brands, though it will be a long time before they are able to buy a real car.[40]

The largest expense for a tween consumer is food, totaling more than $60 billion annually. The next largest expenses are personal care products, entertainment, and reading materials, totally about $43 billion yearly. Clothing follows, at about $22 billion. Households with tweens tend to spend more time than other households browsing and shopping; they especially enjoy new stores. Over 40 percent of tweens buy videogames every year.[41]

After apparel and shoes, entertainment is a major expense for tweens, who spend a considerable amount of their own money. This includes going to the movies, attending sporting events, and eating out at restaurants. Books rank fourth, followed by toys, DVDs and videos, accessories, and music.[42]

To date, no specific events define "the collective past" of tweens, as this group's experiences will be shaped in the future by the effects of decisions made today in politics and elsewhere (e.g., the aftermath of the war in Iraq, the global recession of 2008–11, the 2011 "Arab spring"). However, as a result of the struggling economy, tweens could become less materialistic and consumer driven.[43]

Because technology has replaced historical events as the major defining factor for generational change, the current tween cohort appears to be largely defined by technological fluency, especially in the use of social networking. As the first "digital natives," they have entered a world of information overload, making them so overexposed to commercial messages that only well-targeted messages will reach them.[44] Unlike previous generations, this is also the first generation to see parents and children embrace technology together, as technology substitutes for other teaching aids.

Tweens grow up in a world with widespread equality of the sexes at work and at home. Families are smaller, parents are older, and usually both parents are in the workforce (two-income families). Family, as a matter of fact, is a loose definition to them—single-parent, multiracial, and same-sex parent families are commonplace. "Their parents (usually from Generation X) are older and comfortably affluent, but with big financial commitments. The family works as a unit and relates on an adult level, as if no one has time or space for a childhood. Everybody rushes to work and school in the morning and home at night."[45]

Even more than baby boomers, Generation X and Y parents dote on their children excessively and spend accordingly. However, Generation X parents are reacting against the baby boomers' overindulgent and free-spirited parenting style. While Generation X shares the tendency to be "helicopter parents"—hovering over every aspect of their kids' lives—they are also swinging back to what might be termed traditional values, that is, an emphasis on old-fashioned notions, such as work ethic, etiquette, resilience, fortitude, and taking personal responsibility.[46]

The deluge of media coverage and school projects on climate change will make tweens far more environmentally aware; Many already identify global warming and climate change as the world's biggest issue.[47] The two key influencers of current tweens are their parents and technology, especially the Internet. Researchers and strategists believe that multiplayer computer gaming—which requires collaboration, leadership, and fast strategy switches—will also be influential. Cooperating with others and problem solving will be second nature to them.[48]

The "Cool Factor" and Tween Identity

Today's tweens are encouraged from birth to be unique at the same time that they are involved through technology in interacting with others. Their lives are full of structured activities, and a number of social researchers anticipate that members of this new generation will have a strong social conscience and work ethic.[49] The social environment of tweens is heavy on stimulus, yet weak in face-to-face interpersonal relationships. This is the age in which personalities are beginning to form and where distinctions between family and friends and fitting in versus being unique are emerging. Tweens already have rich online lives (virtual worlds, avatars), and many will have multiple identities for life on- and offline. They are convinced that they can become famous and rich by expressing who they are as individuals and not "following the herd."[50]

Tweens are very creative in making their opinions and ideas heard and seen. They actively produce and share content. They mix their own music, edit their own videos, post their photography on the Internet, and publish blogs and books. This pattern makes it unlikely that a few self-appointed experts will emerge to dictate what is right or wrong. Moreover, the desire to express themselves drives many tweens to conclude that everything is for publication. The phenomenal growth of sites such as MySpace and Facebook (virtual community sites), YouTube and Fliggo (video-sharing sites), Twitter (social networking and microblogging service), Flickr and Photobucket (image and video hosting sites), blogger (blog publishing system), and Wikipedia (a free, open content, community-built encyclopedia) are indicative of a generation that believes that open-source technology is a tool to allow anyone, anywhere, to learn about any topic of possible interest.

Yet when everyone is a creator, everyone is also a judge. The main purpose of tween content producing and publishing is self-expression, rather than making a profit or benefiting society. At the same time, tweens are well aware that a creative contribution is only great until a better one comes along. Playing off the rules of one of this group's favorite TV programs, *American Idol*, the website Idealog puts it this way: "the court of public opinion can vote anyone off at any time (no matter how good one is)."[51] So, the motivation is to be as creative and competitive as possible. Despite the drive that day-to-day life should be challenging, it should ultimately be fun. It somehow needs to involve originality and expression. Nothing is just about work; it's about meaning and transformation. Life for tweens needs to include elements of a game.

The "cool factor" is an important part of any purchase for tweens, even if they do their shopping with parents. Tweens are shaping their identities, and they want things that will help them fit in with peers. Whereas the teen market uses style as an indicator of fashion acceptance, the tween market uses brands. Brands are very important to tweens because their use allows tweens to act like older reference groups and to be accepted by older siblings and friends.[52]

Because buying is entirely discretionary, tweens want products that enhance their communication with others about who they are. Art products, such as scrapbooks and photo albums, allow them to express their creativity. Tweens are also attracted to products that symbolize the positive values that life has to offer: fun, attractiveness, a better life, products that provide comfort and reliable pleasure, and products that are dependable.[53]

More than previous generations, tween girls are concerned with fashion and style. They want to look older but are also self-conscious. Although in a transitional age as far as fashion goes, they still have the desire to be a little bit like everyone else but also start to become their own person. Hence, dressing up is about gaining attention. As a result, tween girls flock to clothing retailers such as Justice, Abercrombie Kids, American Eagle, Hollister, and Limited Too, fashion accessories outlets such as Claire's and Accessorize (boutiques selling jewelry, hair and clothing accessories primarily for young girls), and cosmetics companies such as Bonne Bell, Shimmer City (www.shimmercity. com), and Yofi Cosmetics.[54]

The majority of tweens have a good understanding of what is meant by advertising with specific definitions ranging from something that "tries to get me to buy something" to one that "lets people know about your product." The top five adjectives tweens use to describe advertising are "informative," "funny," "entertaining," "interesting," and "cool."[55]

Tween Communication Habits and Preferred Sources of Information

Tweens act older and grow up faster than previous generations.[56] Peer groups are their first sources outside family with whom they share ideas about trends and styles. The majority of boys' casual talk with friends centers on sports and what to play. Girl tweens, by contrast, report that their number one topic of conversation is boys. Both enjoy sharing entertainment experiences such as TV shows, movies, and music. Because peer acceptance is an essential driver in this age group, tween girls also admit that, when socializing with friends, they love to gossip about other people. Tweens seek connections and identity through virtual networks, talking to friends in chatrooms, on MySpace or Facebook forums, and on instant messaging user lists and others on their so-called buddy lists of 15–50 names.[57]

Tweens are masters of multitasking. They easily combine traditional media with word of mouth via social media, e-mail, online advertising, and other forums for chatting and decision making. In fact, tweens simultaneously spend time engaged with "old," traditional media like TV (about 12.1 hours per week) and use computers and the Internet (about 7.3 hours per week). In addition, tweens spend a growing amount of time playing games, in particular, videogames, alone or—more typically—with friends, whether in person or online.

While two-thirds of tweens do not own a cell phone, 78 percent want one. They want to make sure they know where their friends are and what is going on.[58] Their vocal preferences for specific brands and services have been attributed to consumer behaviors learned from their parents. Based on requests from merchants and tweens, J.C. Penney took Stardoll's fashions for avatars (www.stardoll.com) and made a clothing line for tweens. Tweens request products online, contact companies they see advertised in magazines, and ask directly in stores for their favorite brands.[59] Their favorite magazines, mostly for girls, are *Seventeen, YM, Teen People* and *CosmoGirl*.

Not only do tweens go online to be their own editor and gatekeeper, but they also select the kind of news and opinions that they care about most.[60] They are captivated by the fact that they can post and share their thoughts, ideas, and images globally. This technology and media revolution is being captured in text and on digital still photos and videos, many embedded in cell phones and spread by global networks through blogs, IM (instant messaging), photo and video messaging, and other Web tools.[61] In order to be always "on"—transmit and receive constantly—they spend their days media multitasking.

TV has remained the medium most often paired with usage of other media by tweens.[62] In fact, if a tween were forced to give up some form of entertainment for a month, only 14 percent would give up TV. Three TV shows that have been tops among tweens are *SpongeBob Square Pants, Lizzie Maguire*, and *The Fairly OddParents*. Each program discusses key topics among Tweens: friendships (*SpongeBob*), growing up (*Lizzie McGuire*), and being oneself (*The Fairly OddParents*). Topping the favorite actor list is Frankie Muniz, and Hilary Duff is tweens' favorite actress. The most popular channels in tween households are ABC Family, Nick at Nite, Fox, WB, and PBS. For these networks, 9 to 14 year olds are considered core viewers, and shows are designed especially for this audience.

Tweens are spending a growing amount of time playing mobile videogames. Tweens lead mobile game usage: Among those who play mobile games one or more times per day, they number more than 84 percent, compared with 64 percent as a whole.[63]

Among the 35 percent of tweens who own cell phones, Nielsen found that 5 percent access the Internet on their mobile phone every month. Forty-one percent do so while traveling (e.g., to school), 26 percent while at a friend's house, and 17 percent at social events. Tween mobile users are also using their phones for in-home entertainment. Fifty-eight percent who download or watch TV on their phone do so at home. Sixty-four percent download or play music on their phone at home, and 56 percent access the Internet from home.[64]

The tween cultures of having both "individualistic" (wanting to be different) and "collectivistic" (wanting to fit in) values affect the adoption and consumption of new media (mobile phone, Internet). To enhance uniqueness, tweens use mobile phones and the Internet for interpersonal communication and for enjoyment, while tweens from a collectivist cultural background (e.g., Asian-American or Latino tweens) appear to use the Internet more for educational purposes. For these reasons, the tween consumer segment is definitely not homogeneous.[65]

Riot Connects with Tween Boys

Marketing to a generation of wannabe artists might feel like riding to hell on a skateboard, but smart marketers like Riot Media are finding rich veins for success with tween boys. Riot Media has created the first and only all-encompassing, multimedia lifestyle and entertainment brand for the underserved tween boy market (www.riotgames.com). Riot features an edgy, activity-stuffed website, implemented with a creative viral marketing strategy.

All creative Riot content stems from a central, core story that draws on the universal theme of the battle between good and evil, with powerful villains and underdog heroes. The Riot story is set in a fictional, small American city that is threatened when an evil circus arrives. Faced with this threat, the town's boys rally and fight back—aided by a very special chimp that escapes from the circus and helps the boys in their desperate fight. As the true hero of the story, Riot the Chimp is the proud mascot of the entire Riot brand and is featured prominently in all materials and products.[66]

The over-the-top Riot website is packed with hysterical jokes, funky pictures, stupendous games, weird noises, amazing downloads, and pranks galore. Riotweb.com offers the latest facts about sports and entertainment and always promotes a contest. Kids can browse for exclusive Riot purchase opportunities. Riotweb.com is also the home of the Riot Squad club, an army of Riot loyalists, connected by the common bonds of fart jokes, pop culture passion, and tween fun.[67]

Riot Magazine, a tween guy manifesto stuffed with topical features, gut-busting pranks, entertainment reviews, and, of course, endless humor, reaches tween boys where they shop—more than 5,000 outlets across the country, including Sports Authority, Fred's, and Coconuts. In addition to the website and the magazine, Riot also offers a collectible card game, adventure-themed comic books, a colorful calendar, icky stickers, awesome school supplies, unique mobile wallpapers, and ringtones showcasing wacky Riot humor. RiotSquad apparel, the first line of ultrahip sportswear for tween boys, is available at mass market retailers. The cool, fashionable clothing features hip-hop influence and lots of Riot humor.[68]

To get the word out, Riot hired street teams at the malls of boys age 14 and older as well as advertising (TV, print, online, and direct mail). The company also made innovative use of local retailers, such as Carvel and barbershops—places frequented by tweens. In addition, 20 circus-themed viral mall tours were created, which had tents where boys could learn how to play the Riot collectible card game; Justin Bieber was the celebrity guest for one year's tour. The creator and CEO of Riot Media, Jay Gissen, noted that "boys like getting stuff from other boys rather than parents or from teachers."[69] In sum, Riot uses age- and gender-relevant content, delivered to the target by age- and gender-relevant messengers in age- and gender-relevant locations on- and offline.

Tween Girls: From Dolls to Fashion

Companies that market to tween girls are confronting a phenomenon called KGOY—Kids Getting Older Younger. Examples of products that have sold monumentally well are the Groovy Girls line by the Manhattan Toy Company and a line of dolls called Bratz, introduced in 2001 by MGA Entertainment. Both Bratz and Groovy Girls tend to look ethnically indeterminate, do not have Barbie's pin-up girl measurements, and are designed to portray a positive body image for young girls of all different ethnicities. The dolls all have different skin tones and facial features.

One of the reasons for success with tween girls is both companies' use of transcultural marketing strategies. Their product and communication programs include ancillary videos, books, and websites (vehicles for more advertising) as well as other lines of dolls and products from Gameboy to stationery.[70]

What unites these brands (and other upstart tween brands) is their focus on tween fashion and an attempt to let tweens personalize their looks. EST Today Design Studio Beta and Fashionology (www.fashionology.com) actually allow tweens to create their own clothes.[71] The top fashion magazines that target tween girls are *Seventeen*, *YM*, *Teen People*, *CosmoGirl*. Their combined circulation is over 7 million.

Their success is due to the use of user-generated content, especially online, where site users can collaborate with virtual friends on designs. While tweens are influenced by celebrity fashion, 71 percent of online tweens visit social-networking sites weekly and more than half participate in monthly advertiser-branded interactive activities. Tween fashion marketers use the entire arsenal of contact points and media as well as partnerships and openness to tween ideas in social networking environments and websites. Success comes from their combination of sensitivity to social network users' feelings of ownership, provision of useful information in the form of content and tools, creation of an entertaining environment, treating young people as partners, and innovative ideas that spark tween creativity.

Today's tweens must be reached first at younger ages. In that context, the right "look" and the right "feel" are key elements because tweens follow trends.[72] Since they are at the "in-between" stage, tweens want products that teenagers like but are scaled down and tween-friendly. Products and store layouts not only have to be "cool," but they have to suggest innovation and feel sophisticated. Growing with their tween customer base into the teenage and young adult years affords companies the opportunity to build long-term relationships with these customers.

Visual elements are important in communicating with tweens. On websites and in advertisements, visual imagery should be relevant to tween current likes and aspirations in sports, school, work, and play. Lego had to redesign its classic "human" figure when it decided to target tween girls because they are more likely than tween boys to identify with Legos as avatars. Lego adapted by adding details to the new figure, brighter colors, and book-length biographies.[73] Tweens are quick to detect inconsistencies or exaggerations in marketing communications. If models are used in advertising, their age, culture, and overall appearance are of critical importance. In particular, models should never "look" younger than the targeted tween.[74]

Tweens expect the multicultural environment that they experience in their daily lives to be reflected in the communications that they see. They are critical of the "wrong" type of advertising and are dismayed if there is no cultural diversity in the communications that they receive. Moreover, when it comes to diversity in ads, tween girls are also offended by a lack of variety not only in skin color but also in hair color. All marketing content (stores, webpages, advertising, etc.) must appear "cool" to a tween audience.[75]

Table 5.3 puts into perspective the key decision areas for companies that market to tween consumers. Transcultural marketing involves more than the "traditional 4 Ps." For tweens, some of the avenues for building relationships are not as important as they are for older consumers. For instance, tweens are more focused on their immediate community than corporate aesthetics, financial partnerships of companies, the economic impact of corporate decisions, or financial support for tween causes. For tween consumers, brand names are more important than price/value relationships, marketing communications

Table 5.3

Transcultural Marketing: Cultural Value Propositions for Tweens

Transcultural marketing mix	Tween consumer preferences
Product usage as group marker?	True for all technology-related products and services, music and fashion tastes
Usage variability across diversity within age group	Gender differences most important, age differences for more expensive products
Importance of brand image	Brand choice expresses constructed identity, different brands allow trying on various identities, expresses social acceptance
Memberships in community organizations	Immediate family and friends, online contacts, events for causes, scouting, sports teams
Price/value relationships	Brand name most important
Philanthropic choices	Environment- and disease-related causes
Corporate human resource policies	Little interest
Corporate financial partnerships	Little interest
Support of important causes	Can increase brand recognition, brand loyalty
Local community economic footprint	Can be source of loyalty, pride, or protest, and online buzz
Environmental footprint	Can be source of advantage for building online and event engagement
Relevant messages	Must be age and gender-appropriate content
Media presence/public relations	Can stimulate social network buzz online
Corporate aesthetics	Little interest, but prefer saturated colors and contrasts, visually "interesting"

should stimulate word of mouth, and media choices should include opportunities for interaction and user-generated content.

Brands and marketing tactics that target tweens are real and virtual participants in their lives. Marketing phenomena help tweens shape and express who they want to be and with whom they want to fit. This role in their customers' lives carries a special responsibility for companies that market to tweens. As an important cultural institution in their lives, companies can introduce content that addresses long-term, healthy life skills. Tween marketers can help create a healthier adult generation by subtly but creatively teaching good health practices, life, work, money, and relationship skills. Promoting their customers' best selves while enjoying their current fandom might just make brands less vulnerable to their inevitable chase of "what's cool."

Generation Y Is Creating "What's Cool" in an Insecure World

The term "Generation Y" first appeared in an August 1993 *Advertising Age* editorial to describe children born between 1985 and 1995.[76] The scope of the term has changed greatly since then to include, in many cases, anyone born as early as 1976 and as late as 2000. There is still no precise definition of birth years for Generation Y. Some scholars add a "cusp" generation, the "MTV generation," between Generations X and Y, with a birth range from 1975 to 1985.

This generational cohort has many descriptive names: Echo Boomers, Generation Next, and—in an attempt to tie this generation to key events and cultural trends associated with it—the Millennial Generation, the Internet generation, the Wired Generation, or the Digital Generation. They are best defined by the fact that they graduated from high school around the new millennium. They also grew up during a time of economic growth and stability in the United States, affording them a prosperous childhood. However, they entered the workforce in a time of economic instability and global unrest.[77]

The following quotation best describes the times that have shaped Generation Y:

> Generation Y has never known life without cell phones, pagers, fax machines, and voice mail. Their world has always included minivans, bottled water, cable television, overnight package delivery, and chat rooms. They would have no personal reference for a time before ATMs, VCRs, PCs, CDs, MTV, CNN, SUVs, and TCBYs! And sadly enough, Gen Yers have never known a world without AIDS, crack, or terrorist attacks. They've never known a world where kids don't shoot and kill other kids.[78]

Gen Y Is the 9/11 Generation: Diversity, Dreams, and Family Values

Economic instability and the terrorist attacks of September 11, 2001, are the major events that shape this group's social and cultural values.[79] As a result of the terrorist attacks of September 11, 2001, and the U.S. government actions following the attacks, the United States has shifted toward a more nationalistic and patriotic mood. In 2002 some young adults reported that they felt guilty about not voting in a presidential election. The terrorist attacks, they said, had made them more "politically aware."[80] That showed in their higher participation rates in the 2004, 2008, and 2012 presidential elections.[81] This increased patriotism has also appeared in more positive ratings by this group of American-made products and services.

The experiences of September 11 also increased the prominence of religious beliefs of young Americans. As the most diverse group of Americans, this group is simultaneously more openly tolerant and spiritual.[82] Several studies emphasize the millennials' greater interest in family, religion, and community—at the expense of celebrity role models and their associated brands.[83] There is no one single "American Dream" for this group.[84] Volunteerism is up, and teens now form the most religious age bracket in the United States.[85]

Generation Y is largely characterized as a supersized Generation X. They are greater in number and more diverse, pierced, skateboarding, and in-your-face than Generation X. While members of this generation chart their own course, many Generation Y members openly admit that their parents are their role models. When compared to previous generations, they retain closer parental bonds even after leaving home. They are impatient as a result of being raised in world of instant gratification and blunt and expressive since making a point is most important. They are image-driven, untrusting of major media personalities, and skeptical, but also more adaptable and efficient multitaskers.[86]

As members of Generation Y in the United States began to enter colleges and universities in large numbers, some of their baby boomer parents became helicopter parents. Many college advisers and administrators worry that this could have a negative effect on Generation Y's social progress, ego, and developing maturity. The cell phone has become "the world's longest umbilical cord" between Generation Y and their parents.[87]

Under constant pressure by their parents and society to achieve, millennials find little common ground with the "slacker" archetype of youth displayed by their predecessor generations. In contrast to ultraindividualist Xers, millennials are group-oriented—meaning that they are less interested in an "army of one" and more interested in the "watch *me* become *we*" alternative. Millennials are less hung up on race, gender, or ethnicity than their parents but may increasingly be moving toward increased sensitivity to economic class.[88] Examples of two of their favorite entertainments emphasize "we" over "me": *Dawson's Creek*'s tagline is "Growing up together," and *Black Hawk Down* showed leaving "no one behind."

The millennials are one of the most educated generations yet, and they love to learn. College attendance rates create competition for top schools and top jobs. Generation Y views the four-year degree as a minimum requirement to "get you in the door." Graduate work has become the path to desired careers.[89] Monster.com reported in 2008 that 54 percent of recent graduates did not expect job offers upon graduation, and 19 percent were headed directly to graduate school. Moreover, 52 percent were willing to relocate for a job, and 33 percent were concerned that off-shoring would affect them.[90]

Generation Y wants to start at the top or at least climb the corporate ladder early. They believe that they deserve the position they want, whether experienced or not. The members of Generation Y are not against hard work by any means. This is not a lazy generation, just one that expects immediate gratification, due to a childhood of receiving it. The Generation Y employee does not plan on being at the same location for an extended period and wants to do the work better and faster than his or her coworkers. Being competitive with themselves and others is in their nature. HTC resonated with this group's lifestyles by "offering a phone that is as turbocharged as you." Many millennials would like to be self-employed; making a difference in the world, or the company, is the goal of this generation.

Generation Y as Consumers

Generation Y, with 70 million to 80 million members, is more than three times the size of Generation X and currently comprises about 26 percent of the U.S. population. In 2013, they ranged from 19 to 35 years old (or 13 to 31, according to another source). This generation earns over $200 billion per year and influences $300 billion in family spending.[91] They claim 4–5 percent of all household spending in the United States in men's and women's apparel and footwear but have equally above average consumption in infant apparel, audio equipment, computer technology, alcoholic beverages, and shelter. They voice their opinions about what computer to buy, whom to call for pizza, and where to spend the family vacation.[92]

Marketers too frequently assume that Generation Y responds to brands with hip, edgy statements that cut through media clutter and push the boundaries of style and taste. They are unforgiving of marketers that they think are trying to "trick" them but are so used to reading and writing online customer product reviews that this serves as their main outlet for negative feedback to companies.[93]

They are a high-spending group with large discretionary incomes, but judicious about which brands to purchase.[94] They have been involved in family decisions from a very young age and hence influence a vast majority of household decisions on brands and services. To be perceived as cool, a brand must not only be of high quality but be tailored to people their age. Having grown up in a more media-saturated, brand-conscious world than their parents, members of Generation Y see advertising as important, yet they resent the "hard sell" and are mistrustful of the mass media. Nonetheless, this generation is very involved with advertising and appreciates its informational and entertainment values.

Generation Y's diversity added to the importance of self-expression pose great challenges to marketers. Variety is as preferred in products as it is in media choices and is contributing to the current proliferation of media vehicles. The millennials are also fond of promotions at the expense of brand advertising, partially explaining their lack of brand loyalty.[95] Newer retailers, such as Aeropostale, Urban Outfitters, Anthropologie, or Pacific Sunwear, have become purveyors of Gen Y lifestyles.[96] The food category is a fitting example of Generation Y tastes because pricing and value strategies are more successful than brand loyalty appeals. The pursuit of "what's cool" is constrained by the importance that this group places on family and religion.[97]

The trendsetters for the return of "old-fashioned" values in this ostensibly materialistic generation seem to be ethnic members of Gen Y. More African Americans than white young adults list religion as important, and more Hispanics than white youths mention their greater orientation toward family.[98] Members of Generation Y strongly identify with one another and share a "global inclusivism" as to race, gender, religion, and state of the environment.[99] Thus they look at race quite differently. Compared to white boomers who identify strongly as "white," only 55 percent of white millennials refer to themselves the same way.[100] Time, space, and the social bonds that build families and communities distinguish the Generation Y cohort from previous generations.[101]

Media Choices: Multitasking, Creating Content, and Spreading the "News"

Generation Y is boldly embracing new technologies, entertainment platforms, and communication tools. They prefer integrated platforms, portable media, and "all-in-one" devices. They construct customized media repertoires from combinations of old and new media. Their ability and desire to have instant access to information and entertainment is driving the changed media landscape for all consumers.

Traditional television has suffered from this trend as millennials do not watch scheduled TV programs when they are first broadcast. Gen Y audiences consume their favorite shows either zipping through commercials on DVR-recordings or streaming media on websites. If they catch a show live, they are likely to be multitasking, simultaneously updating their Facebook page or tweeting updates on daily activities to their circle of friends.[102] More important, 64 percent of Generation Yers want to easily connect their home TV to the Internet, 57 percent want an all-in-one device, and 60 percent want to be able to easily move their TV shows, podcasts, movies, and other media content to any devices that they own.[103]

As for music, Generation Y appears to want what is new, original, and different. Indie music—so called to symbolize the out-of-mainstream state of this music and its performers—features artists such as Kanye West, Modest Mouse, Kings of Leon, Vampire Weekend, Lady Gaga, Evanescence, and Good Charlotte. These artists also appear in movies and TV shows that appeal to this generation, which has no definable sound but is fluent "in many sounds."[104] The success with Generation Y audiences of the TV show *American Idol*, where unknown aspiring singing talents have to master various sounds in a competition, seems to support this description of their tastes. This generation's sound is defined by production techniques and newness value; many music acts are new for a season, and then they fade away.

These music trends have heavily affected radio. Because music and information are readily available on the Internet, and they can save individual programs and songs on mp3 players, members of this generation tend to browse and pick their music and news à la carte at any time, so they have less need for commercial radio. This generation is not willing to wait for a particular song or bit of information to be offered on someone else's schedule. They prefer to download it and then listen to it when they see fit, and thus attracting their affiliation and loyalty is challenging.

Generation Y has little time for reading hard copy newspapers and magazines. Given their desire for customization and self-expression, they not only prefer to obtain their news from Web-based sources and blogs but also participate in and comment on the news. The large millennial audience for CNN's "iReports" during the 2008, 2010, and 2012 elections is indicative of this generation's preferred role as "creator-consumer" rather than "consumer" alone, for news.

From the time Gen Yers were young, computer-based games and toys have played a role in their education (LeapFrog) and entertainment (Xbox, Wii, PlayStation). As they grew older, they started using digital devices to communicate, create, and maintain circles of friends. As early as 2007, Gen Y members reported that 87 percent owned a computer, 94 percent owned a cell phone, 76 percent used instant messaging (IM), 75 percent had a Facebook account, nearly two-thirds owned a portable music or video device, and about one-third used the Internet as their primary source of information (which often includes blogs and other privately created information).[105] E-mailing, instant messaging, and gaming are activities via technology that allow them to express themselves in venues such as Facebook and YouTube.

YouTube, for instance, has rapidly become the most popular video-sharing website among Generation Y, as users can upload, view, and share video clips. Videos can be rated, and the average rating and the number of times a video has been watched are both published. The wide variety of site content includes movie and TV clips, music videos, and amateur content such as video blogging and short original videos.

This text-loving generation is obsessed with text messaging on mobile phones. Mobile users not only "text" each other but often opt into free service by companies that automatically "text" users short messages to announce upcoming events in whatever content categories they have indicated interest, such as music, fashion, or local sports. These text messages are often written by peers of the users, known as "mobile correspondents."

Brands Connecting with Generation Y: VW Jetta, Hilfiger, and the "Dew"

Marketing tactics that work with Generation Y are funny, unpretentious, and often confusing to older consumers. The following three examples are different in their approach though they share some elements that success-fully connect with Generation Y. The ads that they most like are irreverent, creative, involved in the generation's lifestyle, and spread trends and ideas by facilitating word of mouth.

Volkswagen's now famous "Da Da Da" commercial, originally titled "Sunday Morning," intrigued, attracted, resonated with, and inspired its Gen Y target audience. It also revived the VW brand as cultural symbol. Although VW did not market directly to teens, both its Golf and Passat models show up on surveys as Generation Y "faves," and many have bought these models after getting their driver's license. In the quirky, edgy "Da Da Da" commercial, two guys drive around aimlessly in a Jetta to the background music of the 1982 German new wave band Trio's hit song "Da Da Da." They pick up a discarded chair on the curb but notice its bad smell while driving on. Having already been alerted to their fastidiousness concerning the cleanliness of the car (one wipes the dash early on), the viewer is not surprised that they drop off the chair a few blocks later. The commercial ends with the message "The Volkswagen Jetta! It fits your life, or the complete lack thereof." The message may be that VW is about driving for pleasure, but the novelty of a commercial that goes nowhere despite its humor is attractive. The ad, funny and oblique, became a favorite among young adults and teens.[106]

Volkswagen linked its advertising in old and new media to its other activi-ties and messages that appeal to Gen Y values. Appealing to Gen Y's taste for music, VW partnered with First Act guitars to build an electric GarageMaster that plugs into the vehicle. They have designed "best practices" programs for the call centers that interface with VW customers and service departments.[107] Their newer Golfs aim to "personalize" the Golf driving experience and match the iPad feel of their infotainment screens.[108] In 2007 the VW Jetta was voted one of the 12 most respected brands of Generation Y, based on its affordability and approachability. However, important, too, were VW's green initiatives and its "fun to drive" motto for the Jetta.[109]

Tommy Hilfiger is another brand whose marketing style intrigues Generation Y. Its distinctive logo-laden shirts and jackets maintain the loyalty of Generation Y by staying ahead of the style curve. Hilfiger achieved this feat by sending researchers to music clubs to see how influential fashion leaders like urban rappers were wearing Hilfiger clothing. It bolstered its traditional mass-media ads with unusual promotions, from giving free clothing to stars on VH1 and MTV, to a deal with Miramax, in which teen film actors appeared in Hilfiger ads. Knowing its customers' passion for computer games, it sponsored a Nintendo competition and installed Nintendo terminals in its stores. Gen Y consumers have rewarded that attentiveness by making Hilfiger jeans their No. 1 brand.[110]

Finally, Pepsi's success with Mountain Dew had little to do with advertising. Instead, kids and young adults found out about Dew from their most trusted endorsers—one another. Mountain Dew executives found out that: "There's a Pavlovian connection between the brand and the exhilarating experience." The company started handing out samples of the soda at surfing, skateboard, and snowboard tournaments, and thereafter drinking "The Dew" was a rush not just because of the caffeine and sugar but because of the hip places where it was first consumed.

> "[Millennials] believed—true or not—that they're the ones who figured out and spread the word that the drink has tons of caffeine," said Marian Salzman, head of the Brand Futures Group at Young & Rubicam Inc. The caffeine thing was not in any of Mountain Dew's television ads. This drink is hot by word of mouth.[111]

Generation Y cannot be reached through traditional marketing channels. Direct mail, print ads, and television advertising have little impact on this group. To break through Generation Y's distrust, marketers need to make their campaigns more subtle, more local, and embedded in high-traffic social media sites. Gen Y also has a strong social conscience and wants to know what companies are doing to address world problems like climate change, poverty, and human rights.[112]

A growing number of advertisers, including Universal Studios, Coca-Cola, and McDonald's, use "street teams." Made up of young people, the teams hang out in clubs, parks, and malls talking to contemporaries about everything from fashion to finance, trying to pinpoint trends as they emerge. Other marketers are trying to build grassroots support for their brands. Following the lead of underground rock bands, mass marketers have taken to "wild postings," that is, tacking up advertising posters on street corners and construction sites. Yet other companies sponsor community events and hand out coupons and T-shirts at concerts and ball games. Another tactic that companies use is asking their street teams to create ads for their website, which look less commercial and more appealing to young consumers.[113]

Meanwhile, computers and other high-tech products are starting to look less industrial and sleeker in an effort to attract younger buyers. Since millennials are constantly comparing the features and styling of their own products with those of their friends, high-tech gadgets need to use color, style, and cool design to attract attention. Gen Y expects convenient access to other customers' reviews and webinars with useful information customized for them.[114]

The Internet's power to reach young consumers is also essential; a well-designed website is crucial for any company hoping to reach Generation Y consumers. They are the pioneers of a digital lifestyle. They were first to use technologies such as QR codes, which allow their mobile devices to link to company websites for more information about products and companies.[115] Since almost everyone has an e-mail address, companies that cannot communicate via e-mail are regarded with disdain by Generation Y.[116] Table 5.4 summarizes Generation Y's marketing preferences for media, messages, brand, and price/value relationships as well as their interest in cultural information such as designs, causes supported by brands, and company policies such as human resources.

What unifies this generation besides its proficiency and seemingly playful use of technology is their belief that they can achieve everything they want and their credo of being unique while totally connected to their social circles. Marketers to Gen Y have learned that success depends on relearning everything about branding and advertising as well as understanding this group's fears and ambitions.

Generation X Cynics Want Straight Talk from Marketers

The birth years of Generation X are not well defined. People born between 1963 and 1978 are generally considered to belong to "Generation X," while others use the term to describe anyone who was in his twenties sometime during the 1990s.[117] According to Neil Howe and William Strauss, Generation X includes anyone born from 1961 to 1981 in the United States. Alternatively,

Table 5.4

Transcultural Marketing: Cultural Value Propositions for Generation Y

Transcultural marketing mix	Generation Y consumer preferences
Product usage as group marker?	Type of leisure and sports activities, school loyalties, fashion, technology, music tastes
Usage variability across diversity within age group	Age- and -gender differences, choice of education versus work after high school, expressions of ethnic pride
Importance of brand image	Do-it-yourself online product research, fashion brands express personal style
Memberships in community organizations	College team sports and alumni organizations, fraternal and religious community organizations
Price/value relationships	Price sensitive but willing to pay for well-known brands
Philanthropic choices	Scholarships, environmental, human rights causes, expect corporate social responsibility commitments
Corporate human resource policies	Important as job candidates and as consumers
Corporate financial partnerships	Little interest
Support of important causes	Can increase brand recognition, brand loyalty
Local community economic footprint	Can be source of loyalty, pride, or protest, online buzz, leadership
Environmental footprint	Can be source of advantage for building online and event engagement
Relevant messages	Cool and hip; don't talk at or down to Gen Y; low key sales pitch, buzzworthy
Media presence/public relations	Can stimulate social network buzz online, street teams, "be where they are"
Corporate aesthetics	Prefer postmodern designs and saturated colors

Meredith and Schewe establish the years from 1966 through 1976 as birth years for Generation X.[118]

The term Generation X was popularized by the Canadian novelist Douglas Coupland in *Generation X: Tales for an Accelerated Culture*, where he portrayed the angst of those born roughly between 1960 and 1965.[119] He described persons who felt no connection to the cultural icons of the baby boomer generation. In Coupland's usage, the X referred to the namelessness of a generation that was becoming aware of its existence as a separate group but was overshadowed by the baby boomers.

Generation X Cynicism Is Based on Their Experiences

Strauss and Howe used cultural trends to define the birth years of Generation X. They identified six forces that shaped "Generation 13": (1) readily accessible birth control, (2) the legalization of abortion on demand, (3) an increase in divorce, (4) an increase in mothers in the workforce, (5) the zero population movement, and (6) "devil-child films."[120] As children in a society in which women were redefining their roles at home and seeking an identity outside it, Generation Xers wondered where they fit and felt unwanted.

The tax and social program cuts of "Reaganomics" were another defining moment for Gen Xers. "Reaganomics" increased the wealth of a few, but the middle class began falling behind. Homelessness and poverty levels increased, while the national debt ballooned. Moreover, in the wake of the stock market collapse of 1987, evidence was uncovered of fraud and insider trading. All of this increased the feelings of bitterness, sarcasm, and hopelessness among those who were coming of age. As a result, Generation X carries a lifelong distrust of institutions.

The AIDS crisis and the *Challenger* explosion in the mid-1980s robbed this generation of the innocence and free spirit that their parents had in their youth. At a time when sexual discovery was supposed to be the norm, fear, anxiety, and uncertainty seemed to overshadow it. AIDS, together with the shuttle explosion, made this generation believe that there were no guarantees in life.

The changes in the communist countries of Eastern Europe and the televised fall of the Berlin wall constituted positive experiences in a sea of negative moments. Finally, the first Gulf War was different from the defining war of the baby boomers—the Vietnam War—in that it was not messy, did not involve a draft, and used surgical smart bombs whose precision hits could be followed on CNN. Since this war did not personally affect many Gen Xers, it was viewed as just another violent confrontation between good and evil, similar to the battles that they simulated in videogames, further desensitizing this generation to violence.

Generation X's lack of optimism about the future, nihilism, cynicism, skepticism, alienation, and mistrust in traditional values led the media to portray them as flannel-wearing, alienated, overeducated, underachieving slackers with body piercings, who chose to work at "McJobs." While these characteristics had some basis in truth, their media repetition led to stereotyping of this generation.[121]

Gen X pointed the finger at the previous generation, baby boomers, who "ruined everything."[122] Even their music grew out of the frustrations and disenchantment that they experienced as young adults. As example, the lead singer of Nirvana achieved cult status among this generation after he committed suicide in 1994. This side of Generation X was described in *Time* during the early 1990s as follows:

> By and large, the 18-to-29 group scornfully rejects the habits and values of the baby boomers, viewing that group as self-centered, fickle and impractical. While the baby boomers had a placid childhood in the 1950s, which helped inspire them to start their revolution, today's twenty-something generation grew up in a time of drugs, divorce and economic strain. They feel paralyzed by the social problems they see as their inheritance: racial strife, homelessness, AIDS, fractured families and federal deficits.[123]

Political-action organizations sprang up during the 1990s to support the libertarian tendencies among many Gen Xers. Instead of seeking careers in big business, they chose alternative paths to success. Some joined nonprofits such as Teach for America in inner-city schools, while others started businesses using their competitive edge over the baby boomers in technology.[124]

Since many in this cohort grew up as "latchkey kids" (children who return from school to an empty home because both parents are at work), they learned at an early age the importance of not depending on external sources of support. Now in their adult years, Generation X works in teams with others on the job, and their free agency and independent spirit often clash with older coworkers and supervisors. As a consequence, many have chosen to be their own bosses as entrepreneurs.[125] Never having enough time at home or at work, Gen X seeks products and services to help manage their busy lives.

Gen X entered the workforce at a volatile time. The Western countries were rapidly deindustrializing and experiencing boom/bust cycles in the 1990s and 2000s. Generation X saw permanent jobs replaced by short-term contracts, and companies opting for offshoring and outsourcing jobs. They had "McJobs" in their youth and, at times, long periods of unemployment. This has left a deep sense of insecurity in Gen Xers, whose usual attitude about work is "Take the money and run."[126] Unemployment and bankruptcy are no longer stigmatizing catastrophes.

Many Gen Xers are indifferent to religion and could be described as atheists. Others, raised in Protestant Christian families, reject the religions of their parents and instead have joined evangelical and "born again" congregations such as those of Joel Osteen or Rick Warren. Still, many Gen Xers do believe in "a higher power" and accept the plurality of world religions.

Generation X as Consumers

Today, most middle-aged adults in the United States are members of Generation X, surrounded by the baby boomers, who are older, and the equally large but younger Generation Y. Yet the absolute size of this market depends on which definition is used regarding its endpoints. Using the start years of 1964–66, Generation X comprises "merely" 42 million–44 million, making it only 19–20 percent of the current adult population. In 2013, members of this generation would be about 34 to 49 years old. However, using Neil and Howe's definition (1961–81) yields a much larger population segment. In this definition, Generation X consists of about 79 million people and accounts for about 35 percent of the adult population. Their age range in 2013 was those 32 to 52 years old.

Like other Americans, many members of Generation X spend more than they earn and are facing mountains of debt from school loans, mortgages, and credit cards.[127] They respond best to visual images and dislike any overstatements; they do not have "role models."

Members of Generation X are willing users of credit, debit, and ATM cards, even when it means carrying a high level of debt. At the same time, Generation X is one of the most financially conservative and pragmatic cohorts since World War II.[128] Members of Generation X were the first to be deeply affected by divorce and the economic and personal turmoil that it creates. Now, however, members of Generation X have become the adults driving the high-tech economy, and they are an increasingly positive economic force. In 2001, the 37 million 25 to 34 year olds had aggregate buying power of over $1.2 billion; in 2011 their purchasing power was reported to exceed $125 billion.[129] Because of their high rates of homeownership, Generation X consumers are having a major impact on furniture, houseware, and home improvement industries.[130] They are also an attractive market for investment and financial advice.

Generation X has been exposed to consumerism and public relations since birth, so they easily see through attempts to manipulate their opinions and purchase behaviors. They are street smart when it comes to advertising and marketing. When watching commercials, they ignore the product and instead deconstruct the marketing techniques.[131] Any kind of hyped sales pitch falls flat with them, but they appreciate the entertainment and informational values of advertising.

Gen Xers are comfortable shopping online for its benefits of ease, value, and convenience. As price-conscious consumers, they look for the best cost-value ratio in products. They are less image-conscious than other age cohorts and shun image over substance and comfort. Nevertheless, Gen Xers are loyal to the brands that deliver good value to them.[132] An advertisement for Volkswagen Jetta used the tagline "first row for the price of nosebleed" to support its value proposition to Gen X car buyers.

Gen X Media and Pop Culture Tastes

Popular culture from 1984 to 1994 reflected Gen X's growing disenfranchisement from a system that they believed had failed them. Their disillusionment was reflected in popular music, movies, books, TV shows, and fashions as well as the way in which Generation X used all media. Movies and TV shows like *Baywatch* and *Beverly Hills 90210* showed Gen X as indifferent, lethargic, and skeptical slackers who passed their ambitionless life in low-paying McJobs.

Popular movies, including *The Terminator, Reality Bites, The Breakfast Club*, and *Chasing Amy,* spoke to the frustration and disappointments of Gen X but in so doing provided a rather distorted and cynical image of this generation. Independent films, like the then-unknown director Quentin Tarantino's *Reservoir Dogs* and *Pulp Fiction*, Richard Linklater's *Dazed and Confused,* and Kevin Smith's *Clerks*, attempted to portray Gen X lifestyles more realistically.[133]

The different speech patterns used by Generation X and baby boomers are partly to blame for their one-sided representation in the media and misunderstandings at work. The following quote describes how their communication style led others to misunderstand them.

> There is a slight pause at the end of the sentence—a pause not long enough to allow more than acknowledgement from the listener but slightly longer than one would normally leave between declarative sentences. . . . And, of course, the speech is peppered with qualifying phrases: perhaps, like, sort of, you know, totally. . . . X'ers speak this way because they find it gentler and more accommodating [because] the listener might have a different opinion. X'ers are more sensitive to diverse points of view, and make a conscious effort not to co-opt the listener.[134]

This special communication pattern sounds like the speaker is uncertain, and so older listeners rush in with advice. However, Gen X speakers know perfectly well what they think and this unsolicited advice is resisted, even resented.

While disappointments with television programming early on led Gen X members to see television (and related entertainment media) as untrustworthy, these media have not lost their fascination. To no surprise, shows such as *The*

Simpsons and *Beavis and Butt-Head* (which showed the edgier mentality of Gen X), *Friends* (which reflected their struggle with careers and relationships), and *The X-Files* (which showed their distrust in authority) had the highest viewer ratings. In spite of the popularity of mass media, this generation has a much different relationship with these media than other age groups. Gen Xers take from the media what they need or what they find entertaining, but they never accept information from the media at face value. They have learned to be critical, to recognize hype and exaggeration, and to control their response to such communications.[135]

For the flannel-and-pierced-nipple set, ever critical about hype and fake idols, Kurt Cobain's 1994 suicide became the only "where were you when it happened" moment. Music companies have tried to recreate the connection that Gen Xers felt with grunge music, but sales continued to fall. Gen X'ers saw their "values" as having created their own musicians, labels, and live music venues (e.g., Lollapalooza), unencumbered by commercialism.

This generation grew up with videogames and the personal computer; Gen Xers were some of the first mainstream users of the Internet and have no fear when it comes to technology. While not quite as at ease with all things online as Generation Y, they are very willing to shop and do research online and, like others, use the Internet as a tool to make their lives easier.[136]

As the older siblings (or parents) of Generation Y, they, too, have a fascination with technological advances, such as high-speed broadband, cloud computing, social networking, portable computing, and smartphones. They respond well to Internet advertising, as it gives them the chance to control information and communication flow. Yet even in this controlled environment, they prefer facts over hype and respond negatively to "in-your-face" approaches.

Building Relationships with Generation X Consumers: Ameritrade, Ford Neon, Holiday Inn

Whether you loved them or hated them, Ameritrade's television commercials featuring the wacky Generation X Stuart and his technologically challenged boss, Mr. P, made Ameritrade a household name. Ameritrade's campaign used a number of lighthearted TV spots to show that trading online can be fun and profitable. The idea that people have the tools that they need to gain control of investing resonated with the "go-it-alone" experiences of Gen X. The most successful campaign of all was "Stuart," which featured the slacker copy guy, a weird-looking twentysomething, photocopying his face. He would then counsel his balding, fifty-something boss on online research and investing, urging him, "Let's light this candle!"

"We want to create brand preference and make Ameritrade look approach-able," explained Tim Smith, the company's manager of integrated media. "We target adults 25–54 with household incomes above $75,000 and some investment knowledge. That demo is reflected in our ads, where you see such things as a boat in a nice neighborhood, a vintage 1940s roadster and Stuart's boss's nice corner office. Our ads are pitched to a cross-section of America. 'Stuart' was young helping old."[137] This campaign helped multiply Ameri-trade's customer base sixfold since it launched in the late 1990s. This ad blitz was carried mostly on cable, a favorite of Generation X.[138] It hit home with Gen Xers because it portrayed them as brilliant but misunderstood.

Other marketing campaigns that have been successful with Generation X include Chrysler's "Hi" campaign for the Neon, showing the car with just the words above it, and Ford's "Have Spot, will travel" campaign for its Focus, which could be customized according to lifestyle (here: dog ownership). The Generation X taste for irony also made a Holiday Inn campaign popular with this age group. The ads featured the slacker character Mark, whose parents taunt him at the end of each spot with the refrain, "What? Does this look like a Holiday Inn?"

In *The Postponed Generation,* Susan Littwin wrote that most Generation X members have a sense of entitlement. "They put great emphasis on the self, dislike answering to others, and they believe that things will somehow work out for the best, that their fantasies will come true."[139] Since Gen Xers today are fairly well off, unlike when they were growing up, they finally have the resources to indulge themselves. National Car Rental's "Your Choice" cam-paign appeals to the Gen X desire to make decisions without expert advice.

Generation X is more willing to take risks and has a greater sense of inde-pendence than the Great Depression cohort (born 1912–1921). Consequently, they are making their own financial contingency plans without counting on federal or other help. Any marketing appeal that puts them in the driver's seat resonates. Gen Xers also learned to count on friends rather than family. Personal relationships have become the most important factor in their lives. Moreover, because they were born into an integrated society, their friends are very likely from various ethnic backgrounds. Promotional campaigns as such do well to portray diverse people socializing together.

Edgy topics and more graphic sexual and violent themes reflect the Gen X acceptance of approaches with shock value. Advertisers should test cam-paigns because the "pushing-the-envelope" style can violate the essential authenticity of the message. This cohort is concerned about the environment and will reward companies that make positive efforts in this regard. They view themselves as part of a global community. Gen Xers are not only curi-ous and accepting about diverse cultural values but concerned about issues such as climate change. Table 5.5 shows the importance of the cultural values proposition for Generation X due to their strong interests in a company's or brand's policies unrelated to traditional marketing variables such as price, message, or brand image. While these are influential in Generation X choices in the marketplace, they are willing to switch to companies that contribute to the causes important to them and whose corporate aesthetics, human resource policies, and financial and strategic partnerships are in line with Generation X's values.

The marketing use of mass customization, where everything from a salad to a car can be customized, is appealing to this cohort as it taps into its affinity for individualism. Brands and marketing tactics that simplify this group's life with straight messages fit its preferred style of marketing communications.

Baby Boomers Grow Old, and Still Try Not to Act It

Much has been written about baby boomers as a generation because they were the first age group whose market-space behavior challenged the understanding of marketers.[140] They simply did not buy or prefer the same things as their elders did at the same age. In fact, boomers rejected the conformity of the Silent Generation and pushed American cultural values toward the individualistic end of the individualism–collectivism continuum.[141] The mark of this post–World War II cohort on American market spaces has been as powerful as its influence on pop culture, lifestyles, and politics.

Their Future Was Bright: Boomers Shaped by Prosperity and Stability

As baby boomers grew up in postwar America, they saw few limitations in an expanding economy with unprecedented job and educational opportunities. Since prosperity was taken for granted, the boomers concentrated on personal growth and instant gratification. They were socially inclusive, assuming that there would be always be enough for all. The realities of life have left many of the boomers' expectations unmet, and they have been scrambling in recent years to learn how to make do with less.

No doubt the baby boomers' quest for "self" has driven the market for new kinds of products and services. Self-improvement activities have had a high priority throughout their lives. Baby boomers define "looking good" as "looking younger." Even while on vacation boomers want to do something different and to have a unique experience. They seek experiences more than goods, though both serve as markers of boomer success.

Baby boomers have dominated schools, mass media characters, and

Table 5.5

Transcultural Marketing: Cultural Value Propositions for Generation X

Transcultural marketing mix	Gen X consumer preferences
Product usage as group marker?	Type of leisure activities, music tastes, use of latest technologies
Usage variability across diversity within age group	Household-type with or without children, expressions of ethnic pride
Importance of brand image	Do-it-yourself product research, brands not always best value,
Memberships in community organizations	Local community and religious organizations, environmental and education causes, other entrepreneurs, libertarian
Price–value relationships	Price and value both important, brand most important in leisure activities
Philanthropic choices	Scholarships, community service organizations, sustainability
Corporate human resource policies	Important as job-seekers and consumers, show cultural diversity
Corporate financial partnerships	Communicates company values
Support of important causes	Can increase brand recognition, brand loyalty, expect commitments to causes
Local community economic footprint	Can be source of loyalty, pride, or protest, online buzz; entrepreneurs admired
Environmental footprint	Can be source of advantage for building online and event engagement
Relevant messages	Provide lots of information and customer reviews for do-it-yourself product research, no hype, reflect importance of family and friends, technology as a way of life
Media presence/public relations	Must be both online and TV
Corporate aesthetics	Prefer postmodern designs and saturated colors

American cultural life since their youth, so they can be expected to reject as many geezer stereotypes as they can. They were the first cohort to engage in active sports participation and fitness programs, and health clubs now focus on meeting their aging needs. While taking care of themselves physically, they also explored their spiritual lives via self-help books, traditional and alternative therapies, guides to happiness, and ways to improve their interpersonal skills.

While they have taught these skills to their children, who cite them as their heroes and role models, their high divorce rates made everyone pay a price.

It is the boomers who challenged American social norms. Until the advent of this group, if you belonged or wished to belong to the "American mainstream," you had to adhere to the tastes and etiquette of upwardly mobile Americans. Divorce, for example, became more acceptable for baby boomers because they preferred not to stay in unhappy marriages as their parents did, "for the children." And many boomers began to recreate themselves postdivorce by changing job or occupation, location, even the gender of live-ins. Although divorce became more acceptable, their children were often left adrift.

Female boomers and their sisters were the leaders of feminism and the first to make their lives more meaningful, comprising more than keeping up one's appearance, good homemaking, and parenting. More than boomer fathers, boomer mothers had a new place in the home: She wasn't always there! And when she was home, she was busier because she had not let go of most of the family's homemaking and parenting tasks.

Baby boomers have driven radical social change and have benefited from the peak times of American invention, creativity, productivity, and global business domination. It is, therefore, surprising that many boomers feel that they somehow have not lived up to their potential. Some are unhappy that their legacy reflects their self-centered life focus. Many members of Generations X and Y see boomers as the cause of the country's exorbitant debt and unfunded commitments left for them to pay. Perhaps this is what is inspiring boomers to continue their spiritual quests as they age and go back to church. Many are involved again with environmental issues, so they like companies that make it easy to have products that both meet personal needs and support environmental causes. They are also opting for second careers rather than retirement.[142] When they spend time with younger family members, they can seem like aliens who have a different language/technology/set of heroes. They share blood but not daily American life and pop cultures.

Baby Boomers as Consumers

The baby boomer cohort is as diverse as other age groups, but in unique ways. Understanding how to segment the boomer market is key for marketers. The composition of current boomer households reflects their current lifestyles rather than ethnic or geographic diversity.

The presence or absence of children living at home is a key factor in purchasing habits and preferences. Food is a product category in which spending increases when there are no children at home; the same is true for alcohol. Baby boomers in general outspend all other age groups in home improvements, electronics, cell phones, and family pets. They will move their savings into more accessible accounts as they retire to less expensive lifestyles. Whether motivated by self-actualization or financial need, most boomers plan to work well into their seventies, shifting to seasonal work, contract labor, and job sharing. Another trend is for boomers to cash in their retirement savings to start their own businesses.[143]

Nielsen segments the boomer market into eight groups, of which four are households with children and four are households without children. In the first group are Single Boomers (one-person households), who constitute about 22 percent of the total. They are among the best educated, and 40 percent of them never married. The so-called Trailing Edge couples, about 15 percent of all boomers, include the highest percentage of unmarried partners and low levels of diversity and education. Leading Edge couples, about 11 percent, are older than Trailing Edge ones, highly educated and have the lowest diversity. Nielsen dubbed households with three or more adults New Family Frontiers. They often include people who are related, such as adult children. Most important for marketers is that over 50 percent of those households have three or more wage earners. This reflects the trend toward adult-only households for empty-nest boomers in the future.

In the second group are Late Blooming Boomers (about 5 percent), that is, highly educated boomers who started their families later in life or were the result of remarriages. Their families tend to be smaller, and one-third of those households are headed by single parents. They include more African Americans, Asian Americans, and U.S. Latinos than other groups. Trailing Edge families (about 15 percent) average four or more people, with more than two young children. They are the most likely group to include U.S. Latinos and are least educated of all boomer households. Leading Edge families (about 10 percent) are headed by older parents and are most likely to have adult children over 18 living at home. Like Trailing Edge families, Leading Edge families are most likely to include U.S. Latinos and have the highest rate of marriage of all boomer households. Last, the boomers who are "Ready to Launch" (about 9 percent) have at least one child over 18 and the most children in their late teens. The parents in this group span the full age range of baby boomers, but they have the lowest incidence of U.S. Latinos and the highest incidence of African Americans.

Many baby boomers expected their children to leave home permanently when they left for college, as they did. However, many of their children are moving back home after college, disrupting their parents' plans for quieter, more adult-focused lives. One ad targeting boomers offered a vacation spot in Illinois for "when the kids move back in."

Baby boomers think of themselves as "getting older" but not "old." That is behind their spending on products that keep them looking young, such as medical enhancements, gym memberships, weight loss programs, and herbal supplements. The "anti-aging" industry was estimated at more than $88 billion in 2010, amid promises that "looking good" equals "looking younger."[144] Forty-six percent of boomers also exercise regularly, and swimming is the most popular sports activity.[145] They like to eat healthfully but give taste high priority, too.[146] While they read and listen to music in their leisure time, they are buying Kindles and iPads to move these habits to updated sources of content.

Boomer Media Habits Slowing Changing

Baby boomers have been slow to update their media habits, but they are online doing many things that they could not do before the development of new technologies. Their children have introduced them to instant messaging, Skype, Facebook, and other online destinations and activities.

Baby boomers still spend the most time with television, though they are beginning to stream programs and movies using Netflix or Hulu, at a special viewing time rather than when first broadcast. Their show preferences have tended toward fiction (*CSI, The West Wing, ER, Friends*) over reality shows, with the exception of *American Idol* and the *Survivor* series. Boomers still listen to radio, though they are spending less time, and they listen to classic rock and talk radio or all-news stations the most. Boomers are avid readers and the core audience for publications such as *Martha Stewart Living, People,* and *Time*. The idealism of their youth has turned into a search for pragmatic solutions to aging, quietly substituting "youthful" for "young."

Having learned to use the computer at work, boomers have been slower than younger consumers to take advantage of it as a source of entertainment. They also support nostalgic websites such as www.boomernet.com or Baby Boomer HeadQuarters (www.bbhq.com). Started out of nostalgia for the 1960s and 1970s, these sites offer discussion forums about current issues and provide services such as discounts or specials and anti-aging products.

Building Loyalty Among Baby Boomers

When shopping, baby boomers value interesting experiences and opportunities for self-discovery. Emotional connections are strongest when a brand and its owners share the boomers' interests in causes and cures, age-fighting products and services, and communication styles that recognize their achievements and search for meaning.

Anthropologie is a retailer whose merchandising targets its customers' right brain, where feelings and emotions are based. This store brand tries to create an "experience that would set up the possibility of change and transformation, where the visitor's imagination was just as important as that of the designer."[147] They use a serendipitous choice of merchandise, mixed up across the store, where it is meant to appeal to the customer's senses. What Anthropologie understands is the three ways in which their customers evaluate themselves and others: what they have, what they do, and who they are. For baby boomers, this means discovering who the real self is, after the social self "retires." Therefore, an important part of a retailer's cultural value proposition to baby boomers is an experience that promises self-discovery.

Table 5.6 illustrates the factors that make a cultural values proposition attractive to baby boomers. Their brand choices reflect their work achievements and volunteer activities. To reach them, marketers should use a combination of online and traditional media with messages that provide a lot of product information. They are community volunteers who value political activism, environmental causes, and religious institutions.

Mature Americans: Meeting Needs While Aging in a Youth-Oriented Culture

In contrast to members of other age subcultures, most senior citizens do not represent themselves as "different." Any marketer who labels them or their needs as distinctive finds out quickly the hazards of old age in a culture that reveres youth. It is being old in a youth-oriented society, not self-identity, that fosters a distinctive subculture for members of the mature market.

Lifestyles and Values of Senior Citizens

Over the course of their lifetime, technology has revolutionized the world around older consumers—the routines and rhythms of daily life; the pace and forms of communication with others; beliefs, heroes, and ideals; how they work, worship, and have fun. Anyone older than 65 in the United States was born before widespread use of computers, smartphones, fast food restaurants, multiplex theaters, the Internet, antibiotics, air conditioning, electric weed trimmers, microwave ovens, credit cards, malls, and other fixtures of twenty-first-century life. Seniors believe that younger Americans take these conveniences for granted and have missed important learning experiences. It is senior citizens themselves who are out of step with "newer is better," the ethos of contemporary America.[148]

Culturally, senior citizens remain invisible, except to their own families. Age discrimination is a common experience of older Americans, even if it is

Table 5.6

Transcultural Marketing: Cultural Value Proposition for Baby Boomers

Transcultural marketing mix	Baby boomer consumer preferences
Product usage as group marker?	Type of leisure activities, travel, music tastes, luxury and vehicle brands
Usage variability across diversity within age group	Household-type with or without children, expressions of ethnic pride, conservative vs. liberal
Importance of brand image	Brand choices show achievements, brand name can be surrogate for product quality
Memberships in community organizations	Volunteer organizations, political activism, environmental causes, religious institutions
Price–value relationships	Respect for well-known brands and perceived as good value
Philanthropic choices	Community service organizations, expect corporate social responsibility commitments
Corporate human resource policies	Important as job-seekers and consumers
Corporate financial partnerships	Communicates company values, impact on 401Ks
Support of important causes	Can increase brand recognition, brand loyalty
Local community economic footprint	Can be source of loyalty, pride, or protest, and online buzz
Environmental footprint	Can be source of advantage for building online and event engagement
Relevant messages	Provide lots of information and customer reviews for do-it-yourself product research
Media presence/public relations	Must be online plus traditional media
Corporate aesthetics	Prefer modern-style designs and colors, anti-aging products

not openly discussed. Older Americans strive to overcome negative stereotypes in the media and workplace, only to find that entertainment, popular leisure pursuits, and music also cater to younger audiences.[149]

Senior citizens exercise important influence over political and civic activities. This group has the highest participation rates in most elections. Their support is important to politicians, and active involvement in the political process via community organizations is an internalized value that they cherish.

Their active voices and organized lobbying efforts give senior citizens unprecedented access to political decision making.[150] Almost half of Americans over 55 are members of AARP, their most vocal advocate. In addition, there are organizations such as the National Council of Senior Citizens and other lobbying groups that represent the interests of older Americans.

In spite of the economic and political power of senior citizens, they are virtually absent from visible participation in American cultural life.[151] This is attributed to the overwhelmingly negative views about aging of young people and the more complex and ambivalent views of the elderly themselves.[152] Because copywriters have an average age below 30, our beliefs about old people reappear as negative images in the media.[153]

The negative view that Americans of all ages share of being old is best observed in the growing difference between chronological and perceived age, as people get older. Most American adults see themselves as 6 to 10 years younger than they actually are; for senior citizens the gap is 15 years.[154] Companies like Jockey feature models who are at least 15 years younger than their target market.[155] Still, chronological age is simply one measure of how old someone is. An alternative is to separate age into: how old someone feels (feel-age), how old someone looks (look-age), age according to a person's activities (do-age), and age corresponding to a person's interests (interest-age).[156]

Different attitudes about the relative importance of saving and consuming show the different worlds of post–World War II cohorts and those born before. These conservative attitudes have made today's senior citizens the most financially secure group of older Americans. They are cautious buyers who seek low risk options. Their home ownership, which is at the highest level among all American adults, is a measure of their preference for secure investments.

Connections to others, particularly to family, are central to the social lives of mature Americans. Family events and holidays spent with family dominate their social calendar and prescribe norms for being "perfect grandparents."[157] Family and friends are important sources of information about products and services for senior citizens; relationships—including those with familiar companies—are important to members of the mature market.

Many researchers have found values-based segmentation superior to age-based approaches in predicting consumer needs. Table 5.7 shows the segments used by two different research groups to help clients target buyers in the mature market. The presumption of each approach is that lifestyles are more predictive of marketplace behavior than are demographic characteristics alone.[158] As noted in the table, mature-market households reflect significant diversity in resources, in attitudes toward other age groups, and in how they adjust to changing environments. Such differences are obvious when comparing senior citizens who

Table 5.7

Values-Based Segmentation of the Mature Market

Six Lifestyles and Values Groups of Older Adults
(1986–1987 National Association for Senior Living Industries)

Attainers (9% of 55+ population)	• Youngest, median age 60 • Most autonomous, healthy • Self-indulgent, wealthy, highest incomes of 55+ • Best-educated, open to change
Adapters (11% of 55+ population)	• Second-highest incomes and home values • Median age 74, tend to be single • Aware of needs, seeking information, highly informed • Open to change, can be demanding consumers
Explorers (22% of 55+ population)	• Middle income, lived 20+ years at current address • Rugged individualists, active, forego children's assistance • Median age 65
Martyrs (26% of 55+ population)	• Low to moderate incomes • Median age 63 • Inward, denying, closed, uninformed about world • Conservative, resistant to change • Divorced or single
Pragmatists (21% of 55+ population)	• Moderate or lower incomes • Median age of 76, likely to be 70+ • Middle of the road, cautious but open to change • Somewhat outgoing but living alone • Moderately demanding
Preservers (11% of 55+population)	• Low income • Median age of 78, three-fourths over 70 • Frightened of change, frail, vulnerable • Least self-indulgent • Living alone or in older adult housing

Life Stages of the Mature Market

Healthy Indulgers (18% of 55+ population)	• Fewest experiences of major life events (e.g. retirement, chronic illnesses, or widowhood) • Most likely to behave like younger consumers • Financially well-off and settled in career • Major focus to enjoy life; seek convenience and personal services • Market for travel services • Interests in reduced-scale, independent housing and security
Healthy Hermits (36% of 55+ population)	• Self-concepts affected by major life events • Resent isolation but choose to withdraw • Do not want to behave like "old people"

	• Least likely to move, market for remodeling
Ailing Outgoers (29% of 55+ population)	• Positive self-esteem despite major life events or health problems • Accepting of "old-age" status • Interested in getting the "most out of life," value their independence • Major market for health-care products and services • Place high value on convenience • Respond to special attention for special diet needs and whatever makes their shopping tasks easier (e.g., catalog and direct marketing)
Frail Recluses (17% of 55+population)	• Accepting of "old-age" status • Lifestyles reflect physical declines and changing social roles • Strong spiritual lives • Need services to assist them in maintenance of house and self • Large market for health-care products and services • Earlier Healthy Indulgers, later as Healthy Hermits or Ailing Outgoers

Sources: J. Gollub, "Six Ways to Age," *American Demographics* (June 1989): 19–23; G.P. Moschis, "Life Stages of the Mature Market," *American Demographics* (September 1996): 44–47, 50. Reproduced by permission of *Advertising Age.* Copyright: Crain Communications Co.

are labeled "Martyrs" with those called "Attainers" or the "Healthy Indulgers" versus the "Frail Recluses." In sum, successful marketing to members of the mature market requires understanding different lifestyles as well as where or when age is a primary determinant of lifestyles and needs.

Older Americans Are the Future Mass Market

Mature Americans (defined as those over 65 years old) will number over 72 million by 2030, compared with 35 million in 2010, an increase of 55 percent. Boomers will soon join the mature market age-wise, but their values will keep them from identifying as older Americans. Women are a majority of this older group, and their proportion increases with age. Today's mature market is mostly white.

The increase in the number of older Americans is most pronounced when observed over time. In 1900, citizens age 65 and older constituted about 4 percent of the total U.S. population. By 1950, this proportion had doubled to 8 percent, and in 1990, it was 12.5 percent.[159] In 2020 it is likely to rise to 16 percent, in 2030 to around 20 percent, and to over 20 percent in the 2050s, or 79 million people, of which 37 million will be older than 85.[160] In the future, more of the young-old (55 to 69 years old) will be caring for the old-old (over 85).

The future mature market will be more diverse than it is today, as members of minority groups age and increase as a percentage of total population. A benefit of more life-saving medicines and treatments, technology has changed the experience of being old, allowing many of these people to live healthy lives for a longer time. Four out of five centenarians are women.

Table 5.8 shows the distribution of older citizens in different American states. In 2010 as well as projected to continue in 2030, the five states with the largest populations over age 65 are California, Florida, Texas, New York, and Pennsylvania. The cities with high percentages of their population consisting of those over age 65 will also remain the same. New York City is home to 2.6 percent of the total American senior population, which constitutes 11.4 percent of New Yorkers. Philadelphia and San Francisco have the largest share of older people in their populations. Marketers can choose to target states with large numbers of senior citizens or states with a high percentage of older Americans, or both.

Mature Consumers Are Constantly Adjusting to a Changing World

Senior citizens place less importance on a brand's ability to reflect social affiliations, but they do not want to be stigmatized by brands that cater to older people's "problems." They value an intangible aspect of customer satisfaction: The shopping experience (such as picking out toys for grandchildren, now conducted online), which leads to other pleasing experiences (spending more time with grandchildren).[161]

Mature consumers represent a growing market for health-related and medical products. They spend more than twice the national average on prescription drugs, and they account for more than 40 percent of all pharmaceutical sales. To take advantage of this and cater to the mature market, Safeway added pharmacy-delivery services in California.[162] The latest trend in assisted living arrangements is "theme" complexes or affinity housing, which offer specialized interests (e.g., country music for the members of the Country Music Association) and targeted neighbors (e.g., Asian Americans or LGBT communities).[163] Health is a major segmentation variable for the mature market. As shown in Table 5.7, health, resources, and connections to others are the most significant differences among members of the mature market.

Major brands are now catering to older consumers. Microsoft offers software tools that make text larger and easier to read. Sony had an ad that showed an older man realizing his dream of going into space and documenting it with a Sony video camera. The Ford 500 (2005–2007) mentioned "high-mounted seats, which permit exceptionally easy entry and exit," thus addressing a

Table 5.8

Top States for the Mature Market

Geographic location	Size of senior population (in 000s)		% of local population		% of U.S. senior population	
	2010	2030	2010	2030	2010	2030
Top ten states	7,300	13,689			18.1	19.7
Florida	3,419	7,769	17.8	27.1	8.5	10.9
West Virginia	292	426	16.0	24.8	0.7	0.6
Pennsylvania	1,956	2,890	15.5	22.6	4.9	4.0
Iowa	450	663	14.9	22.4	1.1	0.9
Maine	212	374	15.6	26.5	0.5	0.5
North Dakota	97	152	15.3	25.1	0.2	0.2
South Dakota	114	185	14.6	23.1	0.3	0.9
Arkansas	412	656	14.3	20.3	1.0	0.9
Hawaii	191	327	14.3	22.3	0.5	0.5
Rhode Island	157	247	14.1	21.4	0.4	0.3
Other states	18,522	32,126			46.0	45.0
California	4,393	8,288	11.5	17.8	10.9	11.6
New York	2,652	3,917	13.6	20.1	6.6	5.5
Texas	2,587	5,186	10.5	15.6	6.4	7.3
Illinois	1,601	2,412	12.4	18.0	4.0	3.4
Ohio	1,587	2,357	13.7	20.4	3.9	3.3
Michigan	1,334	2,081	12.8	19.5	3.3	2.9
New Jersey	1,232	1,960	13.7	20.0	3.1	2.7
North Carolina	1,161	2,173	12.4	17.8	2.9	3.0
Georgia	981	1,908	10.2	15.9	2.4	2.7
Virginia	994	1,844	12.4	18.8	2.5	2.6

Sources: "Table 1.1 Population by Age, Sex, Race and Hispanic Origin: 2006," in *Current Population Survey, Annual Social and Economic Supplement* (Washington, DC: U.S. Census Bureau, 2006); "Table 1: Estimates of the Population by Selected Age Groups for the United States and States and for Puerto Rico: July 1, 2006" (Washington, DC: Population Division, U.S. Census Bureau, May 17, 2007); "Table 5: Interim Projections: Population Under Age 18 and 65 and Older: 2000, 2010, and 2030," In *Interim State Population Projections* (Washington, DC: U.S. Census Bureau, Population Division, April 21, 2005).

feature important to older car buyers. Michelob's Ultra beer was designed to attract older drinkers back to beer by emphasizing its low level of carbohydrates and calories; the campaign was popular with them.

Mature market buyers are skeptical of product claims; in one survey, over 80 percent claimed that products did not work as promised.[164] Furthermore, senior citizens communicate their displeasure with products or sellers to people in their social network (over 75 percent tell others about their marketplace dissatisfactions but do not complain to the company).[165] Their lack of complaints disguises this dissatisfaction from marketers. Mature Americans want to be treated with respect by marketers and their employees, leading retailers such as Walmart, K-Mart, and Target to hire older people as "greeters" and offer "value" over "image" to attract senior citizens.[166]

Many older Americans process advertising in different ways from younger Americans. They typically have a higher need for information before making a purchase. At the same time, mature Americans suffer losses in cognitive processing skills as they age. They may experience few problems in remembering descriptions when given a name, but more trouble in remembering names when given descriptions.[167] Three conditions contribute to positive beliefs about products in response to advertising: actual repetition, perceived repetition, and outside-source attributions.[168]

Another preference of senior citizens is for less visual and verbal embellishment in product advertising. Older consumers do not process ads as quickly as do younger consumers.[169] They avoid interpreting television and radio commercials that they believe are too fast to understand. The art and design tastes of senior citizens were formed before postmodernism, so design is another area for adjustment. It is safe to say that the mature market responds best to straightforward, engaging copy and simple design in marketing communications.

One area of particular opportunity for marketers is the growing number of grandparents (about 70 million) who are living longer than in previous generations and spending more on their grandchildren. Grandparents spent more than $70 billion on their grandchildren in 2009, and many baby boomers have yet to become grandparents.[170] One of the reasons for the growth in grandparent expenditures is the larger role that they are taking in their grandchildren's lives. They are not just buying birthday presents; they are paying for tuition, lessons, and extras that their parents cannot afford. Toy advertisers are missing this opportunity as they place very few dollars in television programs that appeal to older Americans.[171] About 60 percent of grandparents say that the Internet is their top source for information and advice, and they are e-mailing their friends and families at least three to five times a week.[172]

Reaching Mature Americans

While many mature Americans are online daily, their media habits are sustaining traditional media such as magazines, newspapers, and network television. Health and home magazines are most popular with women over 65 while men prefer sports magazines. Travel, science, classic movies, news, and weather are their preferred television entertainments. They respond positively to advertising that is information-, not imagery-based, and it is imperative that older models be shown as active and contributing members of society. The best advice given marketers by an older American is to "talk to my lifestyle, not my age."

Watching television is the most popular leisure activity for senior citizens, rated higher than walking or driving for pleasure. They have the highest readership of newspapers of any age group. The mass media are an extension of the personal networks that senior citizens lose as they age. Media consumption levels are high across all income groups of senior citizens, but the wealthiest tend toward more print media consumption and think the least of advertising in general.[173] Word of mouth is valued highly as an information source for older consumers. While older adults claim that they prefer word-of-mouth sources over advertising for making purchase decisions, actually "past experience" is their most reliable source.[174]

There are other ways to reach mature Americans than choosing media and organizations they support. By understanding what activities carry important value among senior citizens, marketers can adapt messages that will capture their attention. Figure 5.1 shows the kinds of experiences they most enjoy: sharing wisdom and skills, entertaining, and caring for others. Each of the activities listed in the table can be inspirational for product and service development as well as for media, messages, and supportive organizations.

Building Loyalty Among Mature Americans

The past experiences and fiscal conservatism of mature Americans make them risk-aversive consumers, looking for strong incentives to try new products. Many retailers have found in-home trials and money-back and 30-day warranties to have special appeal for older consumers. These incentive programs emphasize value, not the age of buyers.

Senior citizens react strongly to physical features of the shopping environment. Changing a pharmacy from the front to the back of a store, not providing sufficient waiting or sitting areas, and lack of employee assistance

Figure 5.1 **"Being" Experiences of Interest to Mature Adults**

Sharing skills with others	Sharing wisdom with others	Entertaining others	Caring for others
Composing	Collaborating	Acting	Assisting
Creating	Consulting	Arranging	Caring
Decorating	Cooperating	Demonstrating	Catering
Designing	Educating	Hosting	Counseling
Drawing	Influencing	Joking	Curing
Fixing	Proposing	Performing	Encouraging
Painting	Teaching	Public Speaking	Helping
Writing	Training	Singing	Humoring
Staging	Nurturing	Story Telling	Petting
			Supporting
			Tending

Source: Adapted from J. Wonder and P. Donovan, *Whole Brain Thinking* (New York: W. Morrow, 1984), 268; as cited in D.B. Wolfe, *Serving the Ageless Market* (New York: McGraw-Hill, 1990), 216.

in specialty stores have been known to discourage loyal senior clienteles.[175] Losses in problem-solving abilities associated with aging make it more difficult for seniors to recall information and encourage older consumers to use "satisficing" rather than more aggressive strategies of information search.[176] Companies that meet the information needs of older buyers are rewarded with repeat patronage.

An important cultural reference point for the mature market is the experience of sharing in significant family events (weddings, births, graduations). As a result, ads that feature intergenerational settings and nostalgia get their attention. Grandparenting may or may not be central to a senior citizen's self-concept, but an ad that appeals to that role persuades more than others.[177] More than other consumers, they are interested in product features that contribute to their comfort, security, convenience, social interaction, ability to give to others, and independence.[178]

AARP, a nonprofit organization, is the most successful marketer to senior citizens. By developing a community of members whose interests focus on topics relevant to mature Americans, they have a loyal following and an invaluable database. The real success of AARP comes from its aggressive direct marketing to its over 40 million members. Furthermore, AARP positions itself as the spokesperson for a wide variety of issues relevant to senior citizens. In exchange, AARP educates older consumers about topics in which it has an important, powerful competitive position. Senior citizens have been highly responsive to direct marketing appeals via direct mail, telemarketing, and loyal-consumer marketing programs.[179]

Table 5.9 summarizes the cultural value proposition for senior citizens. As

Table 5.9

Transcultural Marketing: Cultural Value Propositions for the Mature Market

Transcultural marketing mix	Mature market consumer preferences
Product usage as group marker?	Health and grandparent roles, music tastes
Usage variability across diversity within age group	Type of housing, level of health
Importance of brand image	Familiar brands preferred
Memberships in community organizations	Volunteer organizations, political activism, donors to legacy and religious institutions
Price–value relationships	Often difficult to assess price–value, so well-known brands most trusted
Philanthropic choices	Community service organizations
Corporate human resource policies	Little interest, but must reflect patriotic values
Corporate financial partnerships	Communicates company values
Support of important causes	Can increase brand recognition, brand loyalty
Local community economic footprint	Can be source of loyalty, pride, online buzz
Environmental footprint	Can be source of advantage for building online and event engagement
Relevant messages	Provide lots of information and expert opinions for these information-intense consumers
Media presence/public relations	Traditional media, some online presence
Corporate aesthetics	Prefer classic designs and subtle colors

noted earlier, health status is an important factor in understanding product preferences and lifestyles for this age cohort. The same is true for its connections to family and other members of society. To achieve a competitive advantage in the mature market, it is advisable to provide information in the media that they consume and offer brands that are familiar. They have preference for American sources of products and services in familiar product categories, but are open to trying new brands when family or friends introduce them to these options. While this group is very active in community organizations, their expectation for companies to have social responsibility commitments is not as high as that of other age cohorts.

Summary

Shared coming-of-age experiences shape consumer subcultures out of different age cohorts. The five age groups of tweens, Generation Y, Generation X, baby boomers, and the mature market have distinctive consumer preferences and media behaviors. The best way to build customer relationships with members of each group is to understand and reflect their worldviews, values, and affiliations. Tweens are creating online content, and brands help them try on various social identities. Generation Y values new technologies and places importance on companies' and brands' social responsibility commitments. As the most diverse cohort, they also expect companies to support diversity in hiring and communications. Generation X likes to do-it-themselves and values other customers rather than experts as sources of product information. They also reward companies and brands that support the causes that interest them. Baby boomers look for products and services that help them age gracefully and that provide rewarding experiences. They are active volunteers and seek corporate support for the issues and causes important to them. The mature market is concentrated in specific states and can be segmented on the basis of health and lifestyle. Seniors prefer familiar brands and product categories, but when they try new products, they rely on family and friends as sources of information.

Notes

The author acknowledges Dr. Olaf Werder, lecturer at the University of Sydney, who contributed research to an earlier draft of this chapter.

1. See, for example, J. Zogby, *The Way We'll Be: The Zogby Report on the Transformation of the American Dream* (New York: Random House, 2008); D.B. Wolfe, *Ageless Marketing: Strategies for Reaching the Hearts and Minds of the New Customer Majority* (Chicago: Dearborn Trade, 2003); G.E. Meredith and C.D. Schewe, *Defining Markets, Defining Moments* (New York: Hungry Minds, 2002); L. Johnson, *Mind Your X's and Y's: Satisfying the 10 Cravings of a New Generation of Consumers* (New York: Free Press, 2003); R.D. Michman, E.M. Mazze, and A.J. Greco, *Lifestyle Marketing: Reaching the New American Consumer* (Westport, CT: Praeger, 2003); J.W. Smith and A. Clurman, *Rocking the Ages: The Yankelovich Report on Generational Marketing* (New York: HarperBusiness, 1997); W. Strauss and N. Howe, *Generations: The History of America's Future, 1584 to 2069* (New York: William Morrow, 1991); W. Strauss and N. Howe, *The Fourth Turning* (New York: Broadway Books, 1997).

2. Strauss and Howe, *Generations*.

3. M.J. Penn, *MicroTrends: The Small Forces Behind Tomorrow's Big Changes* (New York: Twelve, 2007), xi–xxi; A. Ranchhod, "Advertising into the Next Millenium," *International Journal of Advertising* 17, no. 4 (1998), 265–280; J. Wehmann, "Splintering of the Consumer Market," Digital River Blog, March 2, 2011, http://digitalriverblog.com/2011/03/02/splintering-of-the-consumer-market/.

4. Smith and Clurman, *Rocking the Ages,* xii–xiii.

5. Ibid., xv.

6. Ibid., xiii.

7. Ibid., 3.

8. Strauss and Howe, *The Fourth Turning,* 3; Strauss and Howe, *Generations,* 34.

9. Strauss and Howe, *Generations,* 71.

10. G. Hofstede, *Culture's Consequences: Comparing Values, Behaviors, Institutions, and Organizations Across Nations,* 2d ed. (Thousand Oaks, CA: Sage, 2001).

11. Zogby, *The Way We'll Be,* 27–55, 91–119.

12. T.J. Erickson, "Generation Y in the Workforce," *Harvard Business Review* (February 2009): 43–49.

13. M. Gluck, *Why Y Women?* PopSugar Media, October 2009, http://media.onsugar.com/static/imgs/WhyYWomen.pdf.

14. J. Hall, M. Shaw, M. Johnson, and P. Oppenheim, "Influence of Children on Family Consumer Decision Making," in *European Advances in Consumer Research,* vol. 2 (Provo, UT: Association for Consumer Research, 1995), 45–53.

15. F. Francine Russo, "Retro Revival," *Time,* Bonus Section (October 2006): F11.

16. S. Vranica, "P&G Plunges into Social Networking," *Wall Street Journal,* January 8, 2006, B4.

17. K. Naughton, "The Long and Winding Road," *Newsweek,* April 9, 2007, 62–79.

18. Ibid.

19. L.M. Howden and J.A. Meyer, "Age and Sex Composition: 2010," 2010 Census Brief (Washington, DC: U.S. Census Bureau, May 2011), table 2, www.census.gov/prod/cen2010/briefs/c2010br-03.pdf.

20. G. Smith, *Tweens 'R Shoppers: A Look at the Tween Market & Shopping Behavior* (Chicago: Global Association for Marketing at Retail, March 2013), www.popai.com/store/downloads/POPAIWhitePaper-Tweens-R-Shoppers-2013.pdf; J. Preston, "The Rise of the Tween Market," What the Gen?! March 28, 2012, www.genhq.com/rise-tween-market/.

21. C. Dilenschneider, "The Millennials Are Here: Five Facts Businesses and Nonprofits Need to Know," Know Your Own Bone, October 9, 2012, http://colleendilen.com/2012/10/09/the-millennials-are-here-5-facts-nonprofits-and-businesses-need-to-know/; A. de Mesa, "Marketing and Tweens," *Bloomberg Businessweek,* October 12, 2005, www.businessweek.com/innovate/content/oct2005/id20051012_606473.htm.

22. Zogby, *The Way We'll Be,* 77–110; K. Ritchie, *Marketing to Generation X* (New York: Simon & Schuster, 1995); C. Souws, "The 6 Rules of Marketing to Generation X," America's Best Companies, December 22, 2009, www.americasbestcompanies.com/blog/6-rules-marketing-generation-x.aspx; K.E. Klein, "The ABCs of Selling to Generation X," *Bloomberg Businessweek,* April 14, 2004, www.businessweek.com/smallbiz/content/apr2004/sb20040414_0567_sb001.htm.

23. T. Barribeau, "Generation X Not Angst Ridden Slackers After All," io9, October 28, 2011, http://io9.com/5853720/generation-x-not-angst+ridden-slackers-after-all; C. Rampell, "A Generation of Slackers? Not So Much," *New York Times,* May 28, 2012, www.nytimes.com/2011/05/29/weekinreview/29graduates.html.

24. J. Kozar, "Effects of Model Age on Female Consumers' Purchasing Inten-

tions and Attitudes for an Age-Specific Product, Clothing," *International Journal of Marketing Studies* 4, no. 2 (2012): 22–29.

25. U.S. Census Bureau, *American Community Survey, Statistical Abstract: Adult Education and Homeownership* (Washington, DC: U.S. Department of Commerce, Economics and Statistics Administration, 2007).

26. MetLife, "Metlife Mature Market Institute Study Estimates Boomers' Inheritance at $8.4 Trillion," news release, December 14, 2010, www.metlife.com/about/press-room/us-press-releases/index.html?compID=32895/.

27. *American Heritage Dictionary of the English Language*, 4th ed. (Boston: Houghton Mifflin, 2000).

28. "Trends and Issues," JSH&A Public Relations, www.jsha.com/trends/popups/tweens.html, accessed January 5, 2009.

29. J. Hempel, "The MySpace Generation," *BusinessWeek*, December 12, 2005, www.businessweek.com/magazine/content/05_50/b3963001.htm.

30. M. Irvine, "Internet Generation Riding Technological Wave into the Future," *Arizona Daily Star Online*, May 12, 2004.

31. Strauss and Howe, *Generations*.

32. G. Gaddis, "Talking to Generation Now," iMedia Connection, November 14, 2006, www.imediaconnection.com/content/12412.asp.

33. TrendWatching.com, "Generation C," 2009 trend report, http://trendwatching.com/trends/GENERATION_C.htm.

34. T.T. Ahonen and A. Moore, *Communities Dominate Brands: Business and Marketing Challenges for the 21st Century* (London: futuretext, 2005).

35. J. Pearce, "Meet Generation C: Renaissance Revisited," *Idealog* (May/June 2006): 3, 36.

36. Media Center at the American Press Institute, *Meet Generation C* (Arlington, VA: American Press Institute, May 2004).

37. L. Schmidt and P. Hawkins, "Children of the Tech Revolution," *Sydney Morning Herald*, July 15, 2008, www.smh.com.au/news/parenting/children-of-the-tech-revolution/2008/07/15/ 1215887601694.html?page=fullpage#contentSwap1/.

38. Answers.com, "How Much Money Do American Children Spend per Year?" http://wiki.answers.com/Q/How_much_money_do_American_children_spend_per_year_on_average#/; E.E. Clack, "What a Tween Wants . . . Now! Market Research Experts Reveal What's New with This Important Demographic," *Children's Business*, April 1, 2004, http://www.reachadvisors.com/childrensbusinessarticle2.html.

39. A. Sutherland and B. Thompson, *Kidfluence: The Marketer's Guide to Understanding and Reaching Generation Y-Kids, Tweens, and Teens* (New York: McGraw-Hill, 2004).

40. "For Luxury Automakers, Selling Toys Is No Game," *Bloomberg Businessweek*, December 5, 2010, 26–27.

41. Packaged Facts, *The U.S. Teen Market: Understanding the Changing Lifestyles and Trends of 12–19-Year Olds,* 5th ed. (New York: Market Research, August 2002).

42. Clack, "What a Tween Wants . . . Now!"

43. Packaged Facts, *The U.S. Tweens Market,* 2d ed. (New York: Market Research, April 2003).

44. J. Bennett, "Tales of a Modern Diva," *Newsweek*, April 6, 2009, 42–43.

45. R. Beatty, "It Pays to Know Your XYZs," *Melbourne Herald Sun*, June 10, 2008.

46. Schmidt and Hawkins, "Children of the Tech Revolution"; M. Lindstrom with P.B. Seybold, *Brand Child* (London: Millward Brown, 2003), 157–184.

47. A. Walliker, "Get Ready, Here Comes Generation Z," News Digital Media (Sydney, Australia), February 25, 2008, www.news.com.au/national-news-2/get-ready-here-comes-generation-z/story-e6frfkw9-1111115637544/.

48. Schmidt and Hawkins, "Children of the Tech Revolution."

49. S. Fish, "Understanding the New Generations of Young People, Generations Y and Z," EZine Articles, June 7, 2009, http://ezinearticles.com/?Understanding-the-New-Generations-of-Young-People,-Gen-Y-and-Gen-Z&id=2446232/.

50. Pearce, "Meet Generation C."

51. Ibid.

52. B. Nestoras, "The Needy Tween," *Gifts & Decorative Accessories*, January 1, 2007, 8, 28–34.

53. "Trends and Issues"; M. Ritson and R. Elliott, "The Social Uses of Advertising: An Ethnographic Study of Adolescent Advertising Audiences," *Journal of Consumer Research* 26, no. 3 (1999): 260–277.

54. J. O'Donnell, "As Kids Get Savvy, Marketers Move Down the Age Scale," *USA Today*, April 13, 2007, www.usatoday.com/money/advertising/2007-04-11-tween-usat_N.htm.

55. B. Ebenkamp, "Out of the Box: T2: Divide of the Tweens," *Brandweek*, June 30, 2003, 8.

56. Michman, Mazze, and Greco, *Lifestyle Marketing*.

57. D.L. Siegel, T.J. Coffey, and G. Livingston, *The Great Tween Buying Machine* (Ithaca, NY: Paramount Marketing, 2001).

58. J. Jayson, "It's Cooler Than Ever to Be a Tween, But Is Childhood Lost?" *USA Today*, February 3, 2009, http://usatoday30.usatoday.com/news/health/2009-02-03-tweens-behavior_N.htm.

59. "Taking Girls' Internet Fashions to the Mall," *Bloomberg Businessweek*, September 25, 2011, 27–28.

60. N. Kristof, "The Daily Me," *New York Times*, March 18, 2009, A31.

61. Media Center at the American Press Institute, *Meet Generation C*.

62. Ibid.

63. J. Pearce, "Tweens: Generation Mobile," Moco (Mobile Communication) News Net, June 15, 2005, www.moconews.net/entry/tweens-generation-mobile/.

64. Nielsen Media Research, "Kids on the Go: Mobile Usage by U.S. Teens and Tweens," news release, December 3, 2007.

65. L. Andersen, B. Tufte, J. Rasmussen, and K. Chan, "Tweens and New Media in Denmark and Hong Kong," *Journal of Consumer Marketing* 24, no. 6 (2007): 340–350.

66. Riot Media, "www.riotweb.com Goes Live; Riot Media Launches Its New Online Interactive Destination for Tween Boys," PR Newswire, May 5, 2005, www.prnewswire.com/news-releases/wwwriotwebcom-goes-live-riot-media-launches-its-new-online-interactive-destination-for-tween-boys-54300332.html.

67. Lexdon Business Library, "RIOT MEDIA, Inc., the First and Only Lifestyle Brand for and About Tween Boys, Launches Cutting-Edge Website and Magazine," February 27, 2009, www.lexdon.com/article/RIOT_MEDIA_Inc._the_First/20159.html.

68. Writers Write, "RIOT Media Targets Tween Market," Write News, April 16, 2004, www.writenews.com/2004/041604_riot_media.htm.

69. V. VanderZanden, "Tween Boys Have Riot: New Website Caters to Boys' Desires," *Toy Directory Monthly* 4, no. 11 (2005): 15.

70. Interview, "Dan Cook Looks at the Bratz Dolls' Global Popularity," *Global Viewpoint* (Illinois International), May 16, 2007.

71. Fashion Finds, "Trendy Tween DIY Fashion with EST Today Design Studio," Inventor Spot (2008), http://inventorspot.com/articles/trendy_tween_diy_fashion_est_today_design_studio_24773/; E. Magner, "Choose Your Own Tween Fashion Adventure," *JC Report,* March 12, 2009.

72. "Trends and Issues."

73. B. Wieners, "Lego Is for Girls," *Bloomberg Businessweek*, December 19–26, 2011, 66–73.

74. P. Paterson, "Tweens Take Over: Y Generation Is the Wunderkind of Brand Marketing," *Toy Directory Monthly* (June 2003): 2, www.toydirectory.com/monthly/june2003/Tweens_Generations.asp.

75. Siegel, Coffey, and Livingston, *The Great Tween Buying Machine.*

76. P. Markiewicz, "Who's Filling Gen Y's Shoes?"

77. Merrill Associates, "Topic of the Month: Generation Y: The New Global Citizens" (June 1, 2004), www.merrillassociates.net/topic/ 2004/06/01/generation-y-the-new-global-citizens/.

78. E. Chester, *Employing Generation Why?* (Denver, CO: Tucker House Books, 2002), 13.

79. Merrill Associates, Topic of the Month."

80. E. Shearer, "Generation Ignored," *American Journalism Review* (April 2002): 7.

81. M.E. Ross, "A Turned-On Turnout: Young Voters Showed Up Tuesday. Did Celebrities Help?" NBC News, n.d., www.nbcnews.com/id/6400705/ns/politics/t/turned-on-turnout/.

82. Pew Research Center, "Post September 11 Attitudes," December 6, 2001, www.people-press.org/2001/12/06/post-september-11-attitudes/.

83. J.M. Wolburg and J. Pokrywczynski, "A Psychographic Analysis of Generation Y," *Journal of Advertising Research* 41, no. 5 (2001): 33–52.

84. Markiewicz, "Who's Filling Gen Y's Shoes?"

85. Ibid.

86. Michman, Mazze, and Greco, *Lifestyle Marketing.*

87. S. Shellenbarger, "Tucking the Kids In—in the Dorm: Colleges Ward Off Overinvolved Parents," *Wall Street Journal*, July 28, 2005, D1.

88. Markiewicz, "Who's Filling Gen Y's Shoes?"

89. NAS Recruitment Communications, "Generation Y: The Millennials—Ready or Not, Here They Come," NAS Insights (2006), Cleveland, OH, www.permanentsearch.com/designedit/upload/GenerationY.pdf.

90. Monster Intelligence Study, "Entry Level Job Outlook: U.S. Overview," Monstertrack.com (Spring 2008), http://media.monster.com/a/i/intelligence/pdf/TRAK/2008_EntryLevelOutlook_US.pdf.

91. K.W. Escalaera, "Generation Y: Luxury's Most Buoyant Market," *Luxury Society,* May 3, 2012, http://luxurysociety.com/articles/2012/05/generation-y-luxurys-most-buoyant-market/; B. Fields, "Surefire Strategies for Marketing to Generation Y," ArticlesBase.com, November 14, 2007, www.articlebase.com/marketing-tips-articles/10-surefire-strategies-for-marketing-to-generation-y-259464.html.

92. J. Bensley, "Generation Y and Culture: Do They Care?" JB Research (2004), www.jbresearchco.com/GenYArticle.html.

93. M. Fernandez-Cruz, "Advertising Agencies Target Generation Y," Youngmoney.com (2003), http://local.youngmoney.com/Advertising_Agencies/Target/Generation/Y-a1212672.html.

94. K. Cheng, "Setting Their Sights on Generation Y: Should Marketers Hop on the Teeny-Bop," *AdWeek*, August 9, 1999, 15.

95. Wolburg and Pokrywczynski, "A Psychographic Analysis of Generation Y."

96. D. Gill, "Reinvent Brands for Gen-Y Group," *Home Textiles Today* 20, no. 44 (1999): 33.

97. P. Zollo, *Wise Up to Teens: Insights into Marketing and Advertising to Teenagers,* 2d ed. (Ithaca, NY: New Strategist, 1999).

98. Ibid.

99. C. Lim and D.M. Turco, "The Next Generation in Sport: Y," *Cyber Journal of Sport Marketing* 3, no. 4 (1999): 121–135.

100. G. Carroll, "Millennials: The Agency View," *AEJMC Advertising Division Newsletter* (Fall 2008): 7.

101. J. Omelia, "Understanding Generation Y: A Look at the Next Wave of US Consumers," *Drug and Cosmetic Industry* 163, no. 6 (1998): 90–92.

102. R. Junco and J. Mastrodicasa, *Connecting to the Net Generation* (Washington, DC: National Association of Student Personnel Administrators, 2007), http://blog.reyjunco.com/pdf/NetGenerationProof.pdf.

103. Deloitte Media Survey, *The Future of Media: Profiting from Generational Differences* (Australia: Deloitte Touche Tohmatsu, November 2007), www.deloitte.com/assets/Dcom-Australia/Local%20Assets/Documents/Future_of_Media.pdf.

104. R. Hilton, "The Sound of a Generation," All Things Considered (NPR), May 8, 2008, www.npr.org/blogs/allsongs/2008/06/the_sound_of_a_generation.html.

105. A. Herman, *The Hows of Reaching Generation Y* (Kansas City: Barkley, 2009).

106. E. Neuborne and K. Kerwin, "Generation Y: Today's Teens—The Biggest Bulge Since the Boomers—May Force Marketers to Toss Their Old Tricks," *BusinessWeek*, February 15, 1999, http://www.businessweek.com/1999/99_07/b3616001.htm.

107. S.P. Campbell, "Online Broadcast Provides Tips on Driving Customer Service Success with Generation Y," TMCnet, October 10, 2012, www.tmcnet.com/channels/call-center-certification/articles/311449-online-broadcast-provides-tips-driving-customer-service-success.htm.

108. J. LeBlanc, "First Drive: 2014 Volkswagen Golf," Postmedia News, October 12, 2012, http://life.nationalpost.com/2012/10/12/preview-2014-volkswagen-golf/.

109. Auto Channel, "WWJ-VW-GENY," April 26, 2007, www.theautochannel.com/news/2007/04/26/045471.html.

110. Neuborne and Kerwin, "Generation Y: Today's Teens."

111. B. Horovitz, "Gen Y: A Tough Crowd to Sell," *USA Today*, April 21, 2002.

112. Fields, "Surefire Strategies for Marketing to Generation Y."

113. S. Kang, "Trying to Connect with Generation Y," *Wall Street Journal*, October 13, 2005, B3.

114. J. Levitz, "Pitching 401(k)s to Generation Y Is a Tough Sell," *Wall Street Journal,* September 27, 2006, B1–B2.

115. S. Baker, "Channeling the Future," *BusinessWeek,* July 12, 2004, 70–71.

116. Neuborne and Kerwin, "Generation Y: Today's Teens."

117. A. Anushka and V. Thorpe, "Whatever Happened to the Original Generation X?" *Observer* (UK), January 23, 2005, C2.

118. Meredith and Schewe, *Defining Markets, Defining Moments*, 16.

119. D. Coupland, *Generation X: Tales for an Accelerated Culture* (New York: St. Martin's Press, 1991).

120. Strauss and Howe, *Generations*.

121. Coupland, *Generation X*.

122. T. Rall, "Marketing Madness: A Post-Mortem for Generation X," Ted Rall (blog), November 5, 1994, http://rall.com/1994/11/05/marketing-madness-a-post-mortem-for-generation-x/.

123. D.M. Gross and S. Scott, "Proceeding with Caution," *Time,* July 16, 1990, www.time.com/time/magazine/article/0,9171,970634,00.html.

124. Rall, "Marketing Madness."

125. "Reality Bites," *Bloomberg/BusinessWeek,* September 9, 2011; Meredith and Schewe, *Defining Markets, Defining Moments*, 252.

126. Gross and Scott, "Proceeding with Caution."

127. S. Mitchell, *Generation X: Americans Aged 18 to 34,* 3d ed. (New York: New Strategist, 2001), 273.

128. Meredith and Schewe, *Defining Markets, Defining Moments*, 268.

129. A. Raposa, "Approaching Mid-Life, Are Gen-Xers Doomed?" *Forbes,* February 28, 2012, www.forbes.com/sites/kenrapoza/2012/02/28/approaching-mid-life-are-gen-xers-doomed/.

130. Packaged Facts, *The Young Adult Market: Generation X Grows Up* (New York: MarketResearch.com, 2002).

131. D. Rushkoff, comp., *The GenX Reader* (New York: Ballantine Books, 1994), 43.

132. R. Lamb, "Brand Loyalty Highest in Gen X Consumers: eMarketer," *Luxury Daily,* August 25, 2011, www.luxurydaily.com/brand-loyalty-highest-in-gen-x-consumers-emarketer/.

133. Rall, "Marketing Madness."

134. K. Ritchie, *Marketing to Generation X* (New York: Lexington Books, 1995), 164–165.

135. Ibid., 114.

136. Meredith and Schewe, *Defining Markets, Defining Moments*, 266.

137. S. Elliott, "Actor Gets an Encore as Broker's Spokesman," *New York Times,* April 19, 2006.

138. Cable Advertising Bureau, "Campaign Profiles: Multiplying Online Traders," 2006, www.cabletvadbureau.com/Case%20Studies/2000/Ameritrade.htm.

139. S. Littwin, *The Postponed Generation: Why America's Grown-Up Kids Are Growing Up Later* (New York: Morrow, 1986).

140. J. Goldsmith, *The Long Baby Boom: an Optimistic Vision for a Graying Generation* (Baltimore: Johns Hopkins University Press, 2008); L. Steinhorn, *The Greater Generation: in Defense of the Baby Boom Legacy* (New York: St. Martin's Press, 2006); S.M. Gillon, *Boomer Nation: the Largest and Richest Generation Ever, and How It Changed America* (New York: Free Press, 2004); B. Green, *Marketing to Leading-Edge Baby Boomers* (New York: Paramount Market, 2006).

141. Hofstede, *Culture's Consequences*.

142. C. Reynolds, "Boomers, Act II," *American Demographics* (October 2004): 10–11.

143. J. Pethokoukis and E. Brandon, "Going Your Own Way," *U.S. News and World Report*, April 3, 2006, 52–54.

144. "The Old And the Beautiful (Review)," *Bloomberg Businessweek*, August 26, 2010, 90–13.

145. Packaged Facts, *Healthy 50+ Americans: Trends and Opportunities in the Wellness Market* (New York: MarketResearch.com, April 2011), www.packagedfacts.com/Healthy-Attitudes-Activities-6135736/.

146. L. Lee, "Love Those Boomers," *BusinessWeek*, October 24, 2005, 94–102.

147. D.B. Wolfe, *Ageless Marketing*, 56.

148. J. Hammond and J. Morrison, *The Stuff Americans Are Made of* (New York: Macmillan, 1996).

149. R.A. Lee, "The Youth Bias in Advertising," *American Demographics* (January 1997): 46–50.

150. S.C. Lonial and P.S. Raju, "The Decision Process and Media-Related Interactions of the Elderly: A Synthesis of Findings," *Journal of Current Issues and Research in Advertising* 13, nos. 1–2 (1991): 277–312.

151. L.E. Swayne and A.J. Greco, "The Portrayal of Older Americans in Television Commercials," *Journal of Advertising* 16, no. 1 (1987): 47–54.

152. M.L. Hummert, J.M. Wiemann, and J.F. Nussbaum, eds., *Interpersonal Communication in Older Adulthood: Interdisciplinary Theory and Research* (Thousand Oaks, CA: Sage, 1994), 165.

153. K. Goldman, "Seniors Get Little Respect on Madison Ave.," *Wall Street Journal,* September 20, 1993, B6.

154. I.K. Zola, "Feelings About Age Among Older People," *Journal of Gerontology* 17, no. 1 (1962): 65–68.

155. M. Beck, "Going for the Gold," *Newsweek*, April 23, 1990, 74–75; J. Lipman, "Ads Aimed at Older Americans May Be Too Old for Audience," *Wall Street Journal,* December 31, 1991, B4.

156. L.G. Schiffman and L.L. Kanuk, *Consumer Behavior*, 3d ed. (Englewood Cliffs, NJ: Prentice Hall, 1987), 531, as cited by D.B. Wolfe, *Serving the Ageless Market* (New York: McGraw-Hill, 1990), 213.

157. M.M. Walker and M.C. Macklin, "The Use of Role Modeling in Targeting Advertising to Grandparents," *Journal of Advertising Research* 32, no. 4 (1992): 37–43.

158. D.B. Wolfe, *Serving the Ageless Market* (New York: McGraw-Hill, 1990), 100–132; J. Gollub, "Six Ways to Age," *American Demographics* (June 1989): 19–23; G.P. Moschis, "Life Stages of the Mature Market," *American Demographics* (September 1996): 44–50.

159. C. Taeuber, "Table 2.1. Growth of the Older Population, Actual and Projected: 1900 to 2050," in U.S. Census Bureau, *Sixty-Five Plus in America* (Washington, DC: U.S. Department of Commerce, 1993), 2/2–2/3.

160. D. Stipp, "Hell No, We Won't Go! Surprising Demographic Trends Raise a Tough Question: Will the Elderly Live So Long That Society Can't Cope?" *Fortune*, July 19, 1999, 102–108.

161. Wolfe, *Serving the Ageless Market*, 61–76.

162. J. Borzo, "Follow the Money," *Wall Street Journal*, September 16, 2009, R9.

163. H. Barovick, "10 Ideas: Niche Aging," *Time*, March 12, 2012, 86–87.

164. G.P. Moschis, "Survey: Age Is Not Good Indicator of Consumer Need," *Marketing News*, November 21, 1988, 6.

165. Ibid.; Z.V. Lambert, "An Investigation of Older Consumers' Unmet Needs and Wants at the Retail Level," *Journal of Retailing* 55, no. 4 (1979): 35–57.

166. P. Underhill, "Seniors in Stores," *American Demographics* (April 1996): 44–48.

167. G. Cohen, "Age Related Problems in the Use of Proper Names in Communication," in *Interpersonal Communication in Older Adulthood: Interdisciplinary Theory and Research,* ed. M.L. Hummert, J.M. Wiemann, and J.F. Nussbaum (Thousand Oaks, CA: Sage, 1994), 40–57.

168. S. Lawe, S.A. Hawkins, and F.I.M. Craik, "Repetition-Induced Beliefs in the Elderly: Rehabilitating Age-Related Memory Deficits," *Journal of Consumer Research* 25, no. 2 (1998): 91–108.

169. N. Stevens, "The Effectiveness of Time-Compressed Television Advertisements with Older Adults," *Journal of Advertising* 11, no. 4 (1982): 48–55.

170. I. Isidro, "Grandparents: How to Reach This Market for Your Business," PowerHomeBiz.com, November 1, 2009, www.powerhomebiz.com/blog/2009/11/grandparents-how-to-reach-this-market-for-your-business/.

171. J. Brazil, "You Talkin' to Me?" *American Demographics* (December 1998): 54–59.

172. Isidro, "Grandparents: How to Reach This Market for Your Business."

173. J.J. Burnett, "Examining the Media Habits of the Affluent Elderly," *Journal of Advertising Research* 31, no. 5 (1991): 33–41.

174. J.J. Burnett and R.E. Wilkes, "An Appraisal of the Senior Citizen Market," *Journal of Retail Banking* 7, no. 4 (1986): 57–64.

175. P. Underhill, "Seniors in Stores," *American Demographics* (April 1996): 44–48.

176. C.A. Cole and S.K. Balasubramanian, "Age Differences in Consumers' Search For Information: Public Policy Implications," *Journal of Consumer Research* 20, no. 1 (1993): 157–169.

177. M.W. Walker and M.C. Macklin, "The Use of Role Modeling in Targeting Advertising to Grandparents," *Journal of Advertising Research* 32, no. 4 (1992): 37–43.

178. C.D. Schewe, "Get in Position for the Older Market," *American Demographics* (June 1990): 38–41, 61, 63.

179. J. Ostruff, *Successful Marketing to the 50+ Consumer* (Englewood Cliffs, NJ: Prentice Hall, 1989), 249–256; G.P. Moschis, *Marketing to Older Consumers* (Westport, CT: Quorum Books, 1992), 246–255.

6

African Americans

Ethnic Roots, Cultural Diversity

It is a shock for many Americans to learn that race is a socially constructed category and that there is no biological basis for classifying people according to skin color, body form, or any other physical characteristic.[1] All that we measure are the differences in how people look, according to arbitrary, culturally defined criteria, which our society uses to classify physical variations. About 70 percent of cultural anthropologists and half of physical anthropologists reject race as a biological category.[2] Nevertheless, the recognition, even legislation, of racial categories has been a central theme in American history.

The Myth of Race

Americans have historically taken a binary approach to race, assuming that only two races count and that skin color is the dividing line between them. This belief is rooted in the "one-drop rule," a relic of slavery and segregation that classified people as "black" if they had one drop of "black" blood.[3] The "one-drop rule" has not been applied to any other group, whether Native or white Americans or Chinese or Jewish immigrants. The arbitrariness of this definition of race is expressed in Papa Doc Duvalier's alleged answer to a journalist's question about the racial composition of the Haitian population. He replied, "We're 99 percent white, of course, since most of us have mixed blood."[4]

Even peoples who seem indisputably "white" based on skin color have not always been considered "white" in the United States. In 1924 Congress

---

Note: The terms "African American" and "black" are used interchangeably in this chapter to improve readability. They have no other intended significance.

restricted immigration of "inferior races" from southern and eastern Europe (Italians and Romanians).[5] Over time, Italians, Irish, Jews, and Romanians have all been reclassified as "white." Because Americans have traditionally classified anyone with African heritage as "black," most of us do not question the unique treatment of African Americans.[6]

What many Americans perceive as racial differences between blacks and whites are more likely cultural differences and a different basis of ethnic identity. In contrast to other multiracial groups, for African Americans racial and ethnic identity are not distinguished; U.S. Latinos and Asian Americans see their ethnic and racial origins as separate sources of identity. For the majority of whites of European origin, neither race nor ethnicity is as important to social identity as either one is for non-white Americans.[7] These differences indicate why race continues to be perceived as the distinctive characteristic of African Americans, by members of the group and outsiders.

For many African Americans, the physical characteristics associated with "being black" are important to ethnic identity and are learned as distinguishing features of this group as part of the American "experience."[8] While evidence shows that African Americans with darker skin tones continue to experience more discrimination, most African Americans believe that they share the same "race" and heritage of American slavery.[9] While there are endless variations in skin tone among African Americans, most consider themselves "black" Americans, regardless of which label they prefer to use: black, black American, or African American.

The controversy over the interracial heritage of African Americans is a legacy of laws that made it illegal before the 1960s for blacks and whites to marry. Despite the fact that it was illegal, as of the 1960s nearly 75 percent of African Americans had Euro-American ancestors from sexual unions outside legal marriages Most African Americans are "probably as far from the pure Negroid type as from the average Caucasoid type."[10] In addition, a growing number of couples and their offspring are interracial. In 2010 one in ten marriages and one in five unmarried partnerships were interracial, compared with less than 2 percent in 1970.[11] Among those interracial unions in 2010, 20 percent were between blacks and whites and 2 percent black and "other race."[12]

As more people of mixed racial and ethnic background start giving equal weight to each of their respective racial and ethnic heritages, it becomes increasingly difficult to put people into discrete racial/ethnic cells, otherwise known as the "Tiger Woods phenomenon." The famous golfer of mixed racial background has refused to classify himself, or let others classify him, as black, Asian, or any of the racial/ethnic groups represented in his family. Even individuals who belong to a particular ethnic or cultural group may not share the common understanding of that group, and they may even identify with other groups, as is the nature of fluid American social identity.[13]

The Reality of Racial Prejudice in the Marketplace

Even if race is a mythical basis for differences between African and other Americans, it is an invisible cultural boundary that has shaped our shared history. "Other ethnic groups were never slaves in this country, so there is not the moral tension there. Black and White relations are the true test of whether we as a nation are going to be able to overcome racism."[14] It is human nature to prefer people who are like us, but that is not the same as viewing others as inferior. Still, many white Americans hesitate to discuss differences out of fear of being called "racist."

Ethnocentrism refers to our natural human tendency to accept those who seem to be like ourselves and reject those who appear dissimilar.[15] Consumer ethnocentrism describes a preference for companies, brands, or stores owned by people who are most like the shopper or who have the same national (or ethnic) origins.[16] One might expect that African-American consumers with strong African-American racial and ethnic identity would be more likely to prefer African-American–owned businesses. Studies have found that blacks do tend to reduce their purchases from white retailers during periods of racial strife, but under normal circumstances "Buy black" does not drive the purchasing criteria of most African-American consumers.[17]

Motivated by a deep belief in the possibility of racial integration, leaders in the 1960s civil rights movement were convinced that changing laws that regulate public behavior and social relations could uproot racial inequality. It is a paradox of desegregation that our racial divisions have widened. We cling to stereotyped views that suggest there are racial differences between African and other Americans. Television journalists feed racial stereotypes by painting a picture of black men as violent and threatening toward whites and black women as welfare mothers.[18] Repetition of social myths, misconceptions, stupidity, and outright bigotry frame how we perceive our differences.[19]

In recent years, the number of incidents in which members of one ethnic group, as consumers, are engaged in some type of violent confrontation with members of another ethnic group, as storeowners, has increased. Some incidents have involved African Americans and Asian Americans, particularly Korean immigrant storeowners in urban communities.[20] Williams and Snuggs found that African Americans definitely experience discrimination in the marketplace while white Americans think that race has no impact on services provided.[21]

Measures of marketplace discrimination reveal that all consumers are *not* treated equally.[22] Fewer apartments at higher prices are offered to customers of color.[23] Discriminatory practices affect every stage of the mortgage approval process.[24] Both African Americans and women are quoted higher prices than white males for new automobiles.[25] "Hidden camera" investigations on television newsmagazines such as *Dateline* and *20/20* and articles in the popular press have charged that African Americans wait longer or are denied service at restaurants[26] and automobile rental agencies;[27] African-American males are not picked up by taxi drivers;[28] African-American females are not granted fitness club memberships; and restaurants and other businesses refuse to deliver to sections of towns on the basis of race or class alone.[29]

> As young blacks or Latinos walk into a store, security guards nervously shadow them. As they walk toward the cash register and the checkout line, White matrons grip their purses tighter. Video cameras record every step until the teen-agers leave the store.[30]

These incidents create dissatisfied customers who are likely to discontinue patronage and disseminate negative word of mouth. Over 86 percent of African Americans responding to one survey believed that they had been treated differently in retail stores because of race.[31] The long-term consequences of disparate treatment of consumer groups can include organized boycotts, negative publicity, and lawsuits. They constitute a substantial drain on managerial resources. Figure 6.1 describes several incidents and the negative publicity that they generated. If it is true that marketers are "not as concerned about the color of a customer's skin as they are the color of his money," then these incidents trumpet the need to put that philosophy into action.

African-American Diversity

Diverse Heritage and Resources

"Diaspora" comes from a Greek word that describes the scattering of a group of people with a common background. With regard to African Americans, it refers to the great migrations—voluntary and involuntary—of Africans from Africa to other continents. Fifty years ago, most black Americans were descendants of slaves, but today many African Americans can trace their roots directly to the Caribbean and Latin America or are recent arrivals from Africa.[32] What may appear to be a culturally unified group is in fact a mix of peoples who share an African heritage broadly speaking but come from different countries of origin.

Until recently, few African Americans drew a distinction between their

Figure 6.1 **Incidents of Racial Prejudice in the Marketplace**

A black man found himself surrounded by sheriff's deputies, pistols in hand, when bank employees called police, thinking he might be a bank robber because he was sitting in his car outside the bank. Actually he was studying brochures deciding how to invest his savings before entering the bank.[1]

In a shopping mall a security guard stopped two black teenagers when they tried to leave an upscale store, solely on the basis that they were wearing new shirts. He suspected that they had entered the store and exchanged shirts and were now trying to leave. As it turned out, their father had bought the shirts for them the day before.[2]

A video store found itself surrounded by police cars after being called to stop a robbery in progress. The report was traced to a woman who passed the store and saw a large cardboard cut-out of a black man with a gun drawn as a promotion for a recently released video tape (*Lethal Weapon*). She assumed the person in the cut-out was actually a robber and called police.[3]

A black man who was accused of shoplifting and subjected to a strip search along with his 6-year-old son at a New Jersey Bloomingdale's filed a lawsuit against the store and white security guards involved in the incident. On February 10, 1996, Lloyd Morrison was shopping with his son and had already bought him two suits. Morrison left the dressing room to return some pants that didn't fit his son. He was accosted by the security guards who accused him of taking three pair of pants into the dressing room and only returning two. When Morrison said he didn't know what they were talking about, he was ordered to accompany security under threat of being handcuffed, and taken to a room in the back of the store. After Morrison once again insisted that he hadn't done anything, they demanded that he take off his jacket, shirt and ultimately his pants to prove that he wasn't concealing clothes underneath. His son was forced to take his pants off as well.[4]

On October 20, 1995, a young African-American man shopping at an Eddie Bauer outlet was detained and ordered to remove his Eddie Bauer shirt because he could not produce a receipt. Within three months he and two other teens filed an $85 million suit against Eddie Bauer alleging false imprisonment, defamation, and violations of civil rights. A federal jury eventually found in favor of the young men, and awarded the three plaintiffs $1 million. Almost three years later, Eddie Bauer management is still appealing the jury's decision.[5]

A series of "Bud Light Spotlight" commercials were to show actual Bud Light drinkers. A Bud Light film crew picked Dugan's, a sports bar in Atlanta, to participate. The owner was delighted to be included, even though the ad would show the interiors without flashing the bar's name. Representatives from Anheuser-Busch discussed including some of Dugan's employees and 350 predominantly African American clientele in the spot. But when the camera crew showed up, it brought about 25 "real" Bud Light consumers, only two of whom were black. Dugan's no longer serves Bud Light or any other Anheuser-Busch product. "Whoever had the responsibility of setting this up should have been more sensitive" to the bar's regular patrons.[6]

In one court case, a white woman took her two African-American grandchildren and their mother on a weekend trip to the beach. She checked into a motel for two nights while the rest of the family remained in the car. They then deposited their bags in the room and headed for the outdoor pool. Within a few minutes, the desk clerk appeared and demanded that they leave immediately. He refused to respond to their repeated requests for an explanation.[7]

Figure 6.1 *(continued)*

Secretary of State Condoleezza Rice asked to see jewelry at a retail store and the salesclerk brought out only the costume jewelry. When she asked to see the nicer jewels, the clerk grumbled saying something she thought Rice couldn't hear. Rice said: "Let's get one thing straight. You are behind the counter because you have to work for minimum wage. I'm on this side asking to see the good jewelry because I make considerably more."[8]

Sources: E.F. Davidson, "Shopping While Black: Perceptions of Discrimination in Retail Settings," Ph.D. dissertation, University of Tennessee at Knoxville, 2007, http:// trace.tennessee.edu/utk_graddiss/147; G. Schreer, S. Smith, and K. Thomas, "Shopping While Black: Examining Racial Discrimination in a Retail Setting," *Journal of Applied Social Psychology* 39, no. 6 (2009): 1432–1444, www.utexas.edu/features/2006/profiling/ index.html.

[1]J.D. Williams and T. Snuggs, "Survey of Attitudes Toward Customer Service in Retail Stores: The Role of Race," paper presented at Multicultural Marketing Conference, Norfolk, VA, 1996.

[2]Personal experience of Dr. Jerome Williams.

[3]Williams and Snuggss, "Survey of Attitudes Toward Customer Service in Retail Stores."

[4]M. Futterman and M. Nugest, "Shopper Charges Bloomingdale's with Bias and Assault in Search," *Star-Ledger*, September 25, 1997, 33.

[5]R. Castaneda and J. Spinner, "Teens Awarded $1 Million in Bauer Case," *Washington Post*, October 10, 1997, A1.

[6]K. Goldman, "Atlanta Tavern Says Budweiser Was Racially Insensitive on Ad," *Wall Street Journal*, June 4, 1993, B12.

[7]V. Griffith, "The Color of Money," Feature Story, The University of Texas at Austin, October 23, 2006, www.utexas.edu/features/2006/profiling/index.html.

[8]As quoted in G. Kessler, *The Confidante: Condoleezza Rice and the Creation of the Bush Legacy* (New York: St. Martin's Press, 2007), 9.

---

ethnic and racial identity. Any known or perceptible African ancestry made a person "black," with no distinction between those who were born in the United States as descendants of slaves and those who were immigrants or their descendants from Africa, Latin America, or the Caribbean.[33] Only 2.5 percent of U.S. Latinos claimed black as their race in the 2010 census, but for Latinos with origins in the Caribbean, over 10 percent identified their race as black or a combination of races. Blacks who are recent African immigrants or their descendants distinguish themselves from blacks who are the descendants of American slaves. Caribbean and African-origin blacks have this "double identity" that their other African-American cohorts do not share. Caribbean-origin blacks tend to settle in Florida and the Northeast. In Queens, New York, for example, some apartment buildings, city blocks, even neighborhoods, have voluntarily segregated by African-origin black, Caribbean-origin black, and African-American residents.

Table 6.1

African-American Population Growth, 2010–2050
(as a share of total population)

| | | Not of Hispanic origin | | | |
	Total U.S. population	White	Black	American Indian[1]	Asian[2]	Hispanic origin[3]
2010	310,233	66.1%	13.6%	1.6%	5.3%	16.0%
2020	341,387	61.8%	14.0%	1.7%	6.3%	19.4%
2030	373,504	57.5%	14.3%	1.8%	7.3%	23.0%
2040	405,655	53.1%	14.7%	1.9%	8.3%	26.7%
2050	439,010	49.1%	15.0%	2.0%	9.2%	30.2%

Source: U.S. Census Bureau, *Population Projections, 1960–2050* (Washington, DC), www.census.gov/population/www/projections/summarytables.html.
[1]American Indian includes American Indian, Eskimo, and Aleut.
[2]Asian includes Asian and Pacific Islander.
[3]Persons of Hispanic origin may be of any race.

As Table 6.1 indicates, the African-American population of the United States is expected to increase as a share of total population, from about 13.6 percent in 2010 to 15 percent in 2050,[34] Their numbers grew from about 36 million in 2000 and 42 million in 2010 and are expected to reach 45 million by 2030 and 54 million by 2050. The growth rate of the black population is higher than that of the non-Hispanic white population.[35]

African-American households show other aspects of the diversity in this community. The 2010 median income of $29,328 for African-American households was lower than that of any other ethnic group. Yet at the same time the number of poor African Americans in the country decreased, and their real median household incomes improved.[36] African-American household income grew tremendously in the 1990s but lost some of those gains in the recession of 2008–2010. African-American households living below the poverty line comprised only 15 percent of African-American households in 2000, but over 25 percent by 2010. The per capita income of African Americans was $17,033 in 2010, compared with $26,059 for other Americans.[37]

By these yardsticks, African-American disposable income remains lower than that of other Americans. Table 6.2 shows the overall distribution of income in the United States as well as for African-American, non-Hispanic white, Hispanic, and Asian-American households. About 38 percent of black households have income below $25,000 per year, compared with only 25 percent of other Americans. In spite of economic difficulties, black Americans are more optimistic about their progress than are other Americans.[38] Taken

Table 6.2

Household Incomes: Africans Americans Compared with Other Americans

Household income range	Number of all American households	Percentage of all American households	Number of African-American households	Percentage of African-American households	Percentage of non-Hispanic white households	Percentage of Hispanic households	Percentage of Asian-American households
< $25K	29,024	24.8	5,467	37.5	22.9	31.4	20.4
$25–49.9K	29,165	24.9	4,225	28.9	24.5	30.9	19.4
$50–74.9K	20,977	17.9	2,251	15.4	18.4	16.9	15.6
$75–99.9K	14,004	12.0	1,189	8.1	12.5	9.2	12.3
$100K+	14,286	(20.5)	998	(10.0)	21.7	11.7	32.3
$100–149.9K		12.2		6.8			
$150–199.9K	5,250	4.5	309	2.1			
$200K+	4,477	3.8	156	1.1			
Total	117,181	100.0	14,595	100.0	100.0	100.0	100.0

Source: U.S. Census Bureau, *American FactFinder, 2010* (Washington, DC: Department of Commerce, Economic and Statistics Administration, November 2010).

as a whole, total black buying power is expected to reach over $1.1 trillion by 2015.[39]

There are also disparities between black families in different types of households.[40] About half of African-American households consisted of married couples, compared with over 80 percent for Hispanic and non-Hispanic white and Asian households. Over 30 percent of African-American households are headed by women, compared with about 10 percent of households of other Americans.[41] Some 1.4 million black children lived with grandparents and 4 million with both parents. Inner-city households are composed of a variety of related and nonrelated residents, while suburban black households mirror their white counterparts and are more likely to contain two parents and children.

The ratio of black to white median family income varies from 59 percent for female-headed families to 80 percent for married-couple families. While a white family making more than $50,000 is likely to include a husband making $75,000 and a nonworking wife, in African-American families in the same income category, "the husband is likely to be a bus driver earning $32,000, while the wife brings home $28,000 as a teacher or nurse."[42]

Diversity Across Class and Residence

The African-American community has always had significant diversity and stratification. Social distinctions among slaves were based on where they worked (in the fields or the plantation house) and the color of their skin.[43] Early consumer researchers studied low-income blacks mostly in urban areas and mistakenly generalized the results as representative of all African-American consumers.[44] Significant differences across class, geographic location, and age defy the stereotypes about African-American consumers that such extrapolations generate.

A central feature of African-American economic life since the 1960s has been the simultaneous growth of the middle class and an underclass. Civil rights measures led to upward mobility for many African Americans. The middle class grew dramatically, while the really poor tended to stay poor. Middle-class families began to move up and out to the suburbs, to earn more, to send their children to college, and to live better. Meanwhile, the underclass began to sink further into intergenerational poverty, with increasing unemployment rates for young men and a dramatic rise in female-headed families. From 2000 to 2010, the percentage of African Americans living in central cities declined about 10 percent, yet black Americans are still more likely to live in central cities than whites. In 2000 only 29 percent of African Americans lived in the suburbs, while in 2010 more than 50 percent were suburban.[45] These figures for central city and suburban residences are approximately proportionate to the size of the middle-class and poor African-American populations.

Most African Americans are still first-generation middle class. They tend to be employees of others rather than owners and managers and have relatively little accumulated wealth. One difference between middle-class African Americans and whites is the likelihood that more relatives of African Americans come to them for help. Another distinction is that most African Americans lack the resources of people who started life in the middle class.[46] These differences explain why African Americans were harder hit than others by the 2008–11 recession.

A long-standing, if controversial, hypothesis is that the more middle class African Americans are, the weaker their ethnic or race commitment is.[47] Early studies characterized black middle-class life as embodying the "worst of white America" and represented a loss of ethnic identity.[48] The process of African Americans becoming middle class has been treated as analogous to the assimilation process of immigrants, as they, too, become part of the American mainstream over time and generations. Middle-class African Americans are supposedly made to choose between participating in mainstream America or remaining culturally African American, with the result that they are not wholly of either group.[49] Du Bois called this the "double consciousness," of being an American and being black, which leads to perpetual conflict between the two social roles.[50] African-American consumers who have moved up the socioeconomic ladder may have consumption patterns similar to those of their white counterparts, but it does not necessarily mean that they have lost strong ethnic identity.[51]

At the other end of the spectrum are increasing numbers of African Americans who are still trapped in poverty. In 2011 over 27 percent of African-American families had income below the poverty line. While this compares favorably to the 1992 rate of 43 percent, the large percentage of female-headed households among African Americans remains a contributing factor to African-American poverty.[52] Being part of this underclass has other consequences for African Americans. For example, African Americans are disproportionately punished for drug offenses and for crimes committed while they are students. As a result of youthful skirmishes with the justice system, one in 15 African-American men was in prison in 2012, and 1 in 3 African-American men can expect to be incarcerated in his lifetime.[53] Homicide remains the number one cause of death for African-American men age 18 to 29.[54] Black-on-black crime occurs most in cities such as Detroit, Milwaukee, New York, and Chicago, which remain the most segregated cities in the United States, with African Americans concentrated in the inner city and white Americans in the suburbs.[55] Marketers have ignored these urban neighborhoods with low income populations due to the perception that they do not constitute lucrative markets. However, urban neighborhoods often represent more than six times the buying power per square mile of surrounding areas.[56]

The gap between the median net worth of black and white families increased during the 2008–11 recession. During this period, white families lost 19 percent of their net worth, while black families lost 40 percent. One explanation for the gap is that inner-city households are more likely to consist of a single person or a single parent with children than a two-parent household. They are also more likely to be headed by either younger adults (under age 35) or seniors (age 65 or older). And women are significantly more likely to head inner-city households than men.[57] Unemployment among African Americans remained higher in 2012 than for any other Americans. African American unemployment even remained over 15 percent, compared with the national average of 8 percent. The unemployment rate in inner cities can be 30 percent or more.[58] In spite of economic disadvantages, inner-city shoppers do have money to spend—and they spend much of it in their neighborhood. These black inner-city households have more than $122 billion to spend each year, though they represent only 8 percent of the total minority population.[59]

The great migration of blacks from the rural South to Northern cities slowed to a trickle in the 1980s and then began to reverse. Now a steady stream is flowing in the other direction. Affluent blacks are finding the good life in Southern suburbs, and lower-income blacks are looking for a better life in the land of their grandparents. The proportion of blacks living in the South decreased steadily for most of the past century, from 90 percent in 1900 to 53 percent in 1980, but it rose to 57 percent in the 2010 census.[60]

Table 6.3 shows the African-American share of population in several states and in metropolitan areas. As shown in the table, the state with the highest percentage of African Americans is Mississippi (37.6 percent) and the city with the highest percentage is Detroit (84.3 percent). Other states where over 20 percent of the population is African American are Georgia, Alabama, South Carolina, Louisiana, Maryland, Virginia, and North Carolina—all of them Southern states. Western states have the lowest percentage of African Americans. The top ten states are home to almost 60 percent of African Americans, and the top ten cities to over 16 percent.[61]

A growing number of African-American households are affluent, with buying power of over $87.3 billion.[62] In 2010, 7 percent of African Americans were in households that brought home $100,000 or more, and 3 percent were in households with income of more than $250,000.[63] Black households with income of $75,000 or more represent more than 45 percent of all black buying power and are likely to reach that threshold by combining the earnings of two or more workers.[64] In most ways, affluent African Americans are like

Table 6.3

Top African-American Cities and States, 2010

City or state	Total population (in thousands)	Number of African Americans (in thousands)	Percentage of local population	Percentage of all African Americans
Total Population	**308,745.5**			
All African Americans		**42,020.7**	**13.62**	**100.0**
Selected U.S. States				
Top Ten Total		**24,510.4**		**58.33**
New York	19,421.1	3,334.6	17.2	07.93
Florida	18,900.8	3,200.7	17.0	07.62
Texas	25,268.4	3,168.5	12.6	07.54
Georgia	9,727.6	3,054.1	31.5	07.27
California	37,341.9	2,683.9	07.2	06.39
North Carolina	9,565.8	2,151.5	22.6	05.12
Illinois	12,864.4	1,974.1	15.4	04.70
Maryland	5,789.9	1,783.9	30.9	04.25
Virginia	8,037.7	1,653.6	20.7	03.94
Michigan	9,911.6	1,505.5	15.2	03.56
Selected Other States				29.95
Ohio	11,568.5	1,541.8	13.4	03.67
Louisiana	4,553.9	1,486.9	32.8	03.54
Pennsylvania	12,734.9	1,507.9	11.9	03.59
New Jersey	8,807.5	1,300.4	14.8	03.09
South Carolina	4,646.0	1,332.2	28.8	03.17
Alabama	4,802.9	1,281.1	26.8	03.05
Mississippi	2,978.2	1,115.8	37.6	02.66
Tennessee	6,375.4	1,107.2	17.4	02.63
Missouri	6,011.4	747.5	12.5	01.78
Indiana	6,501.6	654.4	10.1	01.56
Massachusetts	6,559.6	508.4	07.8	01.21
District of Columbia	601.7	314.4	52.2	00.75
Selected MSAs				
Top Ten: Total		**6,788.0**		**16.15**
New York	8,175.1	2,228.1	27.3	5.30
Chicago	2,695.6	913.0.	33.9	2.17
Washington, DC	601.7	314.4	52.3	0.75
Philadelphia	1,526.0	686.9	45.0	1.63
Detroit	713.8	602.0	84.3	1.43
Houston	2,099.5	514.2	25.6	1.22
Memphis	646.9	414.9	64.1	1.00
Baltimore	620.9	404.0	65.1	0.96
Los Angeles	3,792.6	402.4	10.6	0.96
Dallas	1,197.8	308.1	25.7	0.73

Source: U.S. Census Bureau, *The Black Population: 2010* (Washington, DC, September 2011).

any other affluent consumers. They are likely to be middle-aged, married, and relatively well educated and to own their own homes. While affluent whites are evenly spread across the country, 45 percent of affluent African Americans live in the South.

Cultural Diversity Across Generations

A teenage boy saunters down the street, his gait and attitude embodying adolescent rebellion. Baggy jeans sag atop over-designed sneakers, gold hoops adorn both ears, and a baseball cap shields his eyes. On his chest, a Tommy Hilfiger shirt sports the designer's distinctive pairing of blue, red, and white rectangles.[65]

Not every African-American person is a basketball player or a thug . . . not all black people speak in slang, wear jeans hanging off them [and are] getting high. That's what's portrayed on TV.[66]

Over 35 percent of African Americans are under age 30. The wedge between African-American generations is hip-hop music and lifestyles, though not all urban youths embrace the culture.[67] Hordes of suburban kids—both black and white—follow their inner-city idols in adopting everything from music to clothing and language, reflected in licensed sports apparel, baseball caps, oversize jeans, and gangster rap music in suburban shopping malls.[68] Although hip-hop got its start in black America, it is now a global phenomenon. An entire generation, black, white, Latino, and Asian, has grown up immersed in hip-hop.[69]

"Urban" is the term used to refer to this market and lifestyle. "Urban" goes beyond racial or ethnic divides and brings together a lifestyle of fashion, attitude, street smarts, and music from all backgrounds. "Urban" has ethnic roots and uses ethnic imagery but is multiracial—black, Latino, Asian. *Vibe, Blaze, XXLMag, The Source*, and *Hip Hop Weekly* are magazines for the hip-hop movement, full of rap music, deejays, and fashion; they target readers of all ethnicities, ages 12 to 24.[70] The hip-hop movement prefers designers and products that do not seem to come from the mainstream, such as Phat Farm, Baby Phat, Stussy, Rocawear, FUBU ("For Us, By Us").[71]

Hip-hop, rap music, and urban lifestyles do not have the same appeal to many older African Americans. If an ad uses an older artist or Motown style of music and fashion for instance, "that's not going to work."[72] Nowhere are the differences across African-American generations more evident than in their choice of entertainment and media sources of information. Table 6.4 indicates that Baby Boomer and senior citizen African Americans spend more

Table 6.4

Generational Differences in African-American Media Use (hours per week)

Media activity	Gen Y	Gen X	Young boomers	Older boomers	Seniors
Watching TV	14	16	15	16	16
Internet: personal	13	14	11	10	9
Internet: work	9	11	10	9	2
Videogames, handheld	4	2	1	1	0
Listening to radio	10	10	9	9	7
Videogames, computer	4	3	2	2	2
Reading magazines	2	2	2	3	3
Reading newspapers	1	2	3	3	5

Source: I. Mitskaviets with J. Anderson, *Online African Americans: A Demographic Profile* (Cambridge, MA: Forrester Research, 2009), www.forrester.com/Online+African+Americans+A+Demographic+Profile/fulltext/-/E-RES54211/.

time with magazines and newspapers than with videogames. The youngest African Americans spend the most time on videogames. All groups spend about the same amount of time watching television, and it is the media activity on which they spend the most time.

Ethnic Identity and African-American Cultural Values

African Roots

Slavery deprived African-American families of the ability to maintain their original African culture—its languages and beliefs. Marriages were not recognized, and groups and families were broken up. Slaves were forced to speak English, to worship in certain ways, and to conform to American beliefs. No other immigrants have met such restrictions limiting their rights. African-American culture has roots in Africa but was constructed in the United States.[73] The infusion of African influences took place in spite of this broken connection, but, unsurprisingly, many African Americans are unaware of how much their African roots shape contemporary behaviors and attitudes.[74]

Writers describe African-American life and cultural style as holistic, with all parts of a person's thinking, feeling, behaving, and being inextricably connected.[75] This interrelated system is the basis of African-origin norms, evident in nine areas, as seen in Table 6.5, The table illustrates how these norms compare to beliefs that dominate other American subcultures. For example, an emphasis on collectivism among U.S. Latinos, Asian Americans, and African Americans contrasts with the individualism of mainstream America. African spirituality and beliefs about expressing emotion are more similar to those of U.S. Latinos than mainstream Americans. Asian and African Americans share attitudes about harmony between man and his environment and the circularity of time. In recent studies, African Americans scored as collectivistic, high on uncertainty avoidance, and power distance, three of Hofstede's cultural value systems.[76]

A growing number of African Americans insist on viewing the world from an "African-centered" perspective.[77] Authenticity, "being real," is essential in Afrocentrism. Significant weight is attached to personal qualities, such as "telling it like it is," "seeing the good as well as the bad," "sharing," "resilience," and "distrust of mainstream institutions" within the African-American community.[78] Assertiveness, speaking up, and expressing emotions are other valued behaviors that are often misinterpreted as aggression in mainstream society.[79] Group rituals that represent passages from one stage of life to another are also important in Afrocentric life, as seen in the importance of African-American funerals and family celebrations of achievements.

Ethnic Identity and Labels

When individuals identify as members of a particular ethnic group, they typically practice and retain the customs, language, and social views of the group.[80] Still, not all individuals in a particular minority culture share all its values and expressions of behaviors: As a result, there may be different degrees of affiliation with the minority culture. For instance, one person may feel a strong identification with African-American culture and less affiliation with the American mainstream, whereas a second may have weak ties to African-American culture and feel more at home with mainstream American values and beliefs.[81] The most common and yet most direct approach to measuring ethnic identity is a single question: "How strongly do you identify with your racial/ ethnic group?" Unfortunately, this does not elicit the dual nature of African-American ethnicity, as seen in preferences for how African Americans are depicted in the media. For example, people who are high African-American identifiers prefer African American-dominant ads in "racially targeted media, while low ethnic identifiers prefer whites in positions of dominance in ads in mainstream media.[82]

For both African and European Americans, ethnic identity is part of social identity but it seems to operate very differently in the two groups.[83] Two central dimensions dominate African-American identity: one political and the other social/personal. In contrast, Euro-American identity has a more integrated structure based on multiple aspects of social life.[84] Higher socioeconomic status is associated with self-perceptions of African Americans that include more "white

Table 6.5

African-Origin Beliefs Compared with Those of Other American Subcultures

African-origin beliefs	American mainstream beliefs	Latin American origin beliefs	Asian origin beliefs
Spirituality			
Powers greater than man exist and are at work	Man can shape his destiny if God is willing	God shapes our destiny	Mixed
Harmony			
Man and his environment are interdependent and connected, as are the parts of one's life	Man can shape his environment for mankind's betterment	Same as American origin	Same as African origin
Movement			
A rhythmic orientation to life, manifested in music and dance, behavior and approach	Life and time are linear; progress is important	Resist change, rely on traditions	Mixed
Verve			

A preference for tuning in to several stimuli rather than a singular orientation; energy and intensity	Achievement and competition directed; specialized roles; play fair; keep busy	Preserve relationships over achievement; individual style important	Preserve group cohesion; self is unimportant

Affect

Emotional expressiveness and sensitivity to emotional cues; feelings and thinking integrated	Feeling and thinking are considered separate processes	Same as African origin	Little emotion expressed

Communalism

Interdependence of people; a social orientation	Individualist orientation	Same as African-origin	Same as African-origin

Expressive individualism

Focus on a person's unique style and spontaneity	Mixture of social conformity and individual expression	Social conformity	Social conformity

Orality

Importance of information learned and transmitted orally; call and response	Low context, words = message; direct; superiority of written word	High context, relationship determines style; indirect	Same as Latin origin

Social time perspective

Time viewed in terms of the event rather than the clock	Linear concept of time and future-orientation	Social time and past orientation	Time is circular and social

Sources: Adapted from N. Carr-Ruffino, *Managing Diversity: People Skills for a Multicultural Workplace* (Cincinnati: South-Western, 1996); M. de Mooij, *Global Marketing and Advertising: Understanding Cultural Paradoxes* (Thousand Oaks, CA: Sage, 1998); J. Hammond and J. Morrison, *The Stuff Americans Are Made of* (New York: Macmillan, 1996); G. Hofstede, *Cultures and Organizations: Software of the Mind*, rev. ed. (New York: McGraw-Hill, 1997); M.G. Willis, "Learning Styles of African American Children: A Review of the Literature and Interventions," in *African American Psychology: Theory, Research, and Practice*, ed. A.K.H. Burlew et al. (Newbury Park, CA: Sage, 1992), 63–86.

traits" than "black traits."[85] Racial inequality may not directly affect personal or racial esteem, but it does influence personal efficacy, the belief that one can accomplish goals and be successful.[86] Other studies show that African Americans have stronger and more positive racial, ethnic, and national identities than European Americans.[87] Perhaps most important, African-American self-esteem and strong ethnic identity are positively correlated.[88] In sum, ethnic identity means very different things in mainstream and nonmainstream groups.

The labels used for African-American self-identification are revealing of shifts in ethnic consciousness and sensitivity to the sociopolitical milieu.[89] Earlier in U.S. history, labels such as *Negro* (from the Latin word *niger*, which is *negro* in Spanish/Portuguese) and *black* or *black* (the English translation of the Spanish word *negro*) *American* derived from European languages.[90] The movement from *Negro* to *black* represented a movement from one European-based language to another but was encouraged by leaders in the community to reflect self-improvement and unity.[91] The grouping of African Americans and other ethnic groups of color into categories such as "minority," "people of color," or "non-white" are believed by some to connote inferior roles and lower importance.[92]

No single identity or label is sufficient to describe the variability of identities among African Americans. Three labels are consistently listed by African Americans to name their ethnic identity: *black, black American*, and *African American*. The preference for these labels has been measured as follows: 61 percent say it does not matter, 13 percent preferred the label *black*, and 24 percent preferred *African American*.[93] Those who chose the label *black* justify their selection by saying it is the right label, generally accepted, reflective of their skin color, and the one that they were taught. Those who selected *black American* explain that the label means being both black and American, and it expresses both patriotism and ethnic pride. Ethnic heritage is the rationale for those using the label *African American*.[94] The use of *black* has been decreasing over time in favor of the label *African American*.[95] Even so, many people still do not identify as African American when they maintain family ties to specific countries of origin.

Language plays an important role in the shifting nature of ethnic identity.[96] Members of language communities maintain linguistic distinctiveness by using a variety of speech and nonverbal markers (e.g., vocabulary, slang, posture, gesture, discourse styles, accent) to create "psycholinguistic distinctiveness."[97] African slaves, who came mostly from West Africa, developed a pidgin English to communicate with their masters. They substituted English for words in their native languages but used the basic structure and idiom of their West African language.[98] Over the years, pidgin English evolved into black English or Ebonics.

Social pressures, often subconscious, exist within the African-American community to maintain black English as a form of group identity and symbol of unity.[99] Many African Americans use some elements of Ebonics, but usage varies significantly in accordance with differences in ethnic identity, social class, gender, age, region, and education level.[100] Black English is used less frequently at places of employment than in school and in conversation with family and friends.[101] Code-switching between the language of mainstream America and black English is often coupled with other communication-style changes, in verbal play, nonverbal symbols, and body language and is the most obvious example of African American communication patterns.

The development of ethnic pride among African Americans is linked to a sense of self and personal worth that explicitly refer to African-American history and consciousness.[102] The communication style of many African Americans shows how language affirms a sense of identity as well as awareness that outsiders do not share that comfort zone of familiar behaviors. There is also a tradition of value placed on verbal skills and oral performances ("stylin'"), call-response patterns of exchange between speaker and audience, and meaningful nonverbal messages communicated by body language, movement, eye contact, and use of time.[103]

Balancing Two Cultures

African Americans grow up as part of, yet apart from, American mainstream society; in it but not of it, included at some levels and excluded at others. This duality is at the heart of an identity struggle that can generate powerful feelings of frustration, anger, and indignation. They must transmigrate back and forth between African-American and Euro-American worlds and find a workable balance between different sets of beliefs as norms for behavior. W.E.B. Du Bois expressed the dilemma that this creates for African-American identity:

> One ever feels his twoness—an American, a Negro; two souls, two thoughts, two unreconciled strivings; two warring ideals in one dark body, whose dogged strength alone keeps it from being torn asunder. . . . The history of the American Negro is the history of this strife—this longing to attain self-conscious manhood, to merge his double self into a better and truer self. . . . He would not Africanize America, for America has too much to teach the world and Africa. He would not bleach his Negro soul in a flood of white Americanism, for he knows that Negro blood has a message for the world. He simply wishes to make it possible for a man to be both a Negro and an American, without being cursed and spit upon.[104]

During the 1960s and early 1970s, scholars assumed that African Americans wanted cultural as well as economic integration. The dominant view was that that blacks "attempt to surround themselves with symbols of whiteness . . . fighting to attain full membership in American society."[105] Consumption of socially visible goods and services easily serve this signaling purpose, not just for African Americans but also for any group that seeks membership in mainstream America. Differences between black and white consumer behaviors were attributed to differences in socioeconomic status rather than cultural differences.[106] Among lower-income blacks there was little pressure to conform to mainstream, middle-class standards; for upper-income blacks, it was important to match accepted, middle-class ideals.[107]

This thinking is consistent with the assumptions of cultural assimilation in which those of the mainstream over time and with economic mobility replace the values and beliefs of an ethnic group. This has not actually been the case among African Americans. After the civil rights movement began some African Americans aggressively began to substitute their own ethnic alternatives to dominant standards of beauty, behavior, and value. Many beliefs were challenged because they did not express "black consciousness."[108] Those people who assert a unique African-American consciousness refute the idea that African Americans are assimilating into mainstream American culture and dropping their unique subcultural values.

Rather than representing either assimilation or separation, most African-American behaviors and beliefs fit a multicultural model of cultural groups coming together.[109] Drawing from extensive socialization and life experiences in the two cultures, African Americans synthesize the experience by existing in two cultural worlds and adopting both value systems simultaneously.[110] This simply means that people who strongly identify as African American will exhibit behavior representative of the African-American cultural script in some situations and behavior representative of mainstream culture in other situations. For example, expenditures on clothing may reflect African heritage while expenditures on food at home mirror European cultural traditions, or vice versa.[111] The behavior of a multicultural person refutes any linear view of acculturation[112] as the choice of appropriate behavior depends on its cultural context.

This discussion of how African Americans adjust to American mainstream life would not be complete without addressing the impact that African Americans have had on mainstream American culture. Music, food, fashion, sports, literature, language, and virtually every sector of American life have been enriched by influences from African-American culture. African-American and urban trends are a primary source of inspiration for American pop culture. "We invent a fashion but white guys manufacture the clothes. We play a game, but white guys own the team. We conceive a music, but white guys market the CDs. We create a catch phrase, but white guys make the T-shirts."[113] Even the way young blacks talk has been adopted in mainstream America. Webster's dictionary includes words such as "homeboy," "dis," and "gangsta" in newer editions.[114] Terms like "hood," "crib," and "bling" have been in *Merriam-Webster's Collegiate Dictionary* since 2007.[115] At the other extreme, "wiggers" is a new term that refers to whites who strive to be black.[116]

African Americans as Consumers

The Legacy of Early Marketing Efforts

As the first beneficiaries of efforts to segment demand on the basis of ethnicity, African-American consumers draw on a variety of experiences in the marketplace. Their cultural symbols have been mocked and distorted in appeals to non–African-American consumers, yet celebrated and embraced by companies seeking African-American loyalty.[117] As a result, many African Americans have a heightened sensitivity to interactions in the marketplace. Consumption can be a medium for simultaneously expressing participation in the mainstream and pride in ethnic roots and accomplishments. The marketplace sends messages of both symbolic and social status content.

As early as the 1940s, mainstream marketers developed strategies to target African-American consumers. In 1946 Pepsi assembled a dozen people in its target marketing team whose job was to make contacts in black communities, black campuses, Elks club meetings, and black churches. The sympathetic black press supported Pepsi and in return benefited from the placement of Pepsi advertisements that portrayed blacks in a positive way. These efforts brought in new customers at a time when Pepsi sales had been falling.[118]

The advertising industry overall, however, has been extremely cautious about developing ties with the African-American community. Even *Ebony*, a black-oriented magazine, carried advertisements with models with predominantly European features; only after the 1960s did these ads give way to models with more typically African features and natural "Afro" hairstyles.[119] Early marketers represented products such as fast foods, tobacco, and alcohol. It was not until long after the 1960s that other mainstream advertisers and agencies developed aggressive, proactive, and positive campaigns for African-American target audiences. Since the 1980s, the increased economic clout of African-American consumers has attracted a growing number of ethnic and mainstream marketers. In spite of the increased attention to this consumer group, African Americans remain almost invisible in mainstream advertising and communications agencies today.[120]

Contemporary marketers must overcome a legacy of earlier insults to African Americans by mainstream marketers. One early print ad showed the bandanna-clad Aunt Jemima smiling on a box of pancake mix. Black women were hired to dress up as traditional "mammies" to cook pancakes at fairs and pose with visitors at Disneyland.[121] Greatly exaggerated physical features such as "saucer" lips and "banjo" eyes were used to depict blacks. Some African-American women still remember how upset they were to see the "most negative, pejorative, derogatory features" of Aunt Jemima projected as the prototype of black women."[122] Brand characters such as Aunt Jemima (pancake mix), Uncle Ben (rice), and Rastus (Cream of Wheat) remain constant reminders of what has been acceptable in mainstream society.[123]

Terms from other eras have also been defamatory to African Americans. Throughout history the slang for Negro has been offensive to blacks. "For black people the n-word symbolizes four hundred years of anti-African racism and cultural repression."[124] Yet around the turn of the twentieth century it was common to see products including the word: Nigger Head canned fruits and vegetables (1905), Nigger Head stove polish (1920), Nigger Head tees (1920), Nigger Head tobacco, and Nigger Head oysters.[125]

Quaker Oats continues to distance its marketing efforts from the early Aunt Jemima. In the 1960s, the company changed Aunt Jemima's bandanna into a headband. Then in 1989 the character became slimmer, exchanged her headband for a perm, and put on pearl earrings to reflect a more professional image. They hired Gladys Knight to pitch the pancakes and syrups. Still, "for some consumers, there's no amount of makeover that would sufficiently offset the stereotypes associated with the name and the picture."[126] The dilemma is what to do about a brand that is synonymous with quality but used a character that is considered a cultural pariah

Most marketers try to avoid insensitivity when marketing to African Americans. Because few African Americans are in key decision-making roles or on staff, marketing mistakes continue to be made. For example, a controversial United Colors of Benetton print ad featured two young girls, one white and the other black. The white girl had golden locks and the light appeared to create a halo around her head. The black girl was not smiling and had her hair shaped into what appeared to be two horns. The image appeared to be an angel and a devil. Not according to Benetton, which reacted to this interpretation with surprise.[127] Walgreen's distributed a flyer during Black History Month that included a coupon for skin lightening cream.[128] And an ad in *Jet* for Toyota Corolla claimed, "Unlike your last boyfriend, it goes to work in the morning." The negative reactions that the ad generated prompted immediate apologies from *Jet*, Toyota, and the agency that created it, Saatchi & Saatchi.[129]

One lesson that mainstream marketers have yet to learn is how to effectively speak the "language of the target." Mainstream marketers have made many mistakes in trying to incorporate the language and behaviors of African Americans into advertising copy. The Pringle's rap to a nongreasy chip was "ridiculous and offensive," as was the Fruity Pebbles cereal commercial featuring the Flintstones character "Barney Rubble" as a rapper.[130] By not speaking in an authentic voice as "extended" member of the African-American community, these marketers actually increased the perceived cultural distance between them and their African-American audience.

Yet other dangers in today's marketplace are "urban legends," reproduced widely and easily in cyberspace. One such myth was the story of Tommy Hilfiger's appearance on "Oprah" in which he allegedly claimed that he did not want "people of color" to buy his clothes. The company, which heavily used e-mail to spread its messages, used the same medium to assure minority consumers that the story was fiction and that they remain valued customers.[131] Tropical Fantasy, a line of low-priced sodas sold in New York's ethnic neighborhoods, attained sales of $2 million a month, until someone started a baseless rumor that the soda was made by the Ku Klux Klan to sterilize black men.[132] Urban legends have always existed, but the Internet spreads them to a global audience.

African-American Consumer Preferences

In 2010, African Americans accounted for 8.5 percent of U.S. consumer spending.[133] Of the more than $1.307 trillion they spent that year, more than $29.3 billion was on apparel, over $65 billion on food, $18.6 billion on telephone services, and $9.7 billion on computers and consumer electronics.[134] Fast food restaurants are the single-largest category in African-American spending from disposable income. In almost every product category black women are the primary decision makers. In 2009 companies spent $87 million targeting black women, and in 2010 over $2.3 billion was spent wooing black consumers. The biggest spenders in the African-American market in 2010 were Procter & Gamble, L'Oréal, Johnson & Johnson, General Motors, McDonald's, Verizon, the U.S. government, AT&T, Berkshire Hathaway, and National Amusements.

Noting the low median household incomes of African-American consumers, some companies decided not to actively pursue them. Based on the 2010 Consumer Expenditure Survey data, in 2010 African-American households, which number some 13.7 million, each spent an average of $35,863, or 27 percent less than the national average of $48,109.[135] Although they spend less per trip, they make more shopping trips than white consumers. In addition, African Americans use fewer coupons or store brands. But their rapidly growing income will allow African-American spending to approach the national average in a few years.[136] Millions of middle- and upper-class African-American households have discretionary income to spend, and the choices that they make raise expenditures above the average for numerous goods and services.[137]

In some product categories, African Americans substantially outspend other consumers and are the trendsetters. For example, a larger percentage of African Americans own smartphones than the national average.[138] This is also true for mobile phone services and personal- and beauty-care products. African Americans spend more than nine times what non–African Americans spend on these products. Within the soft-drink industry, African American and Hispanic consumers purchase some products out of proportion to their representation in the population. The two groups make up 21 percent of the U.S. population, but account for 40 percent of lemon-lime sodas drunk and 50 percent of fruit-flavored (grape and orange) sodas.[139]

The most elusive aspect of African-American consumption patterns concerns whether the differences between African Americans and other consumers are due to cultural or socioeconomic characteristics. Most consumer researchers agree that their consumer behaviors differ, but there is no consensus as to the cause. Some contend that when socioeconomic variables are held constant, the differences are insignificant. Others maintain that there are still behavioral differences attributable to ethnic or cultural differences.[140]

There is also disagreement about what cultural differences communicate about African-American values.[141] When socioeconomic differences are held constant, do consumption differences indicate a desire to remain culturally distinct or does it show that African Americans are less concerned with what others think.[142] Many misconceptions about African-American consumers have been allowed to stand, in spite of the fact that early research focused exclusively on urban and low-income households. That African Americans are "more brand loyal" than other consumers is one such myth. Evidence on their brand loyalty is mixed at best; it is true they buy fewer store brands, but it is also true that they are more likely than other Americans to say, "It's always important to get the best price."[143] More research is the only antidote to inaccurate generalizations about African-American consumers.

Ignoring ethnicity is a different approach to diversity within the African-American market taken by many marketers. Using values measures such as VALS, companies segment African-American consumers and their lifestyles. These segmentation measures do take ethnic or cultural influences into consideration as they translate differences across and within ethnic groups into beliefs and lifestyle choices. Competence, empathy, belonging, and hedonism are four areas researchers have found that effectively group persons with different overall values in the United States, resulting in segments called Hard-Core Traditionalists, Family Values Boomers, Post-Yuppies, and Self-Navigators.[144] The first three groups tend to cross all ethnic groups. The self-navigators are younger (about 50 percent) and have an approach to living that says, "It's up to me to create my own well-being." They are less likely to invest or own many credit cards. The Self-Navigators are 80 percent white, 13 percent black, and 7 percent other.

Tom Burrell found through his agency's focus groups that "status, image, and self-enhancement" are priorities for African Americans. This is consistent with other findings that consumers who have the most rapidly rising income are most likely to spend discretionary income on visible signs of success.[145] Online, African Americans say that "owning the best brand is important to me."[146] As noted earlier, visibly consumed symbols of success are important media for communicating social and economic achievements of African Americans.[147] Consumers who cannot acquire the home they want divert spending to other goods and services that symbolize the "American dream." The active role of the marketplace in African-American social identity creates opportunity for businesses that understand the cultural context of African American expressions of achievement.

An excellent example of the connection between African American social identity and market space choices is the Kwanzaa celebration. In recent years, over 12 million African Americans have set the week after Christmas aside to celebrate Kwanzaa, a festival of "family, roots, and community." Hallmark has been selling Kwanzaa cards with designs by African-American artists as part of its Mahogany line since 1992.[148] An African American–owned publishing company markets 21 styles of Kwanzaa cards and activity books for children. Its Kwanzaa kit comes with a kinara and instructions for novices. Some parents even purchase bicycles and Nintendo sets for Kwanzaa gifts. While some traditionalists disapprove of the commercialization of the festival, it is part of the natural evolution of holiday celebrations.[149] Another important event on the black American calendar is February, Black History Month.

Effective Marketing Means Giving Back to the Community

It may seem obvious, but treating customers with respect is the first principle of any marketing program targeting African-American consumers. Demeaning depictions of African Americans and incidents of racial prejudice are some of the concerns that African Americans have when shopping. That sensitivity is at the forefront of their decision about where to shop. The number one deciding factor for both African-American consumers and their white counterparts is "reasonable pricing." But for whites the second most important factor in deciding where to shop is "availability of quality merchandise," whereas for African Americans, it is "respect" (60 percent). In research and focus groups with African-American consumers, a topic that comes up frequently is either being watched or being ignored.[150]

African-American consumers also place a high value on atmospherics. Shopping meets the need for both information gathering and entertainment. It is hard for customers to have a pleasant shopping experience when they feel mistreated. A pleasant store atmosphere ranks fourth among blacks as a factor in deciding where to shop.[151] Cadillac's programs to attract African-American buyers include sensitivity training for dealership personnel.[152]

A commitment must also be made to having an appropriate product mix and selections that suit African-American tastes. Revlon, Clinique, Prescriptives, and Maybelline have extended their makeup lines with colors and shadings to capture more of the personal-care spending of African Americans.[153] J.C. Penney added a "Fashion Influences" catalog that featured contemporary, African-influenced designs made in the United States. McCall patterns, Spiegel's E-Style clothing catalog, and Sears' African Village clothing line have used Afrocentric themes to appeal to African-American clothing shoppers.[154]

Mainstream companies can find it difficult to "fit in" or use the right language when competing with African American–owned firms. Consumers found some of the greeting card lines as well as fiction paperbacks that mainstream publishers have offered less authentic than the products of proven ethnic marketers.[155] At the same time, African American–owned companies are not always successful because they have a "more ethnic" product. Glory Foods started out selling African-American prepared foods, such as greens and "soul food." Its marketing research discovered a bigger opportunity in convenient alternatives to mainstream American prepared foods, such as broccoli and asparagus.[156]

Having communications with relevant cultural content is another way to tailor marketing programs for African-American consumers. African Americans respond positively to the use of Ebonics in advertising to mainstream audiences that include African Americans and others, but only if it is done well.[157] The "right-on" school of advertising has been known for injecting lexical features of Ebonics into advertising copy. Slang expressions such as "home boys" and "home girls" are used in the copy for products targeted to African Americans.[158] One firm that markets to inner-city African American youth uses street slang to create names and flavors for its potato chips, such as "Chumpies," a commonly used term for "the best of the best," and "Bumpin Barbecue," meaning something "hot and good."[159]

African Americans have been almost invisible in the mainstream media in spite of their heavy consumption of network and cable television programs.

One way to make an impact is to use more inclusive advertising. By placing African-American models in ads, putting them into leading roles instead of the background, using African-American celebrities, and using ethnic-oriented media, a message is sent directly to African-American consumers that their patronage is wanted. Many of McDonald's ads feature only African Americans, and some of the most popular ads overall have all-black casts.[160] Chrysler sponsored the television premiere of the acclaimed documentary "Hoop Dreams," in hopes of reaching millions of African-American teens and their families. The screening was part of a Chrysler-sponsored educational program in schools nationwide. "Programs like this aren't measured by how many cars they sell, but they convey a corporate commitment to things that are important to the African-American community."[161]

Increasing the visibility of African Americans in the media is an important goal of community leaders. In the past, racially exclusive advertisements communicated a "blacks not welcome here" message. This was especially true of real estate, in which potential black renters or home buyers had experienced real discrimination confirming that interpretation. By including African Americans in advertising messages, not only are African Americans more likely to pay attention, they are also more likely to respond to the appeal.[162]

Communication agencies that are either African American–owned or that specialize in the African-American market have been serving major American companies for over forty years. Burrell Communications, the Chisholm-Mingo Group, eMorris Communications, and UniWorld are some of the best known, with clients such as McDonald's, Sears, Coca-Cola, and Procter & Gamble. Despite the growing interest in minority markets, African-American agencies have not flourished to the extent their general and Hispanic market counterparts have.[163]

An important way in which companies "give back" to the black business community is the use of African American-owned media and suppliers. African Americans, U.S. Latinos, and Asian Americans generate combined purchasing power over $1 trillion, yet ethnic radio stations, newspapers, and magazines receive a small portion, if any, of advertising budgets targeting those communities.[164] PepsiCo increased its advertising on black radio stations and ethnic newspapers specifically to expand its influence in the African-American community.

Some large companies have initiated long-term partnerships with institutions in the African-American community. They provide financial support to social, political, and professional associations that represent the interests of African Americans—such as, the NAACP (National Association for the Advancement of Colored People), National Urban League, Rainbow-PUSH Coalition, United Negro College Fund, and Congressional Black Caucus

Foundation. Other important institutions are churches (the historical center of social and political life within African-American communities), schools, sororities and fraternal associations, development programs, and even government agencies. An example of company partnerships with churches is Revlon's sponsorship of gospel conventions, choir robes, and the Stellar Awards, in which product samples are distributed during services. There are also a number of professional associations, such as the National Black MBA Association or the National Association of Black Journalists, that are organized around the interests of African-American members of those occupations. These nonprofit organizations spread the word about which companies are good citizens within the African-American community. Supporting the institutions that build community among black Americans is an opportunity to be seen as an insider for businesses that wish to target African American consumers.

Yet another way in which companies can assist African-American community development is in health and education. Hypertension, diabetes, heart and lung diseases, obesity, and sickle-cell anemia are serious health concerns for African Americans. In addition to donations for research in search of cures and treatments for these diseases, some companies are creating joint ventures with community institutions to educate consumers. Wrigley participated in an advocacy program called Health Watch, whose mission is to encourage African, Asian, and Hispanic Americans to use doctors for regular health maintenance instead of as a last resort.[165]

There are many ways of "giving back" to the community. Le Van Hawkins built a multicity Burger King franchise during the 1990s, and many of the stores were located in the roughest neighborhoods of Detroit, Baltimore, and Washington, DC. The stores offered banana shakes and Cajun fries in addition to Burger King's regular fast-food fare. Klieg lights and neon made the restaurants as "bright as baseball stadiums." Inside, music was all hip hop and R&B, with uniformed Nation of Islam guards providing security. Employees were offered stock options and a path to becoming an owner-operator. Hawkins also made half-million-dollar grants to church foundations and school programs in nearly every neighborhood where he set up shop. The Hawkins philosophy is "to build neighborhoods and self-esteem, not just restaurants."[166]

"Community marketing" is what McDonald's calls its own efforts to participate in African-American communities and institutions. It works with the "A Better Chance Foundation" to offer college and prep school scholarships in underprivileged areas. The company's "Black History Makers of the Future" program highlights 30 African-American children and includes them every year in national television advertising. Coors, Mattel, Kraft/General Foods, and Toyota are other marketers that emphasize the successes of African Americans through scholarships to the American Negro College Fund and school and summer meal programs in inner cities.[167] Dollar General Corporation opens stores near public housing projects in South Carolina, hires residents to work in their stores, and then requires employees to take literacy training.[168]

Information Sources and Media Preferences

Community Networks: An Oral Tradition

Networking within an African American community is an extension of the oral tradition among African Americans. High credibility is given to sources of information from among members and leaders of the African-American community. This is a powerful reason for companies to become visible in African-American targeted media. Often these media offer cost advantages over mainstream media as well. The most trustworthy source of company and product information for African Americans ages 21 to 65 are African American–targeted magazines (87 percent). Next in trustworthiness is *Consumer Reports* (80 percent), followed by news coverage on African-American television stations. African Americans cite local television news and African American magazines as their most frequent sources of company and product information.[169] Networking and word-of-mouth communication are the modern-day versions of "oral tradition."[170] African-American consumers rely more on in-store displays and word-of-mouth communications from salespeople than other Americans.[171] African Americans and U.S. Latinos spend more time on social networking websites than other Americans. All this activity supports the importance to black consumers of "being in the know" and "being the first" to adopt new trends in fashion, music, and pop culture.[172] Black barbershops and beauty salons have always been important parts of the African-American community. Getting a haircut may be secondary to finding out what is going on in the community for African Americans.

African cultures, from which at least some African-American culture is built, make greater distinctions between insiders and outsiders, as do Latin Americans, Asians, and Mediterranean Europeans.[173] Furthermore, there is a long tradition of respect for oral communication in the African-American community.[174] African Americans talk more with family and friends about products, companies, and advertising than other Americans. By comparison, Chinese Americans engage in little consumer talk, Mexican Americans talk more about advertising than products, and white Americans are more likely to discuss negative product experiences.[175] Even parents are cited as valuable sources of product information by black teenagers.[176]

African-American celebrities represent "insider" sources of information to people who identify as African American, and many of them act as celebrity endorsers.[177] Black sports and entertainment personalities dominate annual Q-Ratings, a metric for the popularity of performers as celebrities. Some successful endorsers for mainstream brands, current and past are Halle Berry (Revlon), Janell Monae (Cover Girl), Oprah Winfrey (2012 presidential re-election campaign of Barack Obama), Mary Blige (Burger King), Beyoncé (L'Oréal, American Express, Disneyland), Jay Z (Budweiser, HP computers), Cee Lo Green (Las Vegas tourism), Michael Jordan (Nike), Michael Jackson (Pepsi), Bill Cosby (Jell-O, Kodak), Michael Jordan (Nike, McDonald's), Ray Charles (Pepsi), and Whitney Houston (Coca-Cola).[178] An early study indicated that African Americans were at least twice as likely as whites to rate celebrities as more believable than noncelebrity endorsers. Another researcher reported that celebrity athletes and celebrity entertainers were the most likely advertising spokespersons that would cause African-American consumers to buy a product.[179]

The absence of African Americans in the mainstream media means that the few African-American models and actors have high visibility in those media. Past studies found that less than 10 percent of magazine ads contained blacks, and this percentage dropped to only 2.4 percent when *Ebony* and *Essence* were excluded.[180] Representation of African-American actors in television advertising varies by product category, with overrepresentation in telephone, liquor/wine/beer, and hair product ads and underrepresentation in clothing ads.[181] It also appears that African Americans pay more attention to and recall more from ads with African-American models.[182] This attention to a model's race is extended to the composition of the entire cast in an ad as all-black casts are rarely seen in mainstream advertisements.[183]

Media Use Among African Americans

African Americans spend more time with electronic media such as TV and radio than any other group in the United States. These media provide entertainment as well as product and lifestyle information.[184] Table 6.6 shows media habits of African Americans, compared to non-Hispanic whites and U.S. Latinos. African Americans are more likely to receive news from TV, but they also spend time listening to black-sponsored radio, magazines, newspapers, websites, and blogs. Radio and television have been the primary sources of information about sports, entertainment, and music over the past forty years, and these fields are the places African Americans have made an impact on American popular culture. Thus, these media showcase African-American success in a mainstream context.

Because black viewers indicate such high consumption of network television (40 percent more viewing time than other Americans), many marketers

Table 6.6

African-American Offline Media Habits

Percentage who regularly . . .	Blacks	Non-Hispanic whites	Hispanics
Read a daily newspaper	47	50	34
Watch local TV news	80	74	73
Watch national newscasts	75	68	68
Listen to black news/talk radio	62		
Read a black-oriented magazine	60		
Read a black newspaper	28		
Read black websites or blogs	30		

Source: Pew Research Center, *A Year After Obama's Election: Blacks Upbeat About Progress, Prospects* (Washington, DC, January 12, 2010), 60.

assume that their messages reach African Americans at the same time as the general market audience in that medium. There is significant crossover, but the program tastes of African-American and white audiences differ. In 2010, the favorite types of programs for African Americans were premium cable programming, sports, and reality and award shows. The responses of African Americans to advertisements in mainstream and ethnic media also differ. About 60 percent of African-American consumers reported in a survey that they believe network advertising is designed only for whites. At the same time, a higher percentage of black audiences report paying attention to advertising, suggesting another opportunity for reaching black audiences within mainstream media.[185]

Television and Radio: Entertainment Centers for African Americans

There are dozens of exclusively African American–targeted media for promoting goods and services. Nevertheless, the best medium continues to be network television, where African Americans spend the most time. Even with increasing time online, the average black household has 4 televisions, and spends more than 7 hours per day and over 200 hours per month with network television. Viewers age 12 to 17 and over 50 have the most similar tastes in programs as white audiences.[186] To reach the largest number of potential African American buyers, companies concentrate their media budgets on television. In 2011 more than 46 percent of all advertising toward the African American market was spent on TV, for a total of $916 million.

Choosing which shows to advertise on can be confusing because the preferences of black and white audiences overlap.[187] The top ten shows for black and all U.S. households are similar. However, the programs that African-American audiences prefer are more likely to have multicultural stars, players, or contestants, especially one that is African American.[188] The top five shows among African-American households in 2011 were *The Game Season 4, Real Housewives Atlanta, Let's Stay Together, American Idol*, and *House of Payne*.[189]

Primetime television is "racially divided" in terms of both casts and audiences, and the overall television audience continues to shrink. Networks, under enormous pressure to maximize dwindling profits, have been focusing on reality shows and sitcoms for the more numerous and generally more affluent white households. Because whites rarely watch shows, particularly sitcoms, with largely black casts, the networks broadcast relatively few with black or integrated casts in prime time.[190] As network audiences dwindle, cable offers more options to appeal directly to black viewers.

African Americans subscribe to premium cable at nearly twice the rate of white households. Twenty-two percent of HBO's subscriber base comes from African-American households, and 42 percent of African-American homes subscribe to HBO.[191] African Americans order pay-per-view programs at twice the rates of whites, with Latinos in between. Moreover, 70 percent of African-American households with cable subscribe to other premium services such as HBO compared to about 35 percent for all other households. Subscription to cable services for African-American and U.S. Latino households is higher than for white households at all levels of education or family income.

Cable provides another benefit for African-American and Latino households.[192] If African Americans want to see themselves and their experiences reflected in programming, then subscribing to cable makes sense. Black Entertainment Television (BET) and its affiliated networks reach over 85 million American households. Many of their award-winning shows highlight important issues in the black community.

Radio is another traditional venue for showcasing African American contributions to American pop culture. While white audiences have abandoned radio for online media, black listeners remain more loyal to urban and contemporary hip-hop stations. Black-oriented stations have changed formats in order to broaden their appeal and increase their advertising rates. What used to be called the "urban contemporary" format included a wide range of African American–oriented musical styles, from R&B to jazz, gospel, rap, and hip hop. It has now been replaced by formats that focus on only one or two of those types of music. Rap and hip hop are now part of mainstream popular culture and are the mainstays of the urban-contemporary format. But traditional radio has been hit hard by new technologies. In the black community just as in the rest of society, younger people are listening to downloads on their mobile devices. Disenfranchised older black listeners have fled to talk radio or "light" jazz on the radio, tuned in to Internet radio, or purchased music on compact disks or as downloaded files via iTunes and other online venues.

Print Media: The Community Voice and Expression of Style

Black-targeted magazines, such as *Black Enterprise, Jet, Essence,* and *Ebony,* are a trusted source of company and product information for African-American consumers.[193] A major reason for the trust in African-American magazines and other publications is the important role that a few magazines have had in the African-American community. *Ebony* magazine has been in business for over 60 years and has emphasized topics of special interest to members of the African-American community. The association of brands with these magazines goes beyond mere exposure numbers.[194] Placement of ads for these brands in them communicates to readers that a brand and its owners understand the importance of African-American community institutions.

The 1990s were a boom time for magazines in general and African American–targeted ones in particular. *Forbes* launched a black history magazine, *American Legacy,* and Time Warner developed a magazine called *Savoy.*[195] The publisher of *Prevention* magazine teamed up with an African-American entrepreneur to produce *Heart & Soul,* a black women's health magazine.[196] Black Entertainment Television joined the *New York Daily News* in launching a national weekend magazine called *B.E.T. Weekend* for distribution in city dailies and African-American newspapers.[197] The readership of the new magazines has cannibalized some of the older ones.

African-American magazines reach upscale blacks and tell their stories of achievement. Print ads in these media acknowledge the success stories of African Americans, with copy lines like "State Farm knows you've blazed your own trail" and P&G's "My black is beautiful" campaign. All these magazines have lost readers who now spend more time online. Nevertheless, their online content offers access to middle- and upper-class African-American consumers who are keenly aware of the commitment that such advertisers are making to the African-American community.

African-American newspapers cover local politics, commerce, and community activities. Most do not have large readerships but represent an opportunity for companies to position themselves in the African-American community and can be influential institutions in their own right. At various times African-American newspapers have joined together to pressure mainstream companies to buy advertisements in their publications.[198]

Another effective medium for reaching African Americans, especially in central cities, is the billboard. Large billboards and smaller posters deliver messages to an entire neighborhood and play off the sense of community that is high priority among African Americans.[199] Several studies seem to justify the criticism that there are more tobacco and alcohol billboards in African-American areas of town than in white neighborhoods.[200] The American Public Health Association has called on outdoor advertisers to refrain from targeting minority communities with alcohol and tobacco billboards.[201] In contrast to these perceptions, a content analysis of billboards in San Antonio and Detroit indicated that ethnic and white neighborhoods received similar amounts of tobacco and alcohol advertising.[202]

The controversy about alcohol and tobacco billboard advertising has caused a continuous decline in outdoor spending for these two product categories. Large billboards are being replaced by smaller poster boards. Compared to the large highway billboards, they have an advantage in that they can be placed low and close to the street, thus facilitating greater visibility to passersby of all ages.[203]

One type of marketing that works well with the general population but that has not been effective in marketing to African Americans is direct mail. There are over 15 million African-American households, but direct-mail marketers have few lists of names to target them. Of the $740 million that corporate marketers spent to woo African-American buyers in the early 1990s, less than 0.5 percent went to direct mail. Marketers complain that they have difficulty identifying purchasers as African American.[204] At the same time, African Americans feel more positively about ordering from catalogs, telemarketers, and direct mail than any other group of American consumers.[205]

Black direct-mail entrepreneurs depend heavily on census and zip code information. But because only 30 percent of black consumers live in zip codes that are at least 70 percent black, it can be a costly hit-or-miss exercise. In Chicago, for example, a newspaper coupon insert was mailed to "occupants" in 450,000 households in zip codes that are home to at least 20 percent black residents. "But in my neighborhood, which is 25 percent black, I don't get my own product," said the direct mail company.[206] Essence By Mail, a fashion catalog for black women, has built a list of over 500,000 names, and 80 percent of its customers live in zip codes where less than 70 percent of the residents are black. *Essence* used its subscriber lists to begin selling Afrocentric clothing, accessories, and home decorations by mail.[207]

The Digital Divide Has Disappeared!

Not only have African Americans caught up with other Americans in terms of online activities, but they are now trendsetters in new media. The digital forms of word of mouth include texting, posting videos, blogging, and tweeting, all of which have strong appeal to African Americans. Finding information about products in these places online is often followed up by in-person word of mouth. Over 40 percent of blacks recommend brands and services to others, almost 60 percent "like" companies on social networking websites, and 57 percent talked to others about something they learned from online searches.[208] Consider the following data:

> Once at the epicenter of the digital divide, African-Americans are now 44 percent more likely to take a class online, 30 percent more likely to visit Twitter, and download more movies via the Internet than other ethnic communities. African-American mothers, in particular, are 68 percent more likely to read articles online and 45 percent more likely to listen to music online.[209]

African Americans report they have "liked" a brand, looked up information about a brand, "followed" a brand, and have recommended a brand online.[210]

Personal computer ownership and online activity are the ultimate symbols of the information age. The factor that best explains home computer and online access is income, but with the advent of cheaper tablets and smartphones, that barrier to online participation has fallen.[211] In 2010, 67 percent of whites and 56 percent of African Americans were broadband users.[212]

Not all African Americans are as quick to use online information sources. BET's "African Americans Revealed" study identified four groups online that included 85 percent of all African Americans. They are the Survivors, Conscious Sisters, Techfluentials, and Bright Horizons. Only the last two segments focus on adopting new technologies, and they tend to be 20 to 30 years old, use "technology to positively impact others," and emphasize education, friends, gaming, and, naturally, social media in their leisure time.[213] These last groups are particularly active on social networking sites.[214]

The most frequent online activities for African Americans are researching products and making online purchases. Online videos (YouTube) and social media allow black consumers to engage in conversations on the way to deciding and making purchases. Other popular sites online are yellow pages, job boards, and sites for sharing photos. One major difference from white online shoppers is the positive attitude that black consumers have about advertising. While 60 percent of online users complain about the quantity of advertising, only 39 percent of African Americans complain. They also agree that advertising helps them decide what to buy. Online purchases are one way that African-American consumers have changed their shopping habits in order to save money on the well-known brands that they prefer.[215]

The main reason that African Americans say they do not go online is that they do not see it as relevant to their lives. One possibility is that, despite a range of sites like Africana.com, NetNoir, BlackVoices.com, Black World Today, the African-American Financial Index, BlackPlanet.com, and BET, general purpose search agents may not be an effective way to locate Web content relevant to African-American users.[216] However, the Internet is also attracting African-American entrepreneurs. Their new online content is bringing social networking to the African-American community and is quickly becoming a preferred source of product information.[217]

Nontraditional Media

African-American households report more use of videogame systems than U.S. Latinos, but they also have high rates of renting and buying used games. The TV set serves as the main game technology in the African American home, and extensive recording and streaming of TV programs may represent time shifting in households that stay up late. Videogame players, digital videorecorders (DVRs), mobile phones, and hardware for streaming movies and TV programs are also often purchased, especially if there are children in the African-American household. In households where videos are played often, 52 percent have children present; in households that own video cameras, 41 percent have children present. And even if only 35 percent of households have children under 18, these statistics indicate a lot of video-related activities in homes with children.

African Americans have become early adopters of the latest technology: smartphones. More than 50 percent of African Americans younger than 44 own smartphones.[218] African Americans outdistance other cell-phone users whether counting minutes or text messages. They also use the phone to access the Internet and e-mail, activities that provide opportunities for companies to reach them directly or via cross-platform programs of live TV and social networking sites.

Another nontraditional medium for reaching black consumers is movie theaters. Over 11 percent of heavy moviegoers are African American. They are also more engaged with all movie-related sources of information, paid and viral. Not only do they attend movies, but black consumers more frequently download and rent movies for viewing at home than other American audiences. Like other Americans, they report that their favorite genres of movies are comedies and action adventures, and, of course, movies with an African-American cast.[219]

Two effective ways to integrate communication programs with the needs of African-American community institutions are event sponsorships and philanthropic programs. General Mills uses advertising at various popular sites online, as well as its Feeding Dreams program in four major African-American cities, to enhance its presence among black consumers. Ford sponsors music festivals in partnership with *Essence*.[220] McDonald's offers college scholarships to underprivileged black students and then features the recipients in national television ads. Other companies that have educational programs in African-American communities are Toyota, Chrysler, Coors, Mattel, and Burger King.[221] Many highly respected and well-known black celebrities are involved with community events that are in turn underwritten by companies whose names share the spotlight with these role models.

Caveat Marketer!

Is racial targeting racist? Not if it is done using transcultural marketing techniques to build relationships with black consumers. Too many companies ignore cultural differences when they approve marketing programs and advertising messages for their products. They even ignore important ethnic media that can ensure reach and a culturally compatible editorial environment. When socially desirable products and marketing strategies are directed at disadvantaged consumers, their efforts are praised.[222] However, when targeting involves socially undesirable products or is aimed at consumers who are less knowledgeable, then the practice is viewed as unethical or immoral. Some critics argue that poor, elderly, or uneducated consumers are vulnerable to specific marketing practices;[223] other critics focus on their vulnerability to marketing of potential harmful products.[224]

Since its withdrawal from broadcast advertising in 1971, the tobacco industry has intensified its use of print media and has been one of the heaviest spenders in corporate sponsorships of sports, the arts, and ethnic cultural events. Tobacco companies have increased the use of athletic sponsorships, product placements in movies and cultural events, placements of brand names on clothing or other products, place-based media, contests, and cultural, civic, fashion, and entertainment events. This trend is of particular concern in terms of its impact on African Americans, because they have the lowest success rate in quitting smoking.[225]

As with tobacco, the alcohol industry faces mounting criticism from government agencies, concerned citizens, and the media about the type of advertising that is now targeted at minority groups. Alcohol companies have long pushed malt liquors among urban blacks and Hispanics. Malt liquors contain as much as 50 percent more alcohol than traditional beer. The advertising of malt liquors is unabashedly aimed at inner-city youth, using themes that allude to the potency of the brew and its association with power, sex, hedonism, and even "a drug-like high."[226]

Marketing of legal products such as cigarettes, alcohol, and fast foods have a negative and magnified impact on the health of minorities. Because of this, they will continue to be subject to criticism by African-American and other civic and medical leaders.[227] Philip Morris and Miller Brewing Company have become major contributors to African-American community groups. Whether their philanthropic and community development activities can quiet the criticisms of their products and marketing tactics is yet to be determined.

Summary

African Americans constitute a subculture of many contrasts: black African or Caribbean immigrants and mixed-race descendants of slavery; inner-city, nontraditional households stuck in poverty and successful, middle-class families in the suburbs; young, hip-hop, urban lifestyles and affluent professionals with mainstream tastes; persons with little participation in American mainstream institutions and those who aspire to belong and succeed in the mainstream. Generalizations about African-American beliefs, attitudes, and behaviors, even behavioral norms, mask these vast differences within the community. Nevertheless, African Americans appreciate marketers who solicit their patronage and support African-American media and retailers as well as social and community institutions. The rapid growth of income among African Americans during recent decades presents growing opportunities for companies that are able to understand the paradoxes of the African-American consumer identity.

Notes

The author acknowledges Dr. Jerome Williams, who co-authored an earlier version of this chapter.

1. J.M. Fish, "Mixed Blood," *Psychology Today* (November/December 1995): 55–61, 76, 80.

2. S. Begley, "Three Is Not Enough," *Newsweek*, February 13, 1995, 67–68.

3. T. Morgenthau, "What Color Is Black?" *Newsweek*, February 13, 1995, 62–65.

4. S. Begley, "Scientifically, Race Is Only Skin Deep and Not Very Useful," *Wall Street Journal*, August 1, 2003, B1; J. Tilove, "Jefferson's New Legacy Makes Blood the Real U.S. Melting Pot," *Newark Star-Ledger*, November 8, 1998, 53.

5. E. Cose, "Our New Look: The Colors of Race," *Newsweek*, January 1, 2000, 28–30.

6. F.J. David, *Who Is Black? One Nation's Definition* (University Park: Pennsylvania State University Press, 1991).

7. H. Landrine and E.A. Klonoff *African American Acculturation: Deconstructing*

Race and Reviving Culture (Thousand Oaks, CA Sage, 1996); R.D. Alba, *Ethnic Identity: The Transformation of White America* (New Haven: Yale University Press, 1990).

8. R. James, "Shades of Black-Skin Color Discrimination," YouTube video, December 10, 2010, www.youtube.com/watch?v=E3IzTyjhHLc/; J.L. Hochschild and V. Weaver, "The Skin Color Paradox and the American Racial Order," *Social Forces* 86, no. 2 (2007): 643–670; F.V. Harrison, "Introduction: Expanding the Discourse on 'Race,'" *American Anthropologist* 100, no. 3 (1999): 609–631; J. Wagner and H. Soberon-Ferrer, "The Effect of Ethnicity on Selected Household Expenditures," *Social Science Journal* 27, no. 2 (1990): 181–198.

9. S. Watson, C.G. Thorton, and B.V. Engelland, "Skin Color Shades in Advertising to Ethnic Audiences: The Case of African Americans," *Journal of Marketing Communications* 16, no. 4 (2010): 185–201; M. Keith and C. Herring, "Skin Tone and Stratification in the Black Community," *American Journal of Sociology* 97, no. 3 (1991): 760–778; Hochschild and Weaver, "The Skin Color Paradox and the American Racial Order."

10. N. Carr-Ruffino, *Managing Diversity: People Skills for a Multicultural Workplace* (Cincinnati, OH: South-Western, 1996).

11. CNN Wire Staff, "Number of Interracial Marriages in U.S. Reaches All-Time High," CNN, April 25, 2012, www.cnn.com/2012/04/25/us/us-census-interracial/.

12. Cose, "Our New Look"; C. Leslie, "The Loving Generation," *Newsweek*, February 13, 1995, 72.

13. T. Sasao and S. Sue, "Toward a Culturally Anchored Ecological Framework of Research in Ethnic-Cultural Communities," *American Journal of Community Psychology* 21, no. 6 (1993): 705–726; W.K. Darley and J.D. Williams, "Methodological Issues in Ethnic Minority Research: Changing Consumer Demographics and Implications," in *Marketing and Multicultural Diversity*, ed. C.P. Rao (New York: Quorum Books, 2000): 93–118.

14. S. Shepard, "The Race Issue: More Than a 'Black and White Thing'?" *Austin American-Statesman*, August 3, 1997, J1, J6.

15. G.A. Sumner, *Folkways* (Boston: Ginn, 1907).

16. T.A. Shimp and S. Sharma, "Consumer Ethnocentrism: Construction and Validation of the CETSCALE," *Journal of Marketing Research* 24, no. 3 (1987): 280–289.

17. J.V. Petrof, "The Effect of Student Boycotts upon the Purchasing Habits of Negro Families in Atlanta, Georgia," *Phylon* (Fall 1963): 266–270; J.V. Petrof, "Consumer Strategy for Negro Retailers," *Journal of Retailing* 43 (Fall 1967): 30–38; J.D. Williams and W.J. Qualls, "Middle-Class Black Consumers and Intensity of Ethnic Identification," *Psychology & Marketing* 6, no. 4 (1989): 263–286; D.H. Gensch and R. Staelin, "The Appeal of Buying Black," *Journal of Marketing Research* 9, no.2 (1972): 141–148; G.E. Hills, D.H. Granbois, and J.M. Patterson, "Black Consumer Perceptions of Food Store Attributes," *Journal of Marketing* 37, no. 2 (1973): 47–57; T.W. Whipple and L.A. Neidell, "Black and White Perceptions of Competing Stores," *Journal of Retailing* 47, no. 4 (1971): 5–20.

18. R.M. Entman, "African Americans According to TV News," *Media Studies Journal* (Summer 1994): 8, 29–38.

19. J.L. Dates and E.C. Pease, "Warping the World—Media's Mangled Images of Race," *Media Studies Journal* 8 (Summer 1994): 89–95.

20. E.F. Davidson, "Shopping While Black: Perceptions of Discrimination in Retail Settings" (Ph.D. dissertation, University of Tennessee, Knoxville, 2007),

http://trace.tennessee.edu/utk_graddiss/147/; G. Schreer, S. Smith, and K. Thomas, "Shopping While Black: Examining Racial Discrimination in a Retail Setting," *Journal of Applied Social Psychology* 39, no. 6 (2009): 1432–1444, www.utexas. edu/features/2006/profiling/index.html; M. Dubin, "An Uneasy Coexistence for Blacks and Asians in City," *Philadelphia Inquirer,* August 12, 1990, 1C; M. Dubin and R. Clark, "Shop Owner in Slaying Is Released," *Philadelphia Inquirer,* August 8, 1990, 1B; L. Peñaloza and M.C. Gilly, "Marketer Acculturation: The Changer and the Changed," *Journal of Marketing* 63, no. 3 (1999): 84–104; M. Okazawa-Rey and M. Wong, "Organizing in Communities of Color: Addressing Interethnic Conflicts," *Social Justice* 24, no. 1 (1997): 24.

21. J.D. Williams and T. Snuggs, "Survey of Attitudes Toward Customer Service in Retail Stores: The Role of Race," paper presented at Multicultural Marketing Conference, Virginia Beach, VA, 1996.

22. J. Yinger, "Measuring Racial Discrimination with Fair Housing Audits: Caught in the Act," *American Economic Review* 76, no. 5 (1986): 881–893; J. Williams, W. Qualls, and S. Grier, "Racially Exclusive Real Estate Advertising: Public Policy Implication for Fair Housing Practices," *Journal of Public Policy and Marketing* 14, no. 2 (1995): 225–244.

23. E. Donnerstein, M. Donnerstein, and C. Koch, "Racial Discrimination in Apartment Rentals: A Replication," *Journal of Social Psychology* 96, no. 1 (1975): 37–38; D.A. Johnson, R.J. Porter, and P.L. Mateljan, "Racial Discrimination in Apartment Rentals," *Journal of Applied Social Psychology* 1, no. 4 (1971): 364–377; V.M. Reed, "Civil Rights Legislation and the Housing Status of Black Americans: Evidence from Fair Housing Audits and Segregation Indices," *Review of Black Political Economy* 19, nos. 3–4 (1991): 29–42; W. Berger, "Play Fair in Housing," *Real Estate Today* (April 1992): 15–19.

24. S.L. Myers and T. Chan, "Racial Discrimination in Housing Markets, Accounting for Credit Risk," *Social Science Quarterly* 76, no. 3 (1995): 543–561.

25. I. Ayres and P. Siegelman, "Race and Gender Discrimination in Bargaining for a New car," *American Economic Review* 85, no. 3 (1995): 304–321.

26. C. Hawkins, "Denny's: The Stain That Isn't Coming Out," *BusinessWeek,* June 28, 1993, 98–99; U.S. Attorney General, "7 Asian American and White Syracuse University Students Attacked at Denny's Restaurant After They Were Denied Service," news release, May 14, 1997.

27. "PA Files Complaint Against Avis," *Philadelphia Inquirer,* October 20, 1997; C. Tejada, "HFS Orders Its Avis Unit to End Pact with Franchisee Accused of Racial Bias," *Wall Street Journal,* November 27, 1996.

28. "Cab Company Wary of Blacks Faces Sanction," *New York Times,* February 2, 1995, A16.

29. "San Francisco Tells Pizza Shops to Hold the Excuses," *New York Times,* July 14, 1996, A22.

30. M. Marable, "Reconciling Race and Reality," *Media Studies Journal* 8 (Summer 1994): 11–18.

31. J. Williams, "The Color of Money," 2006, www.utexas.edu. www.utexas.edu/features/2006/profiling/index.html.

32. J.R. Palomo, "Seeds of African Culture Sown in Life, Literature, Language," *Austin American Statesman,* February 18, 1996, A1.

33. F.E. Jandt, *Intercultural Communication: An Introduction* (Thousand Oaks, CA: Sage, 1995).

34. U.S. Census Bureau "Population Projections of the United States by Age, Sex, Race, and Hispanic Origin: 1995 to 2050," U.S. Department of Commerce, Economics and Statistics Administration, Washington, DC, 1996.

35. C. Fisher, "Black, Hip, and Primed to Shop," *American Demographics* (September 1996): 52–59.

36. U.S. Census Bureau, *Money Income in the United States: 1997* (Washington, DC: U.S. Department of Commerce, 1998); idem, *Poverty in the United States: 1997* (Washington, DC: U.S. Department of Commerce, 1998).

37. BlackDemographics.com, "African American Income," 2012, www. blackdemographics.com/income.html.

38. Pew Research Center, *A Year After Obama's Election: Blacks Upbeat About Black Progress, Prospects* (Washington, DC, January 12, 2010).

39. Nielsen, *The State of the African-American Consumer* (New York: Nielsen Company, September 22, 2011): 3, www.nielsen.com/us/en/reports/2011/state-of-the-african-american-consumer.html.

40. H.P. McAdoo, "Upward Mobility and Parenting in Middle-Income Black Families," in *African American Psychology: Theory, Research, and Practice*, ed. A.K.H. Burlew et al. (Newbury Park, CA: Sage 1992): 63–86.

41. U.S. Census Bureau, "Households and Families," in *2010 Census Brief* (Washington, DC: U.S. Department of Commerce, Economics and Statistics Administration, April 2012).

42. D. Gates, "Apartheid, American Style," *Newsweek*, March 23, 1992, 61.

43. A. Pinkney, *Black Americans* (Englewood Cliffs, NJ: Prentice-Hall, 1969).

44. P.A. Robinson and C.P. Rao, "A Critical Review and Reassessment of Black Consumer Behavioral Research," In *Proceedings: Southwestern Marketing Association Conference* (Dallas: Southwestern Marketing Association, 1986), 9–13; I.D. Reid, J. Stagmaier, and C.C. Reid, "Research Design used to Describe and Explain Black Consumer Behavior," in *Cultural and Subcultural Influences*, ed. R.E. Pitts (Chicago: AMA, 1986); J.D. Williams, "African and European Roots of Multi-Culturalism in the Consumer Behavior of American Blacks," in *Historical Perspectives in Consumer Research: National and International Perspectives,* ed. D.T. Tan and J.N. Sheth (Singapore: ACR, 1989): 51–55.

45. "The Changing Color of Cities: Black Flight," *Economist,* March 31, 2011, www.economist.com/node/18486343/.

46. J.E. Ellis, "The Black Middle Class," *BusinessWeek*, March 14, 1988, 62–70; J. Simons, "Even Amid Boom Times, Some Insecurities Die Hard," *Wall Street Journal,* December 10, 1998, A10.

47. E.R. Frazier, *The Black Bourgeoisie* (Glencoe, IL: Free Press, 1957): 13; W.A. Sampson and V. Milam, "The Interracial Attitudes of the Black Middle Class: Have They Changed?" *Social Problems* 23, no. 2 (1975): 153–165; T.E. Ness and M.T. Stith, "Middle-Class Values in Blacks and Whites," in *Personal Values and Consumer Psychology,* ed. R.E. Pitts Jr. and A.G. Woodside (Lexington, MA: Lexington Books, 1984): 231–237; R.E. Goldsmith, J.D. White, and M.T. Stith, "Values of Middle-Class Blacks and Whites: A Replication and Extension," *Psychology & Marketing* 4, no. 2 (1987): 135–144.

48. J. Dollard, *Caste and Class in a Southern Town* (New Haven: Yale University Press, 1937); G. Myrdal, *An American Dilemma: The Negro Problem and Modern Democracy* (New York: Harper & Row, 1944); St.C. Drake and H.R. Cayton, *Black Metropolis,* rev. ed. (New York: Harper & Row, 1962); Frazier, *The Black Bourgeoisie;*

N. Hare, *The Black Anglo-Saxons* (New York: Collier Books, 1970); W.H. Greer and P.M. Cobb, *Black Rage* (New York: Basic Books, 1968).

49. C.G. Woodson, *The Mis-education of the Negro* (Washington, DC: Associated Publishers, 1933); H. Cruse, *The Crisis of the Negro Intellectual* (New York: Morrow, 1967).

50. W.E.B. Du Bois, *Souls of Black Folk* (Chicago: A.C. McLurg, 1903).

51. Williams and Qualls, "Middle-Class Black Consumers and Intensity of Ethnic Identification."

52. Economic Policy Institute, "Poverty Dramatically Higher for Single Mothers: Poverty Rates of Households with Children, Married Couples and Female-Headed Households (Chart)," 2011; http://stateofworkingamerica.org/files/pre-files/poverty_married_and_female_headed_all_years.pdf; A. Thernstrom and S. Thernstrom, *America in Black and White: One Nation, Indivisible* (New York: Simon & Schuster, 1997); Carr-Ruffino, *Managing Diversity.*

53. S. Kerby, "The Top 10 Most Startling Facts About People of Color and Criminal Justice in the United States," Center for American Progress, March 13, 2012, www.americanprogress.org/issues/race/news/2012/03/13/11351/the-top-10-most-startling-facts-about-people-of-color-and-criminal-justice-in-the-united-states/.

54. Henry J. Kaiser Family Foundation, "Race, Ethnicity & Health Care," fact sheet (Washington, DC, July 2006), http://kaiserfamilyfoundation.files.wordpress.com/2013/01/7541.pdf.

55. G. Lubin and C. Jenkins, "The 22 Most Segregated Cities in America," *Business Insider*, April 1, 2011, www.businessinsider.com/most-segregated-cities-in-america-2011-3/.

56. Mintel International Group, "Share of Wallet: Blacks—U.S.," MarketResearch.com, February 1, 2010, www.marketresearch.com/Mintel-International-Group-Ltd-v614/Share-Wallet-Blacks-2610747/.

57. M. Mogelunsky, "Meet the Inner City Shopper," *American Demographics* (December 1998): 38–40.

58. Ibid.

59. A.R. Ramos, "Moving Inner Cities out of the Red, into the Black," *Pacific Standard*, February 12, 2009, www.psmag.com/business-economics/moving-inner-cities-out-of-the-red-into-the-black-3946/; L. Vincenti, "For Merchants, Inner Cities Offer Golden Opportunity," *HFN*, July 6, 1998: 72, 81.

60. C. Tabernese and R. Gebeloff, "Many U.S. Blacks Moving to South, Reversing Trend," *New York Times*, March 24, 2011, www.nytimes.com/2011/03/25/us/25south.html?pagewanted=all/; B. Edmondson, "Black America in 2001," *American Demographics* (November 1996): 14–15.

61. U.S. Census Bureau, *The Black Population: 2010* (Washington, DC: U.S. Department of Commerce, Economics and Statistics Administration, September 2011), tables 5, 8.

62. C. Augustine, "Has Webster's Redefined Urban? Where Are the Black Faces at Urban Outfitters?" *AdWeek*, February 10, 2012, www.adweek.com/sa-article/has-webster-s-redefined-urban-138154/.

63. S. Kraus, "Affluency Survey: Diversity Among Affluent Americans," *AdAge*, April 4, 2012, http://adage.com/article/adagestat/affluency-survey-diversity-affluent-americans/233901/.

64. Mintel International Group, "Share of Wallet: Blacks—U.S."

65. Fisher, "Black, Hip, and Primed to Shop."

66. E. Cose, "The Black Gen X Nobody Knows," *Newsweek*, March 17, 1997, 62.

67. A.K.H. Burlew et al., eds., *African American Psychology: Theory, Research, and Practice* (Newbury Park, CA: Sage, 1992); J. Leland and S. Samuels, "The New Generation Gap," *Newsweek*, March 17, 1997, 51–60.

68. Fisher, "Black, Hip, and Primed to Shop."

69. C.J. Farley, "Hip-Hop Nation," *Time*, February 8, 1999, 54–64.

70. K. Alexander, "Hip-Hop Magazine Gets Fiery Start, Good and Bad," *USA Today*, December 30, 1998, B1.

71. L.E. Wynter, "'Urban' Sportswear Goes Mainstream," *Wall Street Journal*, October 7, 1998, B1; S. Lucas, "For Us, Forever," *Advertising Age*, October 11, 1999, M94–M98.

72. Leland and Samuels, "The New Generation Gap."

73. Jandt, *Intercultural Communication*, 329–345.

74. Palomo, "Seeds of African Culture Sown in Life, Literature, Language."

75. W.A. Boykin, "The Academic Performance of Afro-American Children," in *Achievement and Achievement Motives: Psychological and Sociological Approaches*, ed. J.T. Spence (San Francisco: W.H. Freeman 1983): 321–371; W.W. Nobles, "Extended Self: Rethinking the So-Called Negro Self-Concept," in *Black Psychology* (2d ed.): ed. R.L. Jones (New York: Harper & Row, 1980), 290–315.

76. A. Swaidan, M.Y.A. Rawwas, and S.J. Vitell, "Culture and Moral Ideologies of African Americans," *Journal of Marketing Theory and Practice* 16, no. 2 (2008): 127–137.

77. G. Early, "Understanding Afrocentrism," *Civilization* (July/August 1995): 31–39.

78. M.L. Hecht, M.J. Collier, and S.A. Ribeau, *African American Communication: Ethnic Identity and Cultural Interpretation* (Newbury Park, CA: Sage, 1993).

79. Carr-Ruffino, *Managing Diversity*, 9.

80. G. Devos, "Ethnic Pluralism: Conflict and Accommodation," in *Ethnic Identity: Cultural Continuities and Change*, ed. G. De Vos and L. Romanucci-Ross (Palo Alto, CA: Mayfield, 1975), 69–81.

81. T.E. Whittler, R.J. Calantone, and M.R. Young, "Strength of Ethnic Affiliation: Examining Black Identification with Black Culture," *Journal of Social Psychology* 131, no. 4 (1991): 461–467.

82. C.L. Green, "Ethnic Evaluations of Advertising: Interaction Effects of Strength of Ethnic Identification, Media Placement, and Degree of Racial Composition," *Journal of Advertising* 28, no. 1 (1999): 49–64.

83. J.E. Hofman, "Arabs and Jews, Blacks and Whites: Identity and Group Relations," *Journal of Multilingual and Multicultural Development* 6, nos. 3–4 (1985): 217–237.

84. L.K. Larkey and M.L. Hecht, "A Comparative Study of African American and Euroamerican Ethnic Identity," paper presented at International Conference for Language and Social Psychology, Santa Barbara, CA, 1991; Hofman, "Arabs and Jews, Blacks and Whites."

85. C.L. White and P.J. Burke, "Ethnic Role Identity Among Black and White College Students: An Interactionist Approach," *Sociological Perspectives* 30, no. 3 (1987): 310–331.

86. M. Hughes and D.H. Demo, "Self-Perception of Black Americans: Self-Esteem and Personal Efficacy," *American Journal of Sociology* 95, no. 1 (1989): 132–159.

87. Hofman, "Arabs and Jews, Blacks and Whites"; Larkey and Hecht, "A Comparative Study of African American and Euroamerican Ethnic Identity"; L.E. Smith and J. Millham, "Sex Role Stereotypes Among Blacks and Whites," *Journal of Black Psychology* 6, no. 1 (1979): 1–6.

88. White and Burke, "Ethnic Role Identity Among Black and White College Students"; Larkey and Hecht, "A Comparative Study of African American and Euroamerican Ethnic Identity."

89. M.L. Hecht and S. Ribeau, "Sociocultural Roots of Ethnic Identity: A Look at Black America," *Journal of Black Studies* 21, no. 4 (1991): 501–513; J.S. Jackson and G. Gurin, *National Survey of Black Americans, 1978–1980* (Ann Arbor, MI: Inter-University Consortium for Political and Social Research, Institute for Social Research, 1987); G.D. Jaynes and R.M. Williams Jr., eds., *A Common Destiny: Blacks and American Society* (Washington, DC: National Academy Press, 1989); P.E. Lampe, "Ethnic Labels: Naming or Name-Calling?" *Ethnic and Racial Studies* 5, no. 4 (1982): 542–548; G. Smitherman, "Black Language as Power," in *Language and Power*, ed. C. Kramarae, M. Schulz, and W.M. O'Barr (Beverly Hills, CA: Sage, 1984), 101–115.

90. H. Fairchild, "Black, Negro or Afro-American? The Differences Are Crucial," *Journal of Black Studies* 16, no. 1 (1985): 47–55.

91. S. Carmichael and C.V. Hamilton, *Black Power: The Politics of Liberation in America* (New York: Random House, 1967).

92. V. Gettone, "Negative Label," *Association of Black Psychologists' Newsletter* 12, no. 2 (1981): 3–11; E.E. Dennis, "Racial Naming," *Media Studies Journal* 8, no. 3 (1994): 105–111.

93. F. Newport, "Black or African American?" Gallup News Service, September 28, 2007, www.gallup.com/poll/28816/black-african-american.aspx; Carr-Ruffino, *Managing Diversity.*

94. Carr-Ruffino, *Managing Diversity.*

95. Newport, "Black or African American?"; Hecht and Ribeau, "Sociocultural Roots of Ethnic Identity"; M.L. Hecht and S. Ribeau, "Afro-American Identity Labels and Communicative Effectiveness," *Journal of Language and Social Psychology* 6 (1987): 319–326; M.L. Hecht, S. Ribeau, and J.K. Alberts, "An Afro-American Perspective on Interethnic Communication," *Communication Monographs* 56, no. 4 (1989): 385–410; K.S. Jewell, "Will the Real Black, Afro-American, Mixed, Colored, Negro, Please Stand Up? Impact of the Black Social Movement, Twenty Years Later," *Journal of Black Studies* 16, no. 1 (1985): 57–75; Lampe, "Ethnic Labels: Naming or Name-Calling?"

96. R. Harre, "Language Games and Texts of Identity," in *Texts of Identity,* ed. J. Shotter and K.J. Gergen (Newbury Park, CA: Sage, 1989), 20–35; H. Tajfel, *Human Categories and Social Groups* (Cambridge: Cambridge University Press, 1981); H. Tajfel, ed., *Social Identity and Intergroup Relations* (Cambridge: Cambridge University Press, 2010); J.C. Turner, *Rediscovering the Social Group* (London: Basil Blackwell, 1987); H. Giles, R.Y. Bourhis, and D. Taylor, "Towards a Theory of Language in Ethnic Group Relations," in *Language, Ethnicity and Intergroup Relations,* ed. H. Giles (London: Academic Press, 1977), 307–348.

97. H. Giles and N. Coupland, *Language: Contexts and Consequences* (Pacific Grove, CA: Brooks/Cole, 1991).

98. Smitherman, "Black Language as Power."

99. Carr-Ruffino, *Managing Diversity*; Hecht, Collier, and Ribeau, *African American Communication.*

100. Smitherman, "Black Language as Power."

101. J.D. Williams and K.D. Grantham, "Racial and Ethnic Identity in the Marketplace: An Examination of Nonverbal and Peripheral Cues," in *Advances in Consumer Research,* vol. 26, ed. Eric J. Arnould and Linda M. Scott (Provo, UT: ACR, 1999), 451–454.

102. Whittler, Calantone, and Young, "Strength of Ethnic Affiliation"; A.H. Jenkins, *The Psychology of the Afro-American* (New York: Pergamon Press, 1982); C.W. Thomas and S.W. Thomas, "Something Borrowed, Something Black," in C.W. Thomas, *Boys No More: A Black Psychologist's View of Community* (Beverly Hills, CA: Glencoe, 1971), 98–120; W.E. Cross, "The Negro-to-Black Conversion Experience: Toward a Psychology of Black Liberation," *Black World* 20, no. 9 (1971): 13–27; J. Milliones, "Construction of a Black Consciousness Measure: Psycho-Therapeutic Implications," *Psychotherapy: Theory, Research, & Practice* 17, no. 2 (1980): 175–182.

103. Hecht, Collier, and Ribeau, *African American Communication,* 82–113.

104. DuBois quoted in *A Common Destiny,* ed. Janes and Williams; Carr-Ruffino, *Managing Diversity.*

105. R.A. Bauer and S.M. Cunningham, "The Negro Market," *Journal of Advertising Research* 10, no. 2 (1970): 3–13; R.A. Bauer, S.M. Cunningham, and L.H. Wortzel, "The Marketing Dilemma of Negroes," *Journal of Marketing* 29 (July 1965): 1–6.

106. H.A. Bullock, "Consumer Motivations in Black and White: I and II," *Harvard Business Review* 39 (May/June 1961): 89–104; P.D. Bennett and H.H. Kassarjian, *Consumer Behavior* (Englewood Cliffs, NJ: Prentice-Hall, 1972).

107. Ness and Stith, "Middle-Class Values in Blacks and Whites"; Frazier, *The Black Bourgeoisie*; M. Ramirez, "Assessing and Understanding Biculturalism-Multiculturalism in Mexican-American Adults," in *Chicano Psychology,* 2d ed., ed. J.L. Martinez Jr. and R.H. Mendoza (Orlando, FL: Academic Press, 1984), 77–94; Bauer and Cunningham, "The Negro Market"; L.P. Feldman and A.D. Star, "Racial Factors in Shopping Behavior," in *A New Measure of Responsibility for Marketing,* ed. K. Cox and B. Enix (Chicago: AMA, 1968), 216–225; B.G. Yovovich, "Marketing to Blacks: The Debate Rages on," *Advertising Age,* November 19, 1982, M9; T. Kochman, *Black and White Styles in Conflict* (Chicago: University of Chicago Press, 1981).

108. D.P. Gibson, *$70 Billion in the Black: America's Black Consumers* (New York: Macmillan, 1978).

109. J.D. Williams, "African and European Roots of Multiculturalism in the Consumer Behavior of American Blacks," in *Historical Perspectives in Consumer Research: National and International Perspectives,* ed. C.T. Tan and J.N. Sheth (Singapore: ACR, 1985), 51–55.

110. M. Ramirez III and A. Castaneda, *Cultural Democracy, Bicognitive Development and Education* (New York: Academic Press, 1974).

111. J. Wagner and H. Soberon-Ferrer, "The Effect of Ethnicity on Selected Household Expenditures," *Social Science Journal* 27, no. 2 (1990): 181–198.

112. H. Landrine and E.A. Klonoff, *African American Acculturation*; H. Valencia, "Developing an Index to Measure 'Hispanicness,'" in *Advances in Consumer Research,* vol. 12, ed. E.C. Hirschman and M.B. Holbrook (Provo, UT: ACR, 1985), 118–121; S. Ellis et al., "Cultural Values and Behavior: Chineseness Within Geographic Boundaries," in ibid., 126–128.

113. Carbon Copywriter, "Off-Target: Ghettoizing Black Advertising," *Brandweek* 40 (December 6, 1999): 28–31; L. Pitts, "Motown Still Has a Lesson for African-Americans," *Fort Worth Star-Telegram,* February 13, 1998, 9.

114. K. Chappell, "How the New Generation Changed Black and White America," *Ebony* (November 1995): 190–194.

115. "Hip-Hop Culture," *American Library Newsletter* (October–December 2007).

116. B. Kanner, "On Madison Avenue: An Extremely Hard Sell, Black Ads Go Mainstream," *New York Magazine,* April 11, 1994, 12–13.

117. W.M. O'Barr, *Culture and the Ad: Exploring Otherness in the World of Advertising* (Boulder, CO: Westview Press, 1994): 107–156.

118. "Pepsi Marketers Faced Rebuffs in the Field and in Home Office," *Wall Street Journal,* September 5, 1997, B1.

119. J. Dates, "Advertising," in *Split Image: African Americans in the Mass Media,* ed. J.L. Dates and W. Barlow (Washington, DC: Howard University Press, 1990), 1–25.

120. Ibid.

121. M. Kern-Foxworth, "Plantation Kitchen to American Icon: Aunt Jemima," *Public Relations Review* 16, no. 3 (1990): 55–68; Y. Ono, "Aunt Jemima Brand Hires Gladys Knight," *Wall Street Journal,* September 16, 1994, B3.

122. Ono, "Aunt Jemima Brand Hires Gladys Knight."

123. M. Kern-Foxworth, *Aunt Jemima, Uncle Ben, and Rastus: Blacks in Advertising, Yesterday, Today, and Tomorrow* (Westport, CT: Greenwood, 1994).

124. R. Seltzer and N.E. Johnson, *Experiencing Racism: Exploring Discrimination Through the Eyes of College Students* (New York: Lexington Books, 2009).

125. Kern-Foxworth, *Aunt Jemima, Uncle Ben, and Rastus.*

126. M. Mabry, "A Long Way from 'Aunt Jemima,'" *Newsweek*, August 14, 1989, 34–35; Ono, "Aunt Jemima Brand Hires Gladys Knight."

127. V.T. Berry, "Introduction: Racialism and the Media," in *Mediated Messages and African-American Culture,* ed. V.T. Berry and C.L. Manning-Miller (Thousand Oaks, CA: Sage, 1996), 114–156.

128. "Drug Store Chain Says Ads Not Anti-Black," Reuters, February 24, 1997.

129. "Toyota Ad: Unlike Your Last Boyfriend, It Goes to Work in the Morning," *Jet*, January 25, 1999, 68.

130. Kanner, "On Madison Avenue: An Extremely Hard Sell, Black Ads Go Mainstream."

131. L. McShane, "Fashion Designer Rebuts Racism Allegations on Net," *Philadelphia Inquirer*, March 27, 1998, D1; L.E. Wynter, "Stores Have Different Ideas on African Style," *Wall Street Journal*, October 26, 1993, B1.

132. N. Harris, "Eric Miller Is No Soda Jerk," *BusinessWeek*, August 10, 1997, 28.

133. J.M. Humphreys, "Black Buying Power Continues to Rise," Reaching Black Consumers.com, 2012, www.reachingblackconsumers.com/2012/04/black-buying-power-continues-to-rise/.

134. "New 'Buying Power' Report Shows Black Consumers Spend as Economy Improves," *Target Market News*, August 24, 2012, www.targetmarketnews.com/storyid11011001.htm.

135. U.S. Bureau of Labor Statistics, *Consumer Expenditures in 2010: Lingering Effects of the Great Recession*, Report 1027 (Washington, DC: U.S. Department of Labor, August 2012), www.bls.gov/cex/csxann10.pdf.

136. Nielsen, *The State of the African-American Consumer.*

137. Fisher, "Black, Hip, and Primed to Shop."

138. Nielsen, *The State of the African-American Consumer.*

139. L.E. Wynter, "Blacks and Hispanics Gain Spending Clout," *Wall Street Journal,* September 3, 1997, B1; M. Mogelonsky, "Aficionados de cerveza," *American Demographics* (September 1996): 8.

140. Williams, "African and European Roots of Multiculturalism in the Consumer Behavior of American Blacks."

141. L. Alwitt, W.J. Qualls, and J.D. Williams, "The Susceptibility of Vulnerable Populations to Persuasive Marketing Communications," paper presented at Annual Marketing and Public Policy Conference, Washington, DC, May 1996.

142. T.S. Robertson, J. Zielinski, and S. Ward, *Consumer Behavior* (Glenview, IL: Scott, Foresman, 1984).

143. Nielsen, *The State of the African-American Consumer.*

144. C. Walker and E. Moses, "The Age of Self-Navigation," *American Demographics* (September 1996): 36–42.

145. L.L. Brownlee, "Motorola Gets Signal on Blacks' Pager Use," *Wall Street Journal,* June 24, 1996, B6.

146. I. Mitskaviets, *Online African Americans: A Demographic Profile* (Cambridge, MA: Forrester Research, February 1, 2010), 8.

147. Fisher, "Black, Hip, and Primed to Shop."

148. "Kwanzaa," in Wikipedia, http://en.wikipedia.org/wiki/Kwanzaa/.

149. K.L. Woodward and P. Johnson, "The Advent of Kwanzaa," *Newsweek,* December 11, 1995, 88; J.C. Simpson, "Tidings of Black Pride and Joy," *Time,* December 23, 1991, 81.

150. Fisher, "Black, Hip, and Primed to Shop."

151. Ibid.

152. C. Miller, "Cadillac Promo Targets African-Americans," *Marketing News,* May 23, 1994, 12; J. O'Donnell, "Cadillac Targeting New Groups: Division Making Pitches to Female and Black Buyers," *Plain Dealer,* April 17, 1994, 1F.

153. S. Davis, "Fashions That Fit," *Hartford Courant,* May 3, 1994, D1; F.H. Lowe, "Cosmetics Firms Court Blacks: Hot Sales Bring Competition for Fashion Fair," *Chicago Sun-Times,* April 13, 1994, 65; Wynter, "J.C. Penney Launches Diahann Carroll Line"; L.E. Wynter, "Cosmetics Firms Find Women Blur Color Lines," *Wall Street Journal,* July 3, 1996, B1; Wynter, "Stores Have Different Ideas on African Style."

154. Davis, "Fashions That Fit"; C. Edwards, "Targeting Minority Customers Makes Sense," *Valley Morning Star,* December 22, 1996, E2; L.E. Wynter, "An Untapped Market of 11 Million Homes," *Wall Street Journal,* September 7, 1994, B1.

155. "Reflections in Black: The African-American Greeting Card Market," *Greetings Magazine* 8, no. 5 (1994): 17.

156. L.B. Ward, "Today's Topic: Small Business Working for Glory, Ohio Firm Pioneering Market for African-American Foods," *Cincinnati Enquirer,* July 12, 1994, D01.

157. J.D. Williams et al., "Ebonics and Advertising to the black Consumer: A Need for Research to Analyze Language and Communication Styles in a Linguistic Perspective," in *Developments in Marketing Science, XII. Proceedings of the Thirteenth Annual Conference of the Academy of Marketing Science,* ed. J.M. Hawes and J. Thanopoulos (Orlando, FL: Academy of Marketing Science, 1989), 637–642.

158. "Weekly Almanac: Home Boys," *Jet,* April 2, 1990, 19.

159. V.J. Bush, "Homeboys Inc. Chips in to Help Inner-City Teenagers," *Wall Street Journal,* May 21, 1993, B2.

160. B. Helm, "Ethnic Marketing: McDonald's Is Lovin' It," *Bloomberg Businessweek*, July 10, 2010, 24–26.

161. A.B. Henderson, "Chrysler Backs 'Hoop Dreams' to Court Blacks," *Wall Street Journal*, November 15, 1995, B1.

162. C.L. Green, "Ethnic Evaluations of Advertising: Interaction Effects of Strength of Ethnic Identification, Media Placement, and Degree of Racial Composition," *Journal of Advertising* 28, no. 1 (1999): 49–62; B.S. Tolley and J.J. Goett, "Reactions to Blacks in Newspapers," *Journal of Advertising Research* 11, no. 2 (1971): 11–21; M.J. Schlinger and J. Plummer, "Advertising in Black And White," *Journal of Marketing Research* 9 (May 1972): 149–153; G.J. Szybillo and J. Jacoby, "Effects of Different Levels Of Integration on Advertising Preference and Intention to Purchase," *Journal of Applied Psychology* 59, no. 3 (1974): 274–280; R. Kerin, "Black Model Appearance and Product Evaluation," *Journal of Communication* 29 (Winter 1979): 123–128; Williams, Qualls, and Grier, "Racially Exclusive Real Estate Advertising."

163. Carbon Copywriter, "Off-Target: Ghettoizing Black Advertising."

164. P.A. Harper, "Financial Commitments Emerge That Target Minorities," Associated Press Newswires, January 18, 1999.

165. L.E. Wynter, "Wrigley Ads to Focus on Minority Health," *Wall Street Journal*, June 4, 1997, B1.

166. T.T. Gegax, "Fast-Food Fast Tracker: La-wan Hawkins Thrives by Tweaking a Formula," *Newsweek*, May 26, 1997, 57.

167. M. Campanelli, "The African-American Market," *Sales and Marketing Management* 143, no. 5 (1991): 75.

168. Edwards, "Targeting Minority Customers Makes Sense."

169. "Top Five Most Trusted Sources for Company and Product Information," Minority Markets Alert, December 6, 1998, 12.

170. Hecht, Collier, and Ribeau, *African American Communication*.

171. L.F. Alwitt and T.D. Donley, *The Low-Income Consumer: Adjusting the Balance of Exchange* (Thousand Oaks, CA: Sage, 1996).

172. Futures Company, *Yankelovich Multicultural Marketing Study 2009* (New York: Futures, 2010).

173. M. de Mooij, *Global Marketing and Advertising: Understanding Cultural Paradoxes* (Thousand Oaks, CA: Sage, 1998); G. Hofstede, *Cultures and Organizations: Software of the Mind*, rev. ed. (New York: McGraw-Hill, 1997).

174. Hecht, Collier, and Ribeau, *African American Communication*.

175. W-N. Lee, C. LaFerle, and M. Tharp, "Ethnic Influences on Communication Patterns: Word of Mouth and Traditional and Nontraditional Media Usage," in *Diversity in Advertising*, ed. J.D. Williams, W.-N. Lee, and C.P. Haugtvedt (Mahwah, NJ: Lawrence Erlbaum, 2004): 177–200; G. Williams, "Teens as Consumers: A Survey of Attitudes and Behaviors" (MA thesis, University of Texas at Austin, 1991).

176. "Black Athletes Dominate Top Performer 'Q' Slots," *Jet*, October 31, 1988, 48; "Blacks Again Dominate Top Marketing Q-Ratings," *Jet*, May 22, 1989, 50.

177. Ibid.

178. Ibid.; J. Lipman, "Celebrity Pitchmen Are Popular Again," *Wall Street Journal*, September 4, 1991, B5.

179. J.D. Williams, "Examining the Effectiveness of Celebrity Advertising to Minorities: Entertainers vs. Athletes," in *Minority Marketing: Issues and Prospects: Proceedings of the Academy of Marketing Science Conference,* ed. R.L. King (Charleston, SC: Academy of Marketing Science, 1987), 107–111; S. Hume, "Stars Are Lacking

Luster as Ad Presenters," *Advertising Age,* November 7, 1983, 3; "Survey Measures Blacks' Media, Product Ad Preferences," *Marketing News,* August 21, 1981, 6.

180. J.M. Stearns, L.S. Unger, and S.G. Luebkeman, "The Portrayal of Blacks in Magazine and Television Advertising," in *AMA Educators' Proceedings,* ed. S.P. Douglas and M.R. Solomon (Chicago: AMA, 1987) 198–203; C. Duff, "You, Too, Could Be a Model for Catalogs," *Wall Street Journal,* March 31, 1993, V1; G. Zinkhan, W.J. Qualls, and A. Biswas, "The Use of Blacks in Magazine and Television Advertising 1946 to 1968," *Journalism Quarterly* 67 (Autumn 1990): 547–553; R. Snyder, J.E. Freeman, and S.E. Condray, "Magazine Ad Portrayal Of Blacks: Gender and Readership Effects," in *Proceedings of the Society for Consumer Psychology,* ed. M. Lynn and J. Jackson (Washington, DC: APA, 1991), 81–87; City of New York, *Invisible People: The Depiction of Minorities in Magazine Ads and Catalogs* (New York: Department of Consumer Affairs, 1991).

181. L. Unger and J.M. Stearns, "The Frequency of Blacks in Magazines and Television Advertising: A Review and Additional Evidence," in *Southern Marketing Association 1986 Proceedings,* ed. R.L. King, (Richmond, VA: Southern Marketing Association), 9–13; R.E. Wilkes and H. Valencia, "Hispanics and Blacks in Television Commercials," *Journal of Advertising* 18, no. 1 (1989): 19–25.

182. Tolley and Goett, "Reactions to Blacks in Newspapers"; Schlinger and Plummer, "Advertising in Black and White"; Szybillo and Jacoby, "Effects of Different Levels of Integration on Advertising Preference and Intention to Purchase"; Kerin, "Black Model Appearance and Product Evaluation"; Williams, Qualls, and Grier, "Racially Exclusive Real Estate Advertising"; T.E. Whittler, "Viewers' Processing of Actor's Race and Message Claims in Advertising Stimuli," *Psychology & Marketing* 6, no. 4 (1989): 287–309; T.E. Whittler, "The Effects of Actor's Race in Commercial Advertising: Review and Extension," *Journal of Advertising* 20, no. 1 (1991): 54–60.

183. Snyder, Freeman, and Condray, "Magazine Ad Portrayal of Blacks."

184. D.L. Hoffman, T.P. Novak, and A. Venkatesh, "Diversity on the Internet: The Relationship of Race to Access and Usage," working paper, Aspen Institute's Forum on Diversity and the Media, Queenstown, MD, November 5–7, 1997.

185. K. Goldman, "Burger King Retains Private Eye," *Wall Street Journal,* August 30, 1993, B6.

186. Fisher, "Black, Hip, and Primed to Shop."

187. B. Horovitz, "Marketing," *Los Angeles Times,* May 3, 1994, 1.

188. L.E. Wynter, "Business and Race," *Wall Street Journal,* September 8, 1999, B1.

189. Nielsen, *The State of the African-American Consumer;* L.E. Wynter, "Business and Race," *Wall Street Journal,* April 7, 1999, B1.

190. Nielsen Company, "Television Audience 2009," www.nielsen.com/content/dam/corporate/us/en/newswire/uploads/2010/04/TVA_2009-for-Wire.pdf.; J. Sterngold, "A Racial Divide Widens on Network TV," *New York Times,* December 29, 1998, 1.

191. J.R. Schement, "Thorough Americans: Minorities and the New Media," paper presented at Aspen Institute Conference, Aspen, October 1997.

192. M.L. Mueller and J.R. Schement, "Universal Service from the Bottom Up: A Study of Telephone Penetration in Camden, New Jersey," *Information Society* 12 (1996): 273–292.

193. "Top Five Most Trusted Sources for Company and Product Information," *Minority Markets Alert,* December 6, 1998, 12.

194. C. Brown, "Changing the Face of the Magazine Industry," in *Facing Differences: Race, Gender, and Mass Media*, ed. S. Biagi and S. Kern-Foxworth (Thousand Oaks, CA: Pine Forge Press, 1997), 154–160.

195. P. Reilly, "Spate of Magazines Bet on Black Readers," *Wall Street Journal*, June 2, 1996, B6.

196. L.E. Wynter, "Business and Race," *Wall Street Journal*, February 3, 1999, B1; Reilly, "Spate of Magazines Bet on Black Readers."

197. Reilly, "Spate of Magazines Bet on Black Readers."

198. V. Reitman, "Black Newspaper Group Threatens a Boycott of P&G," *Wall Street Journal,* June 15, 1992, B1.

199. Campanelli, "The African-American Market."

200. C. Schooler and M.D. Basil, "Alcohol and Cigarette Advertising on Billboards: Targeting with Social Cues," paper presented at ICA Conference, Dublin, Ireland, May 1989; *Billboards in Baltimore: Blight on Beauty and a Scourge on Health in Our City* (Washington, DC: National Medical Association, 1989).

201. J.E. Gans and K.L. Shook, eds., *Policy Compendium of Tobacco, Alcohol, and Other Harmful Substances* (Chicago: American Medical Association, 1994).

202. W.-N. Lee and M.F. Callcott, "A Comparative Study of Billboard Advertising in Anglo and Ethnic Minority Neighborhoods," paper presented at the American Academy of Advertising, San Antonio, Texas, 1992.

203. Gans and Shook, *Policy Compendium of Tobacco, Alcohol, and Other Harmful Substances.*

204. Campanelli, "The African-American Market."

205. Lee, LaFerle, and Tharp, "Ethnic Influences on Communication Patterns."

206. L.E. Wynter, "An Untapped Market of 11 Million Homes," *Wall Street Journal,* September 7, 1994, B1.

207. Davis, "Fashions That Fit."

208. Think with Google, *5 Truths of the Digital African American Consumer: A Digital Culture of Change,* Google/GlobalHue/Ipsos OTX MediaCT, U.S. research study, June 2011, http://ssl.gstatic.com/think/docs/five-truths-of-the-digital-african-american-consumer_research-studies.pdf.

209. Nielsen, *The State of the African-American Consumer.*

210. Think with Google, *5 Truths of the Digital African American Consumer.*

211. D.L. Novak and T.P. Hoffman, "Bridging the Racial Divide on the Internet," *Science* 280, no. 5362 (April 17, 1998): 390.

212. A. Smith, *Home Broadband 2010* (Washington, DC: Pew Internet and American Life Project, August 11, 2010), 2, http://pewinternet.org/Reports/2010/Home-Broadband-2010.aspx.

213. Nielsen, *The State of the African-American Consumer.*

214. Think with Google, *5 Truths of the Digital African American Consumer.*

215. Mitskaviets, *Online African Americans.*

216. D. Golden, "Casting a Net: Web Site That Unites Blacks Is Big Ambition of Henry Louis Gates," *Wall Street Journal,* February 17, 2000, A1, A8; R.O. Crockett, "Attention Must Be Paid: The African American Web Community Is Swelling—and Underserved," *BusinessWeek,* February 7, 2000, EB16; L. Castaneda, "African American Financial Index Available on Web," *San Francisco Chronicle,* April 7, 1997; Hoffman, Novak, and Venkatesh, "Diversity on the Internet."

217. Think with Google, *5 Truths of the Digital African American Consumer.*

218. Nielsen, *The State of the African-American Consumer,* 12.

219. Ibid., 17.

220. Nielsen Company, "Television Audience 2009."

221. Campanelli, "The African-American Market."

222. "Retailers Target Ethnic Consumers," *Advertising Age*, September 30, 1991, 50; "After Demographic Shift, Atlanta Mall Restyles Itself as a Black Shopping Center," *Wall Street Journal*, February 26, 1992, B1.

223. F. Korzenny, J. McClure, and B. Razttki, "Ethnicity, Communication, and Drugs," *Journal of Drug Issues* 20 (1990): 87–98; D. Moore, J.D. Williams, and W.J. Qualls, "Target Marketing of Tobacco and Alcohol Related Products to Ethnic Minority Groups in the United States," *Ethnicity & Disease* 6, nos. 1–2 (1996): 83–98; B.M. Scott, R.W. Denniston, and K.M. Magruder, "Alcohol Advertising in the African American Community," *Journal of Drug Issues* 22, no. 2 (1992): 455–469; A.M. Freedman, "Malt Advertising That Touts Firepower Comes Under Attack by US Officials," *Wall Street Journal*, July 1, 1991, B1.

224. Moore, Williams, and Qualls, "Target Marketing of Tobacco and Alcohol Related Products."

225. D.W. Stewart and R. Rice, "Integrated Marketing: New Technologies, Non-Traditional Media, and Nonmedia Promotion in the Marketing of Alcoholic Beverages," working paper, NIAAA Working Group on the Effect of the Mass Media on the Use and Abuse of Alcohol, March 24, 1993.

226. Freedman, "Malt Advertising That Touts Firepower "; A.M. Freedman, "Marketing: Heileman Tries a New Name for Strong Malt," *Wall Street Journal*, May 11, 1992, B1.

227. Moore, Williams, and Qualls, "Target Marketing of Tobacco and Alcohol Related Products."

7

Sexual Orientation
as Community Boundary

LGBT Americans

Lesbian, gay, bisexual, and transsexual (LGBT) consumers constitute one of the most interesting and challenging consumer subcultures in multicultural America. Unlike race, age, or even ethnic origin, sexual orientation is not a characteristic easily observed by other people. Sexual orientation is such a personal topic that only in the past thirty years have more than a few individuals publicly identified themselves or others as "gay." Persons of alternative sexual orientations share "outsider" status and experience discrimination, even persecution, by other Americans. This has provided the catalyst for organizing LGBT communities.

The success of these organizations in representing LGBT rights has, in turn, created a basis for LGBT pride. Open acknowledgment of being lesbian, gay, bisexual, or transsexual and community groups representing the interests of these Americans are the cornerstones of access to this market. In 2014 a mere 18 out of 50 states, plus the District of Columbia, recognized same-sex marriage, civil unions, or domestic partnerships, in effect granting equal rights to LGBT persons.[1]

The existence of a subculture, even a large one, does not necessarily make its members a viable market for partnerships with business and civic organizations. There is no doubt that LGBT persons comprise a difficult market to understand. There are no U.S. Census Bureau data to describe the size and

---

Note: LGBT stands for lesbian, gay, bisexual, and transsexual. For readability, in this chapter we occasionally use the terms "gay" or "gay and lesbian" to indicate all LGBT persons.

growth of the gay population. Even people who are gay disagree about whether a same-sex orientation is a result of genetics or environment. Where do the people who are bisexual fit in? Can marketers reach closeted gay people or only those who are "out"? These are typical questions that firms have when considering a partnership with LGBT consumers.

This chapter first describes events central to the self-identity of homosexuals in contemporary American society. The emphasis is on how individuals integrate their homosexuality with other aspects of social identity and character. The next section describes the controversy over the size of the LGBT population and the difficulties that this creates for marketers. Next, the geography of the LGBT community is described—that is, where in the United States are clusters of gay men and lesbians and what are and are not part of gay-oriented lifestyles and politics. The chapter then turns to the two-way impact of gays on American popular culture and media and to media sources for reaching LGBT consumers. The chapter ends with a discussion of marketing cases in which firms have become identified as members of the extended lesbian and gay community. We also touch on experiences gay men and lesbians have reported that influence their product and brand preferences.

Being Homosexual in a Straight World

Most LGBT Americans see themselves as different—outside the American mainstream, whatever it might be.[2] This recognition is essential to finding and expressing social identity. For some homosexuals, a feeling of being outside the boundary of "typical" Americans is reinforced by real discrimination.[3] For some, it leads to alternative communities where homosexuals constitute a majority. And some gay persons believe that their sexual orientation must always be denied, at least in public.[4] The following quotation expresses the feelings that this experience can engender.

> Being gay may be more acceptable in today's America, but it is still considered a deviation from majority behavior. Consider the following quotation on being gay in American society: "Thus we come to American society, dominated by a white, male, heterosexual, Christian culture. The dominant group expresses its power in and through the control of critical aspects of business, government, home life, education, etc. In addition, the accompanying ideological system often serves to legitimate and support that control. The material and the ideological work in concert with one another, reinforcing the societal hierarchy and making it seem "natural," "right," both to those in the position of dominance and to many of those who are themselves dominated. The ideology is reinforced, the "correctness" of the inequity re-created, over and over again, through the machinations of culture. . . . One gender, one

sexual orientation, one religious affiliation, and one color of skin are seen as mainstream, while all others fall outside this social category.[5]

Acknowledging a Gay Identity

A consequence of socialization with these values can be strong, negative beliefs about being a homosexual.[6] This identity crisis can be particularly difficult as an individual experiences the usual pitfalls of adolescence. Gay persons must ultimately decide on a personal strategy for how to relate to mainstream American culture—assimilate (remain "closeted") or separate (declare shared identity with other homosexuals). In between those two extremes are the 30 percent of men and 15 percent of women who "do not have an exclusive heterosexual history" but who do not consider themselves gay.[7] There is a large difference between these numbers and the much smaller group who identify as gay. Early adolescence is the time when most gay people feel their LGBT identity emerging, but not until late adolescence or early adulthood is this identity consolidated and reinforced. Table 7.1 shows scientific research on median ages in the development of LGBT identity Newer research on this topic is absent, but according to anecdotal accounts the age has dropped for every step in the process of developing and integrating a LGBT identity shown in the table. *The New Gay Teenager* reports that lesbians have their first same-sex contact at age 16 while gay men have their first same-sex contact at age 14.[8] That individuals experience successive stages of LGBT self-awareness, self-labeling, and LGBT behaviors still serves as a template for understanding the process involved in "coming out."[9]

Declaring a gay identity in mainstream society, or "coming out of the closet," has psychological and behavioral dimensions. While "coming out" may be key for integrating a homosexual's self-concept, it has unknown ramifications. Most stressful is not being able to predict the reactions of family and other significant persons. "Passing for straight" is a common coping strategy to deal with this stress, but there are many variations of behavior along a continuum from "straight" to "gay" identity. Some people are in touch with their same-sex orientation earlier or later in life than others, and some choose consciously to deny their sexual orientation at various points in life.[10] Furthermore, homosexuality can be expressed as an identity label, an expression of same-sex desire or same-sex behavior. These differences between how one behaves (homosexual or bisexual sex) and how one sees him- or herself (gender-identity issues for transsexuals) or who one desires create unclear boundaries for who is—and who is not—part of the LGBT community.[11] As example, transgender individuals may never use the "gay" label, engage in same-sex behavior, or have same-sex desires.

Table 7.1

Identity Issues Among Gay Men and Lesbians

	Median age of experience for:	
Stage of gay identity development	Gay men	Lesbians
Initial awareness of same-sex attraction	12–13	14–16
Initial same-sex experience	14–15	20–22
Self-identification as lesbian or gay	19–21	21–23
Initial same-sex sexual relationship	21–24	20–24
Positive gay or lesbian identity	22–26	24–29

Source: L.D. Garnets and D.C. Kimmel, "Lesbian and Gay Male Dimensions in the Psychological Study of Human Diversity," in *Psychological Perspectives on Human Diversity*, ed. J.D. Goodchilds (Washington, DC: American Psychological Association, 1991), 160–180. Reproduced by permission of American Psychological Association.

A significant risk of "coming out" is the homophobia of other people and not being able to trust the strength of family or friendship bonds to overcome a phobic reaction. Men are more homophobic than women, but all heterosexuals express more prejudice against same-sex orientations when it involves their own gender.[12] Some research suggests that "gaydar," the ability to discern another person's sexual orientation, may be scent-based.[13] The need to accommodate these feelings and behaviors results in great variation in how gay identity is expressed. While most conservative estimates of the LGBT population consider adults over age 18, the age for "coming out," the typical age for self-awareness about sexual orientation is as young as 13 or 14.[14] In late 2010, a series of high school and college student suicides occurred after gay persons were bullied or "outed." LGBT persons are frequent victims of hate crimes.[15]

Due to the hostility that homosexuals face in the mainstream world, acceptance by and support of family members is extremely important.[16] At the same time, many gay persons expect rejection of their homosexuality and fear family members' pressure to keep them from "coming out" to other family members. Some homosexuals find family warmth only via a "chosen" and constructed family of friends who accept the whole person. The "extended family" of gay-friendly organizations extends to churches, media, businesses, professionals, and civic and cultural causes as well as to arts organizations, a usually gay-friendly arena.

Being LGBT in a Straight World

A primary issue for LGBT persons is what labels they use for themselves and which ones are acceptable for others to use. For example, "lesbian" and "gay" are terms used for and by people who have a same-sex orientation. Due to the exclusively sexual connotations of the term "homosexual," many men prefer to be called "gay," and women choose "lesbian." "Gay" is acceptable to most men and women of same-sex orientation. "Bisexual" describes people attracted to both men and women. Outside these terms, most of the slang words for members of this subculture are derogative (queer, fag, faggot, pansy, dyke, butch, ad infinitum). Nevertheless, both LGBT and "straight" people sometimes use the more offensive terms; outsiders use them pejoratively, and insiders use them as affirmation of "gay pride." Symbols also serve as markers of gay identity, such as the rainbow, the color lavender, a pink triangle, the number 338, and the Greek sign for lambda. Such labels are also used at times to chastise anyone who does not conform to mainstream gender ideals, especially effeminate men.[17]

It is important to remember that we depend on self-identification in addressing the labeling issue. While some LGBT people wish to be *respected* as a homosexual, many remain afraid of being *labeled* as homosexual. The best solution for marketers may be to use gay-owned or gay-friendly media so that labels are irrelevant. A game played between advertisers and consumers is the use of phrases with meanings specific to insiders of LGBT culture, called "gayspeak." Examples from advertisements are: "Another one coming out"; "Show your pride"; "We are everywhere"; "From an early age, it knew it was different," and "Feeling outrageous?" Even visual images of a sunflower field with only one sunflower above the others or a plane with pink eyelashes and a rainbow below it are used for signaling that the audience includes gay consumers. This strategy, used by both mainstream and gay-oriented advertisers, is an example of how codes and double meanings are a way to show gay consumers that an advertised brand or firm understands LGBT culture.[18]

Kitzinger identified five specific behaviors that result from the experience of being LGBT in a straight world.[19] First is a sense of alienation and self-protection, with a tendency to distrust others. Second is a health consciousness and focus on satisfying needs independently. Third, homosexuals seek affiliation and want group identity, especially with others "out of the closet." This means seeking communications with and loyalty to those who are friendly to the gay community. Fourth, gays generally try new things and want to experience new feelings. Fifth, they try to reduce stress in their lives.[20]

These endless accommodations within a gay person's self-concept mean that there is no such thing as a single gay or lesbian lifestyle. The significance for marketers is that there is a community boundary perceived by many gay and lesbian consumers between themselves and the rest of Americans. Sexual orientation is the characteristic that many homosexuals believe best "defines" them, independent of age, gender, race, or other aspects of identity.[21] In sum, the importance of sexual orientation to personal identity and a perceived community outside mainstream American culture are the foundations of LGBT subculture.

Demographics of LGBT Americans

To whom do the terms "gays and lesbians" or "LGBT Americans" refer? Certainly, they include men and women with same-sex orientations. The term "gay" customarily includes bisexuals (people attracted to both men and women) as well. People with other sexual orientations, such as the transgendered, sadomasochists, fetishists, or pedophiles, are included with homosexuals and bisexuals by mainstream society when referring to people who engage in any alternative (nonheterosexual) sexual practices. Within the LGBT community, however, other labels are used in accordance with the sexual behavior in which a person engages.

"Transgendered" is a term that refers to both transsexuals and cross-dressers. It has been estimated that over 25,000 Americans have had sex-reassignment surgery and at least 2 percent of children have "discomfort with their assigned gender and may experiment with gender roles."[22] Neither the transgendered nor other LGBT persons use the terms "gay" and "lesbian" for effeminate men, "butch" women, hermaphrodites (intersexed persons), or for people who engage in other, alternative sexual practices.

Size of the LGBT Population

There are conflicting estimates of the size of the American gay population. The 1948 Kinsey study estimated the homosexual population at 10 percent, and this proportion was accepted as the "standard" until the 1990s, when several research studies challenged it. In 1993 the Battelle study reported that only 1 percent of male respondents considered themselves exclusively homosexual.[23] Gay activists who claimed that face-to-face surveys inevitably underestimate the incidence of same-sex relations, which are illegal in many states, criticized the methods of the Battelle study. Studies in Europe point to a range of 1 to 4 percent. Lesbians alone were estimated to comprise about 3 million women in the United States in 1993 (about 1 percent of the total U.S. population).[24]

The Yankelovich study in 1994, the first "blue chip" firm to study consumer attitudes of homosexuals, placed the estimate at 6 percent of the U.S. adult population.[25] This figure is consistent with the 6.7 percent figure used by Witeck and Combs (2006), but larger than 2–3 percent estimate of *The Gay & Lesbian Atlas* (2004) published by the Urban Institute. Differences in methodology probably account for some of the different findings, depending on whether they ask a person to categorize him or herself or his or her behavior. Many people who have had homosexual experiences do not consider themselves gay; thus, self-reports tend to be conservative.[26]

The 2010 population of the United States was estimated at 235 million adults over age 18. Based on the discussion above, the LGBT population could vary from 9.4 million (4 percent) to 23.5 million (10 percent). Using the Witeck and Combs calculation of 6.7 percent of those over age 18, the LGBT population in 2010 was more than 15.7 million. Table 7.2 shows these estimates of the size of the LGBT population, at 4 percent, 6.7 percent, and 10 percent of persons age 18 and older. In addition, the table shows the size of the adult LGBT population for the top 25 American cities. It is a conservative estimate of the entire LGBT market's size, yet it is consistent with the Yankelovich finding that gays are concentrated in the top 25 metropolitan areas.[27]

LBGT Geography

The Yankelovich 1994 study estimated that 27 percent of the adult population in cities with a population over 3 million and 34 percent of the population in cities with a population from 1 million to 3 million, were gay.[28] *The Gay & Lesbian Atlas*, however, provides more current details about the LGBT population in specific states, counties, and neighborhoods. The top 10 states with the highest concentration of same-sex couples were Vermont, California, Washington, Massachusetts, Oregon, New Mexico, Nevada, New York, Maine, and Arizona. California has about 15 percent of all LGBT Americans, and New York has 7.8 percent, Texas 7.2 percent, and Florida 6.9 percent.[29] The top 5 Metropolitan Statistical Areas (MSAs) for LGBT persons were San Francisco (16 to 25 percent of adult men), Oakland (CA), Seattle, Fort Lauderdale, and Austin–San Marcos. Among midsize MSAs, the top 5 were Santa Rosa and Santa Cruz, CA, Portland, ME, Madison, WI, and Asheville, NC. The smallest MSAs with significant LGBT populations were Santa Fe, NM, Burlington, VT, Bloomington, IN, Iowa City, IA, and Barnstable–Yarmouth, MA. The distinction for being the "gayest" town was given to Provincetown, MA, where over 1 in 8 households were gay or lesbian (compared to the American average of 1 in 100 households).[30]

Gay and lesbian couples share a preference for living in 5 of the top 10 states with a LGBT concentration: California, Massachusetts, Washington, Arizona, and Vermont. But gay males choose Nevada, Florida, Georgia, Delaware, and New York as their next most populous locations, while lesbians choose New Mexico, Maine, New Hampshire, Oregon, and Colorado. Counties and cities such as San Francisco, Monroe, Florida, the District of Columbia, New York, and Arlington, VA, have large gay male populations, while Hampshire and

Table 7.2

Estimate of Gay and Lesbian Population in Top 25 U.S. Metropolitan Areas, 2010

Metropolitan area	2010 adult population*	4% of adults	6.7% of adults**	10% of adults
Estimate of 2010 U.S. Adult Population	**235,016,000**	**9,400,640**	**15,746,072**	**23,501,600**
Top twenty-five				
New York, NY	12,258,867	245,177	735,532	1,225,887
Los Angeles, CA	10,276,271	205,525	616,576	1,027,627
Chicago, IL	7,377,275	147,546	442,637	737,728
San Francisco, CA	4,513,854	90,277	270,831	451,386
Philadelphia, PA	3,885,962	77,719	233,158	388,596
Detroit, MI	3,111,639	62,232	186,698	311,164
Dallas, TX	2,971,673	59,434	178,300	297,167
Washington, DC	2,943,591	58,872	176,616	294,359
Boston, MA	2,887,604	57,752	173,256	288,760
Houston, TX	2,826,974	56,540	169,619	282,697
Atlanta, GA	2,337,713	46,754	140,263	233,771
Miami, FL	2,217,565	44,351	133,054	221,757
Seattle, WA	1,918,978	38,380	115,139	191,898
Cleveland, OH	1,798,035	35,961	107,882	179,804
San Diego, CA	1,780,259	35,605	106,816	178,026
Minneapolis, MN	1,779,287	35,586	106,757	177,929
Phoenix, AZ	1,666,938	33,339	100,016	166,694
St. Louis, MO	1,589,804	31,796	95,388	158,980
Denver, CO	1,442,217	28,844	86,533	144,222
Pittsburgh, PA	1,409,356	28,187	84,561	140,936
Tampa, FL	1,324,678	26,494	79,481	132,468
Cincinnati, OH	1,184,752	23,695	71,085	118,475
Portland, OR	1,111,965	22,239	66,718	111,197
Kansas City, KA/MO	1,081,818	21,636	64,909	108,182
Milwaukee, WI	1,048,000	20,960	62,880	104,800
Range for size of gay population in 25 metro areas		**1,534,901**	**4,604,705**	**7,674,510**

Source: U.S. Census Bureau, *U.S. Census 2010,* www.census.gov/2010census/; U.S. Census Bureau, "Table 2. Annual Estimates of the Population of Combined Statistical Areas," March 27, 2008,

*Includes only adults 18 or more years old.

**6.7 percent is the conservative estimate of LGBT percentage of adult population used by R. Witeck and W. Combs, *Business Inside Out: Capturing Millions of Brand Loyal Gay Consumers* (Chicago: Kaplan, 2006).

Franklin in Massachusetts, Tompkins in New York, Sonoma and San Francisco in California, are counties with higher-than-average percentages of lesbian households.[31] While these data are based on the 2000 U.S. Census counts of same-sex households, they exclude the 75 percent of gay men and 60 percent of lesbians who were not part of a couple at that point in time.

What is most interesting is that when children are included in gay or lesbian households, those couples are more likely to live in states and metropolitan areas with a relatively low concentration of gay and lesbian households. About one in four of all LGBT couples lives with children, and they are raising them in states such as Mississippi, South Dakota, Alaska, South Carolina, and Louisiana. Individuals over age 55 make up about 30 percent of each state's population of gay and lesbian couples. With this exception—the presence of children—the LGBT population is most likely to live in highly urban and diverse metropolitan areas of the United States and in neighborhoods with above-average housing values, home ownership, and house sizes.

LGBT Incomes: Myth and Reality

Estimates of the spending power of gays and lesbians vary as much as estimates of the size of the population. In 2005 estimates of the gay market's disposable income topped $610 million, up from $580 million in 2004, based on 15.5 million persons.[32] By 2011 the purchasing power of LGBT consumers was estimated at $835 billion[33] by one source, and closer to $780 billion by others.[34] One reason that the estimates of spending power for gays and lesbians are so unstable is that individual and household incomes of LGBTs are used interchangeably.

In the 1990s the gay press publicized its readers as having an average household income almost 70 percent higher than that of heterosexuals.[35] More recent studies have refuted these data. *The Gay & Lesbian Atlas* reports gay men as having less household income than straight men. However, relying again on the Yankelovich Monitor Survey, their reports estimated household income at $37,400 for gay men and $39,300 for straight men, and $34,800 for lesbians, compared to $34,400 for straight women. They also found a higher percentage of gay over heterosexual men with incomes under $25,000, and a higher percentage over heterosexuals for gay and lesbian consumers with incomes above $50,000. Such skewed income distribution suggests that gay consumers include a smaller middle-income group, with larger low- and high-income groups. Ultimately the Yankelovich study, whose sample reflected the total U.S. population, found no significant differences in the incomes of gays and heterosexuals. Myths die hard, and years later the hype about higher LGBT incomes is still around.[36]

One consistency among all studies of the American gay and lesbian population is a finding of higher than average education levels. Fourteen percent of LGBTs attended graduate school, compared to 7 percent of heterosexuals; 49 percent have had some college, compared to 37 percent of the "straight" population, according to the Yankelovich study. As for occupations, 56 percent of gays/lesbians were in professional/managerial jobs versus 16 percent of heterosexuals. They are also more likely to be self-employed and a source of entrepreneurial marketing to fellow members of the LGBT community.

Ethnic Diversity Among LGBT Persons

Very few sources of information exist regarding ethnic differences in the gay and lesbian population. Nevertheless, the work by Beverly Greene is a testimony to cultural diversity in same-sex orientation.[37] In a study of over 700 homosexual African-American couples, she found a significant amount of income, education, and employment diversity. Unlike heterosexual couples, gay couples tended to have more mixed ethnicity. She also found that the income of male same-sex couples was statistically higher than that for female couples.[38] In *The Gay & Lesbian Atlas*, the Southern states and metropolitan areas have higher proportions of African-American gay and lesbian households. The Atlas also found Southwestern states with high concentrations of LGBT-Hispanic population; in addition, LGBT-Hispanics are found in large cities and southern states.[39]

Some Native American tribes have a same-sex tradition of "berdache" ("two-spirit" people) couples. Some African cultures celebrate "woman marriages," and some Asian cultures recognize male pair bonding.[40] Nevertheless, Greene suggests that a larger percentage of homosexuals in American ethnic communities remain closeted. An example of why this may be true is the Latino and Asian importance placed on family and a definition of family that excludes homosexuality.[41] Gender roles in these cultures are tightly defined, and males and females have distinctive role expectations. Disapproval of homosexuality in the Latino community may be more intense than that of non-Latino Americans.[42] "Coming out" for Asian Americans can be seen as a threat to "the continuation of the family line and a rejection of appropriate roles within the culture as well."[43] African and Native American homosexuals do not suffer such strict role definitions and thus may experience fewer fears of the consequence of "coming out" in their respective communities.

The opportunities for marketers who can connect with consumers who prefer LGBT relationships are significant indeed. The demographic profile of the gay market indicates potentially higher average levels of education, disposable income, and more LGBTs in managerial and professional occupations. How much higher these levels are is in dispute, but it translates to heavy product usage of luxury items such as vacation homes, electronic audiovisual equipment, credit cards, liquor and wine, domestic and foreign travel, and sports and fitness activities. A large percentage of readers of gay publications report that they are "very likely" to buy the national products advertised there.[44] London and Paris openly appeal to LGBT travelers, an American segment that spends between $17 billion and $47 billion on travel.[45]

Gay Neighborhoods and Lifestyles

An important aspect of LGBT life is a strong sense of community, as seen in the growing number of gay neighborhoods, activist and networking groups, gay-targeted publications and websites, their personally redefined "families," and special interest lobbying efforts. This unifying force since the 1960s has been building a sense of community among LGBTs, and it was fundamental for fighting the AIDS epidemic among its members.

Gay neighborhoods satisfy the need to reinforce a gay person's sense of identity. As noted earlier, gay males are most likely to inhabit the well-known "gay" neighborhoods.[46] One of the most important reasons for the congregation of LGBT people in urban areas is the greater acceptance of alternative lifestyles. A participant in an earlier study expressed his feelings about gay neighborhoods this way: "the topic is integration versus ghetto. I prefer integration even though it's tougher. First of all, the ghetto makes you forget what society is really like, and you lose the motivation to push for change. Second, if everyone is in the ghetto, who will be the positive gay model for young people trying to come to grips with their identities in Cowtown?"[47]

The following are neighborhoods with high concentrations of gay population: New York's Greenwich Village, SoHo, Brooklyn Heights, Park Slope and Chelsea; San Francisco's Castro, Twin Peaks, Oakland, Mission District, and Haight-Ashbury; Boston's Roxbury, South End, and Jamaica Plain; Houston's Montrose and Heights; Chicago's Lincoln Park and New Town; and Los Angeles' West Hollywood and Silverlake. In addition, there are concentrations of gay-owned property in Fire Island, NY; Provincetown, MA; South Beach, Key West, and Pensacola in Florida; Laguna Beach and Palm Springs in California; Takoma Park, MD, outside Washington; and Royal Oak, MI, outside Detroit.

There is a growing presence of gay people in smaller cities and suburbs, though it is hard to document. The movement out of predominantly gay neighborhoods is a result of increasing tolerance and the desire to achieve the same American "dream house" that nongays prize.[48]

Going to a gay bar is frequently the first public experience for a gay person.[49]

Gay-owned and gay-friendly businesses, especially bookstores and publications, are important components of the LGBT community. Other important organizations include groups formed among computer chatrooms, social networking websites, and political or activist organizations. Even religious groups such as Dignity (www.dignityusa.org), Integrity (www.integrityusa.org), and the Metropolitan Community Church (http://mcchurch.org) are active supporters of LGBT congregations.[50] The Metropolitan Community Church has been a member of the gay and lesbian community since 1968 and includes about 250 congregations in 40 countries worldwide. One of its most worthwhile endeavors is bringing a sense of personal dignity to thousands of LGBT Christians.[51]

Lesbians are more likely than gay men to live in rural and suburban areas, and this is highly correlated with the presence of children in the household. About 20 percent of lesbians have children younger than age 18 in their home, while only 15 percent of gay men have children living with them.[52] Sixty-four percent of lesbians and 46 percent of gay men are in long-term committed relationships, contrary to the stereotype that gays are single and promiscuous.[53]

Many LGBT people speak of a gay or lesbian "sensibility or culture, something beyond the mere question of same-sex sexual acts."[54] Is there such a thing as a gay lifestyle? Early studies confirmed that the process of forming and maintaining relationships is similar whether homosexual or heterosexual.[55] At the same time, there is more role flexibility. Same-sex couples are less likely to internalize stereotypical gender roles.[56] Redefinition of the "family" and the important role of LGBT-identity organizations have created an extensive network of community for gays and lesbians. Success in fighting AIDS was due in part to the access that these community organizations have to members of the gay and lesbian subculture. Table 7.3 lists prominent nonprofit and political organizations in the LGBT community.

Urban gays and lesbians have outgoing lives similar to those of their heterosexual counterparts. But in general they are more active in seeking out new experiences, especially in shopping, food, and entertainment. Stress is a major issue in the lives of LGBT individuals. Security is important to them, whether they are traveling or at home. A strong friendship network is an important antidote to this perceived stress, as are, on occasion, other forms of tranquilizers. For a small minority of the subculture, drug use is a serious hazard, just as it is for heterosexuals. Many LGBT persons are avid consumers of fashion and fitness products. As several gay people have said: "It's a life not a lifestyle." Yet it is not *a particular* lifestyle: "the gay subgroup encompasses as great a variety of appearance and behavior as does the non-gay segment of the population."[57]

Table 7.3

Nonprofit and Political Organizations in the LGBT Community

Organization name	Brief description of purpose or activities	URL
ACLU Gay and Lesbian Rights	Information about gay rights issues	www.aclu.org/lgbt/index.html
Alpha Omega Society	Support for cross-dressers and families	www.aosoc.org
CUAV (Communities United Against Violence)	Addresses and prevents hate violence directed at LGBT persons	www.cuav.org
Gay.com Network or Gay.net	Online chat network. 2,000 affiliates: news, information, and matchmaking	www.gay.com; www.gay.net
GLAAD (Gay and Lesbian Alliance)	Promote fair, accurate and inclusive representation of LGBT individuals and events; media watchdog	www.glaad.org
Human Rights Campaign	Largest LGBT political organization	www.hrcusa.org
International Gay and Lesbian Assn.	Global organization promoting LGBT rights	www.ilga.org
Lambda Legal	Advancing the rights of LGBT persons	www.lambdalegal.org
National Center for Lesbian Rights	Activism on behalf of lesbians	www.nclrights.org
National Center for Transgender Equality	Advocacy, collaboration and equality for transgender people	www.nctequality.org
NGLTF (National Gay and Lesbian Task Force)	Activist group with grassroots organizations and advo-cacy	http://thetaskforce.org
Renaissance Transgender Assn.	Support and information for transgendered individuals and those close to them	www.ren.org
Tri-Ess	Online support for cross-dressers	www.tri-ess.net

Several authors cite the importance of clothes, symbols, and language as important markers of gay identity.[58] An example of the relevance of "style" in communicating a gay aesthetic is parody in the form of camp. Camp is a highly dramatic style in fashion or design that exaggerates, is outrageous, and otherwise celebrates the banal. Meyer claims that "camp" is a critique of society and a vehicle of social mobility for gays. One form of "camp" involves idolizing female stars such as Bette Davis, Mae West, Bette Midler, Madonna, and Lady Gaga, making a parody of these strong, sexually aggressive women who are succeeding in a patriarchal world.[59] Even though the enthusiasm of gay audiences contributes to the popularity of mainstream celebrities, there continues to be censorship of gay themes in art, theater, and even the Internet.

Diverse LGBT Communities, United in Favor of Gay Rights

In the controversy over whether nature or nurture is the source of homosexuality, recent evidence suggests that both contribute.[60] Many gay people feel that their same-sex preferences are as innate as skin or hair color. This view has significant political implications because if being gay is innate, then there is a legitimate argument to be made that legal protections and the right to civil marriage should be extended to LGBTs to prevent discrimination, as it has been used to combat racial and gender discrimination.[61] As of 2013, civil marriages of LGBT persons were recognized in 16 states. "Don't Ask, Don't Tell" was repealed by Congress in December 2010, allowing LGBT persons to serve openly in the military. At the same time, in some states, it is illegal for gay people to adopt children or serve as foster families. Such differences in the rights of LGBT people compared to other Americans motivate activism in the gay community.

While the fight for the equal right to marry is at the top of the LGBT "rights" agenda, all members of the LGBT community face the more mundane issue of violence. In 2008 15.5 percent of 7,222 incidents of bias in the United States were against LGBT individuals.[62] About 60 percent of transgendered persons claimed to have been assaulted at some point in their lives. The gay civil rights movement had its origins in the 1950s, when homosexuals looked inward, seeking tolerance and understanding from outsiders. During the 1960s the movement focused on debates about how to proceed within mainstream society. The Mattachine Society of Washington proposed the first "bill of rights" in 1961. The next major advance was recognition by the American Psychiatric Association that homosexuality was not a mental illness. During the 1970s and 1980s, the gay press focused on the "coming out" process and its importance to self-respect. In this regard, the gay media have played an important role in educating gay people about how to deal with LGBT issues. The gay liberation movement has been committed to changing attitudes, improving communication and community among gay people, and combating stereotypes in mainstream society.

Gay activism today centers on equal rights and the freedom to be "visible in the mainstream world."[63] To that end, more LGBT individuals participate every year in urban events such as marches for LGBT rights, gay history month, and celebrations linked to gay history such as the 1969 Stonewall riots in New York. Another group seeking recognition of their rights are LGBT teenagers; their advocacy groups are the Gay-Lesbian-Straight Education Network and Gay-Straight Alliances. Legal recognition of gay marriage is a portal through which LGBT activists can press for domestic partnership programs and benefits such as health-care and life insurance and leaves for paternity or maternity, illness, and bereavement.

As more people have "come out of the closet," LGBT leaders have encouraged others in the community to support the organizations that contribute to LGBT causes. This has made it less risky for mainstream organizations that target the gay market. In an online survey, almost half of gay respondents said they prefer to buy from companies that support gay community organizations.[64] Mainstream firms such as Absolut Vodka, Benetton, Hiram Walker, American Airlines, Levi's, Virgin Atlantic Airways, Coors, and Philip Morris jumped into the gay market in the early 1990s by supporting nonprofit organizations in the gay community and maintaining a presence in gay media. Absolut Vodka is considered the first mainstream marketer to target gays. Examples of its strong presence in supporting LGBT causes and events are shown in Figures 7.1–7.6. Absolut and other long-term LGBT advertisers have been repaid by the 72 percent of LGBT consumers who prefer brands that directly target them.[65]

The Media: Importance of Endorsement

Gay-oriented media have a long history. *The Advocate* started as an underground newsletter in 1967 that supported gay issues.[66] Its website continues to be one of the few national media websites where LGBTs can become informed about political issues (www.advocate.com). It is also a venue for mainstream politicians to communicate their support of gay issues without the spotlight the mainstream press would put on the politician's position. In early 2009, only *The Advocate* reported that Hillary Clinton was revising policies at the State Department that discriminated against gay people.[67]

Figure 7.1   **In an Absolut World, "Mark, Would You Marry Me? Steve," 2008**

LGBT Media

Gay consumers are more likely to read advertising in gay-oriented media and to find the ads there useful and not boring. Forty-seven percent of those surveyed claim that they trust brands advertised in gay media more than competitive brands, even though they believe that these ads rarely show "people like me."[68] According to *The Advocate*'s media kit, its readers claim that each copy has at

Figure 7.2 **"Absolut Commitment," 2005**

least two readers and over 80 percent say they do not read other national gay and lesbian magazines. And 86 percent of its readers say they are "likely to purchase products or services advertised in *The Advocate*," while 36 percent have actually purchased those advertised products or services. These are some of the reasons advertising dollars in gay media grew three times faster than other advertising from 1996 to 2006. More than $350 million was spent in gay media in 2009, and the market is still growing.[69] Table 7.4 (p. 306) lists the major gay-oriented media in 2012.

In the 1990s a number of national magazines were introduced for LGBT readers. *Out, Girlfriends, Genre, POZ,* and *Deneuve* (later renamed *Curve*) are examples. These publications are slicker and more upscale than the earlier personal ads–based LGBT press. The transformation has not been easy. The publisher of *Genre* discovered that one reason the magazine was not selling well at first was that gay readers were still looking for it in the back, "where they always look."[70] *The Advocate* was hard hit by the new competitors and now emphasizes news, while *Out, Genre*, and *Curve* showcase gay lifestyles.

Figure 7.3 **Sponsorship of Gay Film Festival Is "Absolut Achievement," 2000**

In addition to the national publications, there are more than a hundred local gay newspapers and magazines in the United States.

In 1994 no more than $50 million was spent by national advertisers in all gay-oriented media; by 2009 more than $349 million was being spent in gay media.[71] The gay media focus on editorial content of interest to members of the gay community. Out of total editorial coverage, 23 percent is on the arts, of which movies account for 6 percent, and theater 5 percent. Seventy-two percent of gay men and women attended a movie in the previous year, and 71 percent attended live theater (compared with 21 percent of the American population). Gays were five times as likely as the general population to attend classical music concerts and four times as likely to see dance performances. While only 3 percent of articles in the gay press concern bars, clubs, and restaurants, they generate 23 percent of the advertising.[72] Gay men are seen as "fashion conscious and trendsetting" by other Americans.[73]

Table 7.4

Specialized Media for LGBT Audiences, 2012

LGBT Television networks	LGBT Television programs and characters
Pink	Kings ("Jack")
Logo	Glee
Q Network	The Ellen DeGeneres Show
here! TV (Also Out, The Advocate, and GayWired.com)	Mad Men ("Sal")
PrideVision	Will and Grace

LGBT Radio	LGBT Mailing Lists
QueerNet.org	TWIST (on WLPJ-NY, STAR-LA, Alice-SF)
American List Counsel	Gayradar.com
Metamorphics Media	Sirius Out
	PRIDE-Dallas
	Everyman's Gay Radio
	WBAI (Out-FM Collective @ www.outfm.org)

LGBT Print Media	LGBT Newspapers: National/Regional
Curve (Deneuve until 1998), www.curvemag.com	National Gay Newspaper Guild
The Advocate, www.advocate.com	Texas Triangle
Genre, www.genremagazine.com	
Out, www.out.com	
POZ, www.poz.com	

Stores/Catalogs	LGBT-Oriented Online
AandU America's AIDS Magazine, www.aumag.org	RainbowDepot.com
On Our Backs, www.onourbacks.com	allgaynation.com
Frontiers in LA, www.frontiers publishing.com/2724/index.html	TZABACO
	RainbowShoppingNetwork.com
	GayWallet.com

LGBT Resources Websites	Publishers/Sellers of LGBT Literature
AB Gender.com	lambdarising.com
Planet out.com	Viking/Penguin Press
Gay.com (4 million clicks per month)	Publishing Triangle
Gay.net (subscription website)	
GayWired.com	
AfterElton.com	
biMagazine.org	
TransGenderCare.com	
CDSPub.com	

Print was the mainstay of gay-oriented media until widespread use of the Internet. And even though many gay magazines and newspapers folded during the 2008–11 recession, print is still a cost-efficient way to reach gay consumers. More than 90 percent of gay men and 82 percent of lesbians report

Figure 7.4 **Absolut Vodka Celebrates "Absolut First" in Gay Market, 1981–2004**

reading magazines and books as a hobby. Top nongay magazines among gay readers have been *The New York Times, Men's Health, Entertainment Weekly, People, National Geographic, Esquire, Gentleman's Quarterly, New Yorker, Smithsonian, Vanity Fair,* and *Consumer Reports.* Gay men report a preference for reading nonfiction, while lesbians read more fiction. Several cities have gay-oriented radio and television stations, and there are two gay television networks available on cable or by direct satellite.

There is also a long history of direct marketing to gay consumers. More than 90 percent of *The Advocate* readers claimed to have ordered merchandise by mail or phone in the previous 12 months; 84 percent said they had ordered from a catalog in the previous 12 months. Not only is there a higher than average response rate among gay consumers to direct marketers, but they buy

Figure 7.5   **"Absolut Out" Billboard in the Castro Neighborhood of San Francisco for Gay History Month, October 2003**

more frequently and spend more money per purchase. Catalogs are estimated to reach about 1 million gay and lesbian households. An early catalog that targeted the gay market, Shocking Gray, claimed over 130,000 names on its lists and a 3 percent response rate. Readers of gay media have a higher than average index on renting cars, foreign travel, and hotel and resort stays, and over 50 percent are enrolled in frequent flyer programs. Other important and traditional media in the gay community are the numerous city and national directories, such as the *Gayellow Pages* (www.gayellowpages.com), which list gay-owned or gay-friendly professionals, accommodations, bars, events, organization meeting places, and social groups.

The Internet has become the most efficient way to reach LGBT consumers. In 2007 eMarketer estimated that 7.9 percent, or 12 million, of all adult Internet users were LGBT.[74] In 2011 eMarketer estimated that over 86 percent of LGBT persons could be reached online. This source also reports additional studies that show gays and lesbians lead in the use of social networks and blogs. Furthermore, they are twice as likely to visit a blog and two and half times as likely to have a positive reaction to ads in blogs. Nearly twice as many gays and lesbians say they are online between 24 and 168 hours per week, excluding the use of e-mail.[75] Table 7.3 lists profit and nonprofit web-

Figure 7.6 **"Absolut GLAAD," 2000**

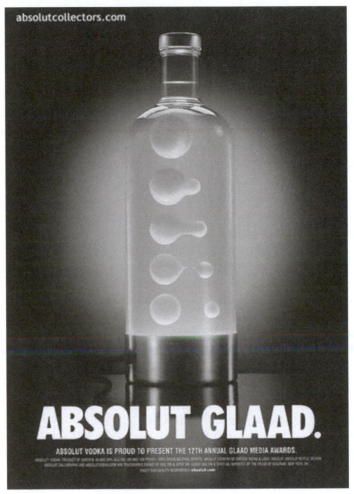

sites that accept advertising that targets the LGBT population. The Internet is the place to be for any organization that wants to reach LGBT consumers, who have more than $660 million in purchasing power and positive attitudes toward advertising and purchasing online.

There are innumerable gay-oriented personal web pages and companies seeking business in the LGBT community. The Internet may be the only place where the "openly closeted" ("out" online only) LGBT population can be reached.[76] An analysis of the web pages of the top mainstream advertisers in the gay market concluded that those firms were communicating information about their products as well as their policies of interest to gay consumers.[77] An early study found that gay people spend more money online than does the general population. Gay.com, PlanetOut, Gay Financial Network, and Online Partners were the first gay businesses to capture the attention of venture capitalists.[78]

Reaching LGBT Audiences Through Mainstream Media

Another way to reach gay consumers is via mainstream programs and entertainment that include gay characters and themes. Popular television programs such as *Glee, Grey's Anatomy*, and *Will & Grace* have included multiple gay characters.[79] Films with gay characters include: *Billy's Hollywood Screen Kiss, Brokeback Mountain, As Good as It Gets, My Best Friend's Wedding, The Opposite of Sex, Love and Death on Long Island, Love Is the Devil, Longtime Companion, The Crying Game, Philadelphia, The Birdcage, In & Out, Gods and Monsters*, and *High Art*. Likewise, well-known gay endorsers such as Greg Louganis, Martina Navratinova, k.d. lang, Anne Heche, or Ellen DeGeneres can reach both gay and mainstream consumers simultaneously.

Images of gay people in mainstream media have come a long way. They must overcome mainstream America's fear that homosexuality is a threat to society. Long-held stereotypes of gay persons include references to being perverted, abnormal, mentally ill, and maladjusted. In research studies, gay women are described as less attractive or feminine than straight women. Media stories speculated that AIDS was spread by homosexuals, and the legitimate fear of all Americans of catching what seemed to be an incurable disease has melted into an intense homophobia among some Americans. The "bathhouse" images of the early 1980s did not help gays gain respectability. A *Life* magazine article in 1964 described the homosexual lifestyle as "obsessive, sadistic, screaming, lewd, aggressive, emotionally unstable, furtive, hazardous, lonely, lazy, luxury-loving, sponging, unwanted, utterly dependent, compulsive."[80] The lack of a clear, "scientific" explanation for same-sex preferences, compounded with a natural fear of those who are "different," translated into a judgment by people who have different behavioral norms that gays are "morally irresponsible."

While it may seem that mainstream media images have hurt the acceptance of homosexuals in American mainstream society, they have also given gays and lesbians a very visible place in our popular culture.[81] "Gayspeak's" secret codes constantly change, but its use is part of youth-centered "urban slang" as well as mainstream media.[82] The episode of *Ellen* in which Ellen "came out" was the highest-rated that year on the ABC television network. Volkswagen kept its "Drivers Wanted" ads on *Ellen* for the "coming out" episode while other big car advertisers (e.g., Chrysler, GM, and Ford) and Wendy's opted out. The reaction among gay viewers was immediate: 18 percent of planned viewers said they would be more likely to buy from advertisers who stayed with the show, and 17 percent said they would be less likely to buy from advertisers who deserted it.[83] This is yet another example of LGBT consumers advocating for "equal rights" with their wallets.

The mainstream media have publicized a number of alternative sexual practices and presented them at times as perverted and at others as just "another wacky lifestyle choice."[84] S&M (sadism and masochism) was the theme behind a Manhattan restaurant "La Nouvelle Justine." And S&M references were prevalent in advertising for Gucci, a Janet Jackson album, and scenes in *Deconstructing Harry*, a Woody Allen movie in the late 1990s. Cross-dressing celebrities like RuPaul and Devine have been mimicked by cross-dressing basketball star Dennis Rodman. As they become part of mainstream popular culture, these references to alternative sexual behaviors lose some of their power to shock.[85]

In the mid-1990s, Hartford Insurance targeted gay consumers via LGBT media but also through mainstream newspapers and outdoor transit and billboards. The campaign for "Diverse Household Auto Insurance" was first introduced by ads in *Out* and *The Advocate* and then was rolled out to selective urban markets. The ad paired various combinations of blue and pink cars (two pink, two blue, and one pink with one blue) with the tagline "Commitment. Bring It On." The fine print offered 25 percent discounts to gay, lesbian, and even "heterosexual couples."[86] The playful use of colors is an example of the "double meanings" that gay consumers can read into mainstream media messages. Encoding mainstream messages with "double entendres" and "gayspeak" is an excellent tactic for capturing the attention of LGBT audiences in mainstream media.

LGBT Sponsorships

While community events are not a "medium" in the traditional sense, for the gay market they have proven an economical way to establish a firm as a supporter and insider in the LGBT community. The Gay Games in 1994 hosted 11,000 competitors from 44 countries, and companies paid over $4 million to be associated with the games, political events, and rallies. In 2010 over 70 countries were represented at the event in Cologne, and advertisers spent over $10 million cash and multiples of that with in-kind donations. Some of the companies represented were American Airlines, Walgreens, Kraft, Pepsi, Sirius, and Disney.

More often, today companies are developing unique ads for these gay events. For example, Anheuser-Busch created an ad with a Bud Light bottle in studded black leather straps and cap, to publicize the Folsom Street Fair, billed as "the world's biggest leather event."[87] The Wyndham Hotel in Palm Springs, CA, has hosted the "White Party," "One Night in Rio," and "A Country Affair" at "Dinah Shore" weekends (to coincide with the Nabisco Dinah Shore LPGA Golf Tournament). This is a "circuit party" for lesbians that has many repeat customers. The "Linashore Golf Classic" is a golf tournament for lesbians held since 1988.[88] Schwab's $40,000 sponsorship of the 19th San Francisco Gay & Lesbian Film Festival brought in over $10 million in new accounts before Schwab had even mailed out a brochure to participants.[89] And art exhibitions such as "In a Different Light" at the University Art Museum of Berkeley are focused exclusively on gay and lesbian artists in mainstream venues.

Marketing Experiences and Responses of Gay Consumers

LGBT and immigrant markets share some similarities. Like immigrants, homosexuals are "birds of a feather." They stick together, support one another, and vote for one another. Like immigrants, they often start their own businesses because it is difficult to find appropriate employment within the mainstream community. Like immigrants, they are proud of their distinctiveness but fear being branded as different. In addition, gay men and lesbians exhibit all the characteristics of an immigrant tribe. They have distinctive mores and fashions, language, signs, symbols, gathering places, and enclaves. If gays are like immigrants, "marketers who study them must think like anthropologists."[90]

Reading the LGBT consumer means understanding the ironies implied above. Gay consumers want to be full-fledged members of the American mosaic, able to express individuality that includes their homosexuality. They may have some unique tastes and behaviors, but they do not want to be branded as outsiders or set apart.[91] This paradox creates a fine line for marketers to walk in recognizing members of the LGBT subculture without threatening members of mainstream society who are the majority of their customers. In the past, old stereotypes have kept mainstream companies out of media such as *Curve* and in denial of this market's potential.[92]

Alternative Strategies for Attracting LGBT Customers

Peñaloza has outlined four alternatives for companies that want to attract LGBT consumers.[93] The first option is to redirect a general market campaign to LGBT media. Without incurring the additional costs of producing distinctive marketing communications for gay and lesbian consumers, many organizations can position themselves as members of the extended gay and lesbian community through a continuing presence in LGBT media.

As noted earlier, LGBT consumers have a high awareness of mainstream companies that advertise in gay-oriented media. In addition, they often prefer to buy from companies with a visible presence in the LGBT community. Miller Lite has been the "beer of choice for lesbians" partly because Miller has been aggressively advertising in gay magazines for over 10 years.[94] In many product categories, such as casual clothes, there are few differences in the tastes of gay and heterosexual consumers.[95] An example of the "standardized message, targeted media" approach to gay consumers is a Saab campaign placed in gay-oriented print media using general market advertisements that read, "Peel off your inhibitions. Find your own road."

A second alternative is to use messages featuring only men or women together to invite gay/lesbian identification. American Express used this kind of ambiguity when it introduced "Checks for Two." The ads showed two male or two female names in the fine print. The advertisements were placed in both mainstream and gay media, doubling the exposure to LGBT consumers.[96] In 1999 Philip Morris added a second man to a couple in the mainstream version of a Parliament ad, when it was featured in gay magazines.[97] A variant of this approach is to use no models at all or figures with no obvious gender.

Yet a third option is to develop a separate marketing communications campaign with distinct and identifiable appeals to members of the lesbian/gay subculture. One example is an ad by Kenneth Cole, featuring pink and black shoelaces in the shape of a triangle. The copy read, "Shoes shouldn't have to stay in the closet either." Gay media are sprinkled with firms using gay symbols like the rainbow, pink triangle, "338," or the Greek sign for "lambda." Advertisements using these symbols, placed in gay-oriented media, or even integrated communications programs incorporating gay-oriented events, support of gay-oriented causes, and other gay-friendly corporate policies, may draw the ire of some mainstream consumers, but more and more firms are willing to take that risk.[98] A 2008 Hilliard and Fleischman study found that 68 percent of heterosexuals would continue to buy from companies that they learn are marketing to gays. IKEA gained a tremendous amount of publicity in the mainstream media when it used an ad openly targeting gay men, in which two men were shopping for furniture.

The fourth approach is to use "gayspeak" coding, such as Miller Lite's "Pour on the Pride."[99] This kind of appeal is easily tied into other elements of an integrated communications campaign within the gay community subculture.[100] AT&T used lavender envelopes in a gay-targeted direct mail campaign. Mainstream marketers have high profiles at events targeting LGBT consumers exclusively, while their messages in mainstream media are subtle. For example, Saturn had a two-page ad in mainstream media that showed a female engineer in a tuxedo. There were no references to gender or sexual orientation, but they believed that lesbians would identify with the woman.

The campaign was followed up by support for a variety of gay-friendly events. Subaru quietly put personalized plates with "SENA LVR" and "P-TOWNIE" and the logo of the human rights campaign on the bumper of cars in its advertising. A spokesperson said: "It's clever and not offensive, and if you're in-the-know, you chuckle."[101] Halloween's popularity in gay subculture has become a mainstream event for heterosexual adults as well, making it a major "gayspeak" opportunity.[102] The use of "gayspeak" sends a message containing the affiliation and acceptance many gay consumers seek.

Regardless of which overall strategy a company uses, other authors suggest that a corporate policy of nondiscrimination in its own operations should be in place first. That step alone places an organization among pioneers in sharing values with members of the LGBT market. Lukenbill suggests the next move should be to publicize and contribute to organizations that defend LGBT rights.[103] The goodwill generated by such gestures is believed to cost little and to go a long way with gay consumers.

Signaling Acceptance to LGBT Customers

Lukenbill also recommends that the specific needs of gay consumers living in "straight" society set the priorities in communication messages: focus on individuality, meet their needs for association, provide solutions for their desire to experience life's diversity, and help alleviate stress by promoting understanding rather than skepticism and mistrust of companies.[104] Using the symbols of gay culture such as the pink triangle without a long history of presence and support in the LGBT community is dangerous. If a firm is committed to diversity, every message does not have to have a "gay spin"; it just has to show diversity.

Table 7.5 suggests several ways to segment the gay and lesbian consumer market. Having a clear target within the LGBT market helps keep the diversity of the group within focus.[105] For example, homosexuals who came of age "pre-Stonewall 1969" are less likely to be "out of the closet." They are more likely to have lived "closeted" lives and to have been part of traditional family structures that conform to heterosexual expectations. They are hesitant participants in the gay pride movement.[106] They are unlikely to participate in activities that endanger their invisibility in the mainstream; in fact, they choose products that help them "pass" for "straight." As a result, this group would prefer a low profile and "less is more" message.

A 2007 study by New American Dimensions identified five segments among LGBT consumers. "Super Gays" (26 percent) are mostly male, well-educated activists. "Habitaters" (25 percent) tend to be older, serious, and in a stable relationship. Those who are members of the "Gay Mainstream" (23 percent)

Table 7.5

Segmentation Within the Gay, Lesbian, Bisexual, and Transsexual Population

Basis of segmentation	Examples of different groups
Gender of consumer	Gay men
	Lesbians
Age of consumer	Teens to early twenties (pre-coming out)
	twenties to forties (cohort most affected by AIDS)
	forties plus (came of age before AIDS)
Household of consumer	One-person household
	DINCs (double income, no children)
	Double income, children present in household
Income of consumer	Under $30,000
	$30,000–$50,000
	$50,000–$75,000
	Over $75,000
Technical literacy	Active online consumers
	Non–technologically literate gays
Neighborhood of consumer	Gay-oriented or gay-tolerant neighborhood
	Gay persons in top 25 cities
	Gay persons in suburban or rural areas
Sexual orientation	Homosexuals
	Bisexuals
	The transgendered
	Other sexual orientations
LGBT lifestyles*	"Super Gays"
	"Habitaters"
	"Gay Mainstream"
	"Party People"
	"Closeted"

Source: *MarketingCharts staff, "Index Seeks to Codify Gay and Lesbian Psychographic, Demographic Data," Marketing Charts, August 16, 2007, www.marketingcharts.com/wp/television/index-seeks-to-codify-gay-and-lesbian-psychographic-demographic-data-1297/.

are low profile and conservative and have a strong gay identity. The "Party People" (14 percent) are risk-taking, cutting-edge, urbanites. The "Closeted" (12 percent) have the lowest gay identity and tend to be older and single. The research suggested that each segment responds differently to imagery and preferred advertising styles.[107]

Younger, affluent gay men and lesbians are spending over $55 billion a year on travel, much of it to destinations or events where there are others like them.[108] The VP for marketing at Carillon Importers described young, affluent, and "out" gay consumers as "a very socially mobile, active, affluent, aspirational segment of the population. They opt for the finer things in life."[109] This may explain their heavy consumption of luxury items such as vacation homes, electronic equipment, credit cards, liquor and wine, and sports and fitness activities. In general, gay consumers reportedly spend more than heterosexuals with the same income, and they are more brand and fashion conscious.[110]

By 2005, at least 175 of Fortune 500 companies advertised in LGBT media. Some examples of firms and their products exclusively marketed to the LGBT community are Community Marketing (travel); Pink, Inc. (personal checks); Everyday Feelings (specialized greeting cards); APP Community Pharmacy (prescription drugs by mail order); Don't Panic Designs! Inc. (gay-theme T-shirts); Community Spirit (calling cards); Alyson Publications (books); Medagenics (nutritional supplements for people with HIV or cancer). In addition, there are several affinity credit cards such as the Rainbow Visa.[111]

Patronizing these and other gay-friendly businesses is one way that the LGBT community has built political and economic clout.[112] The lists of gay-friendly businesses have been instrumental in facilitating a "buy gay" movement. Research and communications firms such as Prime Access, Spare Parts, WinMark, Overlooked Opinions, Direct Male, Mulryan/Nash, aka Communications, and Rivendell Marketing have helped mainstream companies become more experienced in communicating with LGBT consumers.[113] The lists of direct marketers, such as one labeled "AIDS-involved households," are needed for penetrating the significant variety of consumers within the gay market.[114] Several list integrators are shown in Table 7.4.

Several studies assert that clothing and appearance styles are important tools for signaling membership in the gay subculture.[115] Furthermore, aesthetic differences in homosexual and heterosexual men suggest gay men are most likely to be influenced by other gay men, especially those in urban areas with higher incomes. Gay men as trendsetters also influence heterosexual male consumers in areas of style and taste.[116] Other Americans see gay consumers as early adopters and trendsetters. But brands that achieve legitimacy as "gay friendly" within the LGBT community have a clear advantage.[117] Some examples of brands/companies considered "gay friendly" are The Body Shop, Levi's, Absolut Vodka, Cloverleaf tuna, Bravo, Showtime, HBO, Apple, American Express, American Airlines, Target, Saturn, Subaru, and Bacardi. Brands noted as "least gay friendly" were BP, Gillette, Cadillac, Kraft, Olive Garden, Sears, Exxon, Quaker Oats, Samsung, Fritos, Walmart, Dunkin' Donuts, and Cracker Barrel. When asked how the person determines a brand to be "gay friendly," the response included friends, family, community organizations, and ads from those companies.[118]

Preference for Gay-Friendly Businesses

LGBT individuals have years of experience in the mainstream marketplace, where they have not always been well received. As a result, gay-friendly retailers and hospitality and professional service providers have a unique opportunity to meet their need not to receive discriminatory or rude treatment.[119] Growth in the patronage of gay professionals and service firms has been supported by a growing number of local, gay-friendly business directories.[120] Services that concern household finances or retirement plans and wills are particular areas where gay providers may be preferred over others.

Mainstream marketers continue to be reluctant to target gays and lesbians overtly. IKEA and its agency Deutsch received hate mail after the firm's ads aired on television.[121] Norwegian Cruise Lines' gay cruise with 915 men was once denied docking privileges in the Cayman Islands. Visa was a target of the "religious right" for having contributed $10,000 to the Gay Games.[122] Some mainstream firms choose "after 10 p.m. time slots," because protesters are less likely to be tuned in at that time. Gay Day at Disneyworld was a quiet event that had attracted 60,000 participants in the mid-1990s with an estimated $2.4 million in admission ticket sales when this event and Disney's domestic partner benefits policy became the target of boycotts by the Christian Right. Ultimately, Disney, seeing intense competition for talented employees, decided that it had to continue to offer a variety of incentives that were gay friendly.[123] In 2010 on its twentieth anniversary Gay Day hosted 150,000 celebrants.[124] Other companies believe: "Alternative lifestyles have become part of mainstream America."[125] Even with this kind of leadership, interest in the gay and lesbian market seems to ebb and flow, but it responds more to opportunity than threat.

Members of the LGBT population do not necessarily respond to efforts that call attention to the sexual behavior that defines homosexuality. Depicting men or women in erotic contexts is a common visual image used in fashion photography. However, when communications overtly refer to "gay sexuality and behaviors," it can offend both gay and straight audiences. Younger and "out" LGBT consumers may not react as negatively to this kind of advertising, but many other LGBT consumers intensively dislike this approach.

As members of the gay subculture become more accepted by members of mainstream America, how will that affect gay consumers and their preferences in the marketplace? Some marketers fear that as more gay people "come out," they will merge into the general market and lose their interest in companies and products that are now reaching them with gay-specific strategies. Some young professionals refuse to use their sexual orientation as a "personal calling card" and have rejected gay affinity cards and merchandise.[126] However, as long as there are LGBT institutions, causes, and activism at the heart of the LGBT subculture, there will be opportunities to reach LGBT-identified consumers.[127]

Summary

The willingness of consumers to identify as gay or lesbian has made it more practical to target this community. The integration of homosexuality as part of an individual consumer's self-concept is a key step in openness to and preference for gay-friendly marketers. Because the gay population is not counted by independent sources such as the U.S. Census Bureau, there is significant uncertainty over the size of the gay population and important characteristics, such as income, spending patterns, or growth. And in spite of the lack of reliable statistics, mainstream and gay-owned companies alike have increased efforts to attract and retain LGBT consumers. The long-time presence of gay magazines as well as newer media options such as the Internet, gay television networks, multiple directories listing gay-friendly businesses, and direct marketing lists of gay consumers are major avenues for reaching gay consumers.

The gay subculture has its own language of signs and symbols, called "gay-speak," which is visible in gay media and in play as part of American popular culture in mainstream media. The growing unity of the gay community is due to discrimination from outside and to organizations within that represent gay interests to mainstream society. Gay consumers are loyal to organizations that not only recognize members of the LGBT subculture but also support the values and policies important to its members.

Notes

1. National Conference of State Legislatures, "Civil Unions and Domestic Partnership Statues," June 26, 2013, www.ncsl.org/research/human-services/civil-unions-and-domestic-partnership-statutes.aspx (MA, CN, VT, NH, DC, IA, NJ, OR, NV, WA, HW, WI, ME, RI, DL, IL, NY).

2. D. Johnson and A. Piore, "At Home in Two Worlds," *Newsweek*, October 18, 2004, 52; G. Lukenbill, *Untold Millions: Positioning Your Business for the Gay and Lesbian Consumer Revolution* (New York: HarperBusiness, 1995), 103–110.

3. D.G. Embruck, C.S. Walther, and C.M. Wickens, "Working Class Masculinity: Keeping Gay Men and Lesbians out of the Workplace," *Sex Roles* 56 (2007): 757–766; J. Cloud, "The Pioneer: Harvey Milk," *Time,* June 14, 1999, 183–186.

4. T.A. Stewart, "Gay in Corporate America: What's It Like and How Business Attitudes Are Changing," *Fortune,* December 16, 1991, 42–46, 50, 54, 56.

5. J.A. Costa, "Foreword," in *Gays, Lesbians, and Consumer Behavior: Theory, Practice, and Research Issues in Marketing,* ed. D.L. Wardlow (New York: Harrington Park Press, 1996), xvii–xviii.

6. B. Greene, "Lesbian and Gay Sexual Orientations: Implications for Clinical Training, Practice, and Research," in *Lesbian and Gay Psychology: Theory, Research and Clinical Applications,* ed. B. Greene and G. Herek (Thousand Oaks, CA: Sage, 1994), 1–25.

7. F.E. Jandt, *Intercultural Communication: An Introduction* (Thousand Oaks, CA: Sage, 1995), 356.

8. J. Cloud, "The Battle Over Gay Teens," *Time*, October 10, 2005, 42–51.

9. R.T. LeBeau and W.A. Jellison, "Why Get Involved? Exploring Gay and Bisexual Men's Experiences of the Gay Community," *Journal of Homosexuality* 56, no. 1 (2008): 56–76.

10. A. D'Augelli, "Lesbian and Gay Male Development: Steps Toward an Analysis of Lesbians' and Gay Men's Lives," in *Lesbian and Gay Psychology*, 118–132.

11. R. Witeck and W. Combs, *Business Inside Out: Capturing Millions of Brand Loyal Gay Consumers* (New York: Kaplan, 2006), 39.

12. G. Herek, "Gender Gaps in Public Opinion About Lesbians and Gay Men," *Public Opinion Quarterly* 66, no. 1 (2002): 40–66; G. Herek, "Assessing Heterosexuals' Attitudes Toward Lesbians and Gay Men," in *Lesbian and Gay Psychology*, 206–228; "Tuaca Targets Lesbians," *Marketing News*, August 14, 1995.

13. E. Svoboda, "Solving the Mystery of Gaydar," *Psychology Today* (January/February 2008): 73.

14. Witeck and Combs, *Business Inside Out*, 56.

15. K. Webley, "A Separate Peace?" *Time*, October 24, 2011, 40–46; M. Burford, "The Surge in Gary Teen Suicide," AOL, October 12, 2010, www.aolhealth.com/2010/10/12/gay-teen-suicide-surge/; Cloud, "The Battle over Gay Teens"; "Hate Crime," in Wikipedia, http://en.wikipedia.org/wiki/Hate_crime/.

16. J.L. Borgerson, J.E. Schroeder, B. Blomber, and E. Thorssen, "The Gay Family in the Ad: Consumer Responses to Non-Traditional Families in Marketing Communications," *Journal of Marketing Management* 22, no. 9 (2006): 955–578; L. Cobo-Hanlon, "My Child Is Gay, Que Hago?" *Latina* (November 1999): 122–125.

17. T.G. Sandfort, R.M. Melendez, and R.M. Diaz, "Gender Nonconformity, Homophobia, and Mental Distress in Latino and Bisexual Men," *Journal of Sex Research* 44, no. 2 (2007): 181–189; Jandt, *Intercultural Communication*, 357; Greene, "Lesbian and Gay Sexual Orientations."

18. G. Oakenfull and T. Greenlee, "Queer Eye for a Gay Guy: Using Market-Specific Symbols in Advertising to Attract Gay Consumers Without Alienating the Mainstream," *Psychology & Marketing* 22, no. 5 (2005): 421–439.

19. C. Kitzinger, "Social Constructionism: Implications for Lesbian and Gay Psychology," in *Lesbian, Gay, and Bisexual Identities over the Lifespan: Psychological Perspectives*, ed. A.R. D'Augelli and C.J. Patterson (New York: Oxford University Press, 1995).

20. Lukenbill, *Untold Millions*, 106–110.

21. MarketingCharts staff, "Most Gay-Friendly Brands: Bravo, Apple, Showtime, HBO, Absolut, Levi's," Marketing Charts, May 13, 2008, www.marketingcharts.com/wp/direct/most-gay-friendly-brands-bravo-apple-showtime-hbo-absolut-levis-4573/.

22. L. Fitzpatrick, "The Gender Conundrum," *Time*, November 19, 2007, 59; J. Cloud, "Trans Across America," *Time*, July 20, 1998, 48–49.

23. P. Painton, "The Shrinking Ten Percent," *Time*, April 26, 1993, 27–29.

24. E. Salholz and D. Glick, "The Power and the Pride," *Newsweek*, June 21, 1993, 54–60.

25. D. Tuller, "Gays, Lesbians Listed as 6 Percent of Population," *San Francisco Chronicle,* June 10, 1994, A3.

26. Lukenbill, *Untold Millions*, 51; Jandt, *Intercultural Communication*, 353; L. Peñaloza, "We're Here, We're Queer, and We're Going Shopping! A Critical Perspective on the Accommodation of Gays and Lesbians in the U.S. Marketplace," in *Gays, Lesbians, and Consumer Behavior*, 9–41.

27. S. Elliott, "A Sharper View of Gay Consumers," *New York Times*, June 9, 1994, D1, D19.

28. H. Kahan and D. Mulryan, "Out of the Closet," *American Demographics* (May 1995): 40–43, 46–47.

29. G.J. Gates and J. Ost, *The Gay and Lesbian Atlas* (Washington, DC: Urban Institute Press, 2004), 24–30.

30. Ibid., 27.

31. Ibid.

32. E. Duecy, "Attracting the Gay Consumer's Dollars: Lucrative Demographic Drives Marketing Push," *Nation's Restaurant News,* April 18, 2005; PRNewswire. "Buying Power of U.S. Gays and Lesbians to Exceed $835 Billion by 2011," January 25, 2007.

33. "Should You Be Marketing to Gay Consumers?" Electronic Retailer Blog. com, March 25, 2008.

34. Witeck and Combs, *Business Inside Out*, 58.

35. A. Keating and D. McLoughlin, "Understanding the Emergence of Markets: A Social Constructionist Perspective on Gay Economy," *Consumption Markets & Culture* 8, no. 2 (2005): 131–152; R. Alsop, "Are Gay People More Affluent Than Others?" *Wall Street Journal,* December 30, 1999, B1, B3.

36. M. O'Connell and S. Feliz, "Same-Sex Couple Household Statistics from the 2010 Census," SEHSD Working Paper Number 2011–26, U.S. Census Bureau, Washington, DC, September 27, 2011); Alsop, "Are Gay People More Affluent Than Others?"

37. B. Greene, ed., *Ethnic and Cultural Diversity Among Lesbians and Gay Men* (Thousand Oaks, CA: Sage, 1997).

38. L. Peplau, S. Cochran, and V. Mays, "A National Survey of the Intimate Relationships of African American Lesbians and Gay Men," in *Ethnic and Cultural Diversity Among Lesbians and Gay Men,* 11–38.

39. Gates and Ost, *The Gay and Lesbian Atlas*, 50–52.

40. C. Potgieter, "From Apartheid to Mandela's Constitution," in *Ethnic and Cultural Diversity Among Lesbians and Gay Men,* 88–116.

41. Cobo-Hanlon, "My Child Is Gay, Que Hago?"

42. B. Greene, "Ethnic Minority Lesbians and Gay Men: Mental Health and Treatment Issues," in *Ethnic and Cultural Diversity Among Lesbians and Gay Men,* 216–239.

43. Ibid.

44. Community Marketing Inc., Lesbian Consumer Index™ (San Francisco, 2007); Community Marketing Inc., Gay Consumer Index™ (San Francisco, 2007).

45. R. Alsop, "London, Paris Are Burning to Lure Gay Travelers in New Campaigns," *Wall Street Journal,* September 28, 1999, B10.

46. Ibid.; K. Jay and A. Young, *The Gay Report: Lesbians and Gay Men Speak Out About Sexual Experiences and Lifestyles* (New York: Summit, 1979), 796.

47. Jay and Young, *The Gay Report,* 798.

48. Kahan and Mulryan, "Out of the Closet."

49.R.E. Majors, "Discovering Gay Culture in America," in *Intercultural Communication: A Reader,* 7th ed., ed. L.A. Samovar and R.E. Porter (Belmont, CA: Wadsworth, 1994), 165–170.

50. K. McQueeney, "We Are God's Children, Y'all: Race, Gender, and Sexuality in Lesbian and Gay-Affirming Congregations," *Social Problems* 56, no. 1 (2009): 151–173.

51. J.J. McNeill, *Taking a Chance on God: Liberating Theology for Gays, Lesbians, and Their Lovers, Families, and Friends* (Boston: Beacon Press, 1988), 181; Metropolitan Community Churches, "I'm New to MCC," http://mccchurch.org/im-new-to-mcc/; Metropolitan Community Churches, "Who We Are," http://mccchurch.org/overview/.

52. Community Marketing & Insights, *2nd Annual LGBT Community Survey* (San Francisco, 2008), www.communitymarketinginc.com/gay-lesbian-market-intelligence/gay-research-gay-lesbian-consumer-index-demographics-2/.

53. Ibid.

54. Jay and Young, *The Gay Report*, 740–778.

55. J.M. Walters, "The Division of Labor in Same Sex Households: The Role of Gender in Housework" (master's thesis, University of Texas at Austin, 1992), 14.

56. Ibid.

57. Lukenbill, *Untold Millions*, 101; Jandt, *Intercultural Communication*, 357.

58. D. Altman, *The Homosexualization of America: The Americanization of the Homosexual* (New York: St. Martin's Press, 1982); S.M. Kates, *Twenty Million New Customers* (New York: Haworth Press, 1998); and M. Meyer, ed., *The Politics and Poetics of Camp* (New York: Routledge, 1994).

59. Meyer, *The Politics and Poetics of Camp*.

60. R. Kunzig, "Homosexuality May Persist Because the Associated Genes Convey Surprising Advantages on Homosexuals' Family Members," *Psychology Today* (May/June 2008): 89–93; M. Abrams, "The Real Story on Gay Genes," *Discover Magazine* (June 2007): http://discovermagazine.com/2007/jun/born-gay/; S. Begley, "Nature Plus Nurture," *Newsweek*, November 13, 1995, 72; L. Thompson, "Search for a Gay Gene," *Time*, June 12, 1995, 60–61.

61. Thompson, "Search for a Gay Gene."

62. "I. Violent Hate Crimes on the Rise," in Human Rights First, *2008 Hate Crime Survey: U.S.A.* (New York: Human Rights First, 2008), www.humanrightsfirst.org/discrimination/reports.aspx?s=usa&p=violent-hate-crimes-on-the-rise/.

63. J. Greene and M. France, "Culture Wars Hit Corporate America," *BusinessWeek*, May 23, 2005, 90–93; T.A. Stewart, "Gay in Corporate America: What's It Like and How Business Attitudes Are Changing," *Fortune*, December 16, 1991, 42–46, 50, 54, 56.

64. Harris Interactive/Witeck-Combs Communication, "Gay Consumers' Brand Loyalty Linked to Corporate Philanthropy and Advertising," press release, July 22, 2002.

65. Ibid.; S.M. Kates, "Out of the Closet and out on the Street! Gay Men and Their Brand Relationships," *Psychology & Marketing* 17, no. 6 (2000): 493–513.

66. G. Saveri, "The Importance of Being Solvent," *BusinessWeek*, May 29, 1995, 38.

67. "Clinton Pledges Review of LGBT Policies at State Department," *Advocate*, January 15, 2009.

68. D. Gudelunas, "Consumer Myths and the Gay Men and Women Who Believe Them: A Qualitative Look at Movements and Markets," *Psychology & Marketing* 28, no. 1 (2011): 53–68; B.J. Branchik, "Pansies to Parents: Gay Male Images in American Print Advertising," *Journal of Macromarketing* 27, no. 1 (2007): 38–50;

Harris Interactive/Witeck-Combs Communication, "Gay Consumers' Brand Loyalty Linked to Corporate Philanthropy and Advertising."

69. "Advertising in Gay Media Growing Three Times Faster Than Mainstream Media," PR Web, press release, June 4, 2007; www.prweb.com/releases/2007/06/prweb530917.htm.

70. J. Mathews, "From Closet to Mainstream," *Newsweek*, June 1, 1992, 62.

71. D.S. Levine, "Mainstream Advertisers Start to Discover Gay Market," *San Francisco Business Times,* July 21, 1995, 5; Prime Access/Rivendell Media Co., *2009 Gay Press Report* (New York: Prime Access, 2009), http://rivendellmedia.com/documents/gaypressreport2009.pdf.

72. M. Klein, "Gays and the Arts," *American Demographics* (March 1998): 33; Mulryan/Nash, *4th Annual Gay Press Report* (New York: Mulryan/Nash, 1997).

73. Jandt, *Intercultural Communication*, 362.

74. R. Macklin, *Gay and Lesbian Internet Users: The GLBT Community* (New York: eMarketer, November 2007).

75. Ibid.

76. D. Bank, "On the Web, Gay Sites Start to Click," *Wall Street Journal,* September 28, 1999, B1, B6.

77. D. Gudelunas, "Consumer Myths and the Gay Men and Women Who Believe Them: A Qualitative Look at Movements and Markets," *Psychology & Marketing* 28, no. 1 (2011): 53–68; K.L. Smith, "How Advertisers use the World Wide Web to Reach Niche Markets" (MA thesis, University of Texas at Austin, 1998).

78. Bank, "On the Web, Gay Sites Start to Click."

79. Nielsen, "The New Mainstream 28% of TV Watching Spent on LGBT-Inclusive Shows," October 27, 2011, www.nielsen.com/us/en/newswire/2011/the-new-mainstream-28-of-tv-watching-spent-on-lgbt-inclusive-shows.html; J. Poniewozik, "TV's Coming Out," *Time*, October 25, 1999, 116–117.

80. A.D. Winter, "The Gay Press of the United States: A History of the Gay Community and Its Publications" (MA thesis, University of Texas at Austin, 1975), 103–111.

81. J. Flint, "Viacom's Logo Launches with Beer," *Wall Street Journal,* June 28, 2005, B5; Media Education Foundation, *Off the Straight and Narrow: Lesbians, Gays, Bisexuals and Television,* documentary (London: Media Education Foundation, 1998).

82. G. Oakenfull and T. Greenlee, "Gayness Is in the Eye of the Beholder: Using Market-Specific Symbols in Advertising to Attract Gays and Lesbians Without Alienating the Mainstream," *Advances in Consumer Research* 31, no. 1 (2004): 633–653; Lukenbill, *Untold Millions*, 7–16; Jandt, *Intercultural Communication*, 360.

83. S.G. Beatty, "VW Is Not Steering Clear of 'Ellen' Episode," *Wall Street Journal,* April 25, 1997.

84. R. Marin, "Lick Me, Flog Me, Buy Me!" *Newsweek*, December 29, 1997–January 5, 1998, 85; Lukenbill, *Untold Millions*, 17.

85. W.H.S. Tsai, "What Does It Mean to be Gay in American Consumer Culture? Gay Advertising and Gay Consumers: A Cultural Studies Perspective" (Ph.D. dissertation, University of Texas at Austin, 2006).

86. L. Petrecca and J.B. Arndorfer, "Insurer Places Gay-Themed Ads in Mainstream Media," *Advertising Age,* March 2, 1998, 12.

87. R. Alsop, "Brewers Employ in-Your-Mug Approach," *Wall Street Journal,* June 29, 1999, B1.

88. K. Ocamb, "Someone's in the Desert with Dinah," *Advocate* (March 1998), 39–40.

89. Levine, "Mainstream Advertisers Start to Discover Gay Market."

90. Kahan and Mulryan, "Out of the Closet."

91. J.E. Bowes, "Out of the Closet and into the Marketplace: Meeting Basic Needs in the Gay Community," in *Gays, Lesbians, and Consumer Behavior*, 221; A. Freitas, S. Kaiser, and T. Hammidi, "Communities, Commodities, Cultural Space, and Style," in ibid., 83–107.

92. "The Pink Pound in the Americas-In Endless Bloom," *Euromonitor International* (2009), www.euromonitor.com/passport/ResultsList.aspx; R. Alsop, "In Marketing to Gays, Lesbians Are Often Left Out," *Wall Street Journal*, October 10, 1999, B1, B4.

93. Peñaloza, "We're Here, We're Queer, and We're Going Shopping!"

94. B. Chase, "Gay Economy Lures Dollars of Major Advertisers," in *Facing Difference: Race, Gender, and Mass Media*, ed. S. Biagi and M. Kern-Foxworth (Thousand Oaks, CA: Pine Forge Press, 1997), 179–181.

95. N.A. Rudd, "Appearance and Self-Presentation Research in Gay Consumer Cultures: Issues and Impact," in *Gays, Lesbians, and Consumer Behavior*, 129.

96. "Tuaca Targets Lesbians."

97. D. Colman, "Gay or Straight? Hard to Tell," *New York Times*, June 29, 2005, 9-1; R. Alsop, "Cracking the Gay Market Code: How Marketers Plant Subtle Symbols in Ads," *Wall Street Journal,* June 29, 1999, B1, B4.

98. J.L. Borgerson, J.E. Schroeder, B. Blomber, and E. Thorssen, "The Gay Family in the Ad: Consumer Responses to Non-Traditional Families in Marketing Communications," *Journal of Marketing Management* 22, no. 9 (2006): 955–978; S.M. Kates, "Making the Ad Perfectly Queer: Marketing 'Normality' to the Gay Men's Community," *Journal of Advertising* 28, no. 1 (1999): 25–37.

99. D. Clark, "Commodity Lesbianism," *Camera Oscura* 9, nos. 1–2, 25–26 (1991): 183, as cited in Freitas, Kaiser, and Hammidi, "Communities, Commodities, Cultural Space, and Style."

100. Alsop, "Cracking the Gay Market Code."

101. Ibid.

102. Kates, "Making the Ad Perfectly Queer"; V.F. Zonana, "Who Madison Avenue Wakes up with," *Out* (Summer 1992): 40–43.

103. K. Kranhold, "Groups for Gay Employees Are Gaining Traction," *Wall Street Journal,* April 3, 2006, B3; S. Baker and P. Judge, "Where IBM Goes, Others May Follow," *BusinessWeek,* October 17, 1996, 39.

104. Lukenbill, *Untold Millions*, 134–135.

105. S.M. Kates, "The Protean Quality of Subcultural Consumption: An Ethnographic Account of Gay Consumers," *Journal of Consumer Research* 29, no. 3 (2002): 383–399.

106. Kates, *Twenty Million New Customers*, 82–92.

107. MarketingCharts staff, "Index Seeks to Codify Gay and Lesbian Psychographic, Demographic Data," Marketing Charts, August 16, 2007, www.marketingcharts.com/wp/television/index-seeks-to-codify-gay-and-lesbian-psychographic-demographic-data-1297/; B. Vandecasteele and M. Geuens, "Revising the Myth of Gay Consumer Innovativeness," *Journal of Business Research* 62, no. 1 (2009): 134–144.

108. E. Duecy, "Attracting the Gay Consumers' Dollars"; K.T. Drummond, "Not in Kansas Anymore," *Time*, September 25, 1995, 54–55.

109. M. Wolk, "Mainstream Marketers Treat Gay Publications with Respect," *Houston Chronicle*, June 21, 1992.

110. Kates, "Out of the Closet and out on the Street!"; Lukenbill, *Untold Millions*, 35–36.

111. J.S. Hirsch, "New Credit Cards Base Appeals on Sexual Orientation and Race," *Wall Street Journal*, November 9, 1995, B1, B9.

112. "Equal Values (special advertising section)," *BusinessWeek*/GLAAD, September 5, 2011; S. Warren, "Business Owners Cautiously Begin Targeting Pitches To Gay Market," *Wall Street Journal*, October 25, 1995, T1, T4.

113. M. Frazier, "Wal-Mart Partners with Gay and Lesbian Group," *Advertising Age*, August 24, 2006; Alsop, "Are Gay People More Affluent Than Others?"; Peñaloza, "We're Here, We're Queer, and We're Going Shopping!"

114. H. Buford, author interview, New York, September 11, 1999; Alsop, "Are Gay People More Affluent Than Others?"; M. Cox, "New Magazines Cater to People with HIV," *Wall Street Journal*, March 1, 1994, B1.

115. Freitas, Kaiser, and Hammidi, "Communities, Commodities, Cultural Space, and Style."

116. Rudd, "Appearance and Self-Presentation Research in Gay Consumer Cultures."

117. Vandecasteele and Geuens, "Revising the Myth of Gay Consumer Innovativeness"; S.M. Kates, "Dynamics of Brand Legitimacy: An Interpretive Study in the Gay Men's Community," *Journal of Consumer Research* 31, no. 2 (2004): 455–464; MarketingCharts staff, "Gay, Lesbian, Bisexual and Transgender Adults Penalize GLBT-Unfriendly Biz," Marketing Charts, press release, September 27, 2007, www.marketingcharts.com/wp/direct/gay-lesbian-bisexual-and-transgender-adults-penalize-glbt-unfriendly-biz-1812/.

118. MarketingCharts staff, "Most Gay-Friendly Brands: Bravo, Apple, Showtime, HBO, Absolut, Levi's."

119. A.S. Walters and M.C. Curran, "Excuse Me, Sir. May I Help You and Your Boyfriend? Salespersons' Differential Treatment of Homosexual and Straight Customers," in *Gays, Lesbians, and Consumer Behavior*, 144–145; D.A. Jones, "Discrimination Against Same-Sex Couples in Hotel Reservation Policies," in *Gays, Lesbians, and Consumer Behavior*, 153–159.

120. C. Farrell, "Beyond Ozzie and Harriet," *Bloomberg BusinessWeek*, December 14, 2009, 70–71; Lukenbill, *Untold Millions*, 171; and S. Warren, "Business Owners Cautiously Begin Targeting Pitches to Gay Market," *Wall Street Journal*, October 25, 1995, T1, T4.

121. J. Greene and M. France, "Culture Wars Hit Corporate America," *BusinessWeek*, May 23, 2005, 90–93; S. Elliott, "This Weekend, a Business Expo Will Show the Breadth of New Interest in Gay Consumers," *New York Times*, April 14, 1994.

122. Peñaloza, "We're Here, We're Queer, and We're Going Shopping!" 35.

123. S. Gill, "Never Say Never-Never Land," *Out* (March 1998): 70–74, 113.

124. Wikipedia, "Gay Days at Walt Disney World," http://en.wikipedia.org/wiki/Gay_Days_at_Walt_Disney_World/.

125. G. Saveri, "The Importance of Being Solvent," *BusinessWeek*, May 29, 1995, 38.

126. E. Gutierrez, "Beyond Gay: A New Generation of Homosexuals Claim to be Happy Not Being Gay," *Genre* (June 1996): 51–53.

127. G.P. Zachary, *The Global Me* (New York: Public Affairs, 2000).

8

Asian Americans

Realizing the "Asian-American" Dream

The term "Asian American" refers to a broad swath of peoples with origins in Asia, the Indian subcontinent and the Pacific Rim. As a signifier of identity, it is as meaningless as the term "European American." It is useful for comparison with other *Americans*, but it does not capture the vast differences *among* Asian Americans or the ways in which individuals describe themselves. Although Asian Americans are accustomed to filling in forms with the designation "Asian American," virtually no Asian-American family socializes children into "Asian" customs and traditions—only into "Japanese," "Chinese," "Korean," "Vietnamese," "Filipino," (Asian) "Indian," et al., traditions.

As Imada writes, there is no global agreement on which specific groups compose an "Asian" heritage.[1] In this chapter, we employ the definition of "Asian Americans" used by the U.S. Census Bureau, which includes 16 ethnic groups under its designation "Asian American": Asian Indian, Bangladeshi, Cambodian, Chinese, Filipino, Hmong, Indonesian, Japanese, Korean, Laotian, Malaysian, Pakistani, Sri Lankan, Taiwanese, Thai, and Vietnamese.

Table 8.1 shows the Asian American population from eight of these countries of origin. This inclusive definition is an important one for marketers for several reasons. First, grouping consumers with East Asian, Southeast Asian, and Indian heritage is a convenient way to gain insight into their general marketplace preferences and behaviors, but it is not the avenue for reaching them as consumers. Different languages and ethnic-oriented media must be taken into consideration when developing marketing communication programs. Second, the different languages and communities that comprise Asian America are significant enough that marketers must decide whether the costs of attempting to reach all Asian Americans justify the effort. Few economies of scale can be built if an overall strategy must be implemented via messages in various languages and media.

Table 8.1 reveals distinctive patterns of Asian-American presence in different locations. For example, Asian Indian-Americans make up one-fourth of Asian Americans in New York, but only 10 percent of Asian Americans in California. Chinese Americans comprise 40 percent of New York Asian Americans, but significantly less in all other states. Filipinos have the strongest presence in California, Hawaii, and Nevada; Japanese Americans make up the largest percentage of Asian Americans in Florida, Hawaii, and Illinois; Vietnamese favor California, Georgia, and Illinois. Such differences in where Asian-American subgroups cluster makes it expensive to reach Asian Americans in their native languages.

Another reason to question how to target Asian Americans is the "chameleon" behavior of many Asian-American consumers, as described later in this chapter. Their tendency to align with white Americans creates a marketing dilemma: design special communications efforts or stick with a campaign targeted to mainstream Americans? Factors such as whether a product or its purchase reflects status and belonging or is the subject of substantial word of mouth may be more important than consumer ethnicity in reaching Asian-American consumers. Examples of successful marketing efforts using various approaches with Asian American consumers exist, and none is an inherently superior strategy.

Asian America: Diversity of Cultures, Resources, and Experiences

Shared Experience as Twentieth-Century Immigrants

The growth in our Asian-American population has been due primarily to changes in U.S. immigration policy and conflicts in Southeast Asia. Waves of immigration from China and Japan in the nineteenth century were reduced to a trickle by strict quotas set forth early in the twentieth century. A 1965 change in immigration laws in effect reopened migration from the Pacific. The 1965 law allowed members of families already living in the United States, and professionals with needed skills, education, and knowledge, to seek legal residency. Using these family and professional quotas, a great number of Chinese, Koreans, Filipinos, and Asian Indians began migrating to the United States.

U.S. involvement in the Vietnam War resulted in an influx of refugees from Vietnam, Laos, and Cambodia. The Southeast Asian refugees came after 1975, when the war ended for the United States, and another large wave arrived after

Table 8.1

Origins of Asian-American Population: U.S. Total and Top Ten Asian-American States, 2010

State	Total population	Asian Americans	Asian Indian Americans	Chinese Americans	Filipino Americans	Japanese Americans	Korean Americans	Vietnamese Americans	Other Asian Americans*
U.S.	308,745,538 100.0%	17,320,856 5.6%	3,183,063 18.4%	4,010,114 23.2%	3,416,814 19.7%	1,304,286 7.5%	1,706,822 9.8%	1,737,433 10.0%	1,963,298 11.3%
CA	36,308.5	5,555.6 15.3%	10.4%	26.0%	25.2%	6.5%	9.2%	12.0%	10.9%
NY	19,423.9	1,579.5 8.1%	25.2%	40.4%	8.2%	2.9%	9.8%	2.7%	36.8%
TX	23,819.0	1,110.7 4.7%	22.6%	25.2%	17.6%	11.4%	2.2%	7.3%	13.7%
NJ	8,650.5	795.2 8.2%	38.5%	19.3%	17.0%	2.3%	13.2%	3.5%	6.3%
IL	12,785.0	668.7 5.2%	4.7%	31.6%	18.4%	20.0%	3.6%	11.6%	10.5%
HI	1,380.2	780.9 56.6%	.4%	10.6%	35.2%	38.1%	4.7%	1.8%	9.2%
WA	6,465.8	604.3 9.3%	11.4%	20.1%	19.5%	8.7%	13.5%	14%	12.8%
FL	18,222.4	573.1 3.1%	13.8%	28.1%	15.8%	19.7%	3.4%	6.2%	13.2%
GA	9,497.7	365.5 3.8%	15.7%	29.5%	15.0%	6.3%	3.0%	17.1%	13.4%
NV	2,545.8	242.9 9.5%	4.9%	15.3%	51.5%	7.0%	6.4%	4.7%	10.1%

Source: U.S. Census Bureau, The Asian Population: 2010 (Washington, DC, 2012).
*Other Asian Americans include Laotian Americans (199,433, 1.4%), Pakistani Americans (333,064, 2.4%), Cambodian Americans (241,520, 1.8%), Hmong Americans (226,522, 1.6%), Thai Americans (165,371, 1.2%), Taiwanese Americans (98,374, 0.7%), Indonesian Americans (86,973, 0.6%), Bangladeshi Americans (102,983, 0.7%), other Asian Americans (299,259, 2.2%).

passage of the Refugee Act of 1980. In less than 40 years, the Asian-American population was transformed from one that involved a few countries of origin to one that encompasses significant diversity. In 1970, 96 percent of Asian Americans were Chinese, Japanese, or Filipino, and most of their families had immigrated to the United States from the 1850s to the 1930s. In the 1990s, however, these groups accounted for only 54 percent of Asian Americans. By comparison, while in 1980 only 8 percent of all Asian Americans were from Southeast Asia, by 1989 persons from Vietnam, Cambodia, and Laos accounted for 40 percent of Asian-American immigrants.[2] By the time of the 2010 census, those with Chinese, Japanese, or Filipino heritage comprised 50 percent of the Asian-American population, and those with Vietnamese, Cambodian, and Laotian heritage accounted for 13 percent.

Table 8.1 also illustrates how the Asian American population has changed over time. The table shows that Japanese Americans declined from over 40 percent in 1970 to 7.5 percent in 2010. Vietnamese and Asian Indians were not even counted in the 1970 Census, and yet Asian Indians jumped to 18 percent of the 2010 Asian-American population.

Table 8.2 shows the size of the Asian-American population since 1970 and projections for Asian Americans up to 2050. In the decade between 2000 and 2010, the Asian population grew over 45 percent. The census projections in Table 8.2 have the Asian-American population growing from 10.2 million in 2000 to 33.4 million in 2050.[3] Given the radical change in the composition of Asian Americans in the past 30 years, the share for different countries of origin should be expected to continue to fluctuate over the next 35 years.

Annual growth of 4 percent per year during the 1990s made Asian Americans the fastest-growing ethnic group in the United States. Numbering more than 17 million in 2010, the Asian-American population almost doubled since 1990 and now accounts for more than 5.4 percent of the U.S. population. All Asian Americans now number more than Latino immigrants.[4] By 2050, it is estimated that Asian Americans might comprise 8 percent of the U.S. population. The contributions to expected growth from 1990 to 2050 in the U.S. population of five American groups, including Asian Americans, are shown in Table 8.3.[5]

The recent, large increases in the Asian-American population include a large number of those born overseas, currently about two-thirds of the total. Undoubtedly, those born in the United States and those born in Asia who immigrated here have drastically different American experiences. Those born in the country, who may be the second, third, or fourth generation, comprise only about 32 percent of the Asian-American population but comprise nearly 80 percent of Asian Americans under age 18.[6] Although those born here and those born outside the United States may share physical appearances, the

Table 8.2

Asian-American Population Trends, 1970–2020

	1970	1980	1990	2000	2010	2020	2030	2040	2050
Total U.S. population	203,302	226,542	248,709	281,422	308,936	335,805	363,584	391,946	419,854
Total U.S. Asian population	1,357	3,726	7,273	10,243	14,241	17,988	22,580	27,992	33,430
Asian % of U.S. population	0.6	1.6	2.9	3.6	4.6	5.4	6.2	7.1	8.0

Source: U.S. Census Bureau, "U.S. Interim Population Projections by Age, Sex, Race, and Hispanic Origin" (Washington, DC, March 18, 2004) http://www.census.gov/ipc/www/usinterimproj/.

Table 8.3

Comparative Population Growth of American Ethnic Groups, 1990–2050

| | Percentage of U.S. population growth | | | | | |
	Asian American	White American	African American	Native American	U.S. Hispanic	Total (%)
1990–1995	12.8	37.0	16.6	1.0	32.7	100.1
1995–2000	15.2	29.6	16.7	1.0	37.5	100.0
2000–2005	16.5	24.2	16.9	1.1	41.3	100.0
2005–2010	16.6	22.0	16.9	1.2	43.3	100.0
2010–2020	16.6	20.2	16.3	1.1	46.0	100.2
2020–2030	18.4	10.8	16.2	1.2	53.5	100.1
2030–2040	20.0	(X)*	17.0	1.4	63.2	101.6*
2040–2050	20.1	(X)*	17.4	1.4	68.2	107.1*

Source: U.S. Census Bureau, *Current Population Reports: Population Projections of the United States by Age, Sex, Race, and Hispanic Origin: 1995 to 2050*, Report P25-1130 (Washington, DC: U.S. Department of Commerce, 1996), table 1, www.census.gov/prod/1/pop/p25-1130/p251130.pdf.

*Percentages do not add to 100 percent because of the declining size of the "White, not Hispanic" population in these years.

strength of their ethnic identity and relationships to other Americans are very different.

In contrast to the pattern of the late twentieth century, in the next decade the foreign-born segment of the Asian-American population is expected to decline to from 66 percent to 50 percent.[7] The higher relative number of U.S.-born Asian Americans will lower the average age of Asian Americans and increase their exposure to American socialization agents in school and media. We can expect continued changes in their core values, ethnic identities, and marketplace needs and behaviors.

If immigrants are considered "generation 1.0" and native-born Americans are "generation 2.0," what is "generation 1.5"? This nickname is used for foreign-born Americans who immigrate before adulthood. Age of immigration is inversely related to English-language proficiency and closely correlated to acculturation in American culture.[8] In other words, younger immigrants have better English acquisition and adjustment to and understanding of American culture. Highly acculturated individuals behave more like mainstream Americans than do persons from their home countries.[9] Children who grow up in immigrant households often play an important role as a family "change agent," helping the family to adapt to life in America. Their acculturation tends to be greater than that of their parents.[10] At the same time, generation 1.5 does not share the same self-identity as those with ancestry in the same country of origin who were born here. Generation 1.5's identity reflects stronger ties to the country of origin and its cultural norms as well as to global consumer culture.[11]

Paradoxes of the "Model Minority"

The ancestors of Asian Americans include Asian Indians, Pakistanis, Chinese, Filipinos, Japanese, Koreans, Malaysians, Thai, Vietnamese, Cambodians, Laotians, Indonesians, and Guamans as well as subculture groups such as the Hmong of Vietnam, Laos, and Cambodia. The people of these countries of origin have different languages, religions, cultural histories, traditions, and values. To consider Chinese no different from Koreans because they are all Asian Americans ignores important cultural and historical differences among their countries of origin as well as their different histories in the United States.

The Japanese, as the earliest Asian-American community, are significantly different from the Hmong, who are among the most recent Asian immigrants. These differences are reflected in their levels of education, English proficiency, and per capita income. Although education is highly valued among most Asian Americans, actual educational attainment tends to differ greatly among the subgroups. About 91 percent of Japanese Americans have at least a high school education, compared with only 30 percent of Hmong Americans. Japanese Americans have a per capita income three times that of the Hmong.[12] These differences across cultural groups that comprise Asian Americans lead to what appear to be contradictory statistics. For example, median household income of Asian Americans is higher than it is of non-Hispanic whites, while at the same time the poverty rate of Asian Americans is higher (12 percent) than that for all Americans (10 percent). The Hmong's 32 percent family poverty rate is in dramatic contrast to the 5 percent family poverty rate among Filipino Americans.[13]

Tables 8.4 and 8.5 shed more light on education and income levels of Asian Americans, compared with other Americans. About one-fourth of Asian Americans had a bachelor's degree in 2011, compared to about 14 percent of white Americans, about 10 percent of black Americans, and about 8 percent of U.S. Latinos. A little over 50 percent of Asian Americans have either a bachelor's or advanced degree. Asian Americans place a high value on education, as shown by these statistics. For instance, in 2008 about 45 percent of incoming freshmen at the University of California at Berkeley were Asian American compared with white (30 percent), Hispanic (9 percent), and African-American students (4 percent).[14]

On average, Asian Americans also have higher income, and their median family incomes exceed that of all other American ethnicities. Asian Americans had a median income of $72,770, the highest of any group. In

Table 8.4

Education Levels of White, Black, and Asian Americans, 2011

Educational attainment	Total population > 25 years (000s)	% of population > 25 years	% of white population > 25 years	% of black population > 25 years	% of Asian population > 25 years	% of Hispanic population > 25 years
Total population > 25 years	201,543	28	163,979	23,364	9,723	26.672
		100	100	100	100	
Less than high school	17,873	8.9	14.7	18.6	12	38.5
High school diploma	56,404	28	28.1	32	21	27
Some college	34,203.	17.5	16.9	19.8	10.2	13.6
Associate degree	19,046	10.6	9.5	9.9	6.4	6.7
Bachelor's degree	28,733	14.3	14.4	9.8	24.2	7.6
Advanced study/degree	32,611	16.2	16.6	10.0	26.2	6.5
Total		95.5	100.1	100.1	100.0	99.9

Source: U.S. Census Bureau, *Current Population Survey, 2011: Annual Social and Economic Supplement* (Washington, DC, 2011); U.S. Census Bureau, "Table 231: Educational Attainment by Selected Characteristics: 2010" (Washington, DC, 2012), www.census.gov/compendia/statab/2012/tables/12s0231.pdf.

Table 8.5

Median Family Income of White, Black, and Asian Americans, 2011

	Total population (25+)	%	White, not Hispanic	%	Black	%	Asian	%	U.S. Hispanics	%
All families: median incomes	$60,974	100	$69,829	100	$40,472	100	$72,770	100	$40,061	100
	# HHs	%	# HHs	%	# HHs	%	# HHs	%	#HHs	%
# of households	121,084	100	83,573	100	16,165	100	5,705	100	14,939	100
Less than $20,000	23,242		13,387	16.0	5,337	33.02	859	15.06	3,521	23.57
$20,000–$39,999	26,489		17,176	20.56	3,999	24.74	975	17.09	4,149	27.78
$40,000–$59,999	20,160		13,954	16.70	2,527	15.63	801	14.04	2,769	18.54
$60,000–$79,999	15,326		11,173	13.37	1,618	10.01	736	12.90	1,681	11.25
$80,000–$99,999	10,447		7,782	9.31	969	5.99	570	9.99	1,053	7.05
$100,000–$199,999	20,316		15,917	19.05	1,456	9.01	1,358	23.80	1,512	10.12
$200,000 and above	5,106		4,187	5.01	259	1.60	403	7.06	245	1.64

Source: "2011 Household Income Table of Contents," in U.S. Census Bureau, *Current Population Survey 2011: Annual Social and Economic Supplement* (Washington, DC, 2012), www.census.gov/hhes/www/cpstables/032012/hhinc/hinc01_000.htm.
HH = households.

2011 more than 30 percent of Asian-American households earned more than $100,000.[15] High education and income levels not only have attracted marketers to Asian American consumers but also are the basis for their being called the "model minority." About 75 percent of Asian-American buying power is located in the top 10 states.[16] Asian-American purchasing power reached $528 billion in 2009 and $544 billion in 2010 and is expected to exceed $1 trillion by 2017.[17]

High growth, high education, and high income make Asian Americans a desirable market. However, as noted above, not all Asian Americans can currently fit the "model minority" stereotype, as the group comprises both extremely successful and well educated "bananas" (a derogatory term used among Asian Americans for those who are "yellow on the outside but white on the inside," trying too hard to fit into mainstream America) and a large undereducated group of recent immigrants (sometimes called FOBs [fresh off the boat], by other Asian Americans).[18] Some 47 percent are in management, professional, and related occupations.[19] In spite of these successes, Asian Americans occupy less than two-tenths of 1 percent of all corporate director-ships and may face a "glass ceiling" in attempts to reach that level. A large number of Asian Americans have become entrepreneurs, in part as a reaction to this situation.[20] Koreans, in particular, are highly likely to be self-employed (15 percent), compared with all Asian Americans (6.5 percent).[21]

As many of these conflicting statistics suggest, Asian Americans with dif-ferent countries of origin, whether born in the United States or abroad, have different consumer and socialization needs. Differences exist in religion, language, and economic background, even within each cultural group. Asian-American consumers must be thought of, looked at, and talked to in different ways even when considering members of one country-of-origin. It is critical to develop a clear target market among Asian American groups.

The Important Role of Community Among Asian Americans

Asian immigrants prefer to live near friends and family members: because of unique immigration patterns and new immigrants joining family businesses. Asian American populations have tended to concentrate on the West Coast, in particular in gateway cities like San Francisco, Honolulu, Seattle, and Los Angeles, and on the East Coast in New York. Over 4.5 million Asian Americans live in California alone.[22] Table 8.6 lists which states in the United States have the highest concentration of Asian Americans. For example, over 60 percent of Asian Americans live in just five states: California, New York, Texas, New Jersey, and Hawaii. In some communities in Silicon Valley such as Cupertino, CA, the Asian-American population has grown to over 40 percent of the

Table 8.6

Top Asian-American States and Selected Cities, 2010

City or state all Americans	Total population	Number of Asian Americans	Percentage of local Americans	Percentage of all Asian-American population
All Americans (2010)				
All Asian Americans		17,320.9	05.61	100.0
Selected U.S. States				
Top Ten Total		12,584.9		72.67
California	36,961.6	5,556.1	15.0	32.08
New York	19,541.4	1,579.5	08.1	09.12
Texas	15,634.2	1,110.7	07.1	06.41
New Jersey	8,707.7	795.2	09.1	04.60
Hawaii	1,295.2	780.9	60.3	04.51
Illinois	12,910.4	668.7	05.2	03.86
Washington	6,664.2	604.3	09.1	03.49
Florida	18,538.0	573.1	03.1	03.31
Virginia	7,882.6	522.2	06.6	03.01
Massachusetts	6,593.6	394.2	05.9	02.28
Other States		2,666.8		15.40
Pennsylvania	12,604.8	402.6	02.8	02.21
Georgia	9,829.2	365.9	03.4	02.08
Maryland	5,699.5	370.0	05.8	02.08
Michigan	9,969.7	289.6	02.8	01.74
North Carolina	9,380.9	252.6	02.4	01.42
Minnesota	5,266.2	247.1	04.2	01.40
Ohio	11,542.6	238.3	01.9	01.36
Arizona	6,595.8	230.9	03.3	01.35
Nevada	2,643.1	242.9	07.9	01.30
District of Columbia	599.6	26.9	03.8	00.14
Selected Cities (2006)				
Honolulu, HI			64.3	
San Francisco, CA			18.1	
Stockton, CA			15.3	
Yuba City, CA			11.5	
Los Angeles, CA			11.1	
Merced, CA			10.3	
San Diego, CA			10.2	
Salinas, CA			10.1	
Sacramento, CA			9.7	
Fresno, CA			9.3	
New York, NY			6.2	
Seattle, WA			7.7	
Washington, DC			4.8	
Houston, TX			4.8	

Sources: U.S. Census Bureau, *The Asian Population: 2010* (Washington, DC, 2012); U.S. Census Bureau, American FactFinder, 2009, http://factfinder2.census.gov/faces/nav/jsf/pages/index.xhtml; U.S. Census Bureau, "Resident Population by Race, Hispanic or Latino Origin, and State," 2006, www.census.gov/compendia/statab/tables/08s0018.pdf.

total.[23] This extreme concentration makes them easy to reach, even though the population may be small and may speak many different languages.

The Asian-American proclivity for living in established enclaves highlights the cultural importance of community. Ethnic enclaves called "Chinatown," "Koreatown," or "Little Saigon" exist in most cities with large Asian-American populations. These communities not only provide services, housing, and jobs but symbolize cultural unity and provide a physical center for cultural rituals. Bilinguals in these ethnic neighborhoods assist new immigrants in their transition to American life. By 1994, most acculturated Asian Americans were living in suburbs, and today 95 percent of Asian Americans live in metropolitan areas. They continue to prefer ethnic institutions as varied as churches, schools, legal, medical and other professional services, ethnic groceries, and language tutors.[24]

Most Asian suburbanites who live in Western states concentrate in California towns such as Daly City (Filipino), Walnut Creek, San Marino, San Gabriel, Pasadena (Indian Americans), Westminster (Vietnamese), or Monterey Park (Chinese). Seven of the top ten suburbs with a high Asian population are on the Pacific Rim: Los Angeles (CA), San Jose (CA), San Francisco (CA), Honolulu (HI), San Diego (CA), Fremont (CA), and Seattle (CA). But most recent growth in Asian-American population is taking place in middle America.[25] In addition to California, Hmong people are concentrated in the Midwest, in states such as Minnesota, Wisconsin, Michigan, and Colorado, while Laotians are concentrated in Texas, Minnesota, and Washington.

It is no accident that Japanese, Chinese, and Filipinos comprise the majority of Asians who live in Hawaii, California, and Washington state, as these were where earlier immigrants established ethnic neighborhoods. More recent Chinese, Korean, Indian, and Vietnamese and other immigrants live in sizable numbers in Massachusetts, northern New Jersey, and Texas. Asian-American–focused media and merchandise are easier to find in these areas. These communities have the dual roles of continuing country-of-origin lifestyles and cultural traditions as well as easing adjustment to American life.

Another expression of the importance of community in Asian-American life is the concentration of people from a particular country of origin in specific professions or businesses. Typically small business ownership is a way for immigrants to make the best use of available resources such as family labor, but the children of such small business owners often become professionals.[26] Indian Americans work disproportionately in engineering and high technology and Vietnamese Americans in agriculture, fishing, and personal services.

The household is an important unit of consumer decision making and a link to the greater Asian-American and mainstream communities. Asian Americans, especially first-generation immigrants, are more likely than non-Hispanic white

Table 8.7

Household Types: U.S. Averages Compared with Asian-American Averages, 2010

	Total U.S. households		U.S. Asian households	
	#	%	#	%
Family households	77,538.7	66.4	5,222.9	73.1
Married couples	56,510.4	48.4	3,042.7	58.3
Female head of household*	15,250.3	13.1	522.7	10.0
Male head of household*	5,777.6	5.0	253.3	4.8
Nonfamily households	39,177.9	33.6	1,404.3	26.9
Householder alone	31,204.9	26.7	1,007.1	19.3
Female householder, living alone	17,298.6	14.8	530.4	10.2
Male householder, living alone	13,906.3	11.9	476.7	9.1
Total	116,716.3	100.0	4,040	100.0

Source: U.S. Census Bureau, "Profile of General Population and Housing Characteristics: 2010, 2010 Census Summary File 1," American FactFinder, 2011, http://factfinder2.census.gov/faces/tableservices/jsf/pages/productview.xhtml?pid=DEC_10_SF1_SF1DP1&prodType=table/.
    *No spouse present.

Americans to live in extended family households. Consequently, the average Asian-American household is larger (3,98 persons) than the average U.S. family (3.12 persons).[27] As Table 8.7 shows, Asian households contain more married couples and nonfamily households. Several unrelated couples, extended family members, multiple generations, or single people live together to save money. Compared to white or African Americans, fewer Asian Americans live alone.

Continued Traditions

> *"Someday you will see," said my mother.*
> *"It is in your blood, waiting to be let go."*
>
> (Amy Tan, *The Joy Luck Club*)[28]

Confucian Influence on Asian-American Values

Despite having diverse languages, customs, and religions, most Asian Americans share some common values, rooted in the doctrines of Confucius. Confucianism relies on a hierarchical belief system with the emperor (or ruling authority) at the top, and various levels of authority: the son to the father, the younger to the elder, the wife to the husband, and all of society to the throne. It is an overarching system that governs all relationships within the family and society.[29]

Confucianism is also imbued with a conservatism that can delay the adoption of new ideas or innovations. This may be because risk-taking increases the chance of "losing face" when going against community norms. Thriftiness is another tenet of Confucian beliefs and is taught as the norm.[30] This conservatism is reflected in the preferred vehicle for money management among Asian Americans. They typically prefer to save rather than invest in stocks, and investment in land is considered the best way to preserve wealth because "land is the last thing to change." This deeply ingrained Confucian code of manners, social relations, and outlook has a major influence over the ways in which Asian Americans think and act.

Table 8.8 includes some translations of sayings that express the Confucian worldview, contrasted with "lessons" from American sayings. It is interesting to note how unknown people are treated in Eastern and Western cultures. Asians tend to believe in "enemies until friends," while Americans base relationships on the premise that "all men are created equal." The strong "insider" bias of Asians prescribes different codes of behavior for friends and family than for strangers. A byproduct of this cultural norm is the Asian consumer preference for well-known companies and brands.[31] Other interesting differences in cultural teachings are apparent in lessons about the meaning of time (e.g., "time heals all" versus "time is money") and individualism (e.g., "the nail that sticks up gets knocked down" versus "do your own thing" and "be all you can be").

Confucian beliefs provide a layer of similarity for the diverse cultures of Asian America. At the same time, the peoples of Asia and Asian America have widespread differences in religious traditions. The Philippines is predominantly Roman Catholic, India is majority Hindu, Pakistan and Malaysia are Muslim, Thailand, Nepal, and Tibet are Buddhist, Japan has Shinto among other religions, and China, Vietnam, and Korea have Buddhist and Christian traditions. What is most significant is the effects of these differences on Asian American acculturation to mainstream America. Asian Americans who are practitioners of Eastern religions are more likely to continue those traditions and to retain strong ethnic identity and affiliation with the culture of their country of origin. Those who convert to Christianity identify as mainstream Americans more quickly and are more likely to intermarry.[32]

The presence of a close-knit community promotes Asian-American ethnic cohesion within country-of-origin boundaries. The ethnic residential and business communities where new immigrants gather create social interactions that help the residents financially and psychologically. They create community networks for people who share the same interests through churches, schools, and local clubs. What cements these family and community ties is the Asian orientation toward collectivism and a promotion of social harmony.[33] The

Table 8.8

Cultural Lessons in Asian and American Sayings

Subject of American cultural lesson	Asian saying (CH, K, J)	Mainstream saying
Virtues	A good heart always gives a little extra. (CH) Wealth is a treasure for a lifetime, wisdom a treasure for all time. (J)	God helps those who help themselves. He who dies with the most toys wins.
Time	Time is a healer. (K) Time opens every door to him who waits. (CH)	Time is money A rolling stone gathers no moss.
Relationships with others	Enemies until friends. (CH) The nail that sticks up gets knocked down. (K) Everyone has fate bound about his neck. (J) A wise man has long ears and a short tongue. (J) Once a word is out, the swiftest horse cannot overtake it. (CH) Fair without, fair within; foul without, foul within. (K) The face belies the heart. (J)	All men are created equal. Do your own thing! Be all you can be! A squeaky wheel gets the grease. Let's get right to the point. You can't judge a book by its cover. Beauty is as beauty does. There's no fool like an old fool.
Age/wisdom	Of the five blessings, long life is the greatest. (J) Ignore an old man's advice and one day you will be a beggar. (CH)	
Success	Even if you hide yourself in a pot, you will never escape your fate. (K) When the melon is ripe, it will drop by itself. (CH)	If at first you don't succeed, try, try again. Where there's a will there's a way. Take the bull by the horns.
Family	Ice does not freeze on the busy spinning wheel (K) Treat every old man as thy father. (J) Silk clothing warms even a cousin. (K)	Busy hands are happy hands. Blood is thicker than water. You made your own bed, now lie in it.

Sources: G. Althen, *American Ways: A Guide for Foreigners in the United States* (Yarmouth, ME: Intercultural Press, 1988); T.H. Ha, *Maxims and Proverbs of Old Korea* (Seoul: Yonsei University Press, 1970); M. de Mooij, *Global Marketing and Advertising: Understanding Cultural Paradoxes* (Thousand Oaks, CA: Sage, 1998); Y.C. Kim, *Proverbs, East and West: An Anthology of Chinese, Korean, and Japanese Sayings with Western Equivalents* (Elizabeth, NJ: Hollym, 1991); E.C. Stewart and M.J. Bennett, *American Cultural Patterns: A Cross-Cultural Perspective*, rev. ed. (Yarmouth, ME: Intercultural Press, 1991).

Note: CH = Chinese, J = Japanese, K = Korean.

group-centered behavior of Asians is in direct contrast to American indi-vidualism. Asian Americans take responsibility as a group; the basic human unit is not "me" but "us." It is not "my family" or "my house." Instead, it is "our family" and "our house." Some Asians are not really comfortable being identified as individuals. Western cultures penalize those who do not conform to social norms with guilt, while Asian cultures emphasize the shame of not meeting others' expectations.

The Special Role of the Family

Another important Asian-American value is the emphasis on family. Divorce rates and single motherhood among Asian Americans are the lowest for all racial groups in the United States. About one in three Asian households consists of married couples with children, compared to one in four households for the average American.[34] In Asian culture, a hierarchy based on age dictates inter-personal relations. Respect for authority and the elderly are important beliefs common to all Asian ethnic groups. In social relations, younger individuals must be polite to the elderly, either men or women. In business relations as well, those who are new at a company or younger should show respect and be humble. In general, elders are highly respected because they are "wiser." Many Asian-American family members are obligated to work in family-owned businesses, rather than free to pursue their own careers.[35]

Children and parents remain close in traditional Asian-American families. In consequence, parents exert significant influence on their children in many areas, especially in education. Many Asian parents immigrate to the United States not only in the hope of economic gain but also to take advantage of educational opportunities for their children. Some Asian Americans, especially those who lack transferable skills, realize that better education for their chil-dren comes at the price of low-paid, low-status jobs for themselves. Anecdotes about parents paying their children's college tuition in full so that the children can concentrate on studying or mothers coming to cook during exam periods are familiar among college-age Asian-American students.[36] Family-oriented decision making is also apparent in consumer decisions, such as choosing to buy what is good for the family rather than what is good for one member of the family. One ad for Metropolitan Life Insurance said: "Your Metropolitan program is your children's security blanket." This successfully captures the family orientation of Asian Americans.

Generational Differences in Asian America

As Asian-American parents devote their lives to their children, Asian-American households spend 82 percent more on education than any other

American ethnic group.[37] Stereotypes of Asian Americans as science oriented and focused on study have their roots in the high expectations of Asian-American parents.[38] Plenty of Asian-American parents expect their children to attend Ivy League colleges and prefer that they become doctors or engineers.[39] According to the Asian-American work ethic, high socioeconomic status is a respectable and worthwhile achievement. Everyone is believed capable of achieving high status if enough time and energy is devoted to the task. Many role models in the Asian-American community can be cited to support these beliefs.

This orientation toward high academic achievement has also led mainstream Americans to perceive Asian Americans as a "model minority." This is unfortunate because that image gives policymakers the excuse to neglect disadvantaged populations in Asian America. It also fails to acknowledge the extra hurdles of prejudice or discrimination that Asian Americans and all other racial minorities must overcome. Most important, it places pressure on individual Asian Americans to conform to expectations that ignore individual differences in interests and talents.[40]

Another example of strong ties between parents and children is the close supervision of the young by adult members of the family. The rate of pregnancy among unmarried Asian-American women is 8 percent, compared with 20 percent for white Americans. Such low rates of teen pregnancy and single motherhood have positive effects on their subsequent economic status. The social relations of adolescents often come into conflict with the expectations and wishes of Asian-American parents. East Asians have such a strong ethnic identity that they prefer their children not to date people of other ethnicities. In the case of South Asian families, emphasis is placed on marrying not only within the same race or ethnic group but also those with the same religion and class. At the same time, immigrant parents today accept the choice of their U.S-born children to marry outside their ethnicity more frequently than was the case in the past.[41]

In the 1960s and the 1970s, in reaction to the repeal of laws forbidding interracial marriages and to the subsequent rush of movies with romances between Caucasian heroes and Asian women, many East Asian women married white Americans. The large number of intermarriages in the 1960s indicated the desire of second-generation Asian-American women to assimilate.[42] More recently, a sense of ethnic pride and identity among Asian-American youth has experienced a resurgence. Marriage within the same heritage is again in vogue. In the 1960s, Asian culture was embarrassing to the second generation. In the 1990s, the new generations began wearing their Asian background and traditions with pride.[43]

Bridging Two Cultures

Adjusting to American Life

Due to unique customs, history, and language, each ethnic group of Asian Americans has formed its own community-support organizations. Chinese, Japanese, Koreans, Indians, and Vietnamese have their own social networks and leaders. The older generations of Chinese and Japanese Americans have started to lose cohesion and to marry outside their ethnicity. Recent violence against Asians that does not distinguish between the various ethnicities has led Asian Americans to realize that those differences do not matter to outsiders in mainstream America. In many instances, these differences are neither recognized by nor considered significant to other Americans, who sometimes cannot tell who comes from which ethnicity based on their outward appearance.[44]

Violence against Asian Americans first surfaced in the 1980s, when a Chinese-American man was killed by former autoworkers who blamed the loss of their jobs on Japanese auto imports. This case awakened a sense of willingness among Asian Americans to cooperate with one another, as it sent a message that they should move beyond ethnic boundaries and unite as "Asian Americans." Though they still make up a small group relative to other ethnic groups in the United States, joining forces gives Asian Americans better access to political and economic resources.

Espiritu called the move toward creating Asian-American organizations outside country-of-origin boundaries Asian-American Pan-Ethnicity.[45] Some Asian-American leaders advocate the formation of Asian-American Pan-Ethnic organizations to promote cultural awareness and pride, but other Asian Americans want to be treated the same as white Americans and accepted as "nonhyphenated" Americans. This struggle embodies Asian Americans' dual desire to become bona fide members of the mainstream while simultaneously maintaining their cultural heritage.[46]

Few actually call themselves "Asian American." One study found that Vietnamese Americans identify themselves as follows: 42 percent "Vietnamese," 34 percent "Vietnamese Americans," 13 percent as "Asian American," and only 1 percent identify themselves as "American." In contrast, 21 percent of Japanese Americans use "Japanese," 40 percent "Japanese American," about 15 percent of Japanese Americans identify themselves as "Asian American," and 21 percent call themselves "American." Among Chinese Americans, the preferences are 42 percent for "Chinese" and 34 percent for "Chinese American." Korean American self-designations are 41 percent "Korean" and 33 percent "Korean American."[47]

Acculturation describes the process in which those outside mainstream

American society learn about American culture. Acculturation includes learning English and adjusting behaviors to American lifestyles and mannerisms. Marketers play an important role in this process. For example, Albertson's used a print ad in California markets that pictured the "classic" Thanksgiving dinner—how to cook a turkey and what side dishes should go with it. Other sources of information about the American way of life are blogs and websites. Unknown Space LLC is an online billboard site where visitors pose questions about how to find the cheapest car insurance or to how to tell their visiting parents from China not to smoke in the house. Posts on the site are often in "Chinglish."[48]

Typically, someone in the process of becoming acculturated feels excitement over learning the new culture but later goes into culture shock.[49] The acculturation experience brings an infusion of new values and norms that in turn foster conflict within an individual's self-image and sense of security. Cultural stress follows culture shock and may motivate activities to find solutions to the ensuing self-image crisis. Discrepancies between self-image, attitudes, and behaviors are likely to continue until the person achieves a comfortable accommodation to American ways. Some immigrants do not themselves reach this point, but their children do.

The drive and self-confidence of people who have remade themselves by learning and then playing a new role in a new country are the result of having successfully bridged two cultures.[50] Asian Americans deal with acculturation from a practical perspective focused on survival. Success comes from playing this new role with confidence, not from changing into a new person.[51] Such an outlook is the basis of "chameleon" behavior among Asian Americans, although studies of situational ethnicity among other ethnic groups suggest that it is not a unique phenomenon.[52] The ability to switch back and forth between roles in an ethnic culture and in American mainstream culture is another example of consumers transmigrating back and forth across cultural boundaries.

A majority of Asian Americans express a dual desire to be part of the mainstream and to retain their unique cultural heritage. The concept of role switching is a departure from the theory of role transition and assimilation, in which changes are considered permanent and unidirectional.[53] In role switching, depending on the situation, people, and tasks to be performed, Asian Americans can switch between obligations in the Asian-American community to duties as an employee in a mainstream American firm.[54] Table 8.9 compares Asian beliefs to those of the American mainstream and other American subcultures. The table indicates that Asian-American values are more like the worldviews dominant in other American subcultures than those of mainstream society. Because of increasing diversity in the country, American mainstream beliefs are likely to evolve in the direction of Asian ones.

Table 8.9

Comparison of the Dominant Cultural Values in American Subcultures

Cultural value	American mainstream subculture	Asian-American subculture	African-American subculture	U.S. Latino subculture
Personal Identity	Individualistic	Collectivistic, family important	Both	Both
Expressiveness	High but objective	Low, subjective	High	High, subjective
Male-female roles	Overlap	Distinctive	Overlap	Distinctive
Competition as key to success	Important	Not as important	Not as important	Not as important
Role of social networks	Not as important	Very important	Somewhat important	Very important
Power distance	Low	High	Medium	High
Uncertainty avoidance	Low	High	Medium	High
Communication style	Direct	Indirect	Both	Indirect
Relationship to nature	Man dominant	Man-nature in harmony	In harmony	Man dominant
Universal rules of behavior	Yes	No, depends on relationships	No	No
Use of time	Present, future	Past, cyclical	Cyclical	Past, present

Sources: G. Hofstede, *Culture's Consequences* (Beverly Hills, CA: Sage, 1980); E.T. Hall, *The Silent Language* (Garden City, NY: Doubleday, 1959); F. Kluckhohn and F.L. Strodtbeck, *Variations in Value Orientations* (Evanston, IL: Row, Peterson, 1961); F. Trompenaars and C. Hampden-Turner, *Riding the Waves of Culture,* 2d ed. (New York: McGraw-Hill, 1998).

Despite the desire to become part of American society Asian Americans have maintained strong support for cultural ties . . . This is evidenced in continued holiday celebrations such as the Lunar New Year, Moon Festivals, and ceremonies honoring departed family members. Seventy American cities had Chinese Dragon Boat races in 2006.[55] To honor cultural origins, Asian Americans request American assistance for home countries There is once again a preference for marrying other Asian Americans.[56] Attitudes still vary across country-of-origin groups; Indian Americans of Generations 1.5 and 2.0 "may feel more American than Indian. . . . They may listen to American pop music and watch American movies, but they are also comfortable with the popular music and movies of India."[57]

Differences across Asian-Americans can show up in unusual preferences for consumption. For example, McDonald's is the most popular fast food restaurant for all Asian Americans, as it is for other American groups. The second choice for fast food is where differences across Asian American groups arise. In one study, Filipinos would choose local Chinese fast foods second, Indian Americans would go to Pizza Hut, and other Asian Americans would go to other burger chains.[58]

Country-of-origin boundaries replicate differences in preferences for brands, companies, and product usage. For example, among Vietnamese, 78 percent have checking accounts and 58 percent have credit cards, while among Koreans 95 percent have checking accounts and 84 percent have credit cards. Filipino and Vietnamese Americans send international money transfers the most, and Indian and Japanese Americans use them the least. Japanese Americans prefer Sony laptops while others prefer Dell. One-third of Vietnamese-American computer owners did not remember the computer's brand, and Korean Americans are most likely to build their own laptops. United is the preferred airline of Chinese, Indian, and Japanese Americans, Northwest is first choice for Filipino Americans, Korean Air is the choice of Korean Americans, and China Air is the preference of Vietnamese Americans. Indian Americans travel the most domestically and Japanese and Vietnamese Americans travel the most internationally.[59] These numbers reinforce the importance of knowing your Asian American target market's preferences.

Acculturation to American life can be more difficult and take longer for some Asian Americans. English-speaking peoples from Pacific Rim countries have an advantage over non-English-speaking immigrants from Asian countries. Parents encourage their children's fluency in English because it is critical to success in America; at the same time, they do not always teach their children to become fluent in the home-country language. "ABCs" (American-born Chinese) may find themselves "between two cultures," not fitting into either particularly well. They cannot speak with or understand their grandparents, and American friends do not understand their dedication to pleasing their parents.[60]

Asian Influences on Mainstream America

Until recently, Asian Americans have been almost invisible in mainstream American popular culture.[61] Asian-American images in media are typically as "foreigners." When Asians appear in movies and other pop-culture venues, Asian women have been presented as passive, oversexualized, exotic, and humble or as treacherous and evil. Asian men have been stereotyped as incompetent, asexual beings, supremely wise, or martial arts experts.[62] For example, the female character Sun in the series "Lost" was passive and complaisant while her husband, Jin, was incompetent but submissive to his wife. Stereotypes of *Asians* who appear in popular culture vehicles are generalized by other Americans and, unfortunately, applied to the *Asian-American* population.[63]

Stereotyping of Asian Americans has also occurred in advertisements that reinforce simplistic views of Asian Americans. Asian Americans are most often shown in the background of ads and as endorsers of high-technology products. Asian-American women are virtually absent.[64] According to a study of Asian-American portrayals in magazine advertising in 2005, Asian Americans appeared frequently in technology and business product categories.[65] Asian-American actors or models in mainstream television programs or magazines are still limited. Mainstream magazine and television advertisements show few Asians in major selling roles for products.[66] Asian models, especially Asian-American women, are shown in social and home settings or in ads for nontechnical products.[67] Even in marriage and family textbooks, Asian Americans receive little coverage relative to their proportion of the American population.[68]

During the 1990s, this pattern began to change. Asian Americans were seen in a greater variety of roles and began chipping away at stereotypical portrayals. Amy Tan's best-selling novel *The Joy Luck Club* was made into a movie that met with great success. Margaret Cho, a Korean-American comedian, briefly starred in a prime-time television show, *All-American Girl*. Matsuda, Vivienne Tam, Anna Sui, and Josie Natori are counted among today's hottest fashion designers. Lucy Liu, Sandra Oh, B.D. Wong, George Takei, Bruce Lee, and Jason Scott Lee are all stars in mainstream television and film.

Imported movies, games, cuisines, and pop-culture phenomena from the Pacific Rim, including Tamagotchi pets and Pokemon collecting, have made "Asian" influence a trendsetter in American popular culture.[69] Sumo wrestling is now covered in mainstream media and underwritten by Canadian Airlines.[70]

Asian-American entrepreneurs such as James Chu of Viewsonic, Sabeer Bhatia of Hotmail, Vinod Khosla of Sun, Frank Lin of Trident, and Andrew Yang of Yahoo! are role models as high-profile founders of booming high-technology firms and e-commerce ventures. They contribute to a perception of Asian Americans as major architects of the information economy.[71]

Communication Styles of Asian Americans

An important skill in successfully transmigrating between Asian and main-stream culture is the ability to adjust communication style. Mainstream Americans use direct and informal communications and rely on written and verbal parts of messages to decipher intended meaning. At the other extreme, Asian cultures value relationships over communication efficiency, and how something is said is as full of meaning as *what* is said.[72]

High-context cultures, such as those of Asia, Latin America, the Middle East, and Eastern and Southern Europe, value indirect communication. It is considered good manners to be implicit and ambiguous. A message's meaning depends on what the relationship is between sender and receiver, what effects the message might have on that relationship, and whether it is oral or written. Message interpretation in Asian America depends on decoding the message *context* and an overriding need to maintain harmony.[73] Low-context cultures such as those of mainstream America and northern and western Europe, emphasize direct communication.

Members of Asian cultures place a high value on gift giving, exchanging business cards, inquiring about the well-being of family members, and other ritualistic communication behaviors.[74] Mainstream Americans see a person who insists on too much ritual as "too shy," "too polite," or unwilling to disclose. Asians and Asian Americans place more importance on not "losing face" and are reluctant to volunteer personal opinions when the potential consequences are unclear.

Bilingual Asian Americans face many communication dilemmas. First, many concepts do not translate from one language to another. Second, bilinguals may find it difficult to behave as other Americans do when actions come into conflict with Asian-American cultural norms. Asian-American students can be less assertive team members and less verbal overall, compared to their mainstream counterparts. Third, since much of culture is unconscious behavioral programming, Asian Americans misinterpret more communications, experience more discomfort, and frequently find themselves isolated from the important social networks of American organizations.[75]

Second-, third-, and fourth-generation Asian Americans, who speak only English, may use language in an "Asian" way—more indirect, less assertive, and less participative.[76] Awkward and uncomfortable communications between

Asian and other Americans may give the impression that Asian Americans do not want informal contact.

Asian-American Sources of Information and Media Patterns

Source Credibility and the Asian-American Community Network

Psychological distance is important in Asian-American culture. Many Asian Americans recognize a hierarchy from insiders to outsiders, as follows: family, friends from the same village or region in the same country of origin, acquaintances from the same country of origin, individuals from other Asian countries, other immigrants/minorities, white Americans, and, most distant, other American ethnicities. This hierarchy mirrors movement from most to least credible sources of information. From this perspective, Asian-American endorsers are effective in communications because they have higher source credibility than any other experts.[77] Tiger Woods (whose background includes Thai and Chinese ancestry) is a popular endorser of cars, athletic equipment, luxury watches, and even a sports drink. Even after news began to circulate that Tiger had engaged in scandalous behavior off the golf course, sponsors used his consistent dedication and status as a world champion as key themes in ads.

Word-of-mouth marketing is the most cost-effective, productive method of getting the word out in Asian communities. Asian and Asian-American families are "networks within themselves."[78] Several researchers have verified the importance of word-of-mouth communication, advice from friends, and face-to-face personal selling in the Asian-American community.[79] In a study examining information sources used for financial decisions, Asian Americans were found to seek personal advice from friends and relatives; other American investors gave more weight to mass media.[80] Marketers should consider reaching Asian Americans through these community network channels and other grassroots, face-to-face, and personal approaches. These sources have the high credibility that comes from being insiders in Asian-American communities. A "trustworthy relationship" is rated by Asian-American consumers as more persuasive than a sales pitch based on brand attributes.[81]

The preference of Asian Americans for "insider" sources of communication creates bias against non-Asian American people or companies. Americans define people by their profession while Asians view people in terms of the relationship that they have with them.[82] Prejudice against companies that are not part of Asian-American community networks is elastic and depends on the parties involved.[83] A Japanese American may be the "insider" source for a Chinese American in an organization with no other Asian Americans, but he may be the "outsider" in a Chinese-dominant church congregation. It is easier for Chinese Americans (or any other Asian Americans) to recognize subtle differences in physical appearance or body language among Chinese, Korean, Japanese, or other Asian Americans. Indian Americans report the highest attention to ads that use spokespeople of their same heritage while few Japanese Americans pay more attention if the spokesperson is Japanese.[84] Therefore marketers should take care when choosing models or endorsers to appeal to different ethnicities among Asian Americans.[85]

A major obstacle in accessing Asian-American community networks is the low incidence of product- and advertising-related word-of-mouth communications among Asian Americans. In one study of product- and advertising-related talk, at home and with friends, Chinese Americans had the least word-of-mouth communications among four American ethnic groups. The one exception was that they talked more about products and brands with which they were satisfied.[86] The community network in Asian America is invaluable in securing positive recommendations for brands or companies.

Gateways to the Asian community networks are celebrations of culture-based events in Asian America. The Asian-American calendar has many special events, but they vary across ethnicity and religion. Some of the most important holidays are the Lunar New Year, Cherry Blossom Festival, Penitencia in Filipino neighborhoods, the Dragon Boat Festival, the Moon Festival, and the Mid-Autumn Festival. Some of these events are included in promotions and websites sponsored by cities that wish to highlight their Asian-American residents. In addition, many nonprofit organizations develop and supply services for newcomers to Asian-American communities. Korean Baptist churches provide everything from housing assistance to legal advice, doctor referrals, and Korean translators. Asian-American professional and business directories are other venues that "define" the extent of Asian-American community networks.

Ethnic Media Targeting Asian Americans

Cultural background also influences how its members use media. Several studies have indicated that Asian Americans, as well as different subgroups in Asian America, differ from other American subcultures in their patterns of media behavior.[87] This section of the chapter describes ethnic media channels for Asian Americans, while the following one highlights media behaviors among Asian Americans. The availability of targeted media, both ethnic-oriented media in English and in native languages (called in-language media), affect Asian-American media behaviors. Asian immigrants who have spent less than 10 years in the United States prefer to patronize businesses that advertise in their native language.[88] Wherever ethnic media exist, they are not only a conduit to foreign-born Asian Americans but also "competition" for mainstream media in capturing the small amount of time that Asian Americans spend with any media.

Asian Americans are more culturally isolated from mainstream America than are African Americans and U.S. Latinos. These ethnic groups have more visibility in mainstream media and popular culture and share more cultural values with white Americans. African Americans and U.S. Latinos also have a longer history of attention from mainstream marketers, in both ethnic and mainstream media.[89] MTV Desi, MTV Chi, and MTV K represent a new approach: a hybrid of mainstream U.S., foreign, and ethnic programming that represents their "hybrid" target audiences among Indian Americans, Chinese Americans, and Korean Americans. These stations bring global pop culture, musicians, and celebrities to Asian America.[90]

Ethnic-oriented media have two major roles as "cultural institutions" in an ethnic community: (1) to help newcomers learn and adapt to the cultural values and norms of a new country, and (2) to assist in retaining ethnic heritage and ties to a country of origin.[91] In ethnic communities, all media play more diverse roles in addressing their audiences' needs. In Asian America, many entrepreneurs have developed a patchwork of media vehicles in English and native languages to satisfy the needs for social interaction, cultural learning, personal identity, news, and entertainment.[92] They reach both urban and suburban Asian Americans as well as most Asian country-of-origin groups. As early as 1993 approximately 35 to 40 radio broadcasters in New York rented "unused portions of other stations," FM channels called *sideband* radio, and broadcast programming in Asian languages.[93] "Sideband" radio supposedly reaches 40 percent of the Filipino-American population in New York in Tagalog. As long ago as 1997, *Filipinas* magazine reported its reach as 10,100 Filipinos in the San Francisco Bay area.[94]

The geographic concentration of Asian Americans creates an economic bonus for marketers. Because a large majority of Asian Americans live in California, New York, Hawaii, Texas, and Chicago, companies can avoid national media and make smaller buys in local markets.[95] The advertising costs for local, ethnically targeted, in-language media, range from $50 to $500 for a newspaper ad or a 30-second radio spot. These prices are extremely low compared to those in English-language media.

Even with the same number of impressions, in-language media have the advantage of reaching individual consumers who cannot be reached in any English-language medium. A good example is the Chinese and Chinese-

American market in San Francisco. For years, primetime Chinese-language evening news had an audience share average for Monday to Friday that was larger than all other TV stations combined.[96] Even the U.S. Commerce Department reports that over 82 percent of Chinese, Korean, and Vietnamese Americans prefer to communicate and use media in their own language.[97] In-language media are not just a preferred source for newcomers.[98] One more advantage is that tentative evidence suggests that brand or company associations made in native languages result in higher liking of those brands.[99]

Nevertheless, use of in-language, Asian-targeted media has some important drawbacks. Circulation figures for Asian-language newspapers and ratings for Asian-language television programs are not always audited.[100] The media planner's job is more complicated because s/he must analyze which circulation and audience numbers to believe as well as to decide how to optimize limited dollars to meet reach and frequency goals. Today there are hundreds of traditional and nontraditional media vehicles in Asian native languages. The media include in-language newspapers, magazines, television, radio, websites, and newsletters and local bulletins.

Another problem with the use of in-language media is the evidence that other languages use different cognitive routes to memory than English does. For example, Chinese words are interpreted more contextually and rely more on visual or semantic codes than the same English words are. Thus, information learned in Chinese about a brand may not be remembered or recalled in short-term memory without more effort on the part of a consumer and more cues related to context.[101]

Communication service providers such as K&L (www.kanglee.com), InterTrend (www.intertrend.com), AAAZa (www.aaaza.com), Muse Communications (www.museusa.com), and AdmerAsia (www.admerasia.com) have helpful resources on their websites for companies that wish to reach Asian American consumers. Together, these sources can provide a good overview of Asian-American in-language media, as well as current information about population growth, geographic distribution, purchasing power, and cultural environments. Unfortunately, the data are provided mostly by the media themselves and are not audited.

Asian Americans report reading ethnic newspapers and spending more time with this medium.[102] It is impossible to know whether the important role of newspapers in reaching Asian Americans is due to their high literacy rates or the fact that Asian-American newspapers have been the only in-language media available to these consumers until recently. Chinese community newspapers have a long history in cities like New York, San Francisco, and Los Angeles; *India Abroad* has been around for over 25 years. The monopoly of newspapers as in-language media is rapidly declining as electronic media outlets and Internet usage rise.[103] Radio and television have become essential to the Asian media mix since both media achieved full digitalization in 2009, and their audiences can now be measured. It was reported that in 2007 over 69 percent of Asian-American households were online, and 85 percent of Asian-American households had computers, thus web advertising and communications are also critical.[104]

In-language media provide Asian Americans with sources of information relevant to their needs. Yet another reason for the popularity of in-language newspapers has been that many of the larger dailies are supported by parent companies from the country of origin. Some examples include the Japanese newspapers *Yomiuri America* and *Nihon Keizai Shimbun*. Many other in-language local newspapers, typically free weeklies, build circulation by providing a combination of U.S news, local community news, and home-country information.

Several magazines that emerged during the 1990s target Asian Americans, including *A* magazine from New York, *Face* and *Yolk* from California, *Niko* of Texas, and Toronto-based *Typhoon*. In 2008, more than 160 Asian-American–targeted magazines were published. The magazines vary in their focus from fashion to news and entertainment. Faced with increasing competition, the magazines targeting Asian Americans are specializing in narrower targets such as Japanese or Chinese Americans.

As noted earlier, in-language television and radio are rapidly gaining in popularity with Asian-American consumers. Their programs tend to include a combination of satellite news reports or entertainment programs and locally produced news and entertainment shows. Most U.S. cities with a large Asian-American population offer 24-hour multicultural television programming as well as cable access to programming from their countries of origin. Broadcasting from Brisbane, CA, KTSF provides news, information, and entertainment to more than 1.4 million Asian Americans in the San Francisco Bay area.[105] KTSF varies in-language programs throughout the day, thus reaching Chinese, Filipino, Vietnamese, and Korean Americans. The station has the potential to reach 2.75 million households in Northern California. Other popular stations include KIKU in Hawaii and WMBC in New York.

In addition to these stations focused on Asian Americans in general, a growing number of cable companies offer home-country programming as options for their customers. Cable networks such as TVAsia, Eye on Asia, CCTV, and Vision of Asia are available for local subscription in major cities. Video rentals and streaming media are also popular media with Asian Americans due to strong film and television programming industries in Asia.

The Internet adds yet another alternative to the mix for reaching Asian-American consumers. AsianAve.com is a membership community that provides information about careers, money, college, and wellness and has chatrooms for discussing topics such as how Asian Americans are portrayed in the media. Because online penetration exceeds two-thirds of Asian-American households, the Web is an excellent venue for companies to build loyal relationships with affluent Asian-American consumers. Many cities with a large Asian-American population also publicize businesses, community organizations, and ethnic-oriented events on their own websites.

Direct marketing is also an excellent medium for reaching Asian Americans and specific subgroups in Asian America. Some trade publications have reported that Asian Americans are one of the most difficult ethnic groups to reach, but direct marketers have a variety of general market media and lists available for targeting Asian Americans in English.[106] Good sources for mailing lists are the professional organizations among subgroups.[107]

Asian Americans are only beginning to be wooed by marketers with in-language direct mail and telemarketing. In the late twentieth century, in-language databases were scarce, and some Asian Americans did not use credit cards, a prime measure of a target's ability to pay.[108] Nowadays, however, credit cards are in common use among Asian Americans; 80 percent of them prefer to pay for purchases with a credit card.[109]

Last but not least are the ubiquitous yellow-page directories listing Asian-American professionals and Asian-owned businesses. They are mostly distributed free and tend to be subgroup-specific, like the *Houston Korean Journal,* and *Chinese Yellow Pages* in Houston. Local newspapers like *Nikkei West* in California (Japanese Americans), *Orange County Weekly* (Vietnamese Americans), or the Chinese-American newspaper *World Journal,* include directories of local businesses in both English and a native language.[110] Advertisers in these directories are drawn from local community networks and mainstream firms that wish to reach members of the Asian-American communities they represent. They are excellent media for business-to-business marketing.

Asian-American Use of Mainstream and Ethnic Media

A major impediment to making effective media choices for reaching Asian-American consumers has been the absence of Simmons, Nielsen, or IRI data for Asian-American audiences. Nielsen has begun to use people meters in San Francisco and other areas with a large Asian-American population, to better measure local audience programming tastes, but there is still no national coverage of Asian-American media. In addition to the lack of audited audience data, the fragmentation in Asian-American media creates further barriers to economies of scale in media purchases.

Sometimes, the effectiveness of media buys in reaching Asian Americans is apparent even though exposure rates are not measurable. In the late 1990s, Geffen Records ran commercials during *Flames*, a program available on cable from the Filipino Channel. The program appealed to Filipinos in same age demographics as the general-market program *Beverly Hills 90210*. The cable company found that 80–90 percent of subscribers watched the program every day and often tuned to the channel for over six hours per day. For the two weeks that the ads ran, sales shot up but then fell after the commercials stopped appearing.[111]

Asian Americans generally have low levels of consumption of all media types in either English or native languages. Several companies with experience in the market claim that Asian Americans are too busy "getting educated" or "running small businesses." Table 8.10 highlights the weekly media consumption hours of ethnic groups. Asian Americans tend to read newspapers in English (4.72 hours a week) more than do other ethnic groups, exceeding non-Hispanic whites (3.99 hours a week). In terms of magazines, Asian Americans tend to prefer those in English (4.36 hours per week) rather than in-language magazines, and their magazine consumption is higher than that of other ethnic groups. Asian Americans spend more time on the Internet in English (20.33 hours a week) than in native languages (1.28 hours a week). In 2010, 73 percent of Asian Americans had Internet access and 81 percent are expected to be online by 2014.[112] Preference for advertising and media content in foreign languages varies by subgroup, with Vietnamese and Korean Americans consuming the most in-language media.[113]

The implication of data like these is that marketers should minimize media expenditure while putting those budgets to work hiring Asian-American sales personnel, participating in ethnic events, and direct marketing to opinion leaders in Asian-American communities. However, buying in-language media is an efficient way to maximize advertising dollars in the Asian-American market, even though the media are fragmented by language and geographic location. In-language television networks in a few American cities, as well as cable channels, movie rentals, and newspapers are outpacing English-language and ethnic-oriented print media that target Asian Americans.

It would be a mistake to ignore mainstream media in the many vehicles that reach the total Asian-American market. Selective buying of mainstream media in a limited number of cities, in addition to exposure in Asian-oriented media in both English and native languages in those same locations, can deliver wide reach. English-language television is the medium of choice for Indian and Japanese Americans while Chinese and Korean Americans consume more in-language than English-language television.[114] A combination of magazines such as *Masala, Onward*, and *Hum,* which appeal to second-generation Indian Americans, and newspapers such as *India Abroad,*

Table 8.10

Media Usage of U.S. Ethnic Groups, 2007 (hours per week)

	Non-Hispanic whites	Asian Americans	Hispanic Spanish*	Hispanic English**	African Americans
Watching TV in English	22.53	16.83	8.46	16.92	21.02
Watching TV in other language	0.19	2.42	10.81	2.76	0.2
Listening to the radio in English	8.36	7.67	5.32	9.34	8.31
Listening to the radio in another language	0.05	0.61	6.67	2.53	0.15
Reading newspaper in English	3.99	4.72	2.45	4.16	3.91
Reading newspaper in another language	0.04	0.95	2.42	0.47	0.01
Reading magazines in English	2.59	4.36	2.58	3.77	3.74
Reading magazines in another language	0.01	0.68	2.64	0.7	0.04
Using the Internet, including e-mail in English	20.65	20.33	17.22	8.25	19.14
Using the Internet, including e-mail in another language	0.23	1.28	7.96	1.33	0.06

Source: F. Korzenny, B.A. Korzenny, H. McGavock, M.G. Inglessis et al., *The Multicultural Marketing Equation: Media, Attitudes, Brands, and Spending* (Tallahassee: Center for Hispanic Marketing Communication, Florida State University/DMS Research Multicultural Marketing Research Program, 2007). Reproduced by permission.

*Hispanics who completed questionnaires in Spanish.

**Hispanics who completed questionnaires in English.

favored by their immigrant parents, is needed to reach immigrants as well as acculturated Asian Americans. Table 8.11 lists the top ten television markets for Asian-American audiences in 2012–13.

English-language television is the "window on America" for new immigrants, even though they may not speak or understand English well. At the same time, messages in mainstream media do not always resonate with Asian-American values. For example, first-generation Asian Americans were baffled by an AT&T commercial with the theme and music for "Girls Just Wanna Have Fun." They asked: "Where are the husbands? Is it a failed marriage?"[115] Given the fact that Asian Americans spend little time with media and have a multitude of choices, it is especially important to break through the clutter with culturally compatible messages.

The Marketplace as Social Network and Expression of Values

A poll of Asian-American consumers pointed to four important attributes that were the basis of their purchase decisions. They were, in order from most to least important: quality, price for value received, service provided, and convenience. These criteria show no major differences between the preferences of Asian and other American consumers. They also support the proposition that Asian-American consumers do not require significantly different marketing communication messages.[116] At the same time, Asian Americans express a strong need to continue Asian traditions and values. Marketing programs can be adapted to create more culturally compatible relationships with Asian-American consumers in several ways.

First, many foreign-born consumers are not familiar with American brand names. Tactics that build brand recognition are essential before Asian-American consumers can be moved toward brand preference and brand loyalty. Marketers must also become extended members of Asian-American social and professional community networks. JC Penney built traffic among Asian-American consumers by adding well-known Asian brands and a line of cosmetics from Minnesota designed especially for Asian women.[117]

Sears measures its success with Asian-American shoppers by their responses to promotions keyed to important Asian-American holidays. For example, one year during the Moon Festival, it invited Chinese and Vietnamese customers in Los Angeles to bring in coupons and receive traditional items such as mooncakes and lanterns. The promotion was supported by radio and print advertisements. Sales figures for participating stores increased 28 to 30 percent.[118] Tailored promotions like these position mainstream companies as participants in traditions important to Asian-American consumers.

Table 8.11

Top Ten Television Markets for Asian Americans, 2012–2013

Rank	Designated market area	2007–2008 Asian American homes	2012–2013 Asian American homes	% of market area homes, 2012–2013
1	Los Angeles	669,390	789,980	14.6
2	New York	564,370	680,570	12.6
3	San Francisco–Oakland–San Jose	482,320	578,870	10.7
4	Honolulu	220,330	223,270	4.1
5	Chicago	166,080	199,180	3.7
6	Washington, DC	152,880	197,560	3.6
7	Seattle–Tacoma	131,230	168,980	3.1
8	Sacramento–Stockton–Modesto	122,350	148,520	2.7
9	Houston	103,790	145,420	2.7
10	Philadelphia	105,130	134,360	2.5

Sources: Television Bureau of Advertising, Nielsen DMA Ranks (2012), www.tvb.org/measurement/131627/; Nielsen, "Top Ten Markets Ranked by Asian American Homes (Chart)," Marketing Charts.com, September 5, 2007, www.marketingcharts.com/television/hispanic-asian-african-american-tv-households-grow-faster-than-us-average-1499/nielsen-television-dma-asian-american-householdsjpg/.

Second, shopping is a favorite leisure activity for many Asian Americans, who tend to spend a long time browsing and rarely purchase only what they need and then quickly leave the store.[119] Retailers must create a fun and informative atmosphere that meets the needs of Asian-American shoppers. Asian-American consumers respond more positively to deference and "soft sell" from salespeople. National retail stores in ethnic communities should consider hiring personnel who speak and understand the native languages of the subgroup shoppers who live near their stores. When selling services instead of products, it is important to build an association with leaders in the community. MONY Life uses only bilingual salespeople to sell insurance and investment products in Hindi-speaking communities in New Jersey.[120] Too much informality can also get marketers in trouble in Asian America. The assumption that because we "share interests" we are "friends" is not compatible with Asian definitions of friendship or mutual obligation. Nevertheless, tactics such as the use of Asian-American models, a culturally compatible setting, use of cultural symbols, choice of language, or reference to important cultural events show that a brand or company is an "insider" regarding Asian American customs.

A third consideration is the unique focus of Asian-American consumer identity around the family rather than the individual. Asian-American spending on long distance and international calling is much larger than in white households.[121] The top spenders in Asian media have been communication companies: AT&T, Sprint, and Verizon. Favorite possessions of Indian Americans show their owners' emphasis on family and culture and do not serve as expressions of individual identity or style.[122] Emphasis on how a product can increase a consumer's individual freedom may seem self-centered and inconsiderate of others in an Asian-American family. And while many Asian Americans are proud of their cultural heritage, they also might question why marketers single them out for special treatment.[123] Asian Americans are most willing to diverge from majority tastes in the categories that signal personal identity, such as music, clothing, and hairstyles.[124]

Asian American consumers have been described as less venturesome and having a preference for well-known and Asian-owned firms.[125] The role of multiple family members in individual purchase decisions must be taken into consideration in the design of communication messages and marketing programs. In cities like San Francisco, bankers adapt their marketing programs for each branch, using the languages of the country-of-origin populations in surrounding neighborhoods.[126] Some banks use "family banking" products for Asian-American clients that pool the entire family's balance when calculating balance-related charges.[127]

A fourth major difference between Asian and other American consumers is their emphasis on both belonging and achievement. Affluent Asian-American consumers distinguish themselves with luxury goods and high status brands. They buy signature clothing and jewelry, imported automobiles, premium liquor, and so on. "When buying American, they prefer old, established and well-known brands, but new products and services have a good chance if they quickly establish a good reputation for quality and value."[128] Over 50 percent of Crown Royal whisky sales in California come from Korean and Korean-American consumers, who purchase 20 bottles for each one consumed in the general market there. Case sales drop if the prices charged do not represent good value or if the brand is not promoted in media consumed by Korean Americans.[129] Citibank commissioned a unique Swarovski crystal dragon, a symbol of power and beauty among several Asian American subgroups, to use as gifts for consumers opening accounts over a certain amount.[130]

The Asian-American definition of success is framed in material terms, as seen in the high consumption of product categories with strong links to values such as belongingness and education. Status brands are very appealing to Asian-American consumers. A luxury car dealer in Buena Park, CA, claims that 30–35 percent of its business is from Asian-American small business owners. Its customers typically buy an "inexpensive Mercedes for their children and a top of the line one for the business."[131] Direct marketers may find these consumers accessible via current databases, since the most affluent Asian-American consumers are more likely than other consumers to own three or more credit cards.

One innovative use of promotions in Asian America has been the use of scholarships by MetLife. Its Scholar Program targets South Asian Americans. Press releases were sent to publications such as the *India Tribune* in New York, and brochures were distributed at branches and special events and by direct mail. It received over 7,000 application requests, making this an excellent example of tapping into an Asian-American community network and showing emphasis on education and achievement.[132]

Asian Americans share a strong preference for buying from Asian American–owned companies or brands. Wilshire Bancorp, Hanmi Financial, Nara Bancorp, East West Bancorp, Cathay General Bancorp, and Center Financial cater to Asian Americans by providing native-language tellers and signage. At the same time, Asian-American consumers can be activist. At least one in four Asian-American consumers would boycott a company accused of racial discrimination, and one in three Asian Americans would sign petitions in support.

A small but growing portion of business in Asian America comes from cross-ethnic promotions. Asian-owned stores in African-American neighborhoods have begun selling the soul foods of Sylvia Woods Enterprises, and Puerto Rican chicken farmers are finding that Chinese stores are good customers for chicken feet. Corina's in Athens, OH, sells dog treats in flavors including Mongolian beef and Korean barbecue.[133]

Names as well as numbers and colors often have particular significance among Asians and Asian Americans. These symbolic associations can be positive or negative. For example, in several Chinese dialects, the number 7 supposedly brings good luck and 2 and 8 together mean "easy prosperity." Chinese consumers in San Francisco were confused when they received coupons for $28 off their next phone bill; how would a phone bill discount increase their prosperity?[134] The number 3 is a homophone of the word for "life" in Cantonese, while the number 4 sounds like "death" in Mandarin (and it was the "kiss of death" for the Volvo 244DL). In Korean and Chinese, the number 9 is associated with longevity, and 10 with being "guaranteed or assured." The area code for San Gabriel Valley is 818 or "prosperity guaranteed prosperity," a great address for Asian American–targeted companies.[135]

Among Chinese and Japanese people, red stands for joy and happiness, purple is associated with heaven and the emperor, green is associated with health and growth, yellow with the earth, and black with guilt, evil, death, and the direction north. Throughout the Asian world, white is universally associated with funerals, but, at the same time, it stands for purity, innocence, and the direction west.[136] The symbolic meanings of numbers, names, and colors survive Asian Americans' growing use of English. Understanding these possible meanings to Asian-American consumers is important in developing messaging that expresses cultural sensitivity.

As noted earlier, first and second generations as well as urban and suburban Asian Americans have very different lifestyles and values. One marketer has used these differences to define three consumer segments in the Indian-American market. Early immigrants who are affluent and nearing retirement constitute the first group. The main difference between them and the second group is the decade when they came to the United States, and the fact that many members of the second group are married to highly educated women employed outside the home. The third group is made up mostly of relatives of the earlier immigrants. They are often less well educated and are more likely to run small businesses such as motels and convenience stores.[137]

The high ownership of businesses in Asian America is a major opportunity for business-to-business selling. A Chinese proverb states: "There are no prospects in working for others." One source reports that ethnic Chinese and Indian immigrants run almost 25 percent of the high-tech companies started in Silicon Valley since 1980.[138] Indian retailers pool resources and form associations that allow them to buy in bulk and sell at lower prices.[139] Asian-American businesses also take advantage of Small Business Administration programs that give preference to minority-owned firms in selling to government entities.[140] Not only do cultural associations help new immigrants assimilate in Silicon Valley but joining them can offer a major source of business contacts. To summarize, designing marketing programs that fit "the Asian way of life" means hiring ethnic personnel, using ethnic language media, generating word-of-mouth communication through community leaders, and improving postpurchase service.[141]

One of the most valuable sources of information about Asian-American consumers is the growing number of Asian-American–targeted communications, research, and marketing companies (see Asian American Advertising Federation at www.3af.org). In 2009, the companies that spent the most were State Farm, McDonald's, Verizon, Farmers Insurance, MetLife, Toyota, Wells Fargo, New York Life, JC Penney, and Allstate.[142] Asian-American buying power was estimated to exceed $528 billion in 2009 and $750 billion in 2013.[143] Because of their spending in product categories such as phone services at over $1 billion, and overindexing on many other high-cost products and services, Asian-American consumers present a "marketer's dream come true," if companies can master the subtleties of their chameleon behavior.[144]

Summary

Asian America includes peoples from different countries of origin, religions, races, and ethnic identities. It is divided across lines formed by those who were born abroad versus those born in the United States, high versus low economic and educational backgrounds, and immigrants versus second and later generations. One unifying value is the legacy of Confucianism, which gives many Asian Americans a strong commitment to family, hierarchy, and community. Over time and generations, most Asian Americans blend into mainstream America but often retain pride in their heritage and can behave like chameleons, balancing both cultures as required by the situation.

Communication preferences of Asian Americans are distinctive. Their high-context background places more attention on relationships between communicators and to saving face over direct messages. Their insider bias is expressed by a preference for word-of-mouth sources of information, in-language media, and Asian-owned firms. They spend the least time with media of any American ethnic group, making investment in nontraditional media best practice for reaching them. As consumers, they place importance on value received and use well-known brand names as a surrogate measure for product quality. Some Asian-American consumers read symbolic meanings into particular colors, names, and numbers. Support for community events, scholarships, and local promotions present opportunities for cultural partnerships between Asian-American consumers and marketers.

Notes

The author acknowledges Dr. Marilyn S. Roberts, Dr. Eun Soo Rhee, Dr. Wei-Na Lee, Dr. Carrie La Ferle, and Dr. Satomi Furuichi, who all contributed research for earlier drafts of this chapter.

1. B. Imada, "Forget the Asian-American Market Myths—But Remember These Truths," *Advertising Age* 78, no. 44 (2007): 4–14.

2. W. O'Hare and C. Felt, *Asian Americans: America's Fastest Growing Minority Group* (Washington, DC: Population Reference Bureau, 1991), 4.

3. U.S. Census Bureau, "The Asian Alone or in Combination Population in the United States: 2011" (Washington, DC, 2011), www.census.gov/population/race/data/ppl-ac11.html.

4. Pew Research Center, *The Rise of Asian Americans* (Washington, DC: Pew Research Social & Demographic Trends, June 19, 2012), www.pewsocialtrends.org/2012/06/19/the-rise-of-asian-americans/.

5. C. Reynolds, "Far East Moves West," *American Demographics* (October 2004): 56.

6. Packaged Facts, *Asian Americans in the U.S.* (New York: Packaged Facts, 2006).

7. U.S. Census Bureau, "The Asian Alone."

8. D.T.L. Wu, *Asian Pacific Americans in the Workplace* (Walnut Creek, CA: AltaMira Press, 1997), 143–144.

9. J. Berry, "Acculturation as Varieties of Adaptation," in *Acculturation: Theory, Models and Some New Findings*, ed. A.M. Padilla (Boulder, CO: Westview Press, 1980), 9–25.

10. P. Hitch, "Social Identity and the Half-Asian Child," in *Threatened Identities*, ed. G.M. Breakwell (New York: Wiley, 1983), 107–127; J. Hamers and M. Blanc, *Bilinguality and Bilingualism* (Cambridge: Cambridge University Press, 1989).

11 S. Askegaard, E.J. Arnould, and D. Kjeldgaard, "Post-Assimilationist Ethnic Consumer Research: Qualifications and Extensions," *Journal of Consumer Research* 32, no. 1 (2005): 160–170.

12. M. Pfeifer, "An Overview of Recent Developments in Hmong-American and Lao-American Studies Research," presentation (Corpus Christi: Hmong Studies Internet Resource Center, Texas A&M, 2005), http://hmongstudies.org/Hmong-AmericanandLao-AmericanStudiesPresentation.pdf.

13. Ibid.

14. K. Peraino, "Berkeley's New Colors," *Newsweek*, January 7, 2008.

15. D. Anderson, *Asian Persuasion: A Rapidly Growing Influence in the U.S.* (Miami, FL: Nielsen Consumer Panel Services, 2010); B. Kiviat, "Chasing Desi Dollars," *Time Inside Business* (August 2001): A22–A24.

16. Television Bureau of Advertising, "The Asian-American Marketplace," PowerPoint presentation, 2011, www.tvb.org/media/file/TVB_PB_Asian_American.ppt.

17. J.M. Humphreys, *The Multicultural Economy 2012* (Athens: Selig Center for Economic Growth, Terry College of Business, University of Georgia, 2012).

18. E. Lee and K. Li, "The Myth of the Asian American Superstudent," *A Magazine* 1 (1997): 44–47.

19. U.S. Census American FactFinder, 2010, www.census.gov/compendia/statab/tables/08s0631.pdf.

20. A. Ragaza, "I Don't Count as 'Diversity,'" *Newsweek,* February 8, 1999, 13

21. Mintel Oxygen, *Asian-American Lifestyles—US* (London: Mintel Group, October 2007).

22. S.M. Lee, *Asian Americans: Diverse and Growing* (Washington, DC: Population Reference Bureau, June 1998).

23. S. Hwang, "The New White Flight," *Wall Street Journal,* November 19, 2005, A1, A8.

24. W.P. O'Hare, W.H. Frey, and D. Fost, "Asians in the Suburbs," *American Demographics* (May 1994): 33–38.

25. B. Edmondson, "Asian Americans in 2001," *American Demographics* (February 1997): 16–17, 74; O'Hare, Frey, and Fost, "Asians in the Suburbs."

26. E.N. Glenn, "Split Household, Small Producer and Dual Wage Earner: An Analysis of Chinese-American Family Strategies," *Journal of Marriage and Family* 45, no. 1 (1983): 35–45; J.M. Sanders and V. Nee, "Immigrant Self-Employment: The Family as Social Capital and the Value of Human Capital," *American Sociological Review* 61, no. 2 (1996): 231–249.

27. Packaged Facts, *Asian Americans in the U.S.*

28 Amy Tan, *The Joy Luck Club* (New York: G. P. Putnam, 1989), 267.

29. I.H. Park and L.-J. Cho, "Confucianism and the Korean Family," *Journal of Comparative Family Studies* 26, no. 1 (1995): 117–135; A.M. Wong, *Target: The U.S. Asian Market* (Palos Verdes, CA: Pacific Heritage Books, 1993), 69, 83.

30. W.-N. Lee and D. Tse, "Changing Media Consumption in a New Home: Acculturation Patterns Among Hong Kong Immigrants to Canada," *Journal of Advertising* 23, no. 1 (1994): 57–70; B. Mueller, *International Advertising: Communicating Across Cultures* (Belmont, CA: Wadsworth, 1996); M. de Mooij, *Global Marketing and Advertising: Understanding Cultural Paradoxes* (Thousand Oaks, CA: Sage, 1998).

31. D.J. O'Brien and S.S. Fugita, *The Japanese American Experience* (Bloomington: Indiana University Press, 1991); D. Montero, *Japanese Americans: Changing Patterns of Ethnic Affiliation over Three Generations* (Boulder, CO: Westview Press, 1980); L.H. Shinagawa and Y.P. Gin, "Asian American Panethnicity and Intermarriage," *Amerasia Journal* 22, no. 2 (1996): 127–152.

32. D.C. Locke, *Increasing Multicultural Understanding: A Comprehensive Model* (Thousand Oaks, CA: Sage, 1992); W. O'Hare, "Reaching for the Dream," *American Demographics* (January 1992): 32–36.

33. Packaged Facts, *Asian Americans in the U.S.*

34. Ibid.

35. R. Jacob, "Overseas Indians: Make It Big," *Fortune,* November 15, 1993, 168–174.

36. M. Tuan, *Forever Foreigners or Honorary Whites? The Asian Ethnic Experience Today* (New Brunswick, NJ: Rutgers University Press, 1998).

37. Mintel Oxygen, *Asian-American Lifestyles—US.*

38. D. Brand, "The New Whiz Kids," *Time,* August 31, 1987, 42–51; C.R. Taylor and B.B. Stern, "Asian Americans: Television Advertising and the 'Model Minority' Stereotype," *Journal of Advertising* 2, no. 6 (1997): 47–61.

39. Tuan, *Forever Foreigners or Honorary Whites?*; S.J. Ungar, *Fresh Blood: The New American Immigrants* (New York: Simon & Schuster, 1995).

40. Taylor and Stern, "Asian Americans."

41. Tuan, *Forever Foreigners or Honorary Whites?*

42. C. Fong and J. Yung, "In Search of the Right Spouse: Interracial Marriage Among Chinese and Japanese Americans," *Amerasia Journal* 21, no. 3 (1995/1996): 77–98; H.P. McAdoo, ed., *Family Ethnicity: Strength in Diversity* (Newbury Park, CA: Sage, 1993); R. Takaki, *A Different Mirror: A History of Multicultural America* (Boston: Little, Brown, 1993).

43. N. Kibria, "The Construction of 'Asian American': Reflection on Intermarriage and Ethnic Identity Among Second-Generation Chinese and Korean Americans," *Ethnic and Racial Studies* 20, no. 3 (1997): 513–544; Shinagawa and Pang, "Asian American Panethnicity and Intermarriage"; B. Wysocki, "Elite U.S. Immigrants Straddle Two Cultures," *Wall Street Journal*, May 12, 1997, B1, B6.

44. C.J. Yeh and K. Huang, "The Collectivistic Nature of Ethnic Identity Development Among Asian-American College Students," *Adolescence* 31, no. 123 (1996): 645–661; Y.L. Espiritu, *Asian American Panethnicity: Bridging Institutions and Identities* (Philadelphia: Temple University Press, 1992); Tuan, *Forever Foreigners or Honorary Whites?*

45. Espiritu, *Asian American Panethnicity*, 1–18.

46. S. No, Y. Hong, H.-Y. Liao, K. Lee, D. Wood, and M.M. Chao, "Lay Theory of Race Affects and Moderates Asian Americans' Responses Toward American Culture," *Journal of Personality and Social Psychology* 95, no. 4 (2008): 991–1004; Tuan, *Forever Foreigners or Honorary Whites?*; P.G. Min, ed., *Asian Americans: Contemporary Trends and Issues* (Thousand Oaks, CA: Sage, 1995); Takaki, *A Different Mirror*; Wysocki, "Elite U.S. Immigrants Straddle Two Cultures."

47. P.L. Lien, M.M. Conway, and J. Wong, "The Contours and Sources of Ethnic Identity: Choices Among Asian Americans," *Social Science Quarterly* 84, no. 2 (2003): 461–481.

48. L. Yuan, "Web Site Helps Chinese in U.S. Navigate Life," *Wall Street Journal*, October 26, 2004, B1.

49. H.D. Brown, *Principles of Language Learning and Teaching*, 3d ed. (Englewood Cliffs, NJ: Prentice Hall Regents, 1994).

50. D. D'Rozario and S.P. Douglas, "Effect of Assimilation on Prepurchase External Information-Search Tendencies," *Journal of Consumer Psychology* 8, no. 2 (1999): 187–209; Brown, *Principles of Language Learning and Teaching*.

51. L. Lee, "New Immigrants Get Crash Course In Consumerism," *Wall Street Journal*, December 24, 1996, B1; J.K. Matsuoka, "Differential Acculturation Among Vietnamese Refugees," *Social Work* 35, no. 4 (1990): 602–633; W.-N. Lee, "Acculturation and Advertising Communication Strategies: A Cross-Cultural Comparison of Chinese and Americans," *Psychology & Marketing* 10, no. 5 (1993): 381–397.

52. No et al., "Lay Theory of Race Affects and Moderates Asian Americans' Responses Toward American Culture"; D. Stayman and R. Deshpandé, "Situational Ethnicity and Consumer Behavior," *Journal of Consumer Research* 16, no. 3 (1989): 361–371; H.Y. Nahm, "An AsiAm dream," *Transpacific* (1997): 112.

53. D. Luna, T. Ringgberg, and L.A. Peracchio, "One Individual, Two Identities: Frame Switching," *Journal of Consumer Research* 35, no. 2 (2008): 279–293; K. Gergen and M.S. Gibbs, "Role Playing and Modifying the Self-Concept" (paper presented at the Eastern Psychological Association Meeting 1966); K. Oberg, "Culture Shock: Adjustment to New Cultural Environments," *Practical Anthropology* 7 (1960): 177–182.

54. J. Chu and N. Mustafa, "Between Two Worlds: Born in the U.S.A. to Asian

Parents, a Generation of Immigrants' Kids Forges a New Identity," *Time*, January 16, 2006, 64–68; S.J. Yanagisako, *Transforming the Past: Tradition and Kinship Among Japanese Americans* (Stanford: Stanford University Press, 1985), 250–251.

55. A. Bower, "Racing the Dragon," *Time Inside Business* (July 2006): A19–A21.

56. Shinagawa and Pang, "Asian American Panethnicity and Intermarriage."

57. M. Mogelonsky, "Asian-Indian Americans," *American Demographics* (August 1995): 32–39.

58. Cultural Access Group, "Comprehensive Consumer Insights to Expand Your Asian American Consumer Base," ARF Webinar, December 14, 2004.

59. Ibid.

60. J.F.J. Lee, *Asian Americans: Oral Histories of First to Fourth Generation Americans from China, the Philippines, Japan, India, the Pacific Islands, Vietnam and Cambodia* (New York: Free Press, 1992).

61. C.R. Taylor and J.Y. Lee, "Not in Vogue: Portrayals of Asian Americans in Magazine Advertising," *Journal of Public Policy and Marketing* 13, no. 2 (1994): 239–245; I. Cintron, "The World of Commercials Seems Not to Include Asia," *Newsday*, May 20, 1991, 20; C. Martindale, "Only in Glimpses: Portrayal of America's Largest Minority Groups by the *New York Times*, 1934–1994," in *Facing Difference: Race, Gender, and Mass Media*, ed. S. Biagi and M. Kern-Foxworth (Thousand Oaks, CA: Pine Forge Press, 1997), 89–95.

62. C. Spigner, "Race, Gender, and the Status-Quo: Asian and African American Relations in a Hollywood Film," *Explorations in Ethnic Studies* 17, no. 1 (1994): 89–101; P. Lee, "Asian-Americans Decry Stereotypes in TV Ads," *Los Angeles Times*, January 1, 1991, 6.

63. D.Y. Hamamoto, "Kindred Spirits: The Contemporary Asian American Family on Television," *Amerasia Journal* 18, no. 2 (1992): 35–53; L.L. Wang, "Race, Class, Citizenship, and Extra-Territoriality: Asian Americans and the 1996 Campaign Finance Scandal," *Amerasia Journal* 24, no. 1 (1998): 1–21.

64. S.B. Graves, "Diversity on Television," in *Tuning In to Young Viewers: Social Science Perspective on Television*, ed. T.M. MacBeth (Thousand Oaks, CA: Sage, 1996), 61–86; Taylor and Stern, "Asian Americans."

65. K. Lee and S. Joo, "The Portrayal of Asian Americans in Mainstream Magazine Ads: An Update," *Journalism and Mass Communication Quarterly* 82, no. 3 (2005): 654–671.

66. Graves, "Diversity on Television," 68.

67. L. Bowen and J. Schmid, "Minority Presence and Portrayal in Mainstream Magazine Advertising: An Update," *Journalism and Mass Communication Quarterly* 74, no. 1 (1997): 134–146; Taylor and Stern, "Asian Americans"; C.R. Taylor, J.Y. Lee, and B.B. Stern, "Portrayals of African, Hispanic, and Asian Americans in Magazine Advertising," *American Behavioral Scientist* 38, no. 4 (1995): 608–621.

68. R. Bean and R.D. Crane, "Marriage and Family Therapy Research with Ethnic Minorities: Current Status," *American Journal of Family Therapy* 24, no. 1 (1996): 3–8; Shaw-Y. Taylor and N.V. Benokraitis, "The Presentation of Minorities in Marriage and Family Textbooks," *Teaching Sociology* 23, no. 2 (1995): 122–135.

69. J. Yang et al., *Eastern Standard Time: A Guide to Asian Influence on American Culture from Astro Boy to Zen Buddhism* (Boston: Houghton Mifflin, 1997).

70. "First Event Helps Sum Basho Rock Vancouver," *Imprint* (1999/2000, Winter): 16.

71. Wysocki, "Elite U.S. Immigrants Straddle Two Cultures"; S. Thurm, "Asian Immigrants Are Reshaping Silicon Valley," *Wall Street Journal*, June 24, 1999, B6; E. Rivera, "Prototypes of the Asian Century," *Transpacific* (1997): 40–109; D. Takahashi, "Ethnic Networks Help Immigrants Rise in Silicon Valley," *Wall Street Journal*, March 18, 1998, B1, B6.

72. De Mooij, *Global Marketing and Advertising*; G. Althen, *American Ways: A Guide for Foreigners in the United States* (Yarmouth, ME: Intercultural Press, 1988); E.C. Stewart and M.I. Bennett, *American Cultural Patterns: A Cross-cultural Perspective*, rev. ed. (Yarmouth, ME: Intercultural Press, 1991).

73. Wong, *Target*, 178.

74. F. Trompenaars and C. Hampden-Turner, *Riding the Waves of Culture: Understanding Diversity in Global Business*, 2d ed. (New York: McGraw-Hill, 1998); T. Morrison, W.H. Conaway, and G.A. Borden, *Kiss, Bow or Shake Hands: How to Do Business in Sixty Countries* (Holbrook, MA: B. Adams, 1994).

75. Tuan, *Forever Foreigners or Honorary Whites?*; McAdoo, *Family Ethnicity*.

76. Althen, *American Ways*, 21–35.

77. J. Burton, "Targeting Asians: Agencies in U.S. Tailor Messages to New Immigrants," *Far Eastern Economic Review*, January 21, 1993, 40–55; Lee and Tse, "Changing Media Consumption in a New Home"; N. Wang, "From Tennis Rackets to Tinted Contacts," *A Magazine,* October 31, 1994, 31–34, 76.

78. D'Rozario and Douglas, "Effect of Assimilation on Prepurchase External Information-Search Tendencies"; Wong, *Target*, 99.

79. J. Schmid, "Ethnic Niche Catalogs," *Target Marketing,* November 1995, 18; L.P. Tseng and B.B. Stern, "Cultural Differences in Information Obtainment For Financial Decisions—East Versus West," *Journal of Euromarketing* 5, no. 1 (1996): 37.

80. Tseng and Stern, "Cultural Differences in Information Obtainment for Financial Decisions," 37.

81. de Mooij, *Global Marketing and Advertising*.

82. J. Holland and J.W. Gentry, "Ethnic Consumer Reaction to Targeted Marketing: A Theory of Intercultural Accommodation," *Journal of Advertising* 28, no. 1 (1999): 1–14; Althen, *American Ways*, 3–35.

83. J.E. Escalas and J.R. Bettman, "Self-Construal, Reference Groups and Brand Meaning," *Journal of Consumer Research* 32, no. 3 (2005): 378–389; Lee, "New Immigrants Get Crash Course in Consumerism"; de Mooij, *Global Marketing and Advertising*.

84. Cultural Access Group, "Comprehensive Consumer Insights to Expand Your Asian American Consumer Base."

85. A. Bower, "Racing the Dragon," *Time Inside Business* (July 2006): A19–A21; Wang, "From Tennis Rackets to Tinted Contacts."

86. W.-N. Lee, C. LaFerle, and M. Tharp, "Ethnic Influences on Communication Patterns: Word of Mouth and Traditional and Nontraditional Media Usage," in *Diversity in Advertising*, ed. J.D. Williams, W-N. Lee, and C.P. Haugtvedt (Mahwah, NJ: Lawrence Erlbaum, 2004), 177–200.

87. N. Delener and J.P. Neelankavil, "Informational Sources and Media Usage: A Comparison Between Asian and Hispanic Subcultures," *Journal of Advertising Research* 30, no. 3 (1990): 45–52; Lee and Tse, "Changing Media Consumption in a New Home."

88. Wong, *Target*, 49.

89. Bowen and Schmid, "Minority Presence and Portrayal in Mainstream Magazine

Advertising"; Taylor and Stern, "Asian Americans"; Taylor, Lee, and Stern, "Portrayals of African, Hispanic, and Asian Americans in Magazine Advertising."

90. D. Sontag, "I Want My Hyphenated-Identity MTV," *New York Times,* June 19, 2005.

91. Lee, "New Immigrants Get Crash Course in Consumerism"; J.C. Shim, "The Importance of Ethnic Newspapers to U.S. Newcomers," in *Facing Difference: Race, Gender, and Mass Media,* ed. S. Biagi and M. Kern-Foxworth (Thousand Oaks, CA: Pine Forge Press, 1997), 250–255.

92. E. Taylor, "A Cross-Media Study of Audience Choice: The Influence of Traits, Needs, and Attitudes on Individual's Selection of 'Media Repertoires'" (Ph.D. dissertation, University of Texas at Austin, 1999).

93. L.E. Wynter, "Business and Race," *Wall Street Journal,* February 2, 1994, B1.

94. Wong, *Target,* 63.

95. B. Wiesedanger, "Asian-Americans: The Three Biggest Myths," *Sales and Marketing Management* 145, no. 11 (1993): 86–88.

96. S. Gitlin, "Asian Prime Time," *Brandweek* 39, no. 1 (1998): 17.

97. Ibid.

98. Delener and Neelankavil, "Informational Sources and Media Usage."

99. B.H. Schmitt and S. Zhang, "Language Structure and Categorization: A Study of Classifiers in Consumer Cognition, Judgment, and Choice," *Journal of Consumer Research* 25, no. 2 (1998): 108–122.

100. K&L Advertising, www.kanglee.com.

101. N.T. Tavassoli, "Temporal and Associative Memory in Chinese and English," *Journal of Consumer Research* 26, no. 2 (1999): 170–181; Schmitt and Zhang, "Language Structure and Categorization."

102. Delener and Neelankavil, "Informational Sources and Media Usage"; M. Paskowski, "Trailblazing in Asian America," *Marketing and Media Decisions* 21 (October 1986): 74–80.

103. D. Gullapalli, "Indians in U.S. Find New Sidelines: Bollywood Moguls," *Wall Street Journal,* February 21, 2007, A1, A18; "The Rise of Radio in the Asian-American Market," *Brandweek,* April 17, 1995, S2; www.kanglee.com Wiesedanger, "Asian-Americans: The Three Biggest Myths."

104. Anand, "Internet Access Among Different Races in America," Tech Crunchies, May 15, 2008, http://techcrunchies.com/internet-access-among-different-races-in-america/.

105. www.kanglee.com.

106. H. Mummert, "Reaching Ethnic Markets," *Target Marketing News,* November 14, 1995, 18.

107. L.E. Wynter, "Film Distributor Tries to Crack Asian Market," *Wall Street Journal,* June 10, 1998, B1.

108. Mummert, "Reaching Ethnic Markets."

109. Packaged Facts, *Asian Americans in the U.S.*

110. K. Shermach, "Yellow Pages Publishers Find Niches Among Ethnic Groups," *Marketing News,* January 17, 1994, 5.

111. I. Teinowitz, "Multicultural Marketing," *Advertising Age,* November 16, 1998, s1–23.

112. Television Bureau of Advertising, "The Asian-American Marketplace."

113. Ibid.

114. Cultural Access Group, "Comprehensive Consumer Insights to Expand Your Asian American Consumer Base."

115. Teinowitz, "Multicultural Marketing."

116. E.A. Sullivan, "10 Minutes with Vicky M. Wong, President and CEO of DAE Advertising Inc.," *Marketing News,* September 15, 2010, 22–23; Wong, *Target,* 46.

117. N. Crawford, "It's Culture, Not Color," *PROMO Magazine* (January 1998): 47–50, 132.

118. Teinowitz, "Multicultural Marketing."

119. Packaged Facts, *Asian Americans in the U.S.*

120. M. Louis, "Help Wanted: Gujarati Speakers to Sell Insurance," *Wall Street Journal,* October 12, 1999, B1, B16.

121. Insight Research Corporation, *Telecom and Ethnic Groups: Uses of Local, Long Distance, and Wireless Services in Ethnic Communities, 2000–2005* (Durango, CO, 2001), www.insight-corp.com/reports/ethnic2.asp.

122. A. Lindridge and M.K. Hogg, "Parental Gate-Keeping in Diasporic Indian Families: Examining the Intersection of Culture, Gender and Consumption," *Journal of Marketing Management* 22, no. 9 (2006): 979–1008; R. Mehta and R.W. Belk, "Artifacts, Identity, and Transition: Favorite Possessions of Indians and Indian Immigrants to the United States," *Journal of Consumer Research* 17, no. 4 (1991): 398–411.

123. M. Lev, "Asian-Americans' Tastes Are Surveyed by Marketers," *New York Times,* January 14, 1991, B11.

124. J. Berger and C. Heath, "Where Consumers Diverge from Others: Identity Signaling and Product Domains," *Journal of Consumer Research* 34, no. 2 (2007): 121–134.

125. C.B. Bhattacharya and S. Sen, "Consumer-Company Identification: A Framework for Understanding Consumers' Relationships with Companies," *Journal of Marketing* 67, no. 2 (2003): 76–88; Burton, "Targeting Asians"; Lee and Tse, "Changing Media Consumption in a New Home."

126. Wiesendanger, "Asian-Americans," 86–88, 101.

127. Ibid.

128. Wong, *Target,* 40.

129. Y. Zhang and B.D. Gelb, "Matching Advertising Appeals to Culture: The Influence of Products' Use Conditions," *Journal of Advertising* 25, no. 3 (1996): 29–46; Teinowitz, "Multicultural Marketing."

130. Crawford, "It's Culture, Not Color," 47–50, 132.

131. K.W. Lee, "The Rise of the Neo-Mandarins," *A Magazine* (1999): 22–23.

132. Crawford, "It's Culture, Not Color."

133. P. Thomas, "Minority Businesses Increase Cross-Ethnic Marketing," *Wall Street Journal,* April 21, 1998, B2; D. Morse, "Just Sell It: Where Gang Members Are Shoe Salesmen," *Wall Street Journal,* February 19, 1999, A1, A6.

134. M. Boyd, "Incentive Marketing: Asian Dawn," *Incentive* (June 1994): 37–40.

135. S. Berfield, "Hong Kong Plans a Numbers Game," *BusinessWeek,* November 22, 1999, 6; Wong, *Target,* 122–124.

136. Wong, *Target,* 125–126.

137. Mogelonsky, "Asian-Indian Americans."

138. S. Thurm, "Asian Immigrants Are Reshaping Silicon Valley," *Wall Street Journal,* June 24, 1999, B6.

139. Mogelonsky, "Asian-Indian Americans."

140. R. Sharpe, "Asian-Americans Gain Sharply in Big Program of Affirmative Action," *Wall Street Journal*, September 9, 1997, A1, A8.

141. Lee, LaFerle, and Tharp, "Ethnic Influences on Communication Patterns."

142. B. Imada, "Top 10 Corporate Marketers in the U.S. Asian Market," *Advertising Age,* January 20, 2010, http://adage.com/article/the-big-tent/marketing-top-corporate-marketers-u-s-asian-market/141595/.

143. 3Af Webinar, "Asian Americans: A Consumer Segment You Can't Ignore," Asian American Advertising Federation (October 10, 2012), www.3af.org.

144. Wong, *Target*, 24.

Index

Italic page references indicate tables and figures.

About the Author

Marye Tharp studied languages, marketing, and international business with a concentration on Latin America at The University of Texas at Austin, where she received BA, BBA, MBA, and Ph.D. degrees. Her teaching career spans tenured and visiting appointments in 21 countries and includes university courses and executive training. Her publications encompass textbooks for international and multicultural marketing as well as refereed journal articles and conference presentations on the same topics. She serves as strategic planning consultant and speaker for marketing communication agencies, manufacturers, trade associations, and nonprofit organizations.

Dr. Tharp currently lives in the Texas Hill Country and is a senior lecturer in the Marketing Department at The University of Texas at San Antonio.

T - #0045 - 100220 - C0 - 229/152/22 - PB - 9780765643001